CHINA SINCE TIANANMEN

In a new edition of his path-breaking analysis of political and social change in China since the crackdown in Tiananmen Square in 1989, Joseph Fewsmith traces developments since 2001. These include the continuing reforms during the final years of Jiang Zemin's premiership and Hu Jintao's succession in 2002. Here the author also considers social trends and how Chinese citizens are starting to have a significant influence on government policies. As Fewsmith – a highly regarded political scientist and a seasoned China-watcher – observes, China is a very different place today than it was eighteen years ago. In the interim, it has emerged from isolation to become one of the most significant players on the world stage. This book – more than any other – explains the forces that have shaped China since Tiananmen.

JOSEPH FEWSMITH is Professor in the Departments of International Relations and Political Science at Boston University.

Cambridge Modern China Series

Edited by William Kirby, Harvard University

Other books in the series:

Christian Henriot and Wen-hsin Yeh, *In the Shadow of the Rising Sun: Shanghai under Japanese Occuption*

Andrew Scobell, *China's Use of Military Force: Beyond the Great Wall and the Long March*

Andrew H. Wedeman, *From Mao to Market: Rent Seeking, Local Protectionism, and Marketization in China*

Thomas P. Bernstein and Xiaobo Lu, *Taxation without Representation in Contemporary Rural China*

Linsun Cheng, *Banking in Modern China: Entrepreneurs, Professional Managers, and the Development of Chinese Banks, 1897–1937*

Bruce J. Dickson, *Red Capitalists in China: The Chinese Communist Party, Private Entrepreneurs, and Political Change*

Yasheng Huang, *Selling China: Foreign Direct Investment During the Reform Era*

Rachel Murphy, *How Migrant Labor is Changing Rural China*

Warren I. Cohen and Li Zhao, eds., *Hong Kong under Chinese Rule: The Economic and Political Implications of Reversion*

Tamara Jacka, *Women's Work in Rural China: Change and Continuity in an Era of Reform*

Shiping Zheng, *Party vs. State in Post-1949 China: The Institutional Dilemma*

Michael Dutton, ed., *Streetlife China*

Edward Steinfeld, *Forging Reform in China: The Fate of State-Owned Industry*

Wenfang Tang and William Parish, *Chinese Urban Life under Reform: The Changing Social Contract*

David Shambaugh, ed., *The Modern Chinese State*

Jing Huang, *Factionalism in Chinese Communist Politics*

Xin Zhang, *Social Transformation in Modern China: The State and Local Elites in Henan, 1900–1937*

Edmund S. K. Fung, *In Search of Chinese Democracy: Civil Opposition in Nationalist China, 1929–1949*

List of other books in the series continues after the index.

CHINA SINCE TIANANMEN

From Deng Xiaoping to Hu Jintao

JOSEPH FEWSMITH

Boston University

CAMBRIDGE
UNIVERSITY PRESS

CAMBRIDGE UNIVERSITY PRESS
Cambridge, New York, Melbourne, Madrid, Cape Town, Singapore, São Paulo, Delhi

Cambridge University Press
The Edinburgh Building, Cambridge CB2 8RU, UK

Published in the United States of America by Cambridge University Press, New York

www.cambridge.org
Information on this title: www.cambridge.org/9780521686051

© Joseph Fewsmith 2001, 2008

First published 2001
Second edition 2008

Printed in the United Kingdom at the University Press, Cambridge

A catalogue record for this publication is available from the British Library

Library of Congress Cataloging-in-Publication Data

Fewsmith, Joseph, 1949–
China since Tiananmen: from Deng Xiaoping to Hu Jintao / Joseph Fewsmith.
p.   cm.
Includes bibliographical references and index.
ISBN 978-0-521-86693-4 (hardback) – ISBN 978-0-521-68605-1 (pbk.)
1. China–Politics and government – 1976–2002.   2. Political leadership–China.
3. China–History–Tiananmen Square Incident, 1989.   I. Title.
JQ1510.F478   2008
951.05'9–dc22   2007053003

ISBN 978-0-521-86693-4 hardback
ISBN 978-0-521-68605-1 paperback

For Stephanie and Andrew

Contents

Acknowledgments   *page* ix
Chronology   xi
Schematic overview of the Chinese political spectrum   xvii
List of abbreviations and tables   xviii

Introduction   I

PART I   LINE STRUGGLE REVISITED: THE ATTACK
ON DENG'S REFORM PROGRAM

1. Tiananmen and the conservative critique of reform   21

2. Deng moves to revive reform   48

PART II   REDEFINING REFORM: THE SEARCH FOR
A NEW WAY

3. The emergence of neoconservatism   83

4. The enlightenment tradition under challenge   113

5. The emergence of neostatism and popular nationalism   140

PART III   ELITE POLITICS AND POPULAR NATIONALISM

6. Jiang Zemin's rise to power   165

7. Elite politics in an era of globalization and nationalism   197

PART IV A NEW ERA IN CHINESE POLITICS

8.   Hu Jintao takes over: a turn to the left?   231

Conclusion   272

Epilogue: the Seventeenth Party Congress   278

Bibliography   285
Index   325

Acknowledgments

This book has its origins in an earlier attempt to come to grips with the political trends in China since the tragic crackdown on student demonstrations on June 4, 1989, an event usually referred to simply as "Tiananmen" after the central square in Beijing that had been the focus of student activities for the preceding six weeks (though most of the violence took place outside the square). Roderick MacFarquhar asked me to analyze events in the first three years since that time for a revised edition of his *The Politics of China*, which appeared in 1997. I thank him for his encouragement to write that chapter and for his later suggestion to expand that chapter into a book – though doing so took longer and involved more than I had anticipated at the time. His intellectual support and friendship have been critical to that enterprise.

A grant from the Smith Richardson Foundation and a sabbatical leave from Boston University in 1997–8 gave me time to pursue this research. Alas, it became apparent in that year that understanding politics in the years since Tiananmen required delving into the new intellectual moods that grew up in the 1990s and reflected a very different China from the one I had grown accustomed to in the 1980s – and that required additional time and effort. Fortunately, I knew or came to know many of the intellectuals whose works are discussed in the pages that follow. They have helped me understand not only the different ideas that gained currency but also why those ideas came into being and evolved as they have. I hope that I have repaid their time and guidance by conveying the trends of the 1990s accurately.

Since the first edition of this work was published in 2001, much has happened in China. Jiang Zemin has left office and been replaced by Hu Jintao, and the tenor of public discourse has changed significantly. It seemed time to incorporate these changes by updating this work. Accordingly, an eighth chapter has been added and the earlier chapters edited down so that, hopefully, the political history of China in the eighteen years since Tiananmen can be presented coherently. An epilogue has been added discussing

ix

the Seventeenth Party Congress in October 2007. In updating this work I was helped by my stay at the Woodrow Wilson Center for International Scholars in the fall of 2005. I am very grateful to Robert Hathaway and the staff of the center for providing such a hospitable place to study and write.

In trying to understand post-Tiananmen China, I have often worked closely with Stanley Rosen, whose translations of debates in this period are cited frequently in the text. I thank him for his insights and support. I have also benefited from the friendship and support of my colleague Merle Goldman, who read the manuscript in draft form and whose comments have improved the final form. Similarly Cheng Li and Timothy Cheek read the manuscript and provided valuable comments, as did an anonymous reviewer. William C. Kirby supported the project and provided encouragement along the way.

As anyone who has worked on such a book knows, scholarship depends on those who collect, organize, and know the material they put on the shelves of libraries. I have been fortunate to work with the best. Nancy Hearst of the Fairbank Center at Harvard University has provided critical support, not only bibliographically but also by proofreading the final manuscript. James Cheng and his staff at the Harvard-Yenching Library at Harvard have been similarly helpful. Jean Hung and the staff at the Universities Service Center at the Chinese University of Hong Kong were of great assistance in locating much material used in this study, and Annie Chang at the Center for Chinese Studies Library at the University of California at Berkeley has also been of great help in finding material. I also appreciate the help that Jennifer Sova and Luke Wilcox provided in running down sources and checking footnotes.

Parts of this volume are adapted from articles previously published by the National Bureau of Asian Research, the Asia Society, and *Current History*. Permission to do so is gratefully acknowledged.

Mary Child, the editor for Asian Studies, Sociology, and History of Science at Cambridge University Press, provided invaluable guidance and support in the preparation of the first edition of this work, and Marigold Acland has similarly supported the preparation of the second edition.

My wife Irene has been unfailing in her support. Our children, Stephanie and Andrew, have tolerated with uncommon grace my frequent trips to China and the time I have spent locked away in my study. Because of their patience, and just because they are such great kids, this book is dedicated to them.

Chronology

1989

June 4 — Tiananmen crackdown

June 23–24 — Fourth Plenary Session of the Thirteenth Central Committee

November 6–9 — Fifth Plenary Session of the Thirteenth Central Committee

1990

January 10 — Premier Li Peng announces the lifting of martial law in Beijing

September — Economic Work Conference

November — *Yearnings* broadcast

December — National Planning Conference

1991

March 22 — First Huangfu Ping commentary

March — NPC promotes Zhu Rongji to vice premier

July 1 — Jiang Zemin calls for opposing "peaceful evolution"

August 19–21 — Attempted coup d'état in Soviet Union

1992

Jaunary 18–February 21 — Deng Xiaoping's "southern tour"

March 10–12 — Politburo Meeting supports Deng Xiaoping

September 28 — Conservative theoretician Hu Qiaomu dies at age 81

October 12–18 — Fourteenth Party Congress

October 19 — First Plenary Session of the Fourteenth Central Committee

1993

March 5–7 — Second Plenary Session of the Fifteenth Central Committee

Summer	Huntington's article, "Clash of Civilizations?" published
August 3	Chinese ship, *Yin He*, stopped by US Navy
September 23	2000 Olympics awarded to Sydney, Australia, instead of Beijing
November	*Strategy and Management* starts publication
November 11–14	Third Plenary Session of the Fourteenth Central Committee
1994	
March	*Looking at China through a Third Eye* published
September 25–28	Fourth Plenary Session of the Fourteenth Central Committee
1995	
April 10	Chen Yun, advocate of a planned economy, dies at age 90
April 27	Chen Xitong removed as Beijing Party secretary
September 25–28	Fifth Plenary Session of the Fourteenth Central Committee
1996	
March 8	China tests surface-to-surface missiles into sea off the coast of Taiwan
May	*China Can Say No* published
October	*Heart-to-Heart Talks with the General Secretary* published
October 7–10	Sixth Plenary Session of the Fourteenth Central Committee
1997	
February 2	Former Minister of Defense Qin Jiwei dies at age 82
February 19	Deng Xiaoping dies at age 92
May 29	Jiang Zemin speaks at Central Party School
July 1	Hong Kong is returned to China
September 12–18	Fifteenth Party Congress convenes in Beijing
September 19	First Plenary Session of the Fifteenth Central Committee
October 28	Jiang Zemin arrives in Washington, D.C.

1998

February 25–26	Second Plenary Session of Fifteenth Central Committee
March	*Crossed Swords* published
March 5–19	NPC meeting announces major government restructuring
May 4	Beijing University celebrates its 100th anniversary
June 27	President Clinton arrives in Beijing
July 22	Jiang Zemin calls on Chinese military to withdraw from business
September 14	Former president Yang Shangkun dies at age 91
October 12–14	Third Plenary Session of the Fifteenth Central Committee
December 21	Democratic activists Wang Youcai and Xu Wenli sentenced to jail

1999

March 23	United States starts bombing Serbian forces in Kosovo
April 6	Premier Zhu Rongji arrives in Washington to discuss WTO
April 20	Task force established to investigate corruption in Xiamen
April 25	Adherents of Falun Gong demonstrate around Zhongnanhai
May 7	US bombs hit Chinese Embassy in Belgrade
July 9	Taiwan President Lee Teng-hui describes relations with PRC as "special-state-to-state" relations
September 19–22	Fourth Plenary Session of Fifteenth Central Committee
October 1	50th anniversary of the founding of the PRC celebrated
November 15	United States and China reach agreement on China's accession to WTO

2000

January 20	*Wall Street Journal* reports Lin Youfang, wife of Politburo member Jia Qinglin, detained for questioning

February	Jiang Zemin raises "three represents" slogan
March 29	*Enlightenment Daily* carries letter implicitly criticizing Liu Junning
October 9–11	Fifth Plenary Session of Fifteenth Central Committee
2001	
April 1	Chinese F-8 fighter collides with American E-P3 surveillance plane off coast of Hainan
2002	
October 22	Shanghai Party Secretary Huang Ju and Beijing Party Secretary Jia Qinglin are transferred to the center
November 8–14	Sixteenth Party Congress convenes in Beijing
December 4	Hu Jintao, in his first public appearance as general secretary, speaks at celebration commemorating the 20th anniversary of the 1982 constitution
December 5–6	Hu Jintao visits the revolutionary base of Xibaipo
2003	
January 7–9	National meeting of propaganda heads
January 7–8	Rural Work Conference
March 5–11	First Session of the Tenth National People's Congress Meeting. Wen Jiabao is named premier
April 2	Wen Jiabao presides over a State Council meeting that discusses the SARS issue
April 20	Health Minister Zhang Wenkang and Beijing Mayor Meng Xuenong are dismissed from their posts
May 1	Hu Jintao calls to launch a "people's war" against SARS
October 11–14	Third Plenary Session of the Sixteenth Central Committee
2004	
March 2004	*An Investigation of China's Peasants* by Chen Guidi and Chu Tao is banned
September 2	Xiao Weibi, editor of the liberal, Guangdong-based *Tongzhou gongjin* is dismissed for publishing an interview with

	former Guangdong Party Secretary Ren Zhongyi
September 8	*Southern Personalities Weekly* publishes list of the 50 most influential Chinese public intellectuals
September 13	*Yitahutu* chatroom is closed down
September 16–19	Fourth Plenary Session of the Sixteenth Central Committee
September 19	Jiang Zemin retires from the Central Military Commission
September 22	*Strategy and Management* is closed down
November 11	Propaganda Department issues Document Number 29
November 23	Wang Guangze, a journalist at the *21st Century Business Herald*, is fired
December 14	Small- and medium-sized SOEs must clarify who is funding a buyout and who will manage the business before any MBO can be approved
2005	
March 17	Jiao Guobiao is dismissed from Peking University
April 14	Management buyouts of large state-owned enterprises are banned
July 10	Xinhua News Agency issues draft Property Law
August 12	Peking University law professor Gong Xiantian posts letter on Internet attacking the draft property rights law
2006	
March 5–14	Fourth Session of the Tenth National People's Congress meeting discusses Eleventh Five-Year Program
August 10	*Selected Works* of Jiang Zemin are published
September 24	Party Secretary of Shanghai Chen Liangyu is removed from office for his involvement in a security fund scandal
October 8–11	Sixth Plenary Session of the Sixteenth Central Committee

December	Sociologist Lu Jianhua is secretly sentenced to twenty years for leaking state secrets
2007	
March 5–16	Amended property rights law passed at Fifth Session of the Tenth National People's Congress meeting
October 15–20	Seventeenth Party Congress convened in Beijing

Schematic overview of the Chinese political spectrum

Schematic overview of Chinese political spectrum

		STATE		
		The Political Center		
	Left		**Right**	
		Jiang Zemin		
	Li Peng		Zhu Rongji	
		Zeng Qinghong		
The Old Left		Wang Huning		**Liberals**
Deng Liqun	Ding Guan'gen		Wang Daohan	Wan Li
Yu Quanyu	Tang Wensheng		Liu Ji	
Leftist Journals	Wang Renzhi			Li Shenzhi
Contemporary Trends				Shen Jiru
Quest for Truth				Ling Zhijun
Mainstream				Ma Licheng
		SOCIETY		
	The New Left			**Liberals**
New Nationalists	Post-Modernists	Neostatists		Liu Junning
China Can Say No	Wang Hui	Hu Angang		Qin Hui
Wang Xiaodong	Cui Zhiyuan	Wang Shaoguang		Xu Youyu
Yang Ping	Gan Yang			Zhu Xueqin
Fang Ning	Zhang Kuan			Lei Yi

Note: This schematic is arranged horizontally from the center outward, showing those who are far to the left and right of the political center (the Old Left and Liberals respectively) as well as those with left and right tendencies within the political center. Vertically, those farther from the top exercise less political influence. Thus, the Old Left and Liberals influence the political center but are not as powerful, similarly, intellectuals such as Li Shenzhi are not in the same category as former Vice-Premier Wan Li. Other intellectuals, whether New Left or Liberal, are even more distant from the political center and are depicted as societal actors.

Abbreviations and tables

ABBREVIATIONS

ASEAN	Association of Southeast Asian Nations
CAC	Central Advisory Commission
CAS	Chinese Academy of Sciences
CASS	Chinese Academy of Social Sciences
CCP	Chinese Communist Party
CDIC	Central Discipline Inspection Commission
CMC	Central Military Commission
CPSU	Communist Party of the Soviet Union
CYL	Communist Youth League
GATT	General Agreement on Tariffs and Trade
IMF	International Monetary Fund
MOFCOM	Ministry of Commerce
MOFTEC	Ministry of Foreign Trade and Economic Cooperation
NATO	North Atlantic Treaty Organization
NPC	National People's Congress
NMD	National Missile Defense
PBSC	Politburo Standing Committee
PRC	People's Republic of China
SETC	State Economic and Trade Commission
SEZ	Special Economic Zone
SOE	State-Owned Enterprise
SPC	State Planning Commission
TVE	Township and Village Enterprise
TMD	Theater Missile Defense
USTR	United States Trade Representative
WTO	World Trade Organization

TABLES

1 Leadership of the Chinese Communist Party *page* 73
2 Leadership of the Chinese Communist Party following the
  15th Party Congress 202
3 Leadership of the Chinese Communist Party following the
  16th Party Congress 241
4 Frequency of formulations 253
5 Politburo membership before and after the
  17th Party Congress 280
6 The Secretariat 281

Introduction

In the immediate aftermath of Tiananmen, there were widespread predictions among Chinese and foreign observers alike that the Chinese Communist Party (CCP) would collapse within a short period. The harsh repression of student-led dissent, not just in Beijing, which was what most of the world watched, but throughout the major cities of China, could not succeed for long, it was thought. The democratic movement was too strong, public disgust with the corruption and authoritarian policies of the government too great, and the world tide against communist governments – exemplified by the collapse of socialism in Eastern Europe later that same year – too profound for China to resist for long. When it was announced that Jiang Zemin, the Party secretary of Shanghai, had been made general secretary of the CCP, it was widely assumed that he would be a transitional figure, not unlike Hua Guofeng, who had served briefly as chairman of the Party following Mao Zedong's death in 1976.[1]

It was also widely thought that if, through the exertion of pure brute strength, the communist government was able to reassert itself against the societal forces that had been arrayed against it, that the cost would be economic reform and growth. Indeed, such predictions seemed to be borne out as the pace of reform stalled and as administrative measures against inflation bit deeply into China's growth rates. By the summer and fall of 1990, China's growth rates were near zero, by far the slowest rate of growth the Chinese economy had experienced since the start of reform in late 1978.

Such predictions, like so many in the China field, were wrong. The CCP did restore its dominance over society remarkably quickly. The deep differences of opinion within the party were muted if not eliminated by the purge of Party head Zhao Ziyang and other top leaders. Rather than being a transitional figure, Jiang Zemin continued to head the CCP until

---

[1] Michael Weiskopf, "Chief Rose by Following Prevailing Political Winds."

stepping down thirteen years later in 2002, and the Chinese economy not only continued to grow but to stir fears that it had become an unstoppable economic juggernaut as China became the manufacturing center of the world. Whereas per capita income at stood at about $250 in 1989, it had grown to some $1200 by 2006, a remarkable achievement for a country of 1.3 billion people and putting China well on the way toward becoming a middle income country.

Even China's diplomatic pariah status had vanished a decade and a half later as China emerged as an influential presence in world councils, especially in Asia. The change in China's status was strikingly highlighted by the back-to-back appearances of President Bush, who spoke to the Australian parliament 2003, and Chinese president Hu Jintao, who was greeted much more enthusiastically, when he spoke the following day. The conservative Australian paper the *Financial Review* summed up the public mood in its headline: "Bush came, Hu conquered."[2] By 2006, people began talking about China's emerging "soft power."

If it is difficult to make predictions about China, we can at least examine periods of history to better understand the reasons they developed as they did, not only to get a better understanding of the state of Chinese politics and society today but also to raise better questions about its development in the future. That is what this book tries to do. There are at least four essential elements in such an inquiry. The first is politics, particularly elite politics. If Tiananmen reflected a political breakdown, how was the political system put back together? What new understandings of politics emerged to transcend the disputes that had fed into Tiananmen? And how did Jiang Zemin, with little experience in elite political circles and none in military, manage to prevail? The second is changing intellectual concerns. Intellectuals were critics of the state in the 1980s, but by the 1990s and beyond many of them were far more accepting of the state and indeed espousing nationalism in one form or another. How does one explain this change? Third, not only did intellectuals change, but so did the relationship between the state and intellectuals. This relationship became much more complex as both the nature of the state and the intellectual community were changing. And fourth, social change, which has affected the way people have thought about their society and has forced the state to modify its agenda. Not only did new social issues force their way onto the agenda, but the interests that had grown up in the 1990s complicated the state's ability to respond. International relations are not a focus of this book, but,

---

[2] Jane Perlez, "A visitor from China Eclipses Bush's Stop in Australia."

as we will see, China's relations with other countries, particularly the United States, have affected the way people view China's domestic issues, just as those domestic issues influence the way people have seen international relations.

Elite politics have been contentious at best throughout the twentieth century. Neither of Mao Zedong's first two designated successors, Liu Shaoqi or Lin Biao, was successful in replacing Mao. Only Hua Guofeng, chosen as Mao was nearing death, was able to succeed, but he was too junior in the informal political hierarchy to survive for long. And neither Hu Yaobang nor Zhao Ziyang, the heir apparents to Deng Xiaoping, was able to take his place. Such failures manifested a winner-take-all mode of political contestation in which power is conceived of as "monistic, unitary and indivisible."[3] Such a tradition, rooted in the imperial past, but reinforced and indeed heightened by the political struggles of the twentieth century, has undermined the creation of political institutions and the emergence of more pluralistic understandings of politics. The structure of Leninist systems also makes political succession difficult. Overcoming such legacies is not easy, though the creation of institutions, both formal and informal, suggests a possible course of transition to more stable politics.

The history of political contestation in twentieth-century China in general and the heritage of Leninism in particular make it difficult for both institution building and pluralist understandings of political power. The historical record to date suggests that Leninist systems do have difficulty reforming politically. Those in the Soviet Union and Eastern Europe imploded, while those in Cuba and North Korea have resisted reform; China and Vietnam have reformed economically but political reform has been limited (though recently Vietnam has made important strides). Can China chart a path that might lead to liberalization and perhaps to democratization? Can political reform follow the same, incremental path of "crossing the river while feeling the stones" as the economic reforms?

If the rules of political struggle in the twentieth century have been dominated by the perception that actors were in a game to win all, it is nevertheless true that the inauguration of reform has posed a significant challenge to this perception. Indeed, one of the major thrusts of reform was to curtail

---

[3] Tang Tsou, "Prolegomenon to the Study of Informal Groups in CCP Politics," p. 99; and Zou Dang [Tsou Tang], *Ershi shiji Zhongguo zengzhi*, p. 244.

the abuses of authority that had been associated with Mao's rule, particularly during the Cultural Revolution.[4] It was widely believed among the veteran cadres who returned to power in the late 1970s that "normal" Party life had been badly disrupted and was in urgent need of restoration. The mantra of the day was "collective leadership," meaning both that decisions should be made after inner Party discussions in which views could be freely expressed and that those who disagreed with the resulting decision should be allowed to retain their views as long as they agreed to implement the decision. The norm of democratic centralism also contained a sense that there were procedures to be followed in convening Party meetings so that one person could not arbitrarily impose his or her will on the Party or its management – including, for example, such issues as recruitment, evaluation, and promotion of cadres. Although such norms have never been fully adhered to, they continued to exert a moral force. It was toward that end that the Party passed in 1980 the Guiding Rules on Inner Party Life and adopted a new Party constitution two years later. In this way, the reaction of the CCP as an organization paralleled that of the Communist Party of the Soviet Union following Stalin's death in 1953.

Though Deng did not always adhere to the norms of collective leadership – his position as the "core" of the Party connoting something more than simply first among equals – he nevertheless advocated it in principle. Deng voiced the need to create sound political institutions in his famous 1980 speech on reforming the Party and state systems: "If these [leadership] systems are sound, they can place restraints on the actions of bad people; if they are unsound, they can hamper the efforts of good people or indeed, in certain cases, may push them in the wrong direction." It was in deference to these emerging norms of collective leadership that Deng played down the role of personality cult, though it should be noted that he was not above pushing his ideas in a cultlike fashion at critical junctures.[5]

While these inner Party norms were being developed, Chinese society, economy, and culture became far more complex and more integrated with the world. Not only has the Chinese economy more than quadrupled in size since 1978, state control has also retreated significantly from direct management of the economy. Even as late as 1998, there were 64,737, state-owned enterprises (SOEs), employing 110 million workers. By year-end 2005, the number of SOEs had fallen by two-thirds, to 27,477, and the number of workers employed in SOEs had fallen by 40 percent to

[4] Joseph Fewsmith, "The Impact of Reform on Elite Politics."
[5] For instance, the 1983 publication of Deng's *Selected Works* preceded the adoption of the critical Decision on Economic Structural Reform.

64 million. In the same period, the number of private enterprises had grown from 10,667, employing 9.7 million people, to 123,820, employing over 34.5 million workers.

These economic changes, which have been paralleled by social changes less easy to capture with statistics, have forced the Chinese government increasingly to adopt indirect ways of managing the economy, thus changing in important ways the state–society relationship. They have also fostered the growth of law. Since the revival of the National People's Congress (NPC) in the late 1970s, the process of law-making has become more institutionalized and rationalized – though there is still a long way to go.[6]

In addition, the 1978 reform decision to turn from class struggle to economic modernization has gone further than anyone could have predicted at the time. With the emphasis on economic growth has come a change in the basis of the regime's legitimacy. Although the Party still claims legitimacy on the basis of Marxism-Leninism and this claim has important consequences for the political system, everyone is aware that performance legitimacy has become far more important than ideology in justifying the government's continued rule. This was true during the 1980s but has become even more important in the years since 1989, in large part because the Tiananmen Square tragedy destroyed what little belief in Marxism-Leninism was left.

The change in the role of Party ideology, the reassertion of Party norms and the emergence and growth of new norms, the increasing complexity of the society and economy, the growing integration of the Chinese economy into the world economy, the growing body of laws and lawyers, and the increasing role played by quasi-representative organs such as the NPC have all been justly heralded as charting a path of gradual political transition. At the same time, however, it should be recognized that these emerging norms and institutions stand in tension with rule by a Leninist party and the traditional game of winner-take-all politics. Whereas the former trends point to a growing pluralization of Chinese society and governance, the latter suggest a continuing institutional and cultural rejection of pluralism.[7] Although the Jiang Zemin era saw considerable efforts to reconcile these conflicting aspects of the political system, particularly with Jiang's enunciation of the "Three Represents," which permitted entrepreneurs to join the CCP, there has been a surprising re-emphasis on ideology, not to mention a tightened control over media and crackdown on those who pursue rights

[6] Murray Scott Tanner, *The Politics of Lawmaking in China*; Stanley Lubman, *Bird in a Cage*.
[7] Thomas A. Metzger, *A Cloud Across the Pacific*.

even within the framework of the Chinese legal system, in the first years of the Hu Jintao era.[8]

In short, one should not assume that changes observed in the social and economic realms will necessarily be reflected in the Chinese political system; certainly there will not be a one-to-one correspondence. Political systems confronted by socioeconomic change can respond in a variety of ways, not all of which are "rational" from the perspective of enhancing the overall performance of the system. Political systems can simply ignore socioeconomic change, leading to stagnation (both economic and political) and collapse. Individual actors in the political system may also seek personal financial benefit from such changes and so drive what economists call "rent seeking" to new heights, hobbling the emergence of more effective administration. However, political systems can also respond positively, generating more efficient public bureaucracies and more democratic political systems.

How political systems respond depends on a variety of factors, including the perceived threat that socioeconomic changes pose to the political system as well as to individual leaders within that system. Individual leaders will command varying resources and thus respond differently to the challenges confronting the system. Some leaders will resist change while others will seek to respond positively, hoping they can ride such changes to continued or greater success within the political system. In the course of responding to such change, individual leaders are responding within the political culture of the regime – in China's case, within the contours of the CCP and within the context of the winner-take-all rules of the game – even if they are trying to change the system.

There are reasons to believe that over time Chinese politics have become more institutionalized and that conflict among leaders is better contained. But succession in Leninist systems is never easy, and, as we will see, the succession from Jiang Zemin to Hu Jintao, while it has gone better than most, has not been without its tensions. And it is not clear that Hu will be able to pass power on to a successor in a smooth and institutionalized manner.

INTELLECTUAL CONCERNS

The second area that needs to be investigated is that of the changing intellectual attitudes and concerns in the years following Tiananmen. This is

---

[8] Amnesty International, "China: The Olympics Countdown – Failing to Keep Human Rights Promises."

the story most at odds with Western (particularly American) expectations of China, particularly in the first few years after Tiananmen. The student demonstrations in 1989 raised such expectations that it took a long time for Western politicians, editorial writers, and journalists to understand that China was not on the cusp of democratic transition. China may eventually emerge as a democratic nation, but, if so, its path will be longer and more complicated than was so widely assumed in the early 1990s.[9] Contrary to those Western hopes, a significant number of intellectuals in China came to have different comprehensions of their society and the international order than their Western counterparts assumed they had. The story of intellectual development in the 1980s was one of critical self-examination (how could the Cultural Revolution have occurred?), of a cosmopolitan opening to the world, and of democratic hope and aspiration (though a serious investigation of these attitudes needs to include a critical analysis of underlying assumptions about democracy).[10] By the 1990s, many intellectuals were more supportive of their own government and more critical of the West than at any time since the May Fourth Movement of 1919.

Over the past century Chinese intellectuals have worked to create a more open and liberal society, though they have often submerged that quest into what they believed was a broader and more urgent quest for national sovereignty.[11] Nonetheless, whenever international and domestic tensions have relaxed, intellectuals have resumed their efforts to bring greater rationality to the political process, normalize the state–society relationship, and integrate China more fully into the international order. This was certainly the case following the Cultural Revolution. When Mao's death in 1976 brought that cataclysm to an end, intellectuals once again resumed their "proper" role in Chinese society.

Nothing expressed more vividly the hopes for a new era than Deng Xiaoping's humble statement in 1978 that he wished to serve as the "director of support services" for China's scientists and technicians so that they could devote themselves wholeheartedly to their work and to China's modernization.[12] But simple expressions of good wishes could hardly change fundamentally the relationship that had grown up between the Party and intellectuals since the Yan'an era. Mao had made it clear in his 1942 speech to the Yan'an Forum on Literature and Art that intellectuals must overcome

---

[9] In this judgment, I differ from Bruce Gilley, who believes democratic transformation much more imminent. See his *China's Democratic Future.*

[10] Merle Goldman, *Sowing the Seeds of Democracy in China.*

[11] Vera Schwarcz, *The Chinese Enlightenment.*

[12] Deng Xiaoping, "Speech at the Opening Ceremony of the National Conference on Science."

their natural petty bourgeois nature by self-consciously "integrating" themselves with the "masses" – with the Party as judge of how successfully they
had done so.[13] With the perspective of thirty years of persecution, intellectuals naturally were critics of the Party/state even when they served it.
Indeed, some of the most prominent and outspoken of the liberal intelligentsia worked for the state, often in high places, and their self-assigned
mission was to change the state from within. Drawing primarily from the
liberal tradition in Marxism and sometimes on Western liberalism, they
sought to build a state that placed unprecedented emphasis on human
beings – and that meant creating a more liberal, democratic order.

Even as high-ranking cadres, then, such liberal intellectuals were critics
of the state and constituted what X. L. Ding termed a "counterelite."[14] As
critics, they inevitably turned to the May Fourth tradition for moral inspiration – particularly its emphasis on science, democracy, cosmopolitanism,
and the leading role for intellectuals as societal conscience. The May Fourth
Movement (1919) was part of a broader New Culture Movement (1915–20),
which drew inspiration from the European Enlightenment and hence was
dubbed the "Chinese Enlightenment." Accordingly, liberal intellectuals in
the 1980s were often referred to (and saw themselves) as "enlightenment
intellectuals"; indeed, one of the liberal journals founded in the late 1980s
was known as *The New Enlightenment* (*Xin qimeng*).

As the 1980s wore on, China's intellectual establishment diversified.
Anticipating trends that would continue, albeit with significantly different
content, in the 1990s, intellectuals with only minimal attachment to the
state started to become active. The most important of these groups were
gathered around book series and journals: the *Toward the Future* (*Zouxiang
weilai congshu*) book series, created by Jin Guantao and Bao Zunxin; the
Academy of Chinese Culture, organized by Tang Yijie, Li Zhonghua, and
Wang Shucang; and the *Culture: China and the World* (*Wenhua: Zhongguo
yu shijie congshu*) book series, started by Gan Yang and Liu Xiaofeng. These
groups fueled the "cultural fever" (*wenhua re*) of the late 1980s, epitomized
by the film *River Elegy* (*He Shang*).[15] The self-assigned mission of these
groups was to carve out a "public space" that was independent of the state;
it was a mission that assumed a common discourse based on Enlightenment
ideals.

---

[13] Mao Tse-tung [Mao Zedong], "The Yenan Forum on Literature and Art."
[14] X. L. Ding, *The Decline of Communism in China.*
[15] The best discussion of these trends is Chen Fong-ching and Jin Guantao, *From Youthful Manuscripts
to River Elegy.*

The ideals and hopes of these and other intellectuals were shattered by Tiananmen. Some lost their positions (indeed, many had lost them in the course of political battles during the 1980s), some were jailed for various periods of time, and others went abroad. Yet neither political suppression nor exile (voluntary or otherwise) can fully account for the change in intellectual atmosphere in the 1990s or for the changed relationship between the state and intellectuals that began to emerge in the years after Tiananmen. Indeed, the single most important change in China's intellectual scene since then is that the common discourse that had given vitality to discussions in the 1980s has disintegrated as Enlightenment ideals have – for the first time since the May Fourth Movement – been questioned or rejected by a substantial portion of intellectuals. At the start of the new century, liberalism still exists and has even shown signs of vigor at the local level, but it is no longer the common faith of intellectuals. Indeed, it has been subjected to withering criticism by intellectuals, politicians, and popular forces who reject liberalism and the "neoliberal" economics they associate with it. Ironically, even as China entered the WTO, a significant intellectual opposition to capitalism and globalization has emerged. And this critique has grown in the first years of the new century.

As will be discussed in the chapters that follow, some intellectuals changed their minds while others emerged with new ideas. The political atmosphere and concerns changed. Enlightenment intellectuals came increasingly under fire. Just as important, the professionalization of the bureaucracy turned some intellectuals into technocrats; others turned to academic specializations, giving up to some extent the traditional role of social critic. At the same time, the commercialization of culture challenged traditional understandings of the role of intellectuals from below.[16]

The new mood of the 1990s generated a mixture of traditionalism, conservatism, utopianism, and nationalism.[17] The new mix has not extinguished liberalism; indeed, a new generation of liberal intellectuals is emerging to replenish the voices of the 1980s that were silenced by politics or exile. However, for much of the 1990s (except in the economic realm, where liberal ideas continued to receive a good hearing), liberal thinking was largely marginalized in public discourse. Liberal writings continued to be published, though when and to what extent depended very much on the political atmosphere, and some liberals remained optimistic about the

---

[16] Xu Jilin, *Ling yizhong qimeng*, pp. 8–15.
[17] The best compendium of intellectual debates in the 1990s is Zhang Ming and Li Shitao (eds.), *Zhishi fenzi lichang*.

future – though others felt very much besieged. The government encouraged nationalistic feelings through its campaign of patriotic education and generally discouraged writing about the "black spots" in its history.[18] This campaign no doubt encouraged the conservative mood, and to a certain extent the rise of nationalism redounded to the benefit of the government, restoring some of the legitimacy lost in June 1989. But nationalism and utopian strains of thought (which have emerged simultaneously) are clearly double-edged swords, of which the government is very much aware. So even if the decline of Enlightenment thinking has ameliorated some of the alienation between state and society that evolved in the 1990s, the new trends are hardly reassuring in the long run.

The trends in the first years of the new century are no more encouraging. Although most intellectuals remain liberal in their basic orientation, their ability to influence public discourse remains limited. The emergence of the Internet has, of course, allowed much broader circulation of ideas, but the government has fought back vigorously. What is most notable is that the government has become much better at "framing" issues, that is setting out an interpretation of events, whether SARS (Severe Acute Respiratory Syndrome) or China's place in the world, and persuading people to accept at least the rough outlines of the government's views. Of course, the burgeoning economy – contrasted with the difficulties in Russia and many other places – has helped the government make its case.

Probing new intellectual currents and the reasons they have emerged can tell us much about contemporary China, the social problems the state faces, the way social critics see the state, and the issues that arouse political passion and provoke engagement. That alone can clear away some of the gross generalizations that have been made and so give us a more nuanced understanding of present-day China. But intellectual currents and the relationship between intellectuals and the state are also part of the broader problem of institution building. Whether the state can explain its efforts to deal with the problems society faces and secure the acceptance of intellectuals for emerging institutional arrangements are important factors in building legitimacy. To the extent that intellectual currents support state efforts and "public opinion" is mollified, the odds of repeating a Tiananmen-type situation are reduced. Conversely, extreme alienation exacerbates political tensions, while cynicism undermines the effectiveness of nascent institutions. It is open to question whether the turn away from the Enlightenment

---

[18] Suisheng Zhao, "Chinese Intellectuals' Quest for National Greatness and Nationalistic Writing in the 1990s."

ideals of the May Fourth Movement can continue to pressure the political system in ways that promote greater openness, accountability, and restraint. It is also of some concern whether the more illiberal declarations emerging in recent years could form a basis for popular mobilization – as with the demonstrations against Japan in the spring of 2005. In any event, understanding the changes that have already occurred is the first step in thinking more clearly about China's present and future.

THE STATE AND INTELLECTUALS

To look at the evolution of both intellectuals and the political elite is to raise questions about the relationship between these two communities and the ways in which that relationship has changed over time. When Merle Goldman looked at the "democratic elite" in the 1980s, she inevitably turned to "Hu Yaobang's intellectual network" because most of those who were exploring democratization of the political system were tied into this network in some fashion, trying to influence the policies of the CCP.[19] Similarly, when I explored arguments over economic policy in the 1980s, the intellectuals involved were invariably tied into either the conservative network that surrounded Chen Yun, the senior Party leader and economic specialist, or Zhao Ziyang, the premier and later general secretary who led efforts to reform the economy and thus increasingly came into conflict with the policy preferences of Chen Yun.[20] Intellectuals were, to an overwhelming degree, "establishment intellectuals."[21]

This situation began to change in the mid-1980s as intellectuals, frustrated by the lack of political reform, began to carve out an autonomous realm from which they could push for cultural reform. Although the "cultural fever" referred to above allowed for continued links between the state and intellectuals, the growing autonomy of intellectuals soon led them on a collision course with the state.[22]

In some ways, the relationship between the state and the intellectuals in the 1990s continued this trend toward separation, but both the character of the state and that of the intellectuals – not to mention the content of intellectual discussions – have changed greatly, so the relationship between the two arenas is substantially different from what prevailed in the 1980s. On the one hand, political leaders are themselves much better educated than any previous Chinese leadership of the twentieth century. In the 1990s CCP

[19] Goldman, *Sowing the Seeds of Democracy in China.*   [20] Joseph Fewsmith, *Dilemmas of Reform.*
[21] Carol Lee Hamrin and Timothy Cheek (eds.), *China's Establishment Intellectuals.*
[22] Chen Fong-ching and Jin Guantao, *From Youthful Manuscripts to River Elegy.*

general secretary Jiang Zemin was a graduate of Shanghai's famous technical institute, Jiaotong University, while Premier Zhu Rongji was a graduate of the even better known Qinghua University. Today, both Party head Hu Jintao and Premier Wen Jiabao are graduates of Qinghua University. At the same time, many of those who advise the leadership, either from positions within the government or from positions in universities or think-tanks, are highly qualified intellectuals. Nevertheless, they are intellectuals who have gained expertise by dealing with specific issue over long periods of time; they are, in short, not the generalists of before but rather technocrats (though one hastens to add that many continue to keep in touch with broad intellectual trends).[23] As we will see, the emergence of a technocratic elite has not ended the role of intellectual as generalist, for the issues China faces can never be reduced to technocratic issues, but it has diminished this function.

In sum, as government leaders and their advisers have become better educated and more specialized, the distance between them and the broader intellectual community has both narrowed *and* broadened. It has narrowed in the sense that government leaders are themselves often intellectuals and thus share the same general background as other intellectuals. This trend should, *ceteris paribus*, narrow the gap between the two communities and facilitate communication. However, the increasing specialization of many government leaders and advisers means that they are often better informed on specific issues than are their intellectual counterparts. They no longer need to be given broad advice about whether to reform but instead need highly specific advice – which only a few academic specialists are in a position to provide – about *how* to reform.[24] When intellectuals raise broad concerns about the state of contemporary Chinese society – especially about political reform issues – government bureaucrats tend to view them as irrelevant, and in this sense the gap between state and intellectuals is widened.

If the nature of government leadership has changed, then the nature of the intellectual community has changed even more. Several contradictory trends can be observed. First, among some intellectuals there has

---

[23] The important changes that have taken place as a result of generational change are explored in Cheng Li, *China's Leaders*.

[24] There are exceptions to this generalization, as many intellectuals have become much more specialized than before – a trend that reflects an important change in the intellectual community. The government can and does tap the expertise of intellectuals at universities and think-tanks, but such advice tends to be issue-specific rather than the broader advocacy of policy orientation that dominated in the 1980s. This trend toward expertise suggests a maturation in both the government and the intellectual community.

been a distinct trend away from the traditional role of intellectuals as the conscience of society, a role that has deep roots in China's Confucian past. Assaulted by commercialization on the one hand and professionalization on the other, the tradition of the intellectual as generalist giving wise moral advice to the political leadership – the role assigned to the intellectual in the story of Qu Yuan, the second-century BCE adviser who drowned himself when disaster befell the king who had ignored Qu's advice – has faded as many have retreated to the ivory tower. Professionalism, however, is not necessarily contradictory to expressing moral conscience, so a second trend has been the combination of expertise with policy advice. For instance, a substantial number of intellectuals have become experts on one or more aspects of Chinese society, such as rural governance, and have, on the basis of extensive research, raised new ideas for reform. Finally, there is a large and important group of public intellectuals – the "New Left" (a diverse group of intellectuals who are critical of both Marxist orthodoxy and Western liberalism – see Chapter 4) – who continue to articulate what they believe to be the important concerns of the moment if not from the liberal perspective Western observers became accustomed to. Indeed, this book largely focuses on this group of intellectuals. For them, as for their predecessors of the past century and more, the questions of identity continue to loom large: China's relationship to the outside world (inevitably summed up as "the West"), the state's relationship to society, and the present's relationship with the past. This group was largely distanced from the halls of government in the 1990s, but it has emerged as much more influential in the first years of this century.

The role of public opinion remains modest in China, but its significance has clearly grown.[25] One aspect of this growing realm of public opinion has been the commercialization of culture, a trend that has forced intellectuals to compete in or against a real marketplace. As we will see, this too has affected the role of intellectuals in Chinese society. However, the commercialization of culture has not been restricted to the world of entertainment but has also created an audience for a wide variety of ideas – from popular histories to global issues and nationalism. To a certain extent, the government must compete in this marketplace of ideas as well. Thus one finds, for instance, an explosion in the number of books dealing with foreign policy – a subject that was virtually taboo in the 1980s. Some of these works defend the government's position while others are openly critical. In either case, the realm of public opinion can no longer be ignored.

---

[25] Joseph Fewsmith and Stanley Rosen, "The Domestic Context of Chinese Foreign Policy."

Apart from public opinion in the traditional sense, there is also an obvious effort to use publication to bring ideas to the attention of policy-makers or for policy-makers to defend their ideas in public against others in government. The lines linking the state and intellectuals have multiplied, and different interests within the state have tried to manipulate intellectuals to support their preferred positions – just as intellectuals have tried to rally opinion to push their ideas on the state. The interaction between the state and public opinion is complex, subtle, and often obscure to the outside observer; nonetheless, it is an important part of the political process. Still, glimpses can be gained by looking at specific issues and events. Even if our knowledge of this process is not as good as we would like, ignoring it would miss an important dimension of the contemporary scene.

To say that public opinion has been of growing importance is not to say that the political leadership always pays attention to what intellectuals say. Indeed, there are times when political concerns dominate intellectual discussion to the point where the latter are nearly irrelevant. This was largely true of the period immediately following Tiananmen. Intellectuals were largely shocked into silence by the enormity of what had happened; alienated from the political leadership, they had little desire to participate in discussions – and the political leadership, caught up in its own conflicts, had little patience with intellectual expression.

This relative absence of state–intellectual communication in the immediate aftermath of Tiananmen points to the temporal aspect of this relationship. The debate in the wake of Tiananmen was a very political debate that pitted defenders of Marxist orthodoxy (known as the "Old Left" in China) against the reformers allied with Deng Xiaoping. This was the culmination of long-festering differences of opinion that had been building for a decade within the Party, and there was little that intellectuals could do or say to sway the outcome.[26] This period lasted until Deng Xiaoping's famous journey to the south of China in early 1992 and the subsequent affirmation of his views at the Fourteenth Party Congress later that year.

With the basic distribution of power and the affirmation of reform settled by the Congress, at least temporarily, attention could turn to what type of state the political leadership wanted to (or could) build in the post-Tiananmen period. Indeed, these problems were made worse by the lack of attention given to many issues in the 1989–92 period. Given the state's

---

[26] One exception to this generalization is that economists could report and analyze the failings of the economy in this period, thus influencing the debate.

weakened legitimacy and the important role always accorded to ideology in Communist China, there was a role for China's intellectuals to play. What was surprising to outside observers was that, as intellectuals began to partake again in public discourse, much of the antagonism they had directed toward the state only a few years before had largely dissipated. Indeed, one of the real ironies of recent Chinese society is that in the 1980s, a time in which the leadership pushed hard to make reforms against an opposition that was both dubious and entrenched, intellectuals were increasingly alienated by the government and disbelieving of its propaganda.[27] Contrarily, in the 1990s, a time when most outsiders would agree that the government had little interest in political (unlike economic) reform, students and the intellectual community were more believing of government propaganda (despite access to more sources of news) and more supportive of their government generally. The students at Beijing University who questioned American policy and intentions when President Clinton spoke there in June 1998 may have been put to the task by officials, but their cynicism was certainly widespread on college campuses by the middle and late 1990s.[28] Understanding why this new mood has developed is important for those who seek to comprehend contemporary China.

Part of the answer to this question is globalization. As we shall see, a significant portion of Chinese intellectuals (like Western critics of globalization) are very skeptical of the process of globalization – including what it means for China's economic, cultural, and political independence. This orientation dramatically reverses the prevailing mood of the 1980s, and on this point it can be argued that a substantial part of the intellectual community is to the "left" of the governmental mainstream. Worry over globalization partly explains the rise of nationalism in the 1990s.

By the mid-1990s, intellectuals and the state were each exploring in their own ways the issues of state legitimacy, state–society relations, and China's relationship to the outside world. Sometimes there was obvious influence and collaboration; for example, Wang Huning, a well-known political scientist at Shanghai's Fudan University, was invited by Jiang Zemin to join the government in an important think-tank role. Sometimes there seemed to be a commonality of interest, as intellectuals and the government each explored what was considered the baleful influence of the West;

---

[27] Stanley Rosen, "Youth and Social Change in the PRC."

[28] I have no direct knowledge of whether students at Beijing University were told to raise the somewhat hostile questions that they did. I have been told that, when Secretary of State Warren Christopher visited Fudan University and government officials wanted to get a point across, every student in the audience had been given the same question to ask if called on first.

and sometimes there were clashes as government and intellectual views diverged.

By the middle to late 1990s, there was a more obvious contestation over public discourse. Different segments of the intellectual community vied with each other over ideas, while the government (indeed, different parts of the government) reached out to different groups of intellectuals in an effort to influence public discourse. By the end of the decade, there was renewed conflict between at least some intellectuals and the government. Unlike ten years earlier, however, by the end of the 1990s it was the government that was generally more cosmopolitan in its outlook,[29] whereas students and intellectuals took to the streets to angrily denounce the US bombing of the Chinese Embassy and to contest the government's acceptance of American terms for entering the WTO.

In the first decade of the new century, particularly as Hu Jintao took over as general secretary of the CCP and Wen Jiabao replaced Zhu Rongji as premier of the State Council, the government began to absorb at least some of the views of intellectual critics. For instance, concerns about "social justice," raised pointedly by the New Left, have become central concerns of the new administration. This trend suggests that public opinion in a limited but vital sense has become more important in recent years.

SOCIAL CHANGE

Understanding the changing world of China's intellectuals and their relationship to the political system is one aspect of the larger task of looking at a rapidly changing Chinese society, which is the fourth area of concern. In the years since Tiananmen, at least two aspects of social change appear critical. On the one hand, there has been the growth of politically well-connected economic interests. Despite the growth of market forces, cultivating relations with political leaders continues to be an important part of business life in China – and sometimes a short cut to great wealth. There have been spectacular cases of corruption revealed over recent years, such as the Xiamen smuggling operation uncovered in 1998 and the Zhou Zhengyi land development case revealed in Shanghai in 2004. Such cases – and many more – reflect the density of corrupt relationships that bind many

---

[29] I do not want to portray the government as open-minded and "liberal" or to suggest that all intellectuals line up on the side of nationalism. As we will see in later chapters, there is a significant community of liberal intellectuals that has experienced considerable government pressure. I refer here to the growth of nationalism and opposition to the WTO because these attitudes are in such striking contrast to those prevailing a decade ago.

officials and entrepreneurs together. Certainly not all government–business relationships are corrupt, but entrepreneurs do cultivate political relationships and the fabric of such relationships distorts public policy. Interests have become a fact of life in China's political economy.

The other fact about social change in China is that, despite the rapid growth in the economy, inequalities, both interregional and intraregional are growing. The poor may be becoming less poor, but they are doing so only slowly. Rural incomes grew very slowly from the mid-1980s to the early 2000s; meanwhile, urban incomes grew rapidly. Urbanization may be the only long-term solution to this urban–rural gap, but that is a very long-term proposition. Despite the fact that over 100 million people have migrated to the cities, there are today more peasants than there were in 1978. In the 1980s, the rapid growth of township and village enterprises (TVEs) drew nearly 130 million off the land, but the number of jobs being created by TVEs has stagnated now for nearly a decade. Meanwhile, urban layoffs have created an underclass of some 30 million urban poor – a problem China has never faced before.

The juxtaposition of a very wealthy *nouveau riche* urban elite and a still struggling rural population and now a new urban poor class has proven a fertile ground for those who question the direction of reform. In some ways, this questioning is a continuation of previous arguments over reform. There were major debates over reform policy in the 1980s and especially in the wake of Tiananmen when more conservative leaders gained the upper hand.[30] That deadlock was broken by Deng Xiaoping's journey to the south in early 1992, and reform regained momentum. But as social inequalities grew, new doubts and debates broke out, particularly starting in 2004. Unlike the earlier round of debates, the more recent ones have reflected the growth of an urban public opinion and a populist urge backed up by the growth of the Internet and other technologies. Although China remains a state-dominated country, public opinion is challenging and influencing state policy in ways not evident a decade ago.

Whether these trends are "good" depends on where one stands in these policy debates. Although the critics charge that the economic reforms have fostered inequality and corruption, it is not clear that they have clear-cut alternatives that would not lead to worse outcomes. Although their critiques of insider deals and other abuses of reform shine a useful light on the dark corners of reform, it is not yet evident that the exposure of scandals is leading to better corporate governance and healthier legal institutions.

---

[30] On reform debates in the 1980s, see Fewsmith, *Dilemmas of Reform*.

The populist thrust of this critique could even slow the implementation of needed reforms. And the nationalist edge evident in so much of this rhetoric could lead to new frictions in implementing WTO regulations, protecting intellectual property rights, understandings of "economic security," and perhaps national security (which goes beyond the scope of this book).

PART I

Line struggle revisited: the attack on Deng's reform program

Tiananmen and the conservative critique of reform

The violence of June 4, 1989 stunned China's intellectual community. Although reflections and introspections began almost immediately, it would be over two years before intellectuals began to regain their voice, and when they did it was not only a different voice that emerged but also a very changed and divided community. Chinese intellectuals would re-emerge in a very different society, and their reactions to the surrounding socio-economic and political events polarized them in a way not apparent in the 1980s or even, perhaps, before.

The silence and general irrelevance of the intellectual community in the wake of Tiananmen contrasted vividly with the turmoil among the political elite. The Party leadership was neither cowed into silence nor irrelevant, but it was shaken badly. Questions about the goals of reform had simmered just below the surface for years. Was reform, as Party documents repeatedly proclaimed, about the "self-perfection" of socialism or was reform leading China away from socialism? Zhao Ziyang was a lightning rod for such issues. Conservative Party leaders believed that Zhao had been leading reform farther and farther from socialism and that Tiananmen was the inevitable and foreseeable denouement of the reform program that Zhao led and symbolized. It is apparent from the tone of many of the denunciations of Zhao appearing in the weeks and months following Tiananmen that such conservatives resented Zhao personally; they believed that he had ignored and insulted them, treating their concerns contemptuously. But beyond their personal dislike of Zhao was a broader concern about the content of reform as a whole, and that concern centered on the figure of Zhao's patron, senior leader Deng Xiaoping. The question thrown open by Tiananmen, then, was the nature of Deng's leadership and thus whether or not the Party should continue reform as it had been defined by Deng. Many believed that it should not.

The question of the content of reform – or, in Chinese jargon, the political line[1] – was related to a number of state–society questions: the relations between the central government and the localities, the rapidly changing social structure of Chinese society (including the emergence of a *nouveau riche* class, the growing independence of the intellectual elite, and the rising expectations of society), and the very real fears of many people that reform might hurt rather than help their interests. In other words, reform had generated a profound range of social changes, and the question that had racked the Party for years was how it should respond to these changes. How should it channel, suppress, or incorporate the demands that increasingly emanated from this changing society?

Another broad area of questions generated by Tiananmen revolved around China's relations with the outside world. Deng Xiaoping himself raised this issue in his June 9, 1989 address to martial law troops. Deng declared the Tiananmen incident to be "the inevitable result of the domestic microclimate and the international macroclimate."[2] This sense that Tiananmen was influenced (if not instigated) by outside forces raised the issue of readjusting China's relations with the outside world, particularly the United States. The issue of China's relations with the outside world has continued to intrude into Chinese domestic politics throughout the post-Tiananmen period as first Eastern Europe and then the Soviet Union rejected communism, as relations with the United States remained generally strained through much of the 1990s, and as closer ties with East Asia have suggested alternative development models.

In June 1989, a shaken and divided Party leadership tried to begin the process of reconstituting itself while sorting out how its domestic and foreign policies should or should not be changed. This was a highly contentious process. There is little question that Deng's prestige plummeted in the wake of Tiananmen. Deng, however, was not without resources; he was still the "core" of the Party. The term "core" was added to China's political vocabulary by Deng himself, but it clearly reflects a phenomenon that has characterized CCP politics at least since Mao and one that certainly has

---

[1] In the reform period, different conceptions of the scope, pace, and goal of reform grew up around Chen Yun on the one hand and Deng Xiaoping on the other. Although Chen never challenged Deng's "core" status directly, he and his colleagues did develop a systematic critique of Deng's approach to reform. This critique was used to try to limit reform. The conservative critique of reform became the basis for criticizing a whole series of policies, and implicitly Deng's leadership, in the post-Tiananmen period. It thus seems appropriate to refer to this struggle as a "line" struggle, even if it remained implicit. For a discussion of the conflict between Chen and Deng, see Joseph Fewsmith, *Dilemmas of Reform.*

[2] Deng Xiaoping, "Zai jiejian shoudu jieyan budui junyishang ganbu shi de jianghua," p. 302.

roots deep in China's history. Although vague, the term "core" suggests a leader who occupies the center of a wide-ranging web of formal and informal relations that confer an authority not easily displaced.[3] Mao developed his core position in the Party by leading it through the most traumatic phase of its history, bringing the Party back from the debacle in Jiangxi to become a vigorous and growing movement in the heady days of Yan'an and the Sino–Japanese War. In 1943, the Party recognized Mao's unique status by declaring that he would have the decisive vote even if his colleagues on the Secretariat (the equivalent of the later Politburo) disagreed.[4] Mao's immediate successor, Hua Guofeng, never attained core status because he lacked the range of experience and connections essential to that position. Deng did have that status within the Party, and thus replaced Hua and emerged as the core of the "second generation" of CCP leadership (as Deng put it, ignoring the fact that he was really part of the first generation of leadership).

In 1989, Deng could use his core status to stress continuity and to dominate decisions on leadership. When Deng met with leaders of martial law troops on June 9, he declared that the line of "one center and two basic points" (economic development was the center; the two basic points were reform and opening up on the one hand and opposition to "bourgeois liberalization" on the other), which had been officially adopted at the Thirteenth Party Congress in 1987, was correct and that reform and opening up needed to be pursued even more vigorously.[5] Deng also tried to forestall an all-out attack on Zhao's policies (and himself) by declaring that "the political report of the Thirteenth Party Congress was passed by the representatives of the Party to the congress; even one character must not be changed."[6]

JIANG ZEMIN EMERGES AS GENERAL SECRETARY

Perhaps the most important advantage that Deng's core status conferred was the authority to have the final word on high-level leadership decisions. No doubt, given the defense of the Party against the so-called counter-revolutionary rebellion and the discrediting of Zhao Ziyang, conservatives hoped that one of their own – perhaps Premier Li Peng, economic planner Yao Yilin, or even former Propaganda Department head Deng Liqun – might replace Zhao as general secretary. Dashing their hopes, Deng on

[3] Tang Tsou, "Chinese Politics at the Top."   [4] Stuart R. Schram, "General Introduction," p. xix.
[5] Deng, "Zai jiejian shoudu jieyan budui junyishang ganbu shi de jianghua."   [6] Ibid.

May 31 informed Li Peng and Politburo Standing Committee member Yao Yilin that the Party leadership (Deng said that he had conferred with Party elders Chen Yun and Li Xiannian, giving a fairly accurate sense of who constituted the Party leadership) had decided that Jiang Zemin, then CCP secretary of Shanghai, would be plucked from relative obscurity to become the "core" of the third generation of CCP leadership.[7] In explaining the decision, Deng almost contemptuously told Li and Yao, "[t]he people see reality. If we put up a front so that people feel that it is an ossified leadership, a conservative leadership, or if the people believe that it is a mediocre leadership that cannot reflect the future of China, then there will be constant trouble and there will never be a peaceful day."[8]

Thus began Deng's efforts to install a new leadership – his third attempt following the dismissals of Hu Yaobang and Zhao Ziyang – and so guarantee the continuation of his policies after his death. The choice of Jiang Zemin surprised insiders and outsiders alike, but in fact there were not many viable candidates from whom to choose. In 1989 there were five members of the Politburo Standing Committee. Two of these, Zhao Ziyang and Hu Qili, were disqualified because they had been too tolerant toward the Tiananmen demonstrations. Li Peng and Yao Yilin, as Deng scornfully noted, were too conservative to satisfy him. Deng might have added that the choice of either one would have decisively shifted the balance of the Party; maintaining balance – albeit with a bias toward reform – was the only way to maintain both a semblance of stability within the Party and the continuation of Deng's line of reform and opening up. That left Qiao Shi. Some reports maintain that Deng asked Qiao to be general secretary, but that seems unlikely. Qiao seems not to have been the power player that his background in intelligence led many to believe he was, and in any case he was too close to Zhao Ziyang to satisfy conservatives.

Thus, Deng cast his eye toward other members of the Politburo. Chen Xitong might have been a logical choice; he had long served in the Beijing Municipal Party apparatus and had cultivated ties with Deng and other Party elders. However, his well-known hardline response to the student demonstrations undoubtedly disqualified him – as was the case with Li Peng and Yao Yilin. Li Ruihuan was another possibility, but his weak educational background no doubt eliminated him as a serious contender.[9]

---

[7] Deng Xiaoping, "Zucheng yige shixing gaige de you xiwang de ling dao jiti."
[8] Ibid. The full text of Deng's remarks is reportedly far more scathing than the passages included in Deng's selected works.
[9] According to Andrew J. Nathan et al. (eds.), *The Tiananmen Papers*, Deng described Li as "energetic, effective, and thoughtful" (p. 262). Whether or not this is true must remain in doubt as the provenance

Just as Chen and Li were Party secretaries of Beijing and Tianjin, respectively, Jiang Zemin was secretary of China's largest city, Shanghai. If Jiang lacked the illustrious credentials of his revolutionary predecessors, as all members of his generation necessarily did, his background and career were solid. Born in the Jiangsu city of Yangzhou in 1926, Jiang received a mixed classical Chinese and Western education. In 1937 he tested into the prestigious Yangzhou Middle School, where he pursued his interests in literature and music. In 1939, at the age of 13, Jiang was adopted into the family of his uncle, Jiang Shangqing, who had been martyred as a result of his revolutionary activities. In 1943, Jiang began to study electrical engineering at Nanjing's Central University, which was subsequently merged with Shanghai's Jiaotong University. It was at this time that Jiang became actively involved in the Shanghai underground, and in June 1946 he joined the CCP.[10]

In 1947 Jiang Zemin began a career characterized by a gradual climb upward, though mostly in technical fields. In 1953 he was recruited into Shanghai's No. 2 Design Bureau by his political mentor, Wang Daohan (later mayor of Shanghai). In 1955 he was selected to study automotive engineering at the Stalin Autoworks in Moscow. When he returned to China the following year, he was sent to the Changchun No. 1 Automobile Factory, where he spent the next six years. When the Cultural Revolution broke out, Jiang inevitably came under attack as a "person in authority taking the capitalist road," but he quickly resumed his career when he was selected in 1971 to lead a technical delegation to Romania.[11]

In 1980, Wang Daohan was appointed mayor of Shanghai and recommended that Jiang take his place on the State Import–Export Management Commission and the State Foreign Investment Management Commission, organs that were responsible for the newly established Special Economic Zones in Guangdong and Fujian provinces. In 1982, Jiang was appointed first vice-minister of the newly established Ministry of the Electronics Industry and was selected as a member of the CCP Central Committee. He was appointed Minister of the Electronics Industry in June 1983.

---

of these documents remains unclear. According to *The Tiananmen Papers*, Bo Yibo attended the meeting held at Deng Xiaoping's house on the morning of May 17 and quoted his words at that meeting. Zhao Ziyang, however, makes no mention of Bo being at that meeting. It seems unlikely that Zhao simply forgot to mention Bo's presence. See Mei Qiren, *Three Interviews with Zhao Ziyang*, p. 14. See also Alfred L. Chan, "The Tiananmen Papers Revisited," with a rejoinder by Andrew J. Nathan.

[10] Bruce Gilley, *Tiger on the Brink*, pp. 3–23; Yang Zhongmei, *Jiang Zemin zhuan*, pp. 45–59. See also Robert Lawrence Kuhn, *The Man Who Changed China*.

[11] Gilley, *Tiger on the Brink*, pp. 37–62; Yang, *Jiang Zemin zhuan* pp. 70–90.

In 1985, again with Wang Daohan's support, Jiang was named mayor of Shanghai. Two years later, at the CCP's Thirteenth Congress, Jiang Zemin was named as Shanghai CCP secretary and concurrently a member of the Politburo.[12]

In short, Jiang's career was one of steady promotions. His ability to resume his career in 1971 reflects both his junior status and his technical credentials. That he was able to survive in the Ministry of Machine Building in the 1970s no doubt reflects his cautious nature, something that might have cost him further promotion in the reform era if he had not been technically trained and not had the support of patrons such as Wang Daohan. Later, as mayor and then Party secretary of Shanghai, Jiang had many opportunities to host the top leadership when they visited Shanghai. Deng Xiaoping often spent part of the winter there, as did Chen Yun, who was born just outside the city and had spent his early revolutionary career in the city. Jiang's relationship with Li Xiannian seems to have been particularly close. He was thus acceptable to the leading figures in the Party, and that in itself was an important qualification for leadership.

No doubt the single most important reason for Jiang's promotion at that critical time was his decision in May to close down the reform-minded newsweekly *World Economic Herald* (*Shijie jingji daobao*). On April 19, the *World Economic Herald* had convened a joint meeting in Beijing with the *New Observer* (*Xin guancha*) to memorialize Hu Yaobang. Run by the veteran revolutionary Ge Yang, the *New Observer* had been one of the principal outlets for liberal thinking in the 1980s and was at least as controversial as the *World Economic Herald*. In speeches, Su Shaozhi, Yan Jiaqi, Chen Ziming, and others called for "reversing the verdict" on Hu Yaobang as well as negating the 1983 campaign against "spiritual pollution" and the 1987 campaign against "bourgeois liberalization." These speeches were printed in an issue of the *World Economic Herald* that was to go to press on April 24. By this time, there were deepening debates within the Party leadership about how to respond to the student demonstrations, which had started eight days earlier on April 16; on April 25, Deng would endorse a hardline approach by saying that the demonstrations were aimed at "fundamentally negating the leadership of the Chinese Communist Party and at negating the socialist system." It was that judgment, written into a *People's Daily* editorial the next day, that inflamed student opinion and brought the student movement to a new crisis point.[13]

---

[12] Gilley, *Tiger on the Brink*, pp. 64–98; Yang, *Jiang Zemin zhuan*, pp. 106–18, 145–59.
[13] Richard Baum, *Burying Mao*, pp. 251–5.

Aware of the controversies raging within the Party, Jiang Zemin's close confidante Chen Zhili, head of the Shanghai Propaganda Department (and appointed in 1998 to head the Ministry of Education and in 2003 to be a State Councilor), was upset when she saw galley proofs of the forthcoming issue of the *World Economic Herald*, fearing that it would give new stimulus to the demonstrations. On hearing of the situation, Jiang Zemin called the editor of the *World Economic Herald*, Qin Benli, and told him to delete sensitive paragraphs from the offending issue. When, despite Jiang's order, part of the issue was printed and distributed, Jiang immediately ordered the presses stopped and Qin Benli removed from his post. Liu Ji, another close associate of Jiang Zemin who would play an important role in the 1990s, headed a work team that took over the paper. At the time, Liu was deputy head of the Shanghai Propaganda Department. Oddly enough, he was also on very good terms with Qin Benli; not only was Liu himself a contributor to the paper, but Qin's wife had taught Liu in middle school.[14]

The *World Economic Herald* had been one of the icons of liberal reformers in the 1980s and a beacon of expanding press freedom, so the removal of the respected Qin Benli and the paper's closure prompted an immediate outcry among press circles. For the first time since the demonstrations had started, journalists took to the streets. Carrying banners that identified their papers – *People's Daily* (*Renmin ribao*), *Workers Daily* (*Gongren ribao*), *Enlightenment Daily* (*Guangming ribao*), and so on – journalists hoisted signs declaring that they would not be forced to lie again.

At the same time, Zhao Ziyang, who had journeyed to North Korea April 23–30 in one of the worst-timed diplomatic trips imaginable, returned and convened a meeting of the Politburo on May 10. Referring to the *World Economic Herald* incident, Zhao declared that the Shanghai Party Committee had "made a mess of things."[15] Before the meeting concluded, an anxious Jiang followed Li Ruihuan to the men's room to seek his advice. Li, who did not have a good opinion of Jiang, merely laughed.[16] Returning to Shanghai, Jiang tried to repair the damage. Despite interventions by Liu Ji and Su Shaozhi, Qin Benli refused to reconsider his actions, and Jiang seemed to be left hanging.[17] Perhaps, if Jiang's efforts to reverse his "decisive" handling of the *World Economic Herald* case had succeeded, he would not have been chosen as general secretary. However, Jiang emerged looking both decisive in opposing "bourgeois liberalization" and capable in handling the local situation; unlike Beijing, Shanghai was under control.

[14] Gao Xin, *Jiang Zemin de muliao*, p. 207.   [15] Ibid., p. 211.
[16] Ibid., pp. 210–11   [17] Ibid., pp. 211–12.

THE QUESTION OF ZHAO

Following the ouster of Zhao Ziyang and the subsequent crackdown in Beijing and elsewhere, the question of how to deal with Zhao became central. This issue was inevitably linked with the question of Deng Xiaoping's leadership, not just because Zhao's selection first as premier and then as general secretary now seemed to reflect poorly on Deng Xiaoping's judgment (for a second time – the ouster of Hu Yaobang in 1987 marking the first) but also because Zhao had been implementing a political *cum* economic line long supported by Deng.[18] Deng was famous as the exponent of the pragmatic advice, "black cat, white cat, whichever cat catches the mouse is a good cat." Zhao had come to Beijing in 1980 as a pragmatist known for his concentration on economic development.

What lay behind this argument were distinctly different understandings of what "reform" meant. For Zhao – and for Deng – economic development was primary, and the only way to develop the economy was to marketize and join the international economy. In practice, this meant undermining and going around much of the old planned economy, allowing a market economy to grow outside the scope of the planned economy, and thus continuously reducing the relative importance of the planned economy. It also meant, to a greater or lesser extent, playing down much of socialist ideology. For Deng, the "four cardinal principles" (upholding the socialist road, the dictatorship of the proletariat [later, the people's democratic dictatorship], the leadership of the Communist Party, and Marxism–Leninism–Mao Zedong Thought), which he had enunciated in the spring of 1979 to curtail liberal criticisms of Mao and the socialist system, did not constitute a vision of socialist ideology but rather a boundary line defining the limits of acceptable public expression. When expression diverged too far from what he deemed acceptable, Deng cracked down. Such crackdowns allowed more ideologically oriented conservatives to criticize "bourgeois liberalization" for a while, but inevitably Deng would dampen the expression of such themes and re-emphasize economic development. Deng was interested in defining a middle path, using "reform and opening up" to

---

[18] One can draw distinctions between Zhao and Deng, but the similarities predominate. Overall, Zhao appears to have been closer to Deng on most issues than Hu Yaobang. Although Zhao was more open-minded than Deng in his response to the Tiananmen demonstrations, Zhao was hardly a liberal. After all, it was Zhao who sponsored discussions on the "new authoritarianism." The Thirteenth Party Congress, which clearly bears Zhao's imprint, was strongly supported by Deng. On economic issues, Deng was in some sense the more radical, or at least the more impatient, as suggested by his 1988 advocacy of rapid price reform. Certainly in the eyes of their critics, the similarities were far greater than the differences.

oppose "leftism" and using the "four cardinal principles" to oppose "bourgeois liberalization."[19] It was a way to prevent ideological disputes from
tearing the Party apart as they had in the past, and it was a political strategy that allowed Deng to build a coalition that upheld the center of the
political spectrum. The adoption of the formula "one center and two basic
points" in the spring of 1987 (in the course of the campaign against bourgeois liberalization that followed Hu Yaobang's ouster) merely formalized
long-standing practice.

Leftists, on the other hand, emphasized ideology. They did so for several reasons. Many were products of the propaganda "system" (*xitong*) and
thus had a vested interest in maintaining the political relevance of their
competencies. Central ministries also had a vested interest in conservative ideological interpretations, because emphasizing such themes as "the
planned economy as primary" or "state-owned enterprises as pillars of the
economy" bolstered their importance in the political system. Leftist ideology also appealed to the vast numbers of Party cadres who worked in
state-owned enterprises and whose relevance was thrown into question by
the economic reforms. In 1979 Deng had raised the issue of removing Party
committees from enterprises, an issue that continued to fester throughout
the 1990s. Thus, leftists saw Deng's reforms as undermining ideology and
weakening the "fighting strength" of the Party. Market-oriented reforms,
decentralization, and opening to the outside world all threatened these
beliefs and interests.

These very different orientations underlay the mounting tensions in the
Party in the late 1980s, and the anger and frustration of the left wing of
the Party came pouring out in the aftermath of Tiananmen. Even though
much of this hostility was directed at Zhao Ziyang, it was clear that the
criticism of Zhao was also intended to curb Deng's authority. Deng's sharp
defense of the Thirteenth Party Congress resolution – "not one character
should be changed" – was no doubt intended to staunch this anti-reform
tide.

The decision to declare martial law had effectively been made in a meeting at Deng's house on the morning of May 17. Zhao had asked for a meeting
with Deng to explain his views, but instead of meeting individually Deng
notified Li Peng, Yao Yilin, Hu Qili, Qiao Shi – the other members of the
Politburo Standing Committee – and Yang Shangkun. Prior to the meeting, Zhao had canvassed the opinions of his colleagues and found that four
of them – Hu Qili, Qiao Shi, Yang Shangkun, and himself – all opposed

---

[19] Tang Tsou, "Political Change and Reform."

declaring martial law. Only two – Li Peng and Yao Yilin – supported it. But, as Zhao commented in a 1995 interview, "I had been the one to ask for an audience, but he [Deng] had notified so many people, he obviously did not want to hear my opinion." Each expressed his opinion – Qiao Shi and Yang Shangkun changing their minds in the course of the meeting – but it was Deng's views that mattered. As Zhao put it, "Actually, the attitudes of these persons mattered little, as Deng might have imposed military control even if all five had disapproved."[20] A meeting of the Politburo Standing Committee later that evening formally endorsed Deng's view. It was on the morning of the 19th when a tearful Zhao Ziyang appeared in Tiananmen Square, telling students that he had "come too late." Indeed he had; he no longer functioned as general secretary.[21]

According to Party custom, Zhao was expected to support the "majority" opinion, but Zhao embarrassed and angered the Party leadership by failing to attend the public meeting called to announce the implementation of martial law in Beijing on the evening of May 19. He also refused to make the self-criticism that was expected of him. If he had, he probably would have been retained as a member of the Central Committee. Instead, Zhao chose to defend his actions.[22]

Sorting out leadership issues was the task of the Fourth Plenary Session of the Thirteenth Central Committee, which convened in Beijing on June 23–24 following a three-day enlarged meeting of the Politburo. The plenum approved the removal of three Zhao associates: Hu Qili from the Politburo Standing Committee and Rui Xingwen and Yan Mingfu from the Secretariat. Veteran economic planner Song Ping and Tianjin mayor Li Ruihuan were added to the Politburo Standing Committee along with Jiang Zemin, while Li Ruihuan and Ding Guan'gen (Deng's bridge partner) were added to the Secretariat. The new Politburo Standing Committee was more conservative than before, but it was more balanced than might have been expected. Li Peng, Yao Yilin, and Song Ping made up a conservative block, while Li Ruihuan and Qiao Shi represented more moderate views. Jiang Zemin, no ideologue by nature, would have to feel his way in these turbulent waters.

On the question of Zhao, the Fourth Plenum charged that, "[a]t the critical juncture involving the life and death of the Party and state, he made the mistake of supporting turmoil and splitting the Party, and he bears unshirkable responsibility for the formation and development of the turmoil. The

---

[20] Mei, *Three Interviews* with Zhao Ziyang, p. 14.   [21] Author interview.
[22] See Mei, *Three Interviews with Zhao Ziyang*, pp. 15–16; 51–68.

nature and consequences of his mistakes are very serious."[23] The public case for this judgment was made by Beijing mayor Chen Xitong, who presented a long and detailed report to the Standing Committee of the National People's Congress (NPC) on June 30. Despite declaring that Tiananmen had been brewing and had been "premeditated" for a long time, Chen's report focused narrowly on the alleged actions of Zhao and some of his supporters only in the months immediately preceding the crisis and during the demonstration itself. Chen sharply criticized Zhao for his opposition to the closing of the *World Economic Herald*, his speech to the Asian Development Bank, and his revelation to Gorbachev of the Thirteenth Party Congress resolution referring important Party matters to Deng – which Chen described as "deliberately directing the fire of criticism at Deng Xiaoping."[24] In his criticism of some of the intellectuals linked to Zhao, however, Chen hinted at the depth of the struggle within the Party. For instance, referring to a widely publicized conversation between senior intellectuals Yan Jiaqi and Wen Yuankai intimating that Zhao might be removed as Liu Shaoqi had been, Chen declared that this dialogue was intended to "whip up public opinion for covering up Zhao Ziyang's mistakes, keeping his position and power, and pushing bourgeois liberalization even more unbridledly."[25]

Li Peng's report to the Fourth Plenum, which unlike Chen's report to the NPC was not publicized in PRC media, makes it even clearer that the dispute between the two wings of the Party had existed for a long time. Li declared that bourgeois liberalization "spread rampantly" after Zhao became general secretary; Zhao, the premier charged, "accommodated, encouraged, and supported bourgeois liberalization." Specifically, he alleged that, at a Secretariat meeting in January 1987, Zhao had declared that of the four cardinal principles they should emphasize only Party leadership and not mention the other three – the socialist road, Marxism–Leninism–Mao Zedong Thought, and the people's democratic dictatorship. Moreover, Zhao allegedly declared that no one can explain what the socialist road is and, on other occasions, stated that corruption is inevitable at the initial stage of socialism. Li declared that in the future the Party should "carry out the struggle against bourgeois liberalization for a long time to come rather than do it perfunctorily or give it up halfway as in the past."[26]

Zhao Ziyang was allowed to attend the Fourth Plenum and respond to Li Peng's report. Oddly, the *People's Daily* even ran a picture of Party

[23] "Zhongguo gongchandang dishisanjie zhongyang weiyuanhui disice quanti huiyi gongbao," p. 544.
[24] Chen Xitong, "Report on Checking the Turmoil and Quelling the Counter-Revolutionary Rebellion," p. 29.
[25] "Li Peng's Life-Taking Report Lays Blame on Zhao Ziyang," pp. 21, 22, 23.   [26] Ibid., p. 21.

leaders attending the Fourth Plenum that included the back of Zhao's head. Zhao argued that everything he had done had been intended to "ease the confrontation" and to "gradually calm down the student unrest." He also refuted many of the charges raised by Premier Li. For instance, he said that he could not remember ever saying "corruption is inevitable at the initial stage of socialism." He rejected the accusation of neglecting political and ideological education by saying that he was worried that the "old methods" of ideology would not work and "might even arouse people's repugnance." Even while admitting responsibility for grasping economic work firmly but being lax with regard to bourgeois liberalization, he defended himself by citing Deng's words from April 1987, a time when Deng was trying to dampen an earlier campaign against bourgeois liberalization: "The struggle against bourgeois liberalization is a long-term struggle and is also a prolonged process of education. We cannot launch political movements, but should successfully carry out reform and develop the economy, thus demonstrating the superiority of the socialist system. Practice will convince people who doubt the socialist system."[27]

Zhao's speech also reveals that differences of opinion within the Party were long-standing. Describing discussions over the text of Li Peng's "Government Work Report" made to the NPC in the spring of 1989, Zhao said that Li's draft had "repeatedly" used the words "for many years" when discussing problems in economic work. The impasse was resolved by focusing the work report on just the preceding year, but Zhao reported that "[s]ome comrades" had criticized him for not allowing Li to discuss the mistakes of the "past few years" in the report.[28]

Although the Fourth Plenum accused Zhao of supporting the turmoil and splitting the Party – charges Zhao asked the Party to reconsider in his rebuttal – it could not reach a resolution on his case, declaring only that the Party would "continue to investigate his problem."[29] The plenum's failure to conclude Zhao's case reflected the depth of division within the Party. Some wanted to pursue the issue of Zhao's guilt, apparently to the point of criminal prosecution. For instance, Yuan Mu, hardline spokesman for the State Council and protégé of Premier Li Peng, stated that Zhao's case would be handled "in accordance with the criterion based on law," suggesting the possibility of legal prosecution.[30] Some Party elders were even blunter.

---

[27] "Full text" of speech delivered by Zhao Ziyang, pp. 17, 18, 19.   [28] Ibid., p. 17.
[29] "Zhongguo gongchandang dishisanjie zhongyang weiyuanhui disice quanti huiyi gongbao," pp. 543–6.
[30] Xinhua News Service, in Foreign Broadcast Information Service, *China Daily Report* (hereafter FBIS-CHI), July 12, 1989, p. 25.

Li Xiannian, President of the People's Republic of China (PRC), allegedly called Zhao the "root cause of the riots and rebellion," while Party elder Peng Zhen accused Zhao of "attempting to topple the Communist Party and wreaking havoc with the socialist system in coordination with hostile powers at home and abroad."[31]

Putting Zhao on trial, as Deng had the Gang of Four, would have had profound implications for Deng Xiaoping and the continuation of reform. Shortly after such speculation appeared, the PRC-owned Hong Kong paper *Ta kung pao* reported that Deng Xiaoping had set a two-year period for "reflection" and declared that it is "highly unlikely" that Zhao would be put on public trial.[32]

Although Deng's "prediction" that Zhao would not face trial ultimately proved correct, his call for a period of reflection was largely ignored. During the campaign against "bourgeois liberalization" that was unleashed following Tiananmen, it was impossible to separate criticism of Zhao Ziyang from issues of ideology and Party line, and there is every indication that hardliners within the Party wished to press such issues with an eye to curtailing Deng's authority and returning the Party to the more limited notion of reform that had prevailed in the late 1970s and early 1980s. In his 1989 National Day (October 1) address, Jiang Zemin asserted that there were two types of reform: one that upholds the four cardinal principles and one that is based on "bourgeois liberalization." The question, Jiang said, was whether the socialist orientation would be upheld.[33] Deng had opened the way for this line of analysis in his May 31 talk with Li Peng and Yao Yilin. In that talk, Deng said that the "center of their [Zhao Ziyang and others'] so-called 'reform' is to become capitalists. The reform I talk about is different."[34] In picking up Deng's thought and posing the question the way he did, Jiang raised the issue that would dominate Chinese politics for much of the next two years: What was socialist and what was capitalist?

By the same reasoning, if Zhao had advocated a reform that was based on "bourgeois liberalization" and hence was capitalist in nature, then Zhao's mistake would not have been a simple error of implementation (one hand firm and the other lax, as Deng put it) but an error of line. Although the Party, in the interest of putting ideological battles behind it at the

---

[31] Tseng Pin, "Party Struggle Exposed by Senior Statesmen Themselves"; see also *Wen wei po*, July 24, 1989.

[32] *Ta kung pao*, July 22, 1989, trans. FBIS-CHI, July 24, 1989.

[33] Jiang Zemin, "Zai qingzhu Zhonghua renmin gongheguo chengli sishi zhounian dahuishang de jianghua," p. 618.

[34] Deng, "Zucheng yige shixing gaige de you xiwang de lingdao jiti," p. 297.

beginning of the reform era, had ceased to describe intra-Party conflicts as "line struggles," the notion of political line and hence of line struggle remained very much a part of Party life at the elite level.

This assumption about inner-Party struggles comes through clearly in a talk Song Ping gave to a national meeting of organization department heads, where he implicitly criticized Zhao for making line errors. For Song, Tiananmen was the inevitable outcome of a trend of bourgeois liberalization that extended back to the democratic movement of 1978, had never been effectively opposed, and had resulted in such "absurd theories" (*miaolun*) as the "criterion of productive forces." The theory of productive forces, a phrase used (primarily by critics) to describe the view that anything that improves the economy is *ipso facto* socialist, was voiced prominently in an article by Zhao Ziyang that appeared in the *People's Daily* in February 1988,[35] but Song's reference was clearly to Deng Xiaoping as well. This trend of bourgeois liberalization, Song asserted, went against the Marxist political line set by the Third Plenum in 1978, and Tiananmen was the "bitter fruit of violating this [Marxist] *line*" (emphasis added).[36] Similarly, Chen Yun referred to "line struggle" in the "six points" that he conveyed to the Central Advisory Commission in November 1991. The third point reads, "Marxists must admit that there are line struggles within the Party, which is part of normal Party life, and it is necessary to actively launch inner-Party criticism and self-criticism."[37]

Both personal animosity toward Zhao and broader criticism of the "line" that Zhao was supposedly heading came through in press commentary in the summer and fall of 1989. A meeting of conservative writers and artists in July, for instance, declared that Zhao was the "biggest umbrella for bourgeois liberalization in literature and art circles" and accused him of "rudely critic[izing] comrades who adhered to the four cardinal principles" and who, as a result, were "vilified, suppressed, and attacked by others."[38]

Other articles criticized Zhao for putting forth the idea of "transforming the ideological and political work" and thus weakening the Party's ideological work.[39] For instance, one author complained that "[i]n recent years

[35] Zhao Ziyang, "Further Emancipate the Mind and Further Liberate the Productive Forces."

[36] Song Ping, "Zai quanguo zuzhi buzhang huiyi shang de jianghua," pp. 568–9, 574; emphasis added. Contrast Song's emphasis on political loyalty with Li Ruihuan's statement that, "[i]n assessing a leading cadre, his accomplishments in government are primary." See *Nanfang ribao*, October 28, 1989, trans. FBIS-CHI, November 6, 1989, p. 22.

[37] Lo Ping and Li Tzu-ching, "Chen Yun Raises Six Points of View to Criticize Deng Xiaoping."

[38] "More than Seventy Writers and Artists Attend a Forum to Study the Spirit of the Fourth Plenary Session."

[39] Gong Yantao, "The Essence of 'Transformation' Is to Abolish Ideological and Political Work"; Yao Fan, "How Comrade Zhao Ziyang Weakened the Party's Ideological and Political Work"; Liu Shi, "The Purpose of 'Transformation' Is to Pave the Way for Capitalism."

the viewpoint that class struggle in society will certainly find expression within the Party has been criticized as being a 'leftist' viewpoint."[40] The weakening of ideological and political work was held, among other things, to undermine the sense of class struggle, of which Deng was certainly every bit as guilty as Zhao.

DENG'S STRATEGY

In certain ways, the situation following Tiananmen resembled that in 1987 when, in the wake of student demonstrations, Deng and the Party elders had unceremoniously dumped General Secretary Hu Yaobang. After a four-month, often vitriolic, campaign against bourgeois liberalization that targeted three well-known intellectuals – astrophysicist Fang Lizhi, investigative journalist Liu Binyan, and writer Wang Ruowang – Deng and Zhao engineered a dramatic turnaround in the political atmosphere. In April, Deng told visiting Spanish Socialist Workers Party leader Alfonso Guerra that leftism was the "main danger" facing the Party.[41] Shortly thereafter, on May 13, Zhao Ziyang gave a major inner-Party speech, asking rhetorically but sharply: "Who would be responsible if the current [economic] policies were interpreted as liberalization?"[42] On the July 1 anniversary of the Party's founding, the *People's Daily* reprinted Deng's controversial 1980 speech "On Reform of the Party and State Leadership Structure," setting the tone for the upcoming Thirteenth Party Congress, which for the first time addressed the issue of political reform.[43]

In 1989, however, Tiananmen opened divisions within the Party that far exceeded those existing two years before. Among Party conservatives there was a deep sense of "we told you so." Their warnings, they believed, had not been listened to, and Tiananmen was the fulfillment of their predictions. Whereas previously they had held strong reservations about the direction of economic and cultural change in China, in 1989 they were convinced that reform was on the wrong track. Deng Xiaoping's prestige within the Party was correspondingly diminished by Tiananmen and the disgrace of Zhao. Chen Yun summed up the feelings of many conservatives when he accused Deng of being rightist in his economic policies and leftist in his use

---

[40] Dong Jinguan, "The Main Characteristics of Class Struggle at the Present Stage," p. 44.

[41] AFP, April 30, 1987, in FBIS-CHI, May 4, 1987, p. G2.

[42] The sense of Zhao's speech was conveyed by two *People's Daily* editorials: "Deepen the Struggle against Bourgeois Liberalization" and "We Must Not Only Persevere in Reform and Opening Up but Also Speed Them Up." The speech was subsequently published on June 15, 1987. On the drafting, see Guoguang Wu, "Documentary Politics.'"

[43] *People's Daily* restored language that had been deleted when the speech was originally published in 1983. For a comparison, see FBIS-CHI, July 7, 1987, p. K22.

of the military.[44] Unlike before, Deng could no longer dominate China's policy agenda. Turning around the political atmosphere as he had in 1987 would prove far more difficult; indeed, it would take him three years (until 1992).

Deng's task was made even more difficult by the tense international atmosphere that prevailed in the months after Tiananmen. Deng had always coupled "reform" with "opening up" not only because he believed that China's economic modernization needed capital, technology, and export markets that only the West could provide, but because he recognized that jettisoning the Maoist emphasis on international class struggle was necessary for dampening domestic calls for a continuing emphasis on class struggle, something that would (and did) make the implementation of economic reform more difficult, perhaps impossible. The unraveling of communism in Eastern Europe would make Deng's position even more difficult as the dangers of "peaceful evolution" were brought home vividly to China's leaders, Deng included.

In short, in 1989 Deng was fighting a rear-guard action. Although damaged politically, he was hardly without resources. Despite considerable doubt about the wisdom of many of his policies and even a determination to cut back those policies, no one made an effort to remove Deng from his "core" position within the Party. Chen Yun was the only one in the Party with the stature to challenge Deng, but just as he had never challenged Mao, with whom he disagreed, he never challenged Deng's political position. Indeed, Chen seemed to enjoy prestige in the Party at least in part because he was not personally ambitious. Chen was more interested in policy than power, and he seemed both content and determined to force Deng to accept a diminished role in policy-making.

In terms of political strategy, Deng clearly tried to relax the political atmosphere by responding to the popular resentments that had underlain the Tiananmen demonstrations, by trying to play down ideological tensions, and by ameliorating international tensions to the greatest extent possible. On the eve of the Fourth Plenum, Deng urged the leaders not to dissipate the energies of the Party in futile ideological disputes: "If at this time we open up some sort of discussion on ideology, such as a discussion regarding markets and planning, then not only would bringing up this sort of issue be disadvantageous to stability but it would cause us to miss an opportunity."[45] Yet it was, of course, precisely this sort of discussion – whether the given policies were "socialist" or "capitalist" – that was already

---

[44] Baum, *Burying Mao*, p. 319.   [45] Deng Xiaoping, "Disandai lingdao jiti de dangwu zhiji," p. 312.

beginning to fill the media and would dominate policy discussions until Deng's trip to the south in 1992.

Li Ruihuan, the former carpenter whom Deng had put in charge of ideology, made an effort to relax the ideological atmosphere in the summer by calling for a campaign against pornography. The campaign started on July 11, 1989, when the Press and Publications Bureau issued a circular on rectifying the cultural market. Over the summer, Li spoke on the issue of pornography many times.[46] It was a clever ploy that left conservatives nonplussed. After all, pornography was associated with Western influences, but it hardly raised the central ideological issues that conservatives desired to pursue. In September, Li asked in a sharply worded interview with the PRC-owned Hong Kong paper *Ta kung pao*: "Why do we always have to go to excess?" Berating conservative ideologues, Li said that "[w]e must not use dogmatic and rigid methods to criticize bourgeois liberalization."[47]

In Deng's talk on the eve of the Fourth Plenum, he also called for "doing some things to satisfy the people."[48] In response, the State Council in July passed a resolution on resolving problems the people were concerned about, especially restricting the activities of leading cadres' families, and on reorganizing suspect companies.[49]

Similarly, Deng harped on the issue of stability – eventually coining the phrase "stability overrides everything" (*wending yadao yiqie*)[50] – and emphasized the continuity of reform and opening up. In September, on the eve of the Party's Fifth Plenum, Deng told American physicist T. D. Lee that "reform and opening up will certainly be continued."[51] The message of reform and opening up was pressed by a *People's Daily* editorial six days later which strongly reiterated that reform would be continued and declared, "[w]e certainly must not stop eating for fear of choking."[52]

CONSERVATIVES PRESS THEIR ADVANTAGE

As Deng and Li Ruihuan tried to cool the ideological atmosphere and refocus the Party's attention on reform and opening up, conservatives were

---

[46] See, for instance, Beijing television service, August 24, 1989, trans. FBIS-CHI, August 25, 1989, pp. 15–16.

[47] "Li Ruihuan Meets with Hong Kong Journalists."

[48] Deng Xiaoping, "Disandai lingdao jiti de dangwu zhiji."

[49] "Zhonggong Zhongyang, Guowuyuan guanyu jinqi zuo jijian qunzhong guanxin de shi de jueding," pp. 555–7.

[50] Deng apparently first used this phrase in his October 31, 1989 talk with Richard Nixon. See Deng Xiaoping, "Jiesu yanjun de ZhongMei guanxi yao you Meiguo caiqu zhudong," p. 331.

[51] Deng Xiaoping, "Women you xinxin ba Zhongguo de shiqing zuode genghao," p. 327.

[52] *Renmin ribao*, September 22, 1989.

determined to press their advantage. Throughout the reform period a major debate had raged within the Party over the economic line to be pursued. Conservatives, led by Chen Yun, had argued that the "planned economy is primary, the market economy supplementary." That line, which had been enshrined at the Party's 1980 Central Work Conference and the Twelfth Party Congress in 1982, was rejected (albeit implicitly) by the 1984 Third Plenum, which had adopted the "Decision on the Reform of the Economic Structure." The plenum decision endorsed the view that the economy was a "commodity economy" rather than, as conservatives had maintained, a "planned economy."[53] This was a significant ideological breakthrough that served to justify further liberalization of the economy and marked a major parting of the ways.[54] The rift between Deng and Chen widened in the ensuing years.

With the suppression of the protest movement in Beijing and elsewhere and with the ouster of Zhao Ziyang, conservatives seized the opportunity to criticize Zhao's leadership over the economy and impose their own interpretation of economic reform. This effort began with the editing of Deng Xiaoping's remarks. In Deng's June 9 talk, he referred to the "integration of planned economy and market regulation."[55] This expression restored the preferred usage of conservatives, which they had been able to impose during the 1981–2 retreat from more market-oriented reforms.[56] As later revealed, Deng had originally called for the integration of the "planned economy and the market economy," a formulation that put the two economic types on the same plane. However, before his remarks could be published in the *People's Daily*, conservatives edited them to fit their agenda.[57] The term "market economy" would not reappear until Deng's trip to the Shenzhen Special Economic Zone (SEZ) in January 1992.

In November 1989, Chen Yun's economic thought was restored as orthodoxy by the Fifth Plenary Session of the Thirteenth Central Committee. The "CCP Central Committee Decision on Furthering Improvement and Rectification and Deepening Reform" (frequently referred to as "The 39 Points") that was adopted by the plenum laid out a systematic, though implicit, critique of Zhao's management of the economy. That decision, like much commentary in the months since Tiananmen, hinted at the implicit line struggle that had existed within the Party by suggesting that

[53] "Decision of the Central Committee of the Communist Party of China on Reform of the Economic Structure."

[54] Fewsmith, *Dilemmas of Reform*, pp. 133–5.

[55] Deng Xiaoping, "Zai jiejian shoudu jieyan budui junyishang ganbu shi de jianghua," p. 306.

[56] Fewsmith, *Dilemmas of Reform*, chapter 3.   [57] Baum, *Burying Mao*, p. 294.

the economy had begun to go awry in 1984 – when the Decision on the Reform of the Economic Structure was adopted. Since that time, the Fifth Plenum decision declared, economic policy had ignored China's "national strength," allowed aggregate demand to "far, far" exceed aggregate supply, permitted the balance between industry and agriculture to be thrown off, ignored basic industries, and overly dispersed financial resources, thus eroding the state's ability to exercise macroeconomic control. These problems, the decision declared, constituted a "mortal wound" (*zhimingshang*) to the economy.[58] All these charges were part of the conservative critique of reform that had been ongoing at least since 1984.

In Jiang Zemin's speech to the plenum, he declared that the "greatest lesson" to be derived from the PRC's economic past was that the country must not "depart from its national conditions, exceed its national strength, be anxious for success, or have great ups and downs."[59] These, like the charges listed in the preceding paragraph, were all well-known theses of Chen Yun, so Jiang's endorsement of Chen Yun's thought over Deng's line of reform and opening up was apparent.

Just as Party conservatives rejected Deng's economic line, they spurned efforts to lessen ideological tensions. Their rejection of Deng's efforts to reduce tensions was based not only on the depth of division within the Party but also on the collapse of socialism in Eastern Europe.[60] On December 15, Wang Renzhi, the conservative head of the Propaganda Department, launched a blistering attack on bourgeois liberalization in a talk to a Party building class. In direct opposition to Deng's theses that economic development would promote social stability and that ideological debates should be put off – or better, not taken up – Wang argued that stability could only be built on the basis of Marxist ideology. Only in this way, Wang argued, could economic work be carried out without deviating from the socialist orientation. As Wang put it, "[o]nly by criticizing and struggling against the ideological trend of bourgeois liberalization will we be able to consolidate and develop the political situation of stability and unity and to promote the smooth development of socialist construction." In effect, Wang reinterpreted Deng's slogan "stability overrides everything" – a phrase coined to relax ideological tension – as a clarion call for ideological struggle as the

---

[58] "Zhonggong Zhongyang guanyu jinyibu zhili zhengdun he shenhua gaige de jueding (zhaiyao)."

[59] Jiang Zemin, "Zai dang de shisanjie wuzhong quanhui shangde jianghua," p. 711.

[60] Some within the Party argued that the implementation of reform in Eastern Europe had led to the collapse of communism there, while others argued that communism collapsed because the planned economy had continued to prevail in those countries. Wu Jinglian, *Jihua jingji haishi shichang jingji*, p. 41.

basis of some presumed future stability. Lest anyone think that the time had come to relax the campaign against bourgeois liberalization, Wang declared that "[w]e have only just started" to clarify ideological errors and that "[t]he logic of struggle is cruel and merciless."[61]

Wang's speech was followed by a full-page article in the *People's Daily* praising the notorious "Zhuozhuo meeting" of 1987. At that meeting, conservative Party leaders, concerned that Zhao and others would blunt the campaign against bourgeois liberalization that had unfolded in the wake of Hu Yaobang's ouster, tried to breathe new fire into the movement. It was after that meeting, and apparently because of it, that Deng authorized Zhao's famous May 13, 1987 speech that closed off the campaign against bourgeois liberalization and prepared the political atmosphere for the Thirteenth Party Congress in the fall. Now, in the wake of Zhao's ouster, conservative writer Chen Daixi (writing under the pseudonym "Yi Ren") accused Zhao of using "all kinds of dirty tricks with the most malicious motives" to suppress the Zhuozhuo meeting.[62] Obviously, Chen, as well as other conservative writers at the time, was aware that Deng had fully supported the stoppage of the 1987 campaign and they hoped to prevent him from doing so again.

REINFORCING STATE PLANNING

The strength of the conservative wing of the Party in the winter of 1989–90 was indicated not only by the directness of the challenge to Deng's ideological authority but also by a major effort to restore at least a significant measure of state planning to the economy. For years, conservatives had complained that reform had directed investment into small-scale, less efficient industries (mostly township and village enterprises, TVEs) that competed with large- and medium-sized state-owned industries for scarce energy, transportation, and raw materials. As a result, basic energy and material sectors were drained of investment capital while transportation and energy supplies were always strained by demand. Moreover, reform strategy had led to a regional bias as TVEs along the east coast grew and developed while industry and living standards in the interior lagged behind. A major effort to strengthen the "pillars" of the economy, as the large- and medium-sized state-owned industries were called, came in late 1989 when Li Peng announced that a State Council Production Commission

---

[61] Wang Renzhi, "Guanyu fandui zichan jieji ziyouhua." See also the harsh speech Wang delivered to *Qiushi* staffers in August, "Lilun gongzuo mianlin de xin qingkuang he dangqian de zhuyao renwu."
[62] Yi Ren, "Zhuozhuo huiyi de qianqian houhou."

(*Guowuyuan shengchan weiyuanhui*) was being established to "promptly resolve major problems regarding production."[63]

The new commission was headed by Ye Qing, a specialist in the coal industry who had become a vice-minister of the State Economic Commission (SEC) before being named vice-minister of the State Planning Commission (SPC) when the former office was abolished in 1988. The State Council Production Commission incorporated offices that had once belonged to the SEC, including the production control and technological transformation departments, which had been placed under the SPC, and the Enterprise Administration Office, which had been assigned to the State Economic Restructuring Commission.[64]

Rather than resurrecting the SEC, which had often acted as a spokesperson for industry interests and had often clashed with the more conservative SPC, the new State Council Production Commission was clearly intended to be subordinate to the SPC. The idea behind the establishment of the State Council Production Commission was apparently to better coordinate the functions of planning and plan implementation through a newly established "double guarantee" system to be administered by the Production Commission, which in turn would be overseen by the SPC. The double guarantee system was intended, on the one hand, to guarantee the supply of the necessary raw materials and funds to important state-owned enterprises and, on the other hand, for the enterprises to guarantee delivery of profits, taxes, and output to the state.[65] The double guarantee system was initially imposed on 50 major enterprises in northeast China and then extended to cover 234 of China's largest enterprises.

Establishing the Production Commission and implementing the double guarantee system were clear victories for the conservative wing of the Party and especially for Li Peng, who would have a chance to try out his policies for strengthening socialist management. The victory for Li Peng was underscored by the appointment of Zou Jiahua, Li's close colleague of many years, as head of the SPC in December 1989 (replacing the conservative planner, Yao Yilin).

RENEWED DEBATE OVER THE DIRECTION OF THE ECONOMY

In the weeks and months after Tiananmen, there was virtually no debate over the course of the economy – at least not in the major newspapers.

---

[63] *Hong Kong Standard*, December 18, 1989, in FBIS-CHI, December 20, 1989, p. 22; *Ching chi tao pao* 50, December 18, 1989, trans. FBIS-CHI, December 20, 1989, pp. 22–3.

[64] *Ching chi tao pao*, ibid.

[65] *Jinrong shibao*, January 30, 1990, trans. FBIS-CHI, February 14, 1990, pp. 24–5.

In fact, most economic commentaries carried by the *People's Daily* and *Enlightenment Daily* in those early months were by unknown reporters or economists. It was only after the Party's Fifth Plenum in November 1989 that the *People's Daily* began running serious economic commentary again. A number of well-known, if conservative, economists – including Ma Hong, Zhang Zhuoyuan, Li Chengrui, and Wang Jiye – argued the case for the Fifth Plenum's call for continuing retrenchment in measured, academic terms.[66] These economists defended continued retrenchment as more liberal economists began to suggest that the policy of reform and readjustment had already achieved the major goal of controlling inflation and was beginning to hurt the development of the economy by excessively reducing demand. The emergence of this debate over retrenchment policies marked the first time in nearly half a year that a tone of rational discussion had entered the press.

This trend continued the following spring with Li Peng's address to the NPC in March 1990. Although Li was uncompromising on the need to continue "improvement and rectification," the name given to the retrenchment policies adopted in the fall of 1988, he called for finding a way to successfully "integrate" planning and market regulation.[67] This talk inaugurated a public discussion on this topic, the third such discussion in the history of the PRC. The previous two rounds of discussion, however, had been inaugurated in the wake of economic difficulties in 1959 and 1979 and were meant to justify an expansion of market forces. In contrast, this new discussion was intended to justify integration on the basis of planning. But at least an opening for rational discourse on the economy had been created.

Even as Li Peng was seeking to define and defend a policy that would recentralize the economy and reimpose a significant degree of planning, economic trends were revealing just how wrong such conservative views of the economy were. As Naughton has argued, China's economy in 1989 was far healthier than the conservatives' declaration of profound economic crisis would suggest.[68] The harsh restrictions on credit and investment were so successful in reducing demand that, by September 1989, consumer prices were actually falling – though China's planners, calculating inflation on a year-to-year rather than a month-to-month basis, were unaware of this

---

[66] See Ma Hong, "Have a Correct Understanding of the Economic Situation"; Zhang Zhuoyuan, "Promoting Economic Rectification by Deepening Reform"; Li Chengrui, "Some Thoughts on Sustained, Steady, and Coordinated Development"; and Wang Jiye, "Several Questions on Achieving Overall Balance and Restructuring."

[67] Li Peng, "Wei woguo zhengzhi jingji he shehui de jinyibu wending fazhan er fendou."

[68] Barry Naughton, *Growing Out of the Plan*, p. 275.

dramatic turnaround.[69] Even calculating on a year-to-year basis, inflation in the first half of 1990 was only 3.2 percent, making it apparent to everyone that the urgency behind the retrenchment policies had passed. Meanwhile, the profitability of large state firms – the very sector that conservative policies had been designed to shore up – was collapsing. In 1990, profits of in-budget state firms fell 57 percent.[70] At the same time, inventory stocks shot up, enterprise losses jumped 89 percent over the same period the previous year, and the retail sales of commodities fell 1.9 percent.[71] Difficulties in the state-owned sector would force the government to pump an additional 270 billion yuan of loans into that sector in 1990 on top of the 126 billion yuan of loans issued in the fourth quarter of 1989.[72]

The combination of subsiding inflationary fears and stagnating industrial production brought renewed calls to revive reform, although it is surprising how slowly such calls were heeded given the debacle produced by conservative control of the economy. In May and June of 1990, some leaders solicited input from economists by raising the question of whether or not China's economy had come out of the economic trough.[73] This call stirred a new round of economic debate, and that summer the Economic Situation Group of the Chinese Academy of Social Sciences, headed by Liu Guoguang, proposed that the "weight" of reform be increased.[74] This proposal by no means rejected the austerity program adopted in 1988 (indeed, Liu had been one of the authors of that program), but it did emphasize that improvement and rectification were intended to bring about an atmosphere for a market-oriented reform rather than a reinstitution of the planned economy.

CENTER–PROVINCIAL CONFLICT OVER THE EIGHTH FIVE-YEAR PLAN

One of the conservatives' biggest complaints about Zhao's management of the economy was that the strategy of decentralization pursued in the 1980s was leading to Beijing's loss of economic, and perhaps political, control over the provinces. In July 1988, as conservatives were mounting increasing attacks on the economic policies of Zhao Ziyang, Minister of Finance Wang Bingqian complained that the "financial situation is grim," largely because

---

[69] Ibid., p. 281 and p. 347, note 2.   [70] Ibid., pp. 284–5.
[71] Ho Te-hsu, "China Has Crossed the Nadir of the Valley but Is Still Climbing Up from the Trough."
[72] Wu Jinglian, *Jihua jingji haishi shichang jingji*, pp. 12–13.
[73] Ibid., p. 14. Wu does not specify which leaders raised this issue.
[74] Ibid., p. 25; see also "Yi gaige cu wending zai wending zhong fazhan."

decentralization had led to a steady decline of central government revenues as a percentage of national income and as a percentage of all government revenues. The former figure, said Wang, had fallen over the course of reform from 31.9 percent in 1979 to only 22 percent in 1987.[75] Conservative economists complained loudly that the decentralization policies pursued in the course of reform had brought about a system of "feudal-lord economies" (*zhuhou jingji*), where each province was essentially a self-contained economic unit over which Beijing had little control.[76] Conservatives demanded a recentralization of economic and political power.

Conservative complaints were not without some validity. Central government revenues as a percentage of gross domestic product had fallen to under 20 percent by 1990 (from 31 percent in 1978), which put China in a range with such countries as Italy. Some experts predicted that if this trend continued – as indeed it would – it could lead to the virtual inability of the central government to control the macroeconomy.[77] However, the central question was: Which powers were to be recentralized and by what means?

Conservative instincts were to recentralize by exercising more direct control over the economy. This was the route mapped out by the draft of the Eighth Five-Year Plan as it neared completion in the summer of 1990. Zou Jiahua, vice-premier and head of the State Planning Commission (the organization with primary responsibility for drafting the plan), put it as follows: "The integration of central planning and market regulation is a basic principle" of economic policy-making, but "the two do not have equal status. Central planning is of primary importance. Market regulation is supplementary."[78] This, of course, was standard conservative rhetoric.

The difference between this concept of planning and the provincial interest in continuing the existing patterns of reform came to a head at the September 1990 Economic Work Conference. Two issues were central to the conflict. One was an evaluation of reform: whereas Li Peng insisted that reform had led to various "dislocations" in the economy, the provinces insisted that reform be affirmed and written into the Eighth Five-Year Plan. The other issue concerned the financial interests of the provinces. The central government wanted to replace the local financial contract system, under which the provinces were responsible only for delivering a specified sum to Beijing, with a "dual tax system" that would designate clearly

---

[75] Xinhua, July 24, 1988, in FBIS-CHI, July 25, 1988, pp. 42–3.
[76] Shen Liren and Dai Yuanchen, "Woguo 'zhuhou jingji' de xingcheng ji qi biduan he genyuan."
[77] For an influential study of this issue, which will be discussed in Chapter 5, see Hu Angang and Wang Shaoguang, *Jiaqiang zhongyang zhengfu zai shichang jingji zhuanxing zhong de zhudao zuoyong.*
[78] *Jingji daobao*, November 5, 1990, as cited in Willy Lam, *China after Deng Xiaoping*, p. 56.

which taxes would go to the central government and which to the localities. Led by Ye Xuanping (governor of Guangdong), Zhu Rongji (CCP secretary and mayor of Shanghai), and Zhao Zhihao (governor of Shandong), the provinces virtually rebelled against the authority of the central government.[79]

The September work conference is often taken as a symbol of the growing independence of the provinces, and to a certain extent it was. Over the years, reform had allowed the provinces to accumulate considerable resources, primarily in the form of extrabudgetary revenues, which freed them from dependence on the central government. Provincial authorities went to elaborate lengths to nurture (and conceal) such funds, and they would not willingly yield their economic interests.

There was, however, another important aspect of this provincial "rebellion" – namely, that the central government was itself divided, with some political leaders and organizations sympathizing with the provinces. The most important of these was none other than Deng Xiaoping, who feared that the conservative agenda being pushed by Li Peng would negate the contributions of reform (and therefore of Deng Xiaoping) and would also lead to lower growth rates. Throughout the 1980s, Deng had emerged as the champion of higher growth rates, not only because the economic achievements of China would reflect favorably on his own leadership and place in history but also because he believed that, as the economy developed, political and social conflicts would be more easily resolved, thus reducing the possibility that major conflicts could lead to another Cultural Revolution.[80] Thus, on the eve of the Economic Work Conference, Deng sent Yang Shangkun to talk to such provincial leaders as Zhu Rongji and Ye Xuanping, letting them know that they had Deng's support in their opposition to Li Peng.[81]

SINO–US RELATIONS

A significant part of reformers' efforts to regain the initiative in 1990 lay in their hopes to improve Sino–US relations. In the immediate aftermath of Tiananmen, however, Deng Xiaoping appears to have shared some of the suspicions of his more conservative colleagues. In fact, he inadvertently laid

---

[79] Baum, *Burying Mao*, pp. 326–8.
[80] A third reason to support higher growth rates was that a greater percentage of the growth would necessarily occur outside the scope of the plan and thus limit the ability of such conservative bureaucratic organs as the SPC to restrict reform.
[81] Gao Xin and He Pin, *Zhu Rongji zhuan*, p. 212.

the foundation for the campaign against "peaceful evolution" by declaring that the June 4 "storm" had been an inevitable product of the "international macroclimate." A week later, Deng was more explicit, saying that "[t]he entire imperialist Western world plans to make all socialist countries discard the socialist road and then bring them under the control of international monopoly capital and onto the capitalist road"; he stated further that if China did not uphold socialism then it would be turned into an appendage of the capitalist countries.[82] Moreover, in his October 1989 talk with former President Richard Nixon, Deng charged that the "United States was too deeply involved" in the student movement.[83]

Conservative leaders, often quite hostile to the United States, were – on the basis of Deng's comments – able to whip up a campaign against "peaceful evolution." Such conservatives charged that the United States, having failed to contain and overthrow socialism in the 1950s and 1960s, had pinned its hopes on the later generations of Chinese, who might be susceptible to Western influences and thus bring about change from within. Such officials argued in the summer of 1989 that China should reorient its foreign policy away from the West to build better ties with the remaining socialist states and the Third World.[84]

Although such advocates did not carry the day, their views certainly influenced China's top leadership. In Jiang Zemin's October 1, 1989 speech marking the 40th anniversary of the founding of the PRC, the Party general secretary charged that "international reactionary forces have never given up their fundamental stance of enmity toward and [desire to] overthrow the socialist system."[85] Although conservatives were never able to bring about a fundamental reorientation of Chinese foreign policy, they certainly were able to constrain the ability of the Chinese government to take initiatives that might have improved relations. Thus, as Deng told Nixon, "[t]he United States can take a few initiatives; China cannot take the initiative."[86]

The United States responded to Deng's advice by sending Deputy Secretary of State Lawrence Eagleburger and National Security Adviser Brent Scowcroft to Beijing in December 1989. The timing of the trip, it turned out, was not good. The collapse of socialism in Eastern Europe, as noted previously, was provoking new debate in Beijing and bringing about a new

---

[82] Deng Xiaoping, "Disandai lingdao jiti de dangwu zhiji," p. 310.

[83] Deng Xiaoping, "Jiesu yanjun de ZhongMei guanxi yao you Meiguo caiqu zhudong," p. 331.

[84] Harry Harding, *The Fragile Relationship*, p. 236.

[85] Jiang Zemin, "Zai qingzhu Zhonghua renmin gongheguo chengli sishi zhounian dahuishang de jianghua," p. 631.

[86] Deng Xiaoping, "Jiesu yanjun de ZhongMei guanxi yao you Meiguo caiqu zhudong," p. 332.

upswing in conservative influence. Thus, China was able to make only minor concessions in return for the visit: it lifted its own restrictions on cultural and academic exchanges and promised not to sell medium-range missiles to the Middle East.[87] Beijing finally lifted martial law on January 10, 1990. It was not until June 1990 that Fang Lizhi, the Chinese astrophysicist who had taken refuge in the US Embassy in Beijing after the June 4 crackdown, was finally permitted to leave the country.

Fang's release, like the other concessions, was too little and too late to win notice in the US Congress, which was increasingly vocal and hostile, but it did begin to ease the tensions in Sino–US relations. In late 1990, ties improved again with Chinese Foreign Minister Qian Qichen's visit to the United States, which culminated in a meeting with President Bush. After meeting with the president, Qian declared that the visit would "help open vast vistas for bilateral relations."[88] Qian's optimistic appraisal, however, did not materialize. Deep suspicions on both sides kept relations tense, and in China conservatives used opposition to "capitalism" to slow the pace of reform. Even after Deng's reform program was restored in 1992, this hostility left a legacy of suspicion that fed into the very different intellectual atmosphere that would emerge in the 1990s.

[87] Harding, *The Fragile Relationship*, p. 254.   [88] Beijing radio, December 1, 1990.

CHAPTER 2

Deng moves to revive reform

By late 1990, Deng seemed visibly distraught by China's situation and his own inability to reassert his leadership. There were moments of small progress. For instance, in November he met with Jiang Zemin and Yang Shangkun before their trip to Shenzhen to commemorate the tenth anniversary of the SEZs' (Special Enterprise Zones) founding.[1] This meeting no doubt accounts for Jiang's high evaluation of the zones at the meeting later that month.[2] Then, on the eve of the Seventh Plenum in late December, Deng gave a short speech to several leaders emphasizing that planning and markets are not the distinguishing characteristics of socialism and capitalism, respectively. "Don't think that engaging in a little market economy is [taking] the capitalist road; it is not like that," Deng told his colleagues. He also urged his colleagues to be bolder and to take some risks.[3] These remarks evidently caused Jiang Zemin to revise his speech to the Seventh Plenum to declare that it was necessary to persist unswervingly in reform and opening up.[4] One report indicates that Jiang made opening remarks to the plenum – but, if so, they have not been publicized; his closing remarks do contain a section called "firmly persist in reform and enlarge the scope of opening up."[5]

Such verbal reaffirmations of Dengist policy, however, did not amount to a resurrection of Deng's reform line. For instance, whereas the communiqué adopted by the Party's Seventh Plenum in December 1990 "highly evaluated" China's "tremendous achievements" in reform and opening up, it nevertheless went on to stress the "integration of the planned economy with market *regulation*" and to repeat such staples of Chen Yun's economic

---

[1] Lo Ping, "Report on Deng Xiaoping's Behind-the-Scenes Activities."
[2] Guangdong radio, November 27, 1990, trans. FBIS-CHI, November 29, 1990, pp. 36–7.
[3] Deng Xiaoping, "Shicha Shanghai shi de tanhua," p. 364.
[4] Wei Yung-cheng, "Reveal the Mystery of Huangfu Ping," p. 19.
[5] Jiang Zemin, "Zai dang de shisanjie qizhong quanhui bimushi de jianghua."

thought as calling for "sustained, stable, and coordinated" economic development and "acting according to one's capability" (*liangli erxing*).[6]

Such limited endorsement of Deng's views apparently left the patriarch frustrated. "Nobody is listening to me now," Deng allegedly complained. "If such a state of affairs continues, I have no choice but to go to Shanghai to issue my articles there."[7] So saying, Deng traveled to the east-coast metropolis and proceeded to give a number of talks intended to rekindle reform. In his talks, Deng declared that market and planning were both economic "methods" (rather than distinguishing characteristics of capitalism and socialism, respectively) and argued that whatever promoted the socialist economy was socialist. The Hong Kong press quickly dubbed Deng's comments as his "new cat thesis" (because of the idea that anything that promotes production is socialist) after his famous aphorism from the 1960s that the color of the cat does not matter.

The gist of Deng's talks in Shanghai was summarized in four commentaries carried in the Shanghai Party paper, *Liberation Daily*, under the pen name "Huangfu Ping" (which can be translated as "Shanghai Commentator"[8]). Their writing and publication were overseen by Deng's daughter Deng Nan and Shanghai Party secretary Zhu Rongji.[9] The first commentary was published under photographs of Deng Xiaoping, Yang Shangkun, and Li Xiannian conveying lunar New Year's greetings to Shanghai leaders, thus visually emphasizing the authoritative nature of the commentary. Using language not seen since the heyday of reform in the late 1980s, the commentaries excoriated "ossified thinking" and repeatedly called for a new wave of "emancipating the mind." For instance, one article declared that China would "miss a good opportunity" if it got bogged down in worrying about whether something was capitalist or socialist,[10] while another quoted Deng as saying that capitalist society is "very bold in discovering and using talented people" and urging the promotion of a large number of "sensible

---

[6] "Zhongguo gongchandang dishisanjie zhongyang weiyuanhui diqice quanti huiyi gongbao"; emphasis added.

[7] Cited in Liu Pi, "Deng Xiaoping Launches 'Northern Expedition' to Emancipate Mind."

[8] Zhou Ruijin, the deputy editor of Shanghai's *Jiefang Ribao* who headed the three-person writing group that wrote the articles, says that when read in his village dialect, Huangfu Ping can also be understood to mean "receiving the mandate of the people to aid Deng Xiaoping." Zhou Ruijin, *Ning zuo tongku de qingxingzhe*, p. 296.

[9] The four commentaries were published on February 15, March 2, March 22, and April 12, 1991. The writers of the Huangfu Ping articles were Zhou Ruijin, Ling He, and Shi Zhihong. See Wei Yung-cheng, "Reveal the Mystery of Huangfu Ping." According to Gao Xin and He Pin, the galleys of each article were personally approved by Deng's daughter, Deng Nan (see *Zhu Rongji zhuan*, p. 218).

[10] Huangfu Ping, "The Consciousness of Expanding Opening Needs to Be Strengthened."

persons."[11] A third article directly refuted conservative ideologue He Xin's argument (see Chapter 3) that foreign investment had led to the poverty of the Third World by calling on Shanghai leaders to "courageously take a risk, boldly use foreign capital, and turn Shanghai into a commercial, financial, and information center."[12]

RESPONSE FROM THE PROVINCES

It did not take long for several of China's provincial leaders to respond to Deng's initiative. On March 11, 1991 Guangdong's Party secretary Lin Ruo, who had close ties to Zhao Ziyang, published an article in the Guangdong Party paper *Southern Daily* (*Nanfang ribao*) and a shorter, somewhat watered down, version in the *People's Daily*. Lin pointedly attributed the rapid growth that Guangdong had enjoyed over the previous decade to the implementation of market-oriented policies. In the *Southern Daily* version of his article, Lin argued that planning had to be based on "commodity exchange and the law of value" and declared that "this is an objective law whether people recognize it or not."[13]

Another provincial leader who responded to Deng's initiative was Tan Shaowen, the Party secretary of Tianjin. Tan, an ally of Politburo Standing Committee member Li Ruihuan, was subsequently promoted to the Politburo at the Fourteenth Party Congress in 1992 (and then died in February 1993). In a major speech, Tan urged cadres to "emancipate the mind" and declared that "it was because of the reform and opening up that we conducted that we withstood the severe tests of the changes in the international situation, the political storms in the country, and numerous difficulties." In good Dengist fashion, Tan argued that "[e]conomic stability is the foundation of political and social stability."[14]

At the same time that Tianjin publicized Tan Shaowen's address, Hebei governor Cheng Weigao (who would be arrested for corruption in 2003) echoed Deng's Shanghai comments, saying that "the development of the market and display of the market's regulatory functions must not be

---

[11] Huangfu Ping, "Reform and Opening Require a Large Number of Cadres with Both Morals and Talents."

[12] Huangfu Ping, "The Consciousness of Expanding Opening Needs to Be Strengthened."

[13] In making this argument, Lin was paraphrasing, no doubt deliberately, the argument made thirteen years earlier by Hu Qiaomu in his famous 1978 report to the State Council, "Act in Accordance with Economic Laws, Step Up the Four Modernizations." Lin Ruo, "Dui fazhan shehui zhuyi shangpin jingji de jidian renshi."

[14] Tan Shaowen, "Emancipate the Mind, Seek Truth from Facts, Be United as One, and Do Solid Work."

regarded as a practice of capitalism." Reflecting provincial (and Dengist) impatience with conservative leaders, Cheng sharply criticized planners in Beijing who had recentralized authority over the economy, and he demanded that central policies regarding enterprise autonomy be enforced and the Enterprise Law (passed in 1988 but never put into effect) be implemented. Cheng also berated conservatives as people who "have doubts and misgivings" about reform and have "lost the courage to make positive explorations."[15]

Some of the strongest provincial comments came from Jiangxi governor Wu Guanzheng (who would be appointed head of the Central Discipline Inspection Commission in 2002), who called on his colleagues to "emancipate the mind" and "increase the weight of reform." Sharply criticizing those who feared that the economic inequalities brought about by reform would lead to polarization, Wu declared that, "if the work initiative of the workers is not effectively aroused and if production does not grow, there will be only common poverty for all people."[16]

Most surprising of all was the call from Beijing mayor Chen Xitong to "emancipate the mind." One of the most conservative of China's high officials and a hardliner who had actively encouraged the use of force in suppressing the 1989 protest movement, Chen was nevertheless a close follower of Deng and responded to his call. In an interview with *Fortnightly Chats (Banyue tan)*, Chen repeatedly invoked Dengist rhetoric, criticizing "ossified thinking" and giving explicit support to Deng's "new cat thesis."[17] In contrast, Beijing Party secretary Li Ximing, who would be ousted for his conspicuous resistance to Deng's policies following the patriarch's 1992 trip to Shenzhen, avoided the use of similar reformist rhetoric.

ZHU RONGJI ENTERS THE LEADERSHIP

One major success for Deng in the spring of 1991 was the elevation of Zhu Rongji to the position of vice-premier during the annual session of the NPC – though his elevation was balanced by the simultaneous selection of the conservative Zou Jiahua as another vice-premier. After the NPC meeting, there were five vice-premiers: Yao Yilin, Tian Jiyun, Wu Xueqian,

[15] Cheng Weigao, "Further Emancipate the Mind and Renew the Concept, and Accelerate the Pace of Reform and Development."
[16] "Increase Weight of Reform, Promote Economic Development: Speech Delivered by Wu Guanzheng at the Provincial Structural Reform Work Conference."
[17] Luo Xiaolu, "Chen Xitong tan jiefang sixiang." See also Sun Yushan, "Chen Xitong Points Out at a Municipal Supervision Work Conference That Supervision Departments Should Emancipate Their Minds in Carrying Out Work."

Zou Jiahua, and Zhu Rongji. Yao was a member of the Politburo Standing Committee, and Tian and Wu were members of the Politburo. Zou
was a full member of the Central Committee, but Zhu was only an alternate member. It was highly unusual for an alternate member of the Central
Committee to be promoted to vice-premier. Zhu has drawn intense interest
from domestic and foreign observers alike because he is unique in Chinese
politics. Named a rightist in 1957, Zhu nevertheless rose to the inner circles
of power; moreover, Zhu has firm ideas on economic reform and the personality to push them against strong opposition. That Deng would reach
out to such a person suggests his need and determination to counterbalance
the conservative bureaucrats who had come to dominate the top of the system in the wake of Tiananmen – much as Mao decided to dilute Lin Biao's
power by "mixing in sand" to the military command structure in the early
1970s.

Deng appears to have been familiar with Zhu's work and talents since
at least the early 1980s, when Zhu was promoted to vice-chairman of the
State Economic Commission.[18] When the State Economic Commission
was abolished in 1988, Zhu was sent to Shanghai to be mayor. Like Li
Ruihuan in Tianjin, Zhu seems to have drawn Deng's interest by his skillful
handling of the 1989 demonstrations in Shanghai. Despite pressure, Zhu
rejected calls to declare martial law in the city, opting instead for organizing
worker pickets to restore order. After the violent suppression of protesters
in Beijing, Zhu became famous for his ambiguous but suggestive remark
that "the facts will eventually be made clear."[19] But Zhu was no liberal.
When a train accident led an inflamed crowd to beat the driver and set
fire to the train, Zhu oversaw the arrest, conviction, and execution of three
people within eight days.[20]

But conservatives in the capital clearly opposed Zhu's appointment as
vice-premier. Discussions in corridors about who might emerge as "China's
Gorbachev" were directed at Zhu.[21] Li Peng initially declined to assign
him a portfolio. Three months later, under pressure from Deng, Li finally
allowed Zhu to take over the State Council Production Commission, the
group established under the State Planning Commission to oversee implementation of the "double guarantee" system. The Production Commission had failed in that task, allowing interenterprise debts to balloon.[22]

---

[18] Gao Xin and He Pin, *Zhu Rongji zhuan*, pp. 70–2.   [19] Ibid., p. 170.   [20] Ibid., pp. 173–8.
[21] Zhou Ruijin, *Ning zuo tongku de qingxingzhe*, p. 298.
[22] Interenterprise (triangular) debts were debts that accrued between suppliers, producers, and buyers.
These debts accrued as enterprises sent – in accordance with mandatory plans – materials or finished
products to others but received little or no payment in return.

Zhu promptly renamed the group the State Council Production Office (*Guowuyuan shengchan bangongshi*).[23] To put Zhu in charge of the State Council Production Office and of clearing up interenterprise debts marked an obvious policy failure for Li Peng, Zou Jiahua, and Ye Qing, but it did pass the hottest of hot potatoes to their rival Zhu Rongji. Zou maintained his position as a vice-premier and head of the SPC (until 1993), but his influence in policy circles was beginning to fade despite his subsequent elevation to the Politburo (but not its Standing Committee) in 1992.

Nevertheless, Zhu had been given a chance to develop a bureaucratic apparatus. Zhu quickly recruited his former associates from the old State Economic Commission, including former vice-chairmen Zhang Yanning and Zhao Weichen, who were made deputy directors of the new Production Office. The roles of Zhu and the Production Office were further enhanced in May 1993 when the office was expanded and reorganized as the State Economic and Trade Commission. The new office had a bureaucratic standing equivalent to the SPC and effectively marginalized the latter organization by taking over day-to-day management of the economy, leaving the SPC to deal with the macroeconomy.[24] Moreover, Zhu was successful, at least temporarily, in reducing the problem of interenterprise debt. In June 1991, such debts had amounted to some 300 billion yuan; about two thirds of that was cleared by the end of 1992.[25] His successes would eventually allow him to enter the Politburo Standing Committee – a jump of two levels – at the Fourteenth Party Congress in fall 1992.

CONSERVATIVE RESPONSE

Deng's offensive from the fall of 1990 through the spring of 1991 would prove to be a trial run for his efforts of the following year, but in 1991 he came up short. He had indeed used provincial officials to undermine the draft of the Eighth Five-Year Plan and then to publicize and promote his own thought, and he had laid the foundation of a later breakthrough by promoting Zhu Rongji and giving him an institutional base from which to compete with Li Peng. But conservative opposition remained fierce. Despite

---

[23] The Leading Group for the Resolution of Triangular Debt was established in March 1990 with Zou Jiahua in charge. At that time, triangular debt amounted to over 100 billion yuan (up from 32 billion yuan in 1988). Despite a State Council circular setting a four-month deadline for the clearing of such debt and despite state expenditures of about 160 billion yuan, enterprise indebtedness by the end of 1990 was nearing 150 billion yuan. *China Daily*, July 6, 1991.

[24] Gao Xin and He Pin, *Zhu Rongji zhuan*, pp. 242–56.

[25] Zhu Rongji, "Summarize Experiences in Clearing Debt Defaults and Preventing New Defaults to Ensure Sound Development of the National Economy."

Li Ruihuan's formal position as head of the Ideological Leading Small Group, conservatives had dominated the top reaches of the Propaganda and Organization Departments, as well as economic policy-making, since 1989.[26] They would not give up without a fight.

This opposition was led by the father–son combination of Chen Yun and Chen Yuan, then the deputy governor of the People's Bank of China (and, later, the governor of the China Development Bank). Even as Deng carried his message to Shanghai, the *People's Daily* carried a long article by Zhejiang Party secretary Li Zemin disclosing comments made by the normally reclusive Chen Yun the previous year. Chen had long felt that Deng had, like Mao, created his own "one voice chamber" (*yiyantang*) and had thereby not abided by the tenets of collective leadership. Thus, Chen was quoted as saying, "[a]s leading cadres, we must pay attention to exchanging views with others, especially those who hold views opposite from our own."[27]

At the same time that the father's thought was being publicized, the son made a splash in intellectual circles. In December 1990, Chen Yuan organized a forum of many prominent economists at which he presented a paper entitled "China's Deep-Seated Economic Problems and Choices (Outline)." The paper was subsequently published in *China Youth News* in January, in the prestigious economic journal *Economic Research* in April, and in the Party theoretical journal *Seeking Truth* in June. Chen's article picked up where the conservative critique of reform in 1989 and 1990 had left off. Lambasting the decline in central authority that had resulted from a decade and more of devolving economic power, Chen called for a "new centralization" to deal with the emergence of "feudal lords" and "this disintegration of macrocontrol."[28]

In May 1991, the elder Chen was back in the public eye with a rare televised report of Chen meeting with Shanghai leaders. Subtly reiterating his own opposition to Deng's unwillingness to yield to collective leadership, Chen presented Shanghai leaders with a rhymed couplet that enjoined them

---

[26] Defiance of Li Ruihuan's leadership of ideological work was evident not only from the speeches of such leaders as Wang Renzhi and Song Ping and from Gao Di's management of the *People's Daily*, but also from such specific comments as Wang Renzhi's December 1989 claim that the campaign against pornography, championed by Li, "certainly cannot replace opposing bourgeois liberalization." See *Deng Xiaoping lun wenyi yantaohui zaijing juxing.*

[27] *Renmin ribao*, January 18, 1991, trans. FBIS-CHI, January 22, 1991, p. 18.

[28] Chen Yuan, "Wo guo jingji de shenceng wenti he xuanze (gangyao)"; Joseph Fewsmith, "Neoconservatism and the End of the Dengist Era"; Gao Xin and He Pin, *Zhonggong "taizidang,"* pp. 97–124.

to "not simply follow what superiors or books say" but to "act only according to reality."[29]

If Chen's reminders to Deng were gentle – almost obscure – others were willing to be much more direct. Indeed, as soon as the Huangfu Ping commentaries appeared, conservatives launched an investigation into their background, an effort that apparently concluded only when Deng's office let it be known that Deng himself lay behind the commentaries.[30] The knowledge that the commentaries expressed Deng's views apparently did not impress conservative leaders any more than had Deng's previous efforts to promote his views in the capital, and conservatives launched a variety of direct and indirect assaults on Deng's policies and the Huangfu Ping commentaries.

The sharpest attack on them, and hence on Deng, was a commentator article in the conservative journal *Contemporary Trends* (*Dangdai sichao*) that was excerpted shortly thereafter in the *People's Daily*. *Contemporary Trends* was one of several conservative journals that began publication in the wake of June 4 (others include *The Quest for Truth* [*Zhenli de zhuiqiu*] and *Mainstream* [*Zhongliu*]) and was edited by conservative ideologue Duan Ruofei, who had previously worked at the Party journal *Hongqi* (*Red Flag*). Since its founding, *Contemporary Trends* had published several articles by leading hardline officials, including Deng Liqun and Wang Zhen, and had carried numerous articles criticizing bourgeois liberalization in extremely harsh terms.

The April commentator article warned that those in favor of "bourgeois liberalization" remained "resolute" and that "we must be soberly aware that the liberalized trend of thought and political influence, which was once a major trend, will not disappear because we have won a victory in quelling the rebellion, but will again stubbornly manifest itself in a new form, spar with us, and attack us." Harkening back to themes raised by Song Ping and Wang Renzhi the previous year, the commentary argued that opposing bourgeois liberalization – not developing productive forces – was the key to ensuring political stability. Moreover, the article argued that the issue of bourgeois liberalization could never be confined to the ideological sphere

---

[29] Xinhua, May 15, 1991, in FBIS-CHI, May 17, 1991, p. 22. Although there is no obvious difference in meaning between this aphorism and Deng's favorite slogan, "seek truth from facts," Chen always used his own phraseology and never reiterated Deng's slogan.

[30] Liu Pi, "Deng Xiaoping Launches 'Northern Expedition' to Emancipate Mind"; Lam, *China after Deng Xiaoping*, p. 434, note 35.

because it was inherently a political issue involving the question of whether to take the socialist or capitalist road.[31]

REFORM HITS A TROUGH

With the publication of the *People's Daily's* excerpt of the article from *Contemporary Trends* and other attacks on the themes raised by the Huangfu Ping commentaries, reformers fell quiet. For the summer, central and provincial leaders stopped voicing concerns about emancipating the mind or not worrying about whether a given reform was socialist or capitalist. This hiatus in the slow but steady progress that advocates of reform had been making at least since the September 1990 economic conference is difficult to explain. Four explanations seem possible.

The first is that, in the spring of 1991, Deng simply lacked the political strength to reinstate his vision of reform. Such an explanation assumes not only that Deng failed to win over (or intimidate) his opponents, but also that he failed to win the support of the "silent majority" of Party elders who seem to move to one side or the other in periods of political conflict, thereby affecting the political center of gravity. Second and more plausibly, one can assume that Deng, faced with opposition and uncertainty, yielded once again, as he had apparently done several times over the preceding two years – biding his time until a more opportune moment arose to renew his assault. This explanation assumes that Deng possessed the power necessary to prevail (which he would demonstrate a year later), but that he believed the cost in terms of Party unity outweighed the importance of prevailing at that time. As Zhou Ruijin put it, Deng "coolly observed and contemplated" the conflict as it developed.[32] Third, events in the Soviet Union – namely, Gorbachev's turn to the right, which culminated in cracking down on the Baltic republics in January 1991 – may have bolstered conservatives in Beijing, who are likely to have seen such a shift as a sign that the Soviet Union, too, was finally backing away from radical reform.[33] Fourth, the swift American victory in the Gulf War, which caught China off guard,

---

[31] It should be noted that by mid- to late April, just as the *People's Daily* was reprinting the *Contemporary Trends* article, Gorbachev was once again turning toward radical reform – which also scared conservatives into taking a harder line. Though it seems inconsistent, it can be argued that Chinese conservatives reacted to both a tightening up and a political relaxation in the Soviet Union by calling for ideological orthodoxy in China. In the former they would see confirmation of the need to prevent reform from getting out of control, and in the latter they would see a hostile foreign environment that would necessitate a reassertion of socialist values at home.

[32] Zhou Ruijin, *Ning zuo tongku de qingxingzhe*, p. 308.

[33] "Why Must We Unremittingly Oppose Bourgeois Liberalization?"

may very well have renewed fears in Beijing that the world was becoming unipolar and that the United States would apply new pressures on China. Such a concern is likely to have reinforced the tendency among Party leaders to hunker down, assess the situation, and avoid divisive conflicts.

Such explanations are not mutually exclusive, and it is probable that a combination of internal and external factors convinced Deng to back off. In any event, with the publication of Jiang Zemin's speech on the 70th anniversary of the CCP on July 1, 1991, it became clear that reform was once again on hold.

Jiang's speech reflected the sharply conflicting opinions within the Party, affirming reformist themes but stressing conservative concerns. For instance, Jiang paid homage to Deng's emphasis on economic construction, saying that "from beginning to end, we must take economic construction as the center," and he even managed to incorporate (minimally) Deng's remarks in Shanghai by saying, "[p]lan and market are methods of market regulation" and asserting that they "are not signs by which to differentiate socialism and capitalism." Nevertheless, conservative themes predominated. For instance, Jiang returned to the issue he had raised in his 1989 National Day address: the need to differentiate two types of reform. He also linked domestic class struggle to international class struggle and emphasized that "the ideological arena is an important arena for the struggle between peaceful evolution and anti-peaceful evolution." Moreover, with regard to economic policy, Jiang emphasized that "large- and medium-sized state-owned enterprises are the backbone strength of the socialist economy" and that "shaking public ownership of the means of production would shake the economic foundation of socialism and harm the fundamental interests of the whole people, to say nothing of socialism."[34] In short, it was a speech that, despite its bows in a reformist direction, clearly reflected conservative dominance over the overall ideological and policy agenda. More important, whatever reformist sentiments there were in Jiang's speech were soon played down as the Party responded to renewed liberalization in the Soviet Union by circling the wagons even more tightly.

In late July 1991, the Soviet Communist Party (CPSU) surrendered its monopoly on political power and moved its ideological stance toward democratic socialism. This move caused obvious anxieties in China and prompted conservatives to take an even harder line. In particular, an August 16 commentator article in the *People's Daily* put an even more

---

[34] Jiang Zemin, "Zai qingzhu Zhongguo gongchandang chengli qishi zhounian dahuishang de jianghua," pp. 1647, 1640, 1646, 1639, and 1638.

conservative spin on Jiang's CCP anniversary speech, calling for building a "great wall of steel against peaceful evolution" in order to protect the country from "hostile forces" at home and abroad. If such hostile forces won, the commentator article warned, it would be a "retrogression of history and a catastrophe for the people."[35] The tone of other, less authoritative articles likewise suggests a major conservative push in reaction to events in the Soviet Union. For instance, one article made a thinly veiled allusion to the Huangfu Ping commentaries of the previous spring and asked whether the orientation of the author of those commentaries was "socialist or capitalist."[36] Moreover, deputy director of the Propaganda Department Xu Weicheng, writing under his pen name Yu Xinyan, attacked the "Western monopoly capitalist class" for gloating over its success in promoting peaceful evolution, declaring that it had "rejoiced too soon."[37]

THE SOVIET COUP

Given the reaction of Chinese hardliners to what they regarded as the downward spiral of events in the Soviet Union, it is no wonder that they could barely contain their glee when they heard the news of the conservative coup d'état launched on August 19. China's ambassador congratulated the perpetrators of the coup, and conservative elder Wang Zhen, then in Xinjiang, called on China's Party leaders "never to deviate" from Marxism–Leninism–Mao Zedong Thought and to "fight to the death" for communism.[38] During his trip in the province, Wang gave a number of "fiery speeches,"[39] while back in Beijing, leftists called a number of meetings to consider their response.

The ebullient mood did not last long. When the coup collapsed after only three days, Chinese leaders were despondent. Even Deng worried that if Yeltsin banished the CPSU, China would be the only major state practicing socialism. "Then what shall we do?," he reportedly asked.[40] The abortive coup in the Soviet Union posed, in the starkest possible terms, the fundamental question of the period: Should the CCP try to preserve

---

[35] "Build Up a Great Wall of Steel against Peaceful Evolution."

[36] Qin Si, "Wenyiwen 'xingshe haishi xingzi'."

[37] Yu Xinyan, "Preface to Practice and Future of Contemporary Socialism."

[38] Xinjiang television, August 24, 1991, trans. FBIS-CHI, August 27, 1991, pp. 28–9; Wang Youfu, "Wang Zhen Inspects Xinjiang."

[39] See, for instance, Xinjiang television, August 21, 1991, trans. FBIS-CHI, August 22, 1991, p. 20. The *People's Daily* account of Wang's trip deleted most of Wang's harshest language, including his vow to "fight to the death."

[40] *South China Morning Post*, August 26, 1991.

its own rule by emphasizing ideology and socialist values, or should it try to win popular support and strengthen the nation through continued economic reform? Leftists in the Party clearly wanted to take the former route. Chen Yun, in a scarcely veiled attack on newly promoted vice-premier Zhu Rongji, reputedly warned against allowing a "Yeltsin-like figure" to emerge in China.[41]

If Deng was initially despondent over events in the Soviet Union, he did not stay that way for long. Reacting quickly to conservatives' efforts to assert themselves following the Soviet coup, Deng intervened to insist on accelerating reform and opening up. As a PRC-affiliated Hong Kong magazine later put it, "Deng played a crucial role in preventing China from incorrectly summing up the experiences of the Soviet coup and in rendering the 'leftist' forces in the Party unable to use the opportunity to expand their influence."[42] Internationally, Deng reiterated his call for caution, saying that China should "tackle calmly, observe coolly, and pay good attention to our own national affairs."[43] Domestically, he inaugurated a determined campaign to reassert his own leadership and to put his understanding of reform back in the center. That campaign would last from the time of the abortive Soviet coup until the convening of the Fourteenth Party Congress in October 1992.

The first public sign that political winds were shifting came on September 1, when the Xinhua News Service transmitted the text of an editorial to be run the following day by the *People's Daily*. The editorial contained some of the most reformist language to be used since the previous spring, and did so in a more authoritative context. However, the first sentence contradicted and effectively negated the rest of the editorial. It read: "While carrying out reform and opening up to the outside world, we must ask ourselves whether we are practicing socialism or capitalism, and we must uphold the socialist orientation." Seven hours after this version of the editorial was transmitted, Xinhua released a new version in which the first sentence was changed dramatically to read, "While carrying out reform and opening up to the outside world, we must firmly adhere to the socialist course and uphold the dominant role of public ownership."[44] The critical question of whether a reform was "socialist" or "capitalist" had been cut.

---

[41] *South China Morning Post*, September 4, 1991; Baum, *Burying Mao*, p. 333. Note *Wen wei po's* reference to Yeltsin as a "dangerous" person in its examination of the abortive coup. See Cheng Jo-lin, "Short but Strange Coup."

[42] Sun Hong, "Anecdotes about Deng Xiaoping's Political Career and Family Life."

[43] Ho Yuen, "CCP's 'Five Adherences' and 'Five Oppositions' to Prevent Peaceful Evolution."

[44] Both statements were released by Xinhua on September 1, 1991, the first at 0723 GMT and the second at 1456 GMT. See FBIS-CHI, September 2, 1991.

It turned out that the second version was actually the editorial as originally approved, but prior to transmission the director of the *People's Daily*,[45] Gao Di, rewrote the first sentence to insert the conservative's pet thesis. This change was spotted, and at Deng's behest Li Ruihuan ordered that the offending sentence be removed. Thus, the editorial that appeared in the *People's Daily* on September 2 differed from what listeners had heard on the radio the evening before. Deng angrily declared that the "*People's Daily* wants to comprehensively criticize Deng Xiaoping."[46]

This incident underscores the deadly serious nature of "documentary politics" in the PRC, but it also makes clear that reformers were responding quickly to evolving events in the Soviet Union and restoring the push that had stalled the previous spring.[47] In late September, Deng instructed Jiang Zemin and Yang Shangkun to persevere in reform and opening up,[48] and Yang subsequently gave a ringing endorsement of reform on the 80th anniversary of the 1911 Revolution. Reform was, he said, a part of the historical effort to revive and develop China that had begun with Sun Yat-sen.[49]

In its stress on patriotism and its assessment that economic development is the common goal of all Chinese, communist or not, Yang's speech echoed the 1986 Third Plenum resolution on building socialist civilization. That resolution played down the importance of communist ideology in favor of a "common ideal" to which all patriotic Chinese could subscribe.[50] More importantly in terms of the immediate political debate, Yang declared unequivocally that "*all* other work must be subordinate to and serve" economic construction and that the Party must not allow its "attention to be diverted or turned away" from economic construction.[51]

---

[45] In the early 1980s, the editor-in-chief was the highest ranking official of the *People's Daily*. In the wake of the 1983 campaign against spiritual pollution, a separate post of director was created to allow Hu Jiwei, criticized during that campaign, to take up a "second-line" position. Nevertheless, as director, Hu was able to exercise considerable influence over the paper, as evidenced by the selection of the open-minded Qin Chuan as editor-in-chief to replace Hu in that position. Thus, well before Tiananmen the position of director had become the effective head of the *People's Daily*, although the distinction between director and editor-in-chief continued. After the Tiananmen crackdown, Gao Di was named director (replacing Qian Liren), and Shao Huaze became editor-in-chief (replacing Tan Wenrui). In December 1992, Shao replaced Gao as director, and Fan Jingyi became editor-in-chief.

[46] Gao Xin and He Pin, *Zhu Rongji zhuan*, pp. 231–2.   [47] Guoguang Wu, "'Documentary Politics'."

[48] Cited in Baum, *Burying Mao*, p. 334.

[49] Yang Shangkun, "Zai jinian Xinhai geming bashi zhounian dahuishang de jianghua."

[50] See "Resolution of the Central Committee of the Communist Party of China on the Guiding Principles for Building a Socialist Society with Advanced Culture and Ideology."

[51] Yang Shangkun, "Zai jinian Xinhai geming bashi zhounian dahuishang de jianghua."

Despite such clear signals from Deng and his supporters, conservatives continued to resist. During his November visit to Shanghai, Li Peng could not resist telling Zhu Rongji, who had overseen the writing of the Huangfu Ping articles, that "[t]he influence of the 'Huangfu Ping' articles was terrible. It caused the unified thinking that the center had expended a great deal of effort to bring about to become chaotic again."[52]

On October 23, the *People's Daily* published a hard-hitting article by leftist ideologue Deng Liqun, entitled "Have a Correct Understanding of Contradictions in Socialist Society, Take the Initiative in Grasping and Handling Contradictions." In stark contrast to Yang Shangkun's speech two weeks earlier, Deng declared that class struggle was more acute than at any time since the founding of the PRC. An editor's note stated that "the harsh reality of struggle has made clear to us that pragmatism can make a breach for peaceful evolution."[53] The term "pragmatism" seemed a clear allusion to the policies of Deng Xiaoping.

At the meeting of the Central Advisory Commission (CAC) convened on November 29, Party elder Bo Yibo conveyed six points raised by Chen Yun that stressed strengthening Party organization, the threat of peaceful evolution posed by the United States, and the danger posed by overzealous efforts to speed up economic development.[54] In late November, Deng Xiaoping urged the leadership to improve relations with the United States by not raising the issue of peaceful evolution so often and by compromising with the United States on human rights issues. On hearing Deng's suggestion, Party elder Wang Zhen apparently flew into a rage, declaring that Deng's policies were leading the country down the road to capitalism.[55] At the time, as Wang Zhen's outburst showed, the Party remained deeply divided over the danger posed by "peaceful evolution." In September, Propaganda Department head Wang Renzhi and others had organized an "anti-peaceful evolution" study group at the Central Party School which warned that peaceful evolution could be boosted by "pragmatists" in the leadership. Conservatives participating in the group denounced Li Ruihuan as "a person who wants to be Gorbachev" and called Qiao Shi a "fence sitter."[56]

---

[52] Quoted in Gao Xin and He Pin, *Zhu Rongji zhuan*, p. 232.
[53] Ching Wen, "Abnormal Atmosphere in *Renmin ribao*"; Deng Liqun, "Have Correct Understanding of Contradictions in Socialist Society."
[54] Lo Ping and Li Tzu-ching, "Chen Yun Raises Six Points of View to Criticize Deng Xiaoping."
[55] *South China Morning Post*, January 1, 1992, in FBIS-CHI, January 2, 1992, p. 25; Baum, *Burying Mao*, p. 336.
[56] *Tangtai* 14, May 15, 1992, pp. 21–2, trans. FBIS-CHI, May 21, 1992, pp. 18–20.

DENG'S "SOUTHERN TOUR"

On January 19, almost eight years to the day since Deng's first visit to Shenzhen inaugurated a new push in opening China to the outside world, Deng once again set foot in the SEZ. Accompanied by Yang Shangkun and other officials, Deng spent the next several days touring Shenzhen and then the Zhuhai SEZ, talking about the importance of reform and blasting his opponents as he went.

Perhaps the most critical point in his talks was his contention that, without the ten years of reform and opening up, the CCP would not have survived an upheaval such as the Party had faced in spring 1989. This judgment was Deng's response to his opponents' contention that reform had led to the Tiananmen incident and would lead to the downfall of the CCP, just as it had to that of the CPSU and the various communist parties of Eastern Europe.

In order to defend his vision of reform against his critics' arguments, Deng reiterated the theoretically unsophisticated but ultimately effective argument that he had put forth in Shanghai the previous year: planning and markets, far from being distinguishing characteristics of socialism and capitalism, were simply economic "methods" possessed by both types of systems. The two systems, Deng declared, were distinguished by their respective ownership systems – public ownership in the former and private ownership in the latter – rather than by the existence or extent of the market. Moreover, Deng hit back directly at the numerous derogatory criticisms of the so-called "criterion of productive forces" made over the previous two years. In the baldest statement of that thesis since Zhao Ziyang had championed it on the front page of the *People's Daily* four years before, Deng declared that socialism could be defined in terms of three "advantages": whether or not something was "advantageous to the development of socialist productive forces, advantageous to increasing the comprehensive strength of a socialist nation, and advantageous to raising the people's standard of living."[57]

In addition to dismissing conservatives' concerns over whether a particular reform was "socialist" or "capitalist," Deng blasted his cautious colleagues with one of Mao's most famous metaphors. Deng urged them not to act like "women with bound feet"; reform needed to be bolder and the pace of development faster. "To develop a large, developing country like ours," Deng said, "economic development must be a bit faster; it cannot always

---

[57] Deng Xiaoping, "Zai Wuchang, Shenzhen, Zhuhai, Shanghai dengdi de tanhua yaodian," p. 372.

be calm and steady." Underscoring his implicit but pointed criticism of Chen Yun's thought, which had just been endorsed again by the Seventh Plenum in December 1990, Deng went on: "We must pay attention to the steady and coordinated development of the economy, but being steady and coordinated is relative, not absolute." He then called on Guangdong to catch up to the "four small dragons" (South Korea, Taiwan, Singapore, and Hong Kong) in twenty years.[58]

The most eye-catching passages in Deng's talks, however, were his blunt criticisms of the "left." In sharp contrast to the constant criticism of bourgeois liberalization and peaceful evolution over the preceding two years, Deng pointed out that the main danger to the Party lay on the "left." "The right can bury socialism, the 'left' can also bury socialism," declared the patriarch. Moreover, in a direct criticism of Deng Liqun, Deng Xiaoping declared that "saying that reform and opening up is introducing and developing capitalism and believing that the main danger of peaceful evolution comes from the economic arena are 'leftist'." Deng also declared that anyone who opposed reform should "step down" – a threat that would be carried out against several conservative leaders the following fall and was clearly intended to shake up the cautious Jiang Zemin as well. Throwing down the gauntlet, Deng declared: "Whoever changes the line, orientation, and policies of the [1978] Third Plenum will be stopped by the common people [*lao baixing*] and will be struck down."[59]

THE STRUGGLE FOR DOMINANCE

Initially, the PRC media did not report Deng's trip and the CCP did not relay his comments internally. It was only after the Hong Kong media began reporting on Deng's trip that the PRC-owned Hong Kong papers *Wen wei po* and *Ta kung pao* began covering it. *Wen wei po* claimed that the failure of the PRC media to cover Deng's trip was at Deng's insistence.[60] If that was the case (and it seems highly unlikely), Deng soon changed his mind.

The obvious resistance to publicizing Deng's trip – and the subsequent process of yielding partially while continuing to resist – reflects the very ambiguous nature of authority relations at the highest level of the CCP in the early 1990s. Deng began to shed his formal authority by stepping down from the Politburo Standing Committee at the Thirteenth Party Congress in September 1987 and then yielding leadership over the Party's Central

---

[58] Ibid., p. 377.   [59] Ibid., pp. 370–83.
[60] "Deng Xiaoping's Visit to Special Zones Shows China Is More Open."

Military Commission (CMC) to Jiang Zemin in November 1989. However, it seems that Deng was unwilling to shed all vestiges of formal authority and rule solely through informal politics. Thus, the Thirteenth Party Congress passed a secret resolution to refer all major decisions to Deng Xiaoping as the "helmsman" of the Party.[61] The authority conferred by this resolution is ambiguous, though, since "helmsman" was not a formal position and it was not clear whether Deng's wishes still needed to be obeyed in the same way as before his retirement. With the Tiananmen incident, Deng's prestige within the Party plummeted, weakening his ability to exercise informal authority. Conservative strategy in the three years following that incident was apparently to hamstring Deng's ability to exercise authority but not to challenge directly his "core" position. The effort was to turn Deng into the titular leader of the Party, much as Liu Shaoqi and Deng himself may have hoped to do to Mao in the early 1960s.

As the struggle for dominance in the spring of 1992 would show, Deng had (or had regained) enough authority to force nominal compliance with his wishes but not enough to immediately subdue opposition. Unlike in the spring of 1991, when Deng had backed off from a decisive confrontation with his opponents, in 1992 – with the Fourteenth Party Congress looming on the horizon – Deng was determined to raise the stakes to the level of a contest for Party leadership. In such a contest, the advantages of being "core," ambiguous as they were, would eventually secure the victory for Deng, but his opponents would not yield without staunch resistance.

A turning point in this struggle for dominance – the first of several – came when a Politburo meeting on February 12, 1992, under obvious pressure from Deng, decided to relay the content of Deng's talks orally only to cadres at or above the ministerial, provincial, and army ranks.[62] This limited dissemination of Deng's views reflected a pattern that would hold throughout most of the spring: namely, yielding to pressure from Deng (thereby sidestepping direct confrontation) but doing so only as little as possible (in the hopes that Deng would yield to resistance).

In the face of this passive resistance, Dengist forces used local media to step up the pressure on Beijing's still silent official media. On February 15, Shanghai's *Liberation Daily* (*Jiefang ribao*) published a full page of pictures of Deng taken by Yang Shaoming, Yang Shangkun's son. Five days later, on February 20, Shenzhen's paper launched a series of eight articles that gave

---

[61] Beijing television, May 16, 1989, trans. FBIS-CHI, May 16, 1989, p. 28; *Renmin ribao*, May 17, 1989, trans. FBIS-CHI, May 17, 1989, p. 16.

[62] Suisheng Zhao, "Deng Xiaoping's Southern Tour," p. 751.

new details about Deng's visit and summarized the content of his remarks – the first such coverage in PRC media.[63]

Finally, the *People's Daily* began to yield to the pressure. On February 22, it published an authoritative editorial, apparently reflecting the Politburo meeting ten days earlier, that called for strengthening reform. In contrast to the emphasis on slow and steady economic growth that had dominated press coverage in recent months, the *People's Daily* now declared that "the fundamental point for upholding socialism is developing the economy as fast as possible."[64] The editorial made clear its criticism of "leftists" within the Party by pointing out the "catastrophes" caused in the past by "taking class struggle as the key link." Two days later, a second editorial urged people to "be more daring in carrying out reform" and cited the Dengist dictum, "Practice is the sole criterion of truth."[65]

What attracted even greater attention, though it carried less weight, was a vigorous defense (the likes of which had not been seen in over two years) of learning from capitalism by Fang Sheng, an economist at Chinese People's University. Decrying "leftist" influences in the past that had led China to take a "tortuous" path, Fang urged "absorbing certain views, models, and methods from contemporary bourgeois economic theories" – even if it meant that "exploitation" would exist in China for a while.[66] However, despite publication of the two editorials and of Fang Sheng's article, Beijing's media remained silent about Deng's trip to the south, indicating the deep opposition within the Party to Deng and his views. Indeed, Deng's opponents took active measures to resist Deng's new offensive. Deng Liqun made his own trip, visiting the cities of Wuhan and Xining, where he declared, "[t]here is the core of economic work but also another core of fighting peaceful evolution and waging class struggle. And sometimes, the campaign against peaceful evolution is more important."[67] Chen Yun himself presided over a meeting of the CAC held in Beijing on February 17 at which he declared that the only way for the CCP to avoid a CPSU-style collapse was to emphasize communist ideology and strengthen Party building. Thirty-five senior leaders at the meeting drafted a strong letter to Deng demanding that communist ideology continue to be propagated

[63] The first three of these are translated in FBIS-CHI, February 24, 1992, pp. 27–30. A report on the fourth appears in FBIS-CHI, February 26, 1992, p. 16, and the fifth and sixth are translated in FBIS-CHI, March 2, 1992, pp. 33–4. The seventh is translated in FBIS-CHI, March 4, 1992, p. 19, and the eighth in FBIS-CHI, March 10, 1992, p. 16.
[64] "Adhere Better to Taking Economic Construction as the Center."
[65] "Be More Daring in Carrying Out Reform."
[66] Fang Sheng, "Opening Up to the Outside World and Making Use of Capitalism."
[67] *South China Morning Post*, May 11, 1992, in FBIS-CHI, May 11, 1992, pp. 16–17.

and that the Party strongly oppose peaceful evolution.[68] It was not until March 1 that Deng's remarks were officially spread within the Party in the form of Central Document No. 2. This official compilation followed the dissemination of Deng's remarks in five versions in different bureaucratic hierarchies and was intended not only to put out an official version but also to delete some of Deng's harshest comments. Nonetheless, the propaganda system limited circulation of the document.[69]

Yet the dissemination of Document No. 2 did not squelch opposition. Conservative Party elder Song Renqiong declared in early March that he could not detect leftist influences in current political, ideological, and economic work.[70] Similarly, the conservative director of the *People's Daily*, Gao Di, declared on March 9 that "[w]e have already published two or three comments, and that is enough for the moment. No more articles will be published."[71]

In the midst of this acrimonious dispute, an enlarged meeting of the Politburo was convened for March 10–12. Yang Shangkun, Deng's close associate and permanent vice-chairman of the CMC, led the charge by demanding that the body endorse Deng's view of economic work at the center. Jiang Zemin offered a self-criticism for his laxity in promoting reform and opening and echoed Yang's views.[72] Politburo member and NPC chairman Wan Li also strongly endorsed Deng's views, and Politburo Standing Committee member Qiao Shi argued pointedly that the leadership of the Party remained hindered by leftist ideology that interfered with the effective implementation of the Party's principles and policies. In opposition, Politburo Standing Committee member Yao Yilin argued that Deng's comments on guarding against leftism referred to the economic field; there were no indications of leftism in other fields. Yao's comments were echoed by Song Ping, also a member of the Standing Committee.[73] The outcome favored Deng. The communiqué issued by the Politburo meeting endorsed the "necessity" of upholding the "one center" of economic development and called on the Party to "accelerate the pace of reform and opening to the outside world." Moreover, it affirmed Deng's thesis that the main danger the Party faced was leftism.[74] Accordingly, China's central media finally publicized Deng's trip. On March 31, the *People's Daily* reprinted a long,

---

[68] Zhao, "Deng Xiaoping's Southern Tour," p. 754.
[69] *Ming pao*, March 7, 1992, trans. FBIS-CHI, March 9, 1992, pp. 26–7.
[70] Ling Hsueh-chun, "Wang Zhen and Li Xiannian Set Themselves Up against Deng."
[71] Ching Wen, "Abnormal Atmosphere in *Renmin ribao*," p. 21.
[72] Xinhua, March 11, 1992; Baum, *Burying Mao*, p. 347.
[73] Jen Hui-wen, "Political Bureau Argues over 'Preventing Leftism'."
[74] Zhao, "Deng Xiaoping's Southern Tour," p. 752.

flowery but detailed account of Deng's activities in Shenzhen entitled, "East Wind Brings Spring All Around: On-the-Spot Report on Comrade Deng Xiaoping in Shenzhen."[75]

Despite this important endorsement, the meeting decided to delete a reference to guarding against leftism from the draft of Li Peng's Government Work Report to the upcoming session of the NPC on the grounds that it would be inappropriate to include any reference to differences of opinion in a government (as opposed to Party) work report.[76] A fusillade of criticism from the floor, clearly abetted by NPC chairman Wan Li, forced the premier to add a warning to his report that the main danger lay on the left – as well as to make 149 other large and small changes.

The enormous stakes involved and Deng's willingness to use any and all methods to carry the day were clearly revealed at the NPC meeting when Yang Baibing, vice-chairman of the CMC, declared that the People's Liberation Army (PLA) would "protect and escort" (*baojia huhang*) reform.[77] This military intervention in domestic politics was a clear indication of the degree of tension in the Party and perhaps of the political ambitions of the Yang brothers. Moreover, the military kept up the pressure and, in doing so, went too far. Over the ensuing months, four delegations of senior PLA officers visited the Shenzhen SEZ to demonstrate their support for reform and opening up; also, the army newspaper, the *Liberation Army Daily*, repeatedly ran articles in support of reform.[78] The effort to professionalize and depoliticize the military, which had suffered badly with its crushing of the 1989 movement, was again set back. If military support was useful to Deng in 1992, it also suggested that the military could support or withhold support from political leaders at will, a violation of the stricture that the Party controls the gun. Deng would have to address this problem for the sake of future political stability.

---

[75] *Renmin ribao*, March 31, 1992. The article had originally appeared in the *Shenzhen tequ bao* (*Shenzhen Special Economic Zone Daily*) on March 26. By merely reprinting the article, the *People's Daily* demonstrated its desire to keep an arm's length from the content.

[76] Jen Hui-wen, "Political Bureau Argues over 'Preventing Leftism'."

[77] Xinhua, March 23, 1992. Note that the *Jiefangjun bao* editorial hailing the close of the NPC prominently played the theme of "protecting and escorting" reform. See "Make Fresh Contributions on 'Protecting and Escorting' Reform, Opening Up, and Economic Development."

[78] The first group of PLA leaders visited Shenzhen in late February, and the fourth group visited Shenzhen in early June. See *Wen wei po*, April 16, 1992, p. 2, trans. FBIS-CHI, April 16, 1992, p. 38; Xinhua, May 19, 1992, in FBIS-CHI, May 21, 1992, pp. 31–2; *Xinwanbao*, June 11, 1992, p. 2, trans. FBIS-CHI, June 16, 1992, pp. 32–3. On *Jiefangjun bao*'s support for reform, see Shi Bonian and Liu Fang, "Unswervingly Implement the Party's Basic Line"; He Yijun, Jiang Bin, and Wang Jianwei, "Speed Up Pace of Reform, Opening Up"; and Lan Zhongping, "Why Do We Say That Special Economic Zones Are Socialist Rather than Capitalist in Nature?"

The March 1992 Politburo meeting and the subsequent NPC session marked important, if not unambiguous, victories for Deng. The battle over reform continued. On April 8, members of the CAC held a meeting to draft a letter to the Central Committee, which was subsequently forwarded on April 14. The letter warned against the tendency to "completely negate" the theories of Marxism–Leninism–Mao Zedong Thought and declared, in direct opposition to Deng's comments in Shenzhen, that "the biggest danger is the 'rightist' tendency and bourgeois liberalization in the last 10 years."[79]

Shortly thereafter, on April 14, the *People's Daily* ran a long article by Li Peng confidante Yuan Mu, head of the State Council Research Office. Entitled "Firmly, Accurately, and Comprehensively Implement the Party's Basic Line," Yuan's article did to Deng what Deng had previously done to Mao: reinterpreted the leader's thought by insisting that it be viewed "comprehensively." For instance, while endorsing Deng's view about the importance of guarding against the left, Yuan went on to stress the need to maintain "vigilance against bourgeois liberalization" in order to prevent the sort of "evolution" experienced by Eastern Europe and the Soviet Union.[80] Similarly, a joint Propaganda Department and State Council Information Office writing team published an article by Leng Rong, who was then working in the Party Literature Research Center and who would emerge in 2004 as the head of a newly established Marxism-Leninism Academy in CASS (see Chapter 8), that used Deng's words to blunt Deng's own offensive. The article cautioned against bourgeois liberalization by quoting Deng as saying, "[h]enceforth, if necessary, when elements of turmoil just emerge, we must go to any lengths to eliminate them as soon as possible." This was not the message that Deng was trying to promote in the spring of 1992.[81]

In response, Deng's supporters rallied. On April 6, Qiao Shi – in an apparent criticism of Jiang Zemin – derided "some leading comrades" who only feign compliance with the line of reform and opening up. Such people, Qiao urged, should step down from power.[82] Similarly, during his

[79] Yueh Shan, "Central Advisory Commission Submits Letter to CCP Central Committee Opposing 'Rightist' Tendency."

[80] Yuan Mu, "Firmly, Accurately, and Comprehensively Implement the Party's Basic Line."

[81] Leng Rong, "To Realize Lofty Aspirations and Great Ideals of the Chinese Nation." See also *Xinbao*, May 4, 1992, trans. FBIS-CHI, May 4, 1992, pp. 19–21.

[82] Lin Wu, "Deng's Faction Unmasks Face of 'Ultraleftists'."

April 16–22 tour of Shanxi province, Qiao touted Dengist themes, calling for an "ideological leap" in people's awareness of the need for reform.[83] On April 13, Gong Yuzhi (former deputy head of the Propaganda Department and a long-time supporter of Deng) gave a talk called "Emancipate Thought, Liberate Productive Forces" at the Central Party School. Gong sharply criticized those who questioned further reform on the grounds that it was capitalist, saying that such views had prevented the emergence of reforms for many years prior to the 1978 Third Plenum. China needed to renew the spirit of "emancipating the mind" that had prevailed then. This talk marked an important signal to intellectuals and opened the way to harsher attacks on leftism.[84]

In late April, Vice-Premier Tian Jiyun went to the Central Party School and lambasted leftists for having "basically repudiated all the most fundamental and substantial elements that we have upheld since reform and opening up." In a barb apparently directed at General Secretary Jiang Zemin, Tian declared that "[t]o do away with 'leftist' influence, one must particularly guard against those who bend with the wind, the political acrobats who readily vacillate in attitude." With a parody rare in Chinese politics, Tian told his listeners that leftists should go to a "special leftist zone" in which there would be total state planning, supplies would be rationed, and people could line up for food and other consumer items.[85] Soon, pirated copies of Tian's talk were being sold on the streets of Beijing.

Deng's demonstration that he would not back off this time, underscored by the mobilization of the army on his behalf, stirred Chen Yun to make some concessions. Appearing in Shanghai on the eve of Labor Day, the Party elder encouraged leaders there to "emancipate their minds" and "take bold steps." According to one report, Chen's declaration came on the heels of a high-level meeting with Deng, Peng Zhen, Li Xiannian, Bo Yibo, and Yang Shangkun.[86] Chen, who in 1978–9 had opposed the establishment of the SEZs and especially opposed the establishment of one in Shanghai, was now quoted as saying, "I very much favor the development and opening of Pudong!"[87]

Despite Chen's partial concession in Shanghai, Deng Xiaoping obviously remained frustrated at the lack of meaningful response from the leadership.

[83] Xinhua, April 22, 1992, in FBIS-CHI, April 23, 1992, pp. 11–12.

[84] Gong Yuzhi, "Emancipate Our Minds, Liberate Productive Forces." See also Lu Yu-shan, "Chen Yun Responds to Document No. 2."

[85] *South China Morning Post*, May 7, 1992, in FBIS-CHI, May 7, 1992, pp. 22–3; "Summary of Tian Jiyun's Speech Before Party School"; Baum, *Burying Mao*, p. 353.

[86] Jen Hui-wen, "There Is Something Behind Chen Yun's Declaration of His Position."

[87] Xinhua, May 1, 1992, in FBIS-CHI, May 1, 1992, pp. 18–19.

On May 22, Deng showed up at Capital Iron and Steel (usually referred to by its Chinese abbreviation, Shougang) and listened to Zhou Guanwu, the long-time leader of the model enterprise, report on the enterprise's reform experience. Deng complained that many leaders were "merely going through the motions" of supporting reform and that they were in danger of losing their jobs.[88] Just as important, Deng signaled his strong support for Zhu Rongji, whom he had sponsored to become vice-premier in March 1991. Zhu, Deng said, was "quite capable" in economics.[89]

Deng's criticism of China's leadership finally stirred Jiang Zemin to action. On June 9, the general secretary followed in the wake of Qiao Shi and Tian Jiyun by giving a major speech at the Central Party School. Jiang at last openly endorsed the view that the "primary focus must be guarding against the 'left'." Quoting liberally from Deng's talks in Shenzhen, Jiang now argued that reform is like "steering a boat against the current. We will be driven back if we do not forge ahead." The Party chief nevertheless refrained from calling for a "socialist market economy," which would become the keynote of the Fourteenth Party Congress, continuing to refer instead to "market regulation" (though he dropped the formulation "integration of planned economy and market regulation").[90] Jiang's speech was the occasion of the *People's Daily*'s first authoritative comment on reform since February.[91]

Reform was given new momentum in late May with the circulation of Document No. 4, "The CCP Central Committee's Opinions on Expediting Reform, Opening Wider to the Outside World, and Working to Raise the Economy to a New Level in a Better and Quicker Way." The document, apparently drafted under the auspices of Zhu Rongji, marked a major new stage in China's policy of opening to the outside by declaring that five major inland cities along the Yangtze and nine border trade cities would be opened and that the thirty capitals of China's provinces and municipalities would enjoy the same preferential treatments and policies as the SEZs. Moreover, the document stated formally what Deng had said in January – namely, that Guangdong was to catch up with the four small dragons in twenty years.[92]

---

[88] Deng's comments were reported by Hong Kong media in May but were not publicized by PRC media until early July, when Shanghai's *Jiefang ribao* finally broke the long silence. See *Ming pao*, May 28, 1992, trans. FBIS-CHI, May 28, 1992, p. 15; *South China Morning Post*, May 28, 1992, in FBIS-CHI, May 28, 1992, p. 15; and AFP, July 7, 1992. The following month, Deng followed up his trip to Shougang with a trip to the northeast. See *South China Morning Post*, June 24, 1992.

[89] Yen Shen-tsun, "Deng Xiaoping's Talk during His Inspection of Shoudu Iron and Steel Complex."

[90] Xinhua, June 14, 1992, in FBIS-CHI, June 15, 1992, pp. 23–6.

[91] See "New Stage of China's Reform and Opening to the Outside World."

[92] Hsia Yu, "Beijing's Intense Popular Interest in CPC Document No. 4"; "The CCP Issues Document No. 4."

The more open political atmosphere of the spring encouraged long-silenced liberal intellectuals finally to raise their voices again in protest against leftism. A collection of essays by such famous intellectuals as Wang Meng (former Minister of Culture), Hu Jiwei (former editor-in-chief of the *People's Daily*), and Sun Changjiang (former deputy editor of *Science and Technology Daily* [*Keji ribao*]) created a storm when it was published under the title *Historical Trends*.[93] The book's sharp criticism of leftism quickly brought the wrath of the Propaganda Department, which banned the book.[94] Shortly after the book's publication, Yuan Hongbing – the law lecturer from Beijing University who had edited the book – presided over a gathering of more than 100 well-known intellectuals in Beijing. Such people as Wang Ruoshui, the former deputy editor of the *People's Daily*, and Wu Zuguang, the famous playwright who had been expelled from the Party in 1987, addressed the forum.[95] In the months that followed, other books denouncing leftism came off the press.[96]

The renewed activities of such liberal intellectuals was certainly grist for the leftists' mill. Shortly after the forum in Beijing, Deng Liqun launched a new attack. In an internal speech at the Contemporary China History Institute, Deng called for "extra vigilance over the recent rise in rightist tendencies."[97]

Many intellectuals had taken heart from Deng Xiaoping's trip to the south and his harsh denunciations of the left. They hoped that the patriarch would at last deal a fatal blow to such leftist leaders as Deng Liqun, Wang Renzhi, and Gao Di. Deng's calculus, however, remained different from that of the intellectuals. Deng's goals were twofold. First, he wanted to reassert his dominance in the Party. His southern tour, his harsh rhetoric, and his willingness to use the military in an intra-Party struggle demonstrated his determination; the Fourteenth Party Congress' enshrinement of Deng's thought would signal his success. Second, however, Deng sought a path that might ensure stability after his passing, and the terrible intra-Party struggles that Tiananmen and the ensuing changes in the international environment had set off demonstrated just how precarious that goal was. In 1989 Deng had endorsed the concept of neo-authoritarianism, the idea that the authority of the state could be used to build a strong economy and stable society à la the authoritarian regimes on China's periphery. During

[93] *Lishi de chaoliu bianweihui* (ed.), *Lishi de chaoliu.*
[94] Lu Ming-sheng, "Inside Story of How *Historical Trends* Was Banned."
[95] *Ming pao*, June 15, 1992, trans. FBIS-CHI, June 15, 1992, pp. 26–7.
[96] See Zhao Shilin (ed.), *Fang "zuo" beiwanglu*; Wen Jin (ed.), *Zhongguo "zuo" huo*; and Yuan Yongsong and Wang Junwei (eds.), *Zuoqing ershinian.*
[97] *South China Morning Post*, June 24, 1992. See also Meng Lin, "Deng Liqun Reaffirms Disapproval of Phrase 'Deng Xiaoping Thought'."

his trip to the south, Deng praised the example of Singapore. During his visit to Shougang, he signaled that he had found his tool to build such a society: Zhu Rongji.

Thus, the Fourteenth Party Congress that convened in October 1992 sought to attain two seemingly contradictory goals: establish the dominance of Deng (and his line of reform and opening up) over the left and deny the fruits of victory to the "bourgeois liberals" within the Party.

THE FOURTEENTH PARTY CONGRESS

Deng's efforts over the preceding year and more, starting with his early 1991 trip to Shanghai and building momentum following the abortive coup in the Soviet Union and with his trip to Shenzhen, finally culminated in October 1992 with the adoption by the Fourteenth Party Congress of the most liberal economic document in CCP history. Whereas a year earlier Deng Liqun had been calling reform and opening up the source of peaceful evolution,[98] the Fourteenth Party Congress report declared that "the most clear-cut characteristic of the new historical period is reform and opening up" and that the "new revolution" inaugurated by Deng Xiaoping was "aimed at *fundamentally* changing the economic structure rather than patching it up." Underlining the profound changes called for by Deng's revolution, the political report endorsed the creation of a "socialist *market* economic system" as the goal of reform, thereby advancing well beyond the 1984 thesis of building a "socialist planned commodity economy" – which had itself been a controversial step forward.[99]

Moreover, the political report endorsed the important theses of Deng Xiaoping's southern tour, including his statement that planning and market are merely economic "means" for regulating the economy, his proposition that the 1978 Third Plenum line should be pursued for 100 years, and – most important – that it was necessary "mainly to guard against 'leftist' tendencies within the Party, particularly among the leading cadres."[100]

The Fourteenth Party Congress was certainly a personal victory for Deng. Although his policies had been under nearly constant attack since 1989 and Chen Yun's economic thought had been repeatedly written into speeches and policy documents, the Fourteenth Party Congress lauded Deng for his "tremendous political courage in opening up new paths in socialist construction and a tremendous theoretical courage in opening up a new

---

[98] Baum, *Burying Mao*, p. 334.
[99] "Political Report" to the Fourteenth Party Congress. Quotes taken from pages 25 and 24, respectively.
[100] Ibid., p. 29.

Table 1: *Leadership of the Chinese Communist Party*

Prior to the 14th Party Congress	Following the 14th Party Congress
Politburo	
Standing Committee	Standing Committee
Jiang Zemin (age 66)	Jiang Zemin (66)
Li Peng (64)	Li Peng (64)
Qiao Shi (68)	Qiao Shi (68)
Yao Yilin (76)	Li Ruihuan (64)
Song Ping (76)	Zhu Rongji (64)
Li Ruihuan (59)	Liu Huaqing (76)
	Hu Jintao (50)
Other Full Members	Other Full Members
Li Tieying (57)	Chen Xitong (62)
Li Ximing (67)	Ding Guang'gen (59)
Qin Jiwei (79)	Jiang Chunyun (62)
Tian Jiyun (64)	Li Lanqing (60)
Wan Li (77)	Qian Qichen (64)
Wu Xueqian (72)	Tan Shaowen (63)*
Yang Rudai (67)	Tian Jiyun (64)
Yang Shangkun (86)	Wei Jianxing (61)
	Wu Bangguo (51)
	Xie Fei (60)
	Yang Baibing (72)
	Zou Jiahua (66)
Alternate Member	Alternate Members
Ding Guan'gen (59)	Wang Hanbin (67)
	Wen Jiabao (50)
Secretariat	
Ding Guan'gen (59)	Hu Jintao (50)
Li Ruihuan (59)	Ding Guan'gen (59)
Qiao Shi (68)	Wei Jianxing (61)
Yang Baibing (73)	Wen Jiabao (51)
	Ren Jianxing (67)
Alternate Member	
Wen Jiabao (50)	

*Died February 1993

realm in Marxism." No other plenum or congress report in the reform era had been so personal or so laudatory. Rhetorically at least, Deng's status became comparable to, if not higher than, that of Mao.

Personnel changes at the Fourteenth Party Congress (see Table 1) supported to some extent the policies favored by Deng. Conservative leaders Yao Yilin and Song Ping were removed from the Politburo Standing

Committee and Zhu Rongji, Liu Huaqing (a senior military modernizer who was also promoted to be vice-chairman of the CMC), and Hu Jintao (then a 50-year-old former Communist Youth League cadre and former Party secretary of Tibet to whom Deng had taken a liking) were added. The conservative Li Ximing, targeted by Deng during his southern tour, was removed from the Politburo and subsequently replaced as Beijing Party secretary by Chen Xitong, who had responded loyally to Deng's "emancipate the mind" campaign in 1991, despite his hardline stance during the 1989 protest movement. Overall, the number of full Politburo members was increased to 20 from 14 as a number of provincial and younger leaders joined the august body while several elders retired (Yang Shangkun, Wan Li, Qin Jiwei, Wu Xueqian, and Yang Rudai).[101] Moreover, the Central Advisory Commission, of which Chen Yun was the head and which had long served as a bastion of conservative opposition to Deng, was abolished.

Although these changes reflected a major shift in China's top-level policy-making body, Deng stopped short of a fundamental overhaul. In particular, Deng was determined to prevent supporters of former general secretary Zhao Ziyang from moving into the highest positions. Thus, Vice-Premier Tian Jiyun, a protégé of Zhao who had pushed Deng's themes with such devastating effectiveness the previous spring, was denied a Politburo Standing Committee seat. Moreover, such Zhao associates as Hu Qili and Yan Mingfu, partially rehabilitated in June 1991, did not rejoin the Politburo and Secretariat (respectively) as some had hoped.[102] Indeed, the promotion of Hu Jintao to the Politburo reflected this effort to make sure that Zhao would never stage a comeback. As a Communist Youth League (CYL) leader, Hu had good ties with Hu Yaobang and other reformers, but he had emerged following the Cultural Revolution as head of the CYL in Gansu province, where the conservative Song Ping was Party secretary. Hu, who is open-minded but circumspect, got along well with Song, and Song became his primary supporter. In the period prior to Tiananmen, Zhao Ziyang arranged for Hu to go to Guizhou as Party secretary, much to Hu's dismay. Hu was a victim of the internecine battles then raging between Hu Yaobang and Zhao Ziyang. Hu Jintao's turn came following Tiananmen, when Jiang and others needed cadres who were hostile to Zhao. By

---

[101] Joseph Fewsmith, "Reform, Resistance, and the Politics of Succession," pp. 8–11.
[102] Former Politburo Standing Committee member Hu Qili, purged for his support of Zhao during the 1989 demonstrations, was appointed vice-minister of the Ministry of the Machine-Building and Electronics Industry. Yan Mingfu, former member of the Secretariat and head of the Party's United Front Work Department, was appointed a vice-minister of Civil Affairs. A third Zhao associate, Rui Xingwen, was named vice-minister of the SPC at the same time. Xinhua, June 1, 1991, in FBIS-CHI, June 4, 1991, p. 30.

using Hu, Jiang was able to appease those in Hu Yaobang's camp, appeal to conservatives like Song Ping, and freeze out supporters of Zhao.[103]

Most importantly, the changes stopped short of affecting the "Jiang–Li structure" at the top of the system. Many had expected Zhu Rongji or Tian Jiyun to be elevated to the second slot, in line to succeed Li Peng as premier, at the NPC meeting the following spring. Such predictions *cum* hopes were unrealistic. Zhu had already made a "helicopter"-like ascent by jumping two levels from alternate member of the Central Committee to the Politburo Standing Committee; to go one level further would have roused intense opposition. And Tian had offended many conservatives by his caustic ridicule – not to mention by his close relationship with Zhao.

Deng's most important consideration, however, may have been to maintain balance between reformers and conservatives. As the well-known writer Bai Hua put it: "It was as though he [Deng] were afraid that once the leftists had been wiped out, the [factional] balance would be upset and another wave of 'bourgeois liberalization' would set in."[104] Bai's estimate was, no doubt, correct.

Deng did at least two things that bolstered Jiang. After thinking seriously of removing Jiang from office, Deng was persuaded not only to retain him but also to strengthen his position by removing Yang Baibing as vice-chairman of the powerful CMC, a move that also undercut the authority of Yang Shangkun, Deng's long-time confidant and supporter. Yang Baibing had made no bones about his disdain for Jiang Zemin, conferring major promotions himself rather than deferring to Jiang as head of the CMC, and that meant the leadership situation was unstable. In addition, there was growing resentment in the military establishment at the concentration of authority in the hands of the Yang brothers (who were derided for creating a "Yang family army"). This antagonism was particularly concentrated among veterans of the New Fourth Army who had fought in east China during the war against Japan. These veterans, who included Zhang Aiping, Li Xiannian, Ye Fei, Hong Xuezhi, and Zhang Zhen, resented being passed over by the Yang brothers, who had risen through the ranks as political commissars rather than as commanders.[105] They also rallied to Jiang Zemin as one of their own. Zhang Aiping, one of the founders of the PLA Navy and a leader of China's nuclear program, had been close to Jiang Zemin's uncle, Jiang Shangqing. Zhang had served as commander of the Fourth

---

[103] On Hu Jintao, see Cheng Li, *China's Leaders*. For Hu's relations with Song Ping and Zhao Ziyang, I have relied on a number of interviews.

[104] Quoted in Lam, *China after Deng Xiaoping*, p. 171.

[105] Gao Xin, *Jiang Zemin quanli zhi lu*, pp. 58–80.

Division of the New Fourth Army. Li Xiannian was commander of the Fifth Division, Ye Fei was commander of the First Division, and Hong Xuezhi was chief of staff of the Third Division. Zhang Zhen, who would be promoted at the Fourteenth Party Congress, had been Zhang Aiping's chief of staff.

Moreover, senior conservative Party leaders also supported Jiang Zemin. The key person was Bo Yibo, the veteran economic planner who somehow maintained close relations with both Chen Yun and Deng Xiaoping. When Jiang first came to Beijing as general secretary, he cultivated a close relationship with Bo, often visiting his house and seeking his guidance. Now Bo supported Jiang. In a reference to Deng's removal of first Hu Yaobang and then Zhao Ziyang, Bo told Deng that he could not repeatedly (*yi er zai, zai er san*) change general secretaries. No doubt Bo's advice reflected the counsel of other conservative leaders.

To turn against his long-time associate Yang Shangkun and support Jiang Zemin, whose desultory support of reform had prompted Deng's trip to the south, must have been difficult. In retrospect, it appears to have been Deng's most statesmanlike act. Perhaps he reflected on the unstable situation Mao had left behind and worried that if he, Deng, left a situation of political tension then his legacy might well end up like that of Mao – overturned.

To replace the Yangs, Deng turned to the elderly (76 in 1992) Liu Huaqing, who was given a Politburo Standing Committee seat and named vice-chairman of the CMC, and Zhang Zhen (78 in 1992), who was named second vice-chairman of the CMC. The surprise elevation of Liu and Zhang certainly underscored a renewed professionalism in the PLA (Liu is one of the leading modernizers in the PLA – particularly of the navy, which he led for many years – and Zhang was commandant of the National Defense University before his promotion), but their promotion also highlighted the inability to turn the leadership of the military over to a younger generation, even as the age of the civilian leaders of the country continued to fall.

Second, in order to stabilize the political situation, Deng limited his purge of leftists. As noted previously, Song Ping and Yao Yilin were removed from the Politburo Standing Committee, and the CAC, a bastion of conservative influence, was abolished. In addition, Li Ximing was removed from the Politburo and from his position as secretary of the Beijing Municipal CCP Committee, and Gao Di was removed as director of the *People's Daily*. These moves already cut deeply into conservative influence, so Deng allowed others to remain in influential positions. For instance, Xu Weicheng, who had once written on behalf of the Gang of Four and more recently had been editor of the conservative *Beijing Daily*, remained as deputy head of the Propaganda Department. Wang Renzhi, who had excoriated Deng's policies as head of the Propaganda Department, was removed from that position (he was replaced by Deng loyalist Ding Guan'gen) but took over as Party secretary of the Chinese Academy of Social Sciences (CASS). Moreover, Deng Liqun organized many of his leftist colleagues – including former State Education Commission head He Dongchang, former CASS vice-president You Lin, former vice-chairman of the State Planning Commission Fang Weizhong, and director of the Party Literature Research Center Pang Xianzhi – into a newly established PRC Historical Society. It was apparent that this group of leftists intended to maintain a voice in Party councils and to maintain vigilance against bourgeois liberalization.[106]

BACK TO THE MIDDLE

The effort to strike a new balance was apparent in the aftermath of the Fourteenth Party Congress. Whereas Deng's new reform push had dominated Chinese politics since his trip to Shenzhen at the beginning of the year, China's leaders began to warn liberal intellectuals not to go too far shortly after the congress closed. Thus, in late November, Jiang Zemin warned cadres to exercise caution in criticizing Marxism–Leninism–Mao Zedong Thought, saying that their viewpoints represented "the most updated reflection of class struggle inside society and inside the Party in a certain realm." Similarly, Chen Xitong, who had come out in vigorous support of Deng's "emancipate the mind" campaign in the spring of 1991, told a December 1992 meeting of the Beijing Party committee that "[t]he bourgeois liberalization elements in some superstructure departments and activists in the 1989 counterrevolutionary riot have resumed their activities again, and have dished up all sorts of viewpoints on thoroughly dumping Marxism, while propagating a Western capitalist multiparty system."[107]

As the political atmosphere began to shift in a more conservative direction, Yao Yilin, who had stepped down from the Politburo Standing Committee at the Fourteenth Party Congress, sharply criticized economic czar Zhu Rongji at a State Council meeting and then at a conference for Politburo members and state councilors. Yao argued that capital investment had exceeded the plan by too much (38 percent), that bank credits had likewise greatly exceeded the plan (120 percent), and that debt chains and

---

[106] He Po-shih, "The Army Reshuffle Was Carried Out to Pacify the Leftist Faction."
[107] Lo Ping, "Blowing of the 'Left' Wind, and the Four-Horse Carriage."

stockpiles were again building up. His criticisms were echoed by Wang Bingqian, the conservative former minister of finance, who warned against a repetition of the sort of fevered atmosphere that had prevailed during the Great Leap Forward in the late 1950s. Zhu reportedly defended himself by arguing that, although there were problems with the economy, it was not "overheated."[108] Nevertheless, both Jiang Zemin and Li Peng warned at the year-end National Planning Conference and National Economic Conference against the "overheated economy."[109]

This renewed attack on rapid economic growth, which can be directly attributed to Deng's efforts to build momentum for reform in 1992, prompted the patriarch to intervene again. For the third year in a row, Deng appeared in Shanghai to encourage high growth and reform. This time, Deng was quoted as saying, "I hope you will not lose the current opportunities. Opportunities for great development are rare in China." Deng also used the occasion to heap praise on Shanghai, which had grown a remarkable 14.8 percent since his last visit: "In 1992 people in Shanghai accomplished what other people could not do."[110]

Deng's intervention was apparently intended not only to keep up reform momentum in general but also specifically to influence the NPC meeting scheduled for March. In early March, the Second Plenary Session of the Fourteenth Central Committee met to consider policy prior to the NPC and endorsed Deng's view that "at present and throughout the 1990s, the favorable domestic and international opportunities should be grasped to speed up the pace of reform, opening up, and the modernization drive." On the basis of this optimistic assessment, the plenum endorsed an upward revision of the annual growth target set by the Eighth Five-Year Plan (1991–5) from 6 percent to 8–9 percent.[111]

The issues that roiled the political elite in the years from 1989 to 1992 were basically those that had shaped Chinese politics from the late 1970s until Tiananmen. On the one hand, those who looked to the 1950s as a "golden age" emphasized ideology, political loyalty, and the planned economy, whereas those who believed in more radical change stressed "reform and opening up." The tensions between these two lines had coursed through

---

[108] Cheng Te-lin, "Yao Yilin Launches Attack against Zhu Rongji, Tian Jiyun"; Jen Hui-wen, "Deng Xiaoping Urges Conservatives Not to Make a Fuss"; Chen Chien-ping, "Zhu Rongji Urges Paying Attention to Negative Effects of Reform."

[109] Xinhua, December 27, 1992, in FBIS-CHI, December 28, 1992, pp. 34–6.

[110] China Central Television, January 22, 1993, trans. FBIS-CHI, January 22, 1993, pp. 20–1.

[111] Xinhua, March 7, 1993, in FBIS-CHI, March 8, 1993, pp. 13–14.

Chinese politics for more than a decade before exploding in the cataclysm of Tiananmen and the vitriolic struggles of the years immediately thereafter.

Deng won the battle. His ideas were enshrined in the Fourteenth Party Congress report. Targets for growth were raised, new measures to attract foreign investment were adopted, and, most important, the non-state sector would be permitted to develop – indeed, explode. But in another sense, the Fourteenth Party Congress really marked the end of the Dengist era (though Deng would not die until 1997). Although the issues with which that congress dealt would remain relevant throughout the 1990s, they would be joined by new issues as the problems bequeathed by the Dengist reforms became increasingly apparent. Income inequality, corruption, and decline of state revenues could not be addressed adequately simply by more reform and opening up, at least as that program had been understood in the 1980s, and greater efforts at state building did not necessarily mean a retreat from reform and opening. Moreover, the changed international environment of the post-Cold War era began to have a profound impact on the thinking of Chinese elites, and a new nationalism inevitably emerged. In short, a rethinking of the issues of domestic reform and China's place in the world would mark the 1990s as a very different decade from the one before it. The post-Deng era was arriving in China even as Deng had his greatest personal success in forging the Fourteenth Party Congress report. To understand the issues that shaped the post-Deng era, we need to shift our attention from the rarefied atmosphere of elite politics to the broader arena of intellectual contention. The next three chapters explore the reshaping of the intellectual landscape that occurred in the 1990s.

PART II

Redefining reform: the search for a new way

CHAPTER 3

The emergence of neoconservatism

In the years following Tiananmen, new currents of thought began to emerge and play a significant role in social, intellectual, and political circles. Most of these currents had roots in the 1980s, but either they were more peripheral ideas that moved toward the center of intellectual concern or they underwent a significant evolution in the context of post-Tiananmen China, or both. In all cases, they reflect an effort to come to grips intellectually with the political failure of reform in the 1980s, the economic and social problems that emerged (or became more acute) in the 1990s, and the type of political system that might be effective in coping with the problems facing China, both domestically and internationally. As we will see in this and the next two chapters, deep divisions opened up within the intellectual community, even as the place of that community in Chinese society changed significantly. In broad terms, even as the government maintained its own ideological line, a new arena of public discourse developed. Over time, the government took increasing account of this public opinion, sometimes absorbing ideas from it, sometimes engaging it, and sometimes suppressing it. The purpose of Part II is to focus on intellectual developments in the 1990s; in Part III, we will look more closely at the government–intellectual interaction.

One trend that emerged in the 1980s was that of "new authoritarianism," which re-emerged in the 1990s as "neoconservatism." Although few in government, or even in intellectual circles, would lay claim to the title "neoconservative," the impact of the ideas associated with it on the thinking of the political leadership was clear, particularly in the early to mid-1990s.

The first public glimpse of this trend came on January 16, 1989, when Shanghai's reform-oriented newspaper, the *World Economic Herald*, published an article by Wu Jiaxiang, then a young researcher with the General Office of the Central Committee. In a self-conscious imitation of *The Communist Manifesto*, Wu began, "there is a strange spirit that has sprouted wings and flown through the forest of the intellectual world, and that is the intellectual tide of the new authoritarianism" (*xin quanwei zhuyi*). Society needed to develop through three stages, Wu maintained: first a stage of traditional authoritarianism, then an intermediate stage in which individual freedom could develop under the protection of new authoritarianism, and finally a stage of freedom and democracy. The intermediate stage of new authoritarianism was necessary, Wu argued, because otherwise the crumbling authority of traditional authoritarian rule would be captured by a variety of social structures and forces, preventing both individual freedom and necessary central authority. Freedom would not develop and authority would be dispersed. The "new" in new authoritarianism referred to self-conscious use of authority to guide society through this treacherous intermediate stage, blocking those forces that would otherwise prevent the development of individual freedom from forming and thus guiding society safely through to a free, democratic, and modern society.[1]

Chinese intellectuals began exploring the idea of new authoritarianism in 1986. Wu himself refers to a 1986 report written by Wang Huning – then a professor of international politics at Fudan University and, after 1995, head of the Political Section of the Central Committee's Policy Research Office under Jiang Zemin (and then promoted to be director of the Central Policy Research Center in 2002) – discussing the need for "necessary concentration" of central authority in the course of reform.[2] Wang's report set off a major internal policy battle when it was read by Hu Qili. Hu was favorably impressed by the report and forwarded it to Hu Yaobang. The general secretary, however, was not impressed and referred to it, in a marginal note, as "rubbish." Later he took Hu Qili to task for accepting the ideas in the report.[3]

At roughly the same time that Wang was forwarding his report to the top leadership, another intellectual, Zhang Bingjiu (then a Ph.D. candidate at Beijing University) wrote an article saying that China needed a "semi-authoritarian" (*banjiquan*) political system in order to develop a commodity (i.e., market-oriented) economy.[4] What Zhang meant by the creation of a semi-authoritarian political system was the separation of politics from economics. In traditional authoritarian systems, Zhang maintained, economics and politics were conflated so that economic units could not have real autonomy. Democracy could only develop on the basis of such economic autonomy, so the current need was to use the political system to consciously separate politics from economics. Zhang believed – similarly

[1] Wu Jiaxiang, "Xin quanwei zhuyi shuping."
[2] Ibid., p. 4. Yu Guanghua, "Xin quanwei zhuyi de shehui jichu ji huanxiang."
[3] Author interview.   [4] Gu Xin, "Xin quanwei zhuyi de lilun kunjing," p. 46.

to Wu – that if China tried to move too quickly to democracy then the conflation of economics and politics would continue and there would be no basis for real, stable democracy. Just as Yuan Shikai in 1915 could abort Song Jiaoren's efforts to bring about a democratic system by ordering his assassination, so democracy would not have an adequate foundation today unless the political elite consciously used the political system to force through the separation.[5]

Following Hu Yaobang's ouster as general secretary, Zhao Ziyang felt the need to concentrate greater authority in his office, both to be able to push reform forward against the resistance of local officials and to ward off political threats at the central level. Thus, a debate on the merits of new authoritarianism opened up among Zhao's advisers, with some favoring the concept and others opposed. Zhao indicated his sympathy for the concept by reporting on the discussion in April 1989 to Deng Xiaoping. Deng indicated general agreement, saying "[t]his is also my idea" while registering reservations about the terminology (saying that the "specific word for this notion can be reconsidered").[6]

Over the early months of 1989, the pages of China's newspapers and journals filled with discussions of new authoritarianism and related issues. The emphases of different authors varied. Some favored "elite democracy"[7] while others emphasized "strongman politics."[8] However, the basic thrust of these various discussions was that, at this particular stage in China's reform, it was necessary to have a powerful, authoritarian central government to push through economic reforms and bring about full marketization. Advocates of the new authoritarianism argued that unless a powerful central government could oversee the implementation of market-oriented reforms, the reform process itself might stall and a democracy might never appear. Those in favor of the new authoritarianism were not opposed to democracy but, on the contrary, believed that only a step-by-step, gradualist approach could ultimately achieve it.[9]

The contentions of the new authoritarians were quickly challenged by liberal intellectuals. For instance, Yu Haocheng, a legal scholar and chief

---

[5] Zhang Bingjiu, "Jingji tizhi gaige he zhengzhi tizhi gaige de jincheng yu xietiao."

[6] "Deng Xiaoping on Neoauthoritarianism"; Stanley Rosen and Gary Zou, "The Road to Modernization in China Debated."

[7] Chen Yizi, Wang Xiaoqiang, and Li Jun, "The Deep-Seated Questions and the Strategic Choice China's Reform Faces."

[8] Dai Qing, "From Lin Zexu to Jiang Jingguo."

[9] On the debates in this period, see Mark Petracca and Mong Xiong, "The Concept of Chinese Neo-Authoritarianism"; Liu Jun and Li Lin (eds.), *Xinquanwei zhuyi*; and Qi Mo (ed.), *Xinquanwei zhuyi*.

editor of the Masses Publishing House (*Qunzhong chubanshe*), argued that the new authoritarians fundamentally misunderstood their facts; the conditions in the "four small dragons" (South Korea, Taiwan, Singapore, Hong Kong), on which much of the new authoritarian thinking was modeled, were fundamentally different from conditions in China.[10] In the four dragons, the economy was free and so intertwined with the international economy that their governments really could only have a "minuscule" impact on determining their economies. The example of a "honeymoon" period between the common citizens and monarchs of Europe (another argument made by the new authoritarians) was irrelevant to China, which had not had a manorial economy in the two millennia since the first emperor of the Qin. What China had seen was an autocratic government and a lack of democracy. Indeed, it was this lack of democracy, Yu argued, that had led to the alternation of autocracy and anarchy in Chinese history. Only by developing democracy could this cycle be broken. Contrary to the reasoning of the new authoritarians, Yu argued that only a democratic system could bring the stability and solidarity desired by the new authoritarians, and democracy could not be achieved by building a new autocracy.[11]

Proponents of the new authoritarianism and of democracy each focused on real, but different, features of the Chinese polity in the late 1980s. New authoritarians worried about two problems. On the one hand, they worried that the decentralizing reforms that reformers themselves had helped bring about were now creating new centers of power at lower levels that were preventing the continuation of marketizing reforms. Whereas lower levels had welcomed reforms earlier in the decade, now they had developed interests in the semireformed institutions of local society and opposed efforts that would erode their newfound power. New authoritarians hoped to use the power of the state to break through these obstacles and push marketization forward. On the other hand, both the reform program and individual reformers, particularly Premier (and then General Secretary) Zhao Ziyang, were facing a rising barrage of criticism. Some advocates of the new authoritarianism no doubt hoped to use the theory to concentrate greater power in Zhao's hands and thus turn back challenges to his authority. For them, Zhao's personal role and the fate of marketizing reforms were two sides of the same coin.

---

[10] On Yu's background, see Merle Goldman, *Sowing the Seeds of Democracy*, pp. 70–1. Most of the liberal critics of the new authoritarianism were related in some fashion to Hu's intellectual network, while most of the advocates of the new authoritarianism (at least in Beijing) were tied in some fashion to Zhao Ziyang. This debate therefore reflected the deepening divisions among reformers in the late 1980s.

[11] Yu Haocheng, "Zhongguo xuyao xin quanwei zhuyi ma?"

Liberal intellectuals, such as Yu Haocheng, saw the same problems but arrived at very different conclusions. In their opinion, political reform had to precede economic reform. Unless the political system could be democratized, they believed, there could never be guarantees for the sanctity of law or property, without which a market economy could never function well. Moreover, they believed that a recentralization of authority, however good the intentions of the new authoritarians might be, would inevitably lead China back into the sort of autocracy from which the country had only recently begun to escape.

It might be said that the new authoritarians underestimated the likelihood that a recentralized authority would be used to shore up personal authority (not necessarily that of Zhao Ziyang!) instead of being used to push through the marketizing reforms that they hoped for, just as liberal intellectuals underestimated the very real problems in maintaining social stability and in continuing economic reform – some of which required the creation of a stronger, or at least more effective, state. Both new authoritarians and liberal intellectuals were strongly influenced by the example of the "East Asian development model" that had seemed so effective in that part of the world, but whereas new authoritarians hoped to emulate their neighbors, liberal intellectuals stressed the differences between China and its neighbors. Liberal intellectuals contrasted the independence of state administration, law, market institutions, and "civil society" in other East Asian societies with the pervasive role the CCP played in China and concluded that China could not follow the developmental path of its neighbors; without political reform, the Chinese Communist Party could not be extricated from the other institutions of society and hence China could never develop either a market economy or a professional state administration.

Although the public nature of this debate ended with the crackdown of June 1989, the themes that it raised informed thinking among intellectuals and policy-makers alike and laid the bases for new debates in the 1990s, debates that reprised the themes of those debates on new authoritarianism but also developed in new directions. By the 1990s, there were new concerns with the problems of stability, the complexities of reform, and the difficult international environment. Whereas reformers in the 1980s had largely seen themselves as moving away from the planned economy and ideological orthodoxies of the past, by the 1990s the problems of partial reform had become evident; the need to build a new system, rather than merely tear down the old one, came to the fore. This trend had been evident in the discussions of the new authoritarianism, but it was the trauma of Tiananmen that imparted new urgency to the task.

In the immediate aftermath of Tiananmen, as described in Part I, there was a knee-jerk effort to reimpose ideological orthodoxies and strengthen planning. By late 1990, the failure of that effort was evident, though it took until 1992 for the Dengist reform program to be publicly reaffirmed. But even the reaffirmation of reform did not mean a return to the problematique of the 1980s. Below the highest levels, policy-makers and intellectuals – sometimes in conjunction but more often following their own paths – began to chart policies and rationales that could no longer be understood simply in terms of "reform" measures and "conservative" opposition.

There were many issues driving this new agenda. First and foremost was the issue of stability. In the 1980s, the only choices appeared to be between "reform" and "conservatism"; Tiananmen and the subsequent collapse of the Soviet Union confronted Chinese policy-makers and intellectuals alike with the specter of an unpleasant third alternative: social and political collapse. Foreign observers, focusing on hopes for political democratization, tend not to consider the downside risk of political change, in part because worries about "chaos" can and have been used by the political authorities in Beijing to justify repressive measures. Chinese policy-makers (not just "hardliners") and intellectuals, however, are keenly aware of the turmoil of twentieth-century politics and worry openly about the costs of political implosion. Even such a liberal observer of contemporary China as Ding Xueliang has warned: "If an anarchic situation appears in China, the violence that Chinese will inflict on each other will far exceed the barbarism inflicted by the Japanese army when it invaded in the 1930s."[12]

The shock of Tiananmen, which was soon followed by the collapse of socialism in Eastern Europe and the subsequent disintegration of the Soviet Union, led many in China to rethink the course of reform. This rejection of enlightenment thinking (which stressed science and democracy) and at least partial reaffirmation of more statist approaches to reform has often been referred to as neoconservatism. Neoconservatism must be understood as a loose term, indicating a set of concerns and a broad intellectual orientation rather than a well-developed and consistent body of thought. In general, neoconservatism indicated a desire to find a middle path between the traditional conservatism of the Old Left (as exemplified ideologically by more orthodox Marxist–Leninists such as Hu Qiaomu and Deng Liqun and economically by such traditional planners as Chen Yun) and "radical reformers" (as epitomized culturally by the film *River Elegy* and economically by advocates of privatization). In general, neoconservatism accepted

[12] Ding Xueliang, *Gongchanzhuyihou yu Zhongguo*, p. xxii.

market economics, albeit with some caveats, but desired a greater role for the state. Here, it is useful to view the development of neoconservatism by looking at the following themes: incrementalism, central–local relations, its roots in the new authoritarianism, state-centered nationalism, and the turn away from cultural cosmopolitanism.

INCREMENTALISM

The disintegration of the Soviet Union stood in stark contrast to China following Tiananmen. Whereas the Soviet Union broke up into its fifteen constituent republics, lost its superpower status, and experienced rapid economic and social decline, China held together and after a short while resumed an impressive rate of growth. Although some argued that such a contrast justified the Tiananmen crackdown, most people drew the more modest but nevertheless potent lesson that "incremental" reform was better than "shock therapy" (the idea of instituting price and property reforms in a short period of time). This was a lesson that perhaps came easily to Chinese, for it seemed embedded in their reform experience: "Crossing the river by feeling the stones" (*mozhe shitou guohe*) was the mantra of the 1980s. Moreover, it did not take long before foreign economists affirmed the wisdom of their Chinese counterparts.[13]

The transformation of incremental reform from a necessity of circumstance into a distinct "Chinese model"[14] was rooted in the economic discussions of the 1980s. In the first decade of reform, young and middle-aged economists increasingly introduced Western neoclassical economics in opposition to the political economy of Marxism. Although some focused more on macroeconomics while others emphasized microeconomics, there was a common understanding among these reformers that economics as developed in the West was applicable to China. By 1986–7, however, "institutional economics" as developed by Ronald Coase, James Buchanan, Mancur Olson, Douglass North, and others came increasingly to the attention of young economists, many of whom had studied overseas. Institutionalist economics appealed to Chinese economists because it provided a framework for studying China's transition to a market economy. As Sheng Hong (a leading institutional economist and former student of Ronald Coase) wrote, neoclassical economics "supposes that institutions are constant factors, that transaction costs are zero, and that a human being's rationality is

[13] John McMillan and Barry Naughton, "How to Reform a Planned Economy"; Chen Kang, Gray Jefferson, and Inderjit Singh, "Lessons from China's Economic Reform."

[14] Sheng Hong, "Zhongguo de guodu jingjixue," p. 4.

perfect; it also ignores research into the distribution of interests."[15] These were all dubious assumptions in the very imperfect market conditions in China, and they did not explicate the problems China faced in the course of transition. Perhaps more importantly, then, institutional economics provided an intellectual rationale for rejecting "shock therapy." Neoclassical economics, in Sheng's opinion, lacked a concept of time; shock therapy was thus a logical corollary to neoclassical economics – and neither was suitable to China.[16]

What was striking about the Chinese "model" of incremental reform for Sheng and many others was that China had gone a long way toward the reform of prices, property rights, stock markets, and so forth at a relatively low cost. This was particularly important in light of Tiananmen, which, as Sheng wrote, "raised from a negative perspective the question of the cost of reform" and caused "some young economists to give up their romantic attitude toward reform issues."[17] The experience of Tiananmen persuaded some economists not only to doubt neoclassical economics but also to pay increasing attention to avoiding conflicts of interest and reducing the cost of reform.[18] One might say that incremental reform was elevated from an unarticulated strategy to a theory, one that some economists held was applicable not just to China but elsewhere as well.[19]

For Sheng Hong, there was also an important cultural dimension to China's transition. For Sheng, who would soon draw widespread attention as a cultural nationalist, China's culture emphasizes the harmony between individuals, reconciling their interests and promoting cooperation. This cultural disposition, in Sheng's opinion, forms a broad background to government efforts to work out reforms in a way that maximizes benefits and minimizes costs.[20] Whether or not China's culture has influenced its reform strategy, Sheng's attitude toward China's culture has certainly influenced his advocacy of transitional economics as a model. There is an evident self-satisfaction in the rejection of "romantic" notions of reform derived from Western neoclassical economics and in the identification of a uniquely "Chinese" path to reform.

---

[15] Sheng Hong, "A Survey of the Research on the Transitional Process of Market-Oriented Reform in China," p. 10.

[16] Ibid., p. 13.   [17] Sheng Hong, "Zhongguo de guodu jingjixue," p. 5.   [18] Ibid.

[19] Lin Yifu, Cai Fang, and Li Zhou, "On the Gradual-Advance Style of Economic Reform in China"; see also Sheng Hong, "Cong jihua junheng dao shichang junheng." Fan Gang takes an opposing point of view in "Liangzhong gaige chengben yu liangzhong gaige fangshi."

[20] Sheng Hong, "A Survey of the Research on the Transitional Process of Market-Oriented Reform in China," p. 11.

If a belief in incrementalism derived primarily from China's reform experience, it also had roots, perhaps ironically, in a historical and cultural critique of the Chinese revolution. Cultural debates in the 1980s, as noted in the Introduction, were dominated by a cosmopolitanism, a desire to "enter the world" (*zouxiang shijie*), and a corresponding fervor to critique the "feudal" values of China's past. By the late 1980s, however, some were questioning this cosmopolitan orientation. One critique came from a group of scholars, many of whom were based abroad, who argued that China needed to revive its traditional Confucian values. This interest in Confucianism, as we will see in the next chapter, was inspired by the same search for values that underlay much of the cultural fever in the 1980s. Such scholars argued that China needed to recover those timeless Chinese values that could be of value in the present. They believed that the loss of values felt by so many intellectuals was because the Chinese revolution had moved too far from China's tradition – indeed, that the revolution in 1949 had marked a radical rupture in China's cultural history.

This argument was presented most forcefully by Princeton University Professor Yu Yingshi in a speech presented at the Chinese University of Hong Kong in 1988 (though not published until almost two years later). Yu argued that Chinese intellectual thought in the twentieth century has been characterized by the dominance of radicalism and that it became increasingly radical from the late nineteenth century through the Cultural Revolution. Yu firmly placed the origins of this trend in the reform movement of 1898, led by Kang Youwei and Liang Qichao. At this time, the demand was for "rapid change." Kang had argued that incremental change was useless; change must be immediate and comprehensive. Of all the leaders of the reform movement, the one who most thoroughly exemplified the radical spirit of the times was Tan Sitong, whose 1897 *Study of Humaneness* (*Renxue*), in Yu's opinion, "completely denied 2,000 years of Chinese tradition" (*yi kou foukenle Zhongguo liangqian nian de chuantong*).[21] From political radicalism, China moved to cultural radicalism in the May Fourth Movement, and then to social radicalism with the victory of the communist revolution. The Cultural Revolution, in Yu's opinion, was the logical culmination of this century of unchecked radicalism. In a follow-up article, Yu took issue with trends in contemporary American studies of China that see contemporary China as a continuation of tradition. Yu held a completely opposite view: "Since 1949, a group of marginal people in China, relying on an especially radical theory and using a new type of totalitarian

---

[21] Yu Yingshi, "Zhongguo jindai sixiangshi zhongde jijin yu baoshou," p. 139.

organization, completely destroyed the traditional social structure of China."[22]

Yu's ideas certainly had an impact on mainland scholars. "Incrementalism" began to have much more positive connotations. The French Revolution, glorified in the Chinese Marxist tradition, began to lose its luster, while the English Revolution, previously denigrated as insufficiently radical, came to be seen in a much more positive light. Some years later, the impact of Yu's ideas was clearly visible in Li Zehou and Liu Zaifu's controversial 1996 book *Farewell to Revolution* (just as Li Zehou's ideas had an impact on Yu's thinking). Li and Liu argued that most of China's political difficulties over the past century have been caused by a powerful tendency to see problems in revolutionary terms. That is to say, when confronted by obstacles or opposition, there has been a tendency to see the solution not in discussion and compromise but in terms of "struggle" and revolution. Political conflicts become total: "You die and I live." Tracing the modern history of this revolutionary impulse, Li and Liu, like Yu, found its *locus classicus* in Tan Sitong. Reviewing the history of the period, they arrived at the controversial conclusion that the revolution of 1911 was "not necessarily necessary,"[23] a judgment that undermined the legitimacy of the communist revolution as well.

CENTRAL–LOCAL RELATIONS

As stability and incrementalism became one important impulse informing Chinese discourse in the 1990s, concern over the changing relationship between the central government and the local governments was another. Between 1978 and 1992, central government revenues as a percentage of GDP had fallen from 31.2 percent to 14.7 percent, suggesting that the central government had been weakened to the extent that it could no longer maintain control over macroeconomic policy – and inflation was then a major concern. The publicity given to several major instances of regional protectionism (the "cocoon war," the "cotton war," etc.) all reinforced the notion that the central government was losing control over the provinces. In 1988, CASS economists Shen Liren and Dai Yuanchen, in a highly influential article, introduced the term "feudal lord economy" (*zhuhou jingji*) to describe this phenomenon.[24]

---

[22] Yu Yingshi, "Zailun Zhongguo xiandai sixiang zhongde jijin yu baoshou," p. 146.
[23] Li Zehou and Liu Zaifu, *Gaobie geming*.
[24] Shen Liren and Dai Yuanchen, "Woguo 'zhuhou jingji' de xingcheng jiqi biduan he genyuan."

In the wake of Tiananmen, conservatives had (as discussed in Chapter 1) tried to turn the clock back, but even they soon realized that the goal of restoring anything resembling the old planned economy was no longer practical. This realization prompted new efforts to explore ways of combining political control and economic marketization and to justify a tightening of central control. One of the most important exponents of neoconservative thinking in this area was Chen Yuan, son of Party elder and economic policy specialist Chen Yun.

Born in 1945, Chen Yuan entered the department of automatic control (*zidong kongzhi*) at Qinghua University in 1965. Chen received his degree in 1970, even though classes were suspended because of the Cultural Revolution, and was sent to work in a factory in Hunan. In 1973 he returned to Beijing to work as a technician in the Aeronautics Ministry. When entrance exams were restored in 1978, Chen tested into the economic management department of the graduate school at CASS, where he studied under the guidance of senior economists Ma Hong and Yu Guangyuan (interestingly, Zhu Rongji was in the same institute at that time). After a short stint in the State Planning Commission, Chen was appointed deputy and then first Party secretary of the West City District Party Committee in Beijing. In 1984 he became head of Beijing Municipal Commerce and Trade Department (*bu*) and concurrently deputy director of the city Economic Reform Commission (under then-mayor Chen Xitong). At this time, Chen organized a group of people as the Beijing Young Economists Association (*Beijing qingnian jingji gongzuozhe xiehui*) to study economic theory and formulate Beijing development strategy. This organization was intended to serve as Chen Yuan's own think-tank, and many of the connections between Chen and young economists in the late 1980s continued into the 1990s.

In 1987, in one of the first uses of multicandidate elections (*cha'e xuanju*, which have more candidates than positions though not as many as two candidates for each position), Chen Yuan failed to be elected to the Beijing Party Committee. Chen's failure was primarily a reflection of widespread resentment of the rapidly growing power of the children of high-level cadres (*taizi*, "princes"), a trend that continues to this day. In the same election, Chen Haosu (son of Marshal Chen Yi) and Bo Xicheng (son of Party elder Bo Yibo) both withdrew their names from consideration rather than face defeat; Chen Yuan proved overly confident. With Chen's defeat, Zhao Ziyang quickly arranged a position for him as vice-governor of the People's Bank of China; Zhao's concern was motivated by his desire to placate Chen Yun, with whom he was then having increasing difficulties.

In the summer of 1987, Chen Yuan organized a large-scale seminar to discuss a "Report on the Stages of the Socialist Economic Operating Mechanism." At this seminar, Chen presented a report stressing that the chief characteristic of China's economy in the primary stage of socialism is the "tightness" of the economy. That is to say, the "primary contradiction" facing China's economy is "shortage" created by growing aggregate social demand and the limited resources available to produce the requisite supply. This was, in Chen's view, a structural problem that could not be allowed to continue without serious social consequences, including inflation and the distortion of the structure of production. The solution to this problem, Chen argued, was to strengthen planning and thereby gradually build the capacity to meet demand. Only planning would allow China to use its scarce resources in a way that would maximize supply in a socially beneficial manner.[25]

In December 1990, Chen Yuan presented a paper entitled "China's Deep-Seated Economic Problems and Choices – Several Issues Regarding China's Economic Development Situation and the Operating Mechanism (Outline)," which decried many of the decentralizing consequences of reform. As pointed out in the previous chapter, this paper was very much a part of the critique of the Dengist reform program that unfolded in the period after Tiananmen. Although it was no doubt connected with his father's (Chen Yun's) critique of Deng, it was not simply a repetition of his father's formulations. Rather, Chen Yuan was exploring an approach that was conservative in terms of its critical evaluation of Deng's decentralizing policies but also more accepting of Western economics. In this way, Chen Yuan's paper tried to lay out a neoconservative approach to economic policy.

Chen objected to decentralization both on the grounds that it led to local protectionism and the fragmentation of the national market and, more seriously, on the grounds that the erosion of central resources was resulting in a "weak and powerless central government" surrounded by numerous "feudal lords." These trends would, he warned, result in "the great socialist mansion that we have built laboriously over many years collapsing" if nothing were done.[26] Faced with this dire situation, Chen recommended a "new centralization," but one, he declared, that would be different from the old planned economy.[27] Although Chen wanted to recentralize authority and use the power of the state to readjust China's industrial structure, he was also very clear that he wanted to develop the

---

[25] Gao Xin and He Pin, *Zhonggong "taizidang,"* pp. 112–13.
[26] Chen Yuan, "Wo guo jingji de shenceng wenti he xuanze (gangyao)," pp. 18–19.
[27] Ibid., p. 19.

role of the market (by breaking down local protectionism and ministerial interference in enterprises) even as he would give a greater role to the state.

Chen obviously had the East Asian developmental state in mind. He argued that the successful experiences of the late industrializing nations proved that the central government has certain unique functions; not everything can be left to the whims of the market.[28] Chen's understanding of the role of the central government was also influenced by his view of China's role in the world economy: whereas China should participate in the international division of labor and economic exchange, at the same time, "China must develop as an economic great power that is not dependent on any other country or group of countries." China's developmental path cannot be like that of small countries; China must have a complete and fairly advanced industrial system.[29] Market forces alone will never bring about such an economic system; the government should have a clear industrial policy and should direct scarce resources to strategic industries.

A year later, Chen Yuan reflected on the usefulness of Western economics for China in another article. He firmly rejected the ideas of deficit financing and expansionary monetary policy that were then closely associated with the name of Keynes, but he praised Keynes for "pointing out in clear-cut terms that the function of macroeconomic quantitative regulation and control can only be performed by the government, not the market mechanism." He praised Milton Friedman for his emphasis on monetary control but rejected his *laissez-faire* economic philosophy. By selecting what was useful and rejecting the rest, Chen argued that "Western economics can be turned to serve our socialist revolution." It is difficult to imagine Chen Yuan's father citing the works of Keynes or Friedman, but not difficult to imagine the elder Chen agreeing that the state is an "indispensable actor" and not simply a "passive referee."[30]

NEW AUTHORITARIANISM AND NEOCONSERVATISM

While Chen Yuan began to articulate a neoconservative vision of economics in the post-Tiananmen period, others began to explore the political dimensions. As just discussed, intellectuals such as Wu Jiaxiang and Zhang Bingjiu argued that authority needed to be recentralized in the hands of the central government – not, as conservatives would have it, to restore the old Marxist–Leninist order, but to use the strength of the central government to

---

[28] Ibid., p. 20. [29] Ibid., p. 23.
[30] Chen Yuan, "Several Questions on Methods and Theory Regarding Studies in Economic Operations in China," pp. 40–1.

push the marketization of the economy against local forces that supported decentralization but not marketization. Although such people argued for strengthening the center's authority, there was a liberal goal within their vision. The marketization of the economy would lead to the growth of a middle class, which in turn would foster the growth of democratic governance. This was the lesson that many intellectuals at the time had drawn from the development of several East Asian economies and the wave of democratization then starting to spread across the region. For these intellectuals, the government would take the place of the middle class until a middle class could develop.

Although the public discussion on new authoritarianism is generally identified with a number of intellectuals close to then-General Secretary Zhao Ziyang, the earliest discussions were held in Shanghai. Two important people in these discussions were Wang Huning and Xiao Gongqin.

Wang Huning, who in 1995 was to be brought to Beijing by Jiang Zemin in order to head the Political Section of the CCP's Policy Research Office, was born in 1955. He entered Shanghai's East Normal University during the Cultural Revolution as a "worker-peasant-soldier student" in 1974. After three years of studying French, Wang studied for a master's degree at Fudan University's Department of International Politics. Completing the program, he stayed on at Fudan University, eventually heading the Department of International Politics.[31]

In the late 1980s, Wang wrote a series of essays that drew attention to himself as one of the bright young lights on the intellectual scene. Political science was a new and precarious discipline in China, and it was impossible to write rigorous political science. Nevertheless, Wang managed to infuse his writings with some of the concerns of Western political science, giving his essays a freshness lacking in many of the writings then being published. Many of these essays appear in *The Collected Writings of Wang Huning*, which was published in 1989. Written mostly in 1987 and 1988, a time when discussion of political structural reform filled the air, these essays give the sense of a liberal, open-minded writer. Pointing to phenomena as diverse as the call for further democratization by the 27th Party Congress of the CPSU, the implementation of multicandidate elections in Hungary, the election of the French Socialist Party, and the democratic movement in South Korea, Wang declared that political reform is a universal phenomenon in the world. China's culture itself is changing from being "conservative, closed, subjective, and arbitrary" to one that is "renewed,

---

[31] Gao Xin, *Jiang Zemin de muliao*, pp. 284–6.

open, objective, and democratic." "Without a highly democratic political system," Wang warned, "it is difficult to establish oneself as a modernized, strong country among the advanced people of the world."[32]

Unlike much of the democratic discussions then taking place in China, however, Wang constantly registered a note of caution. First, Wang's notion of democracy, though never explicitly defined, appears to be one of substantive rather than procedural democracy. Wang seemed more interested in building a stable and efficient government that could make good decisions based on widespread consultation – what might be called "elite democracy" – than democracy per se. For instance, Wang called for better policy research and brain trusts, powerful and effective administrative organs, effective propaganda to win the trust of the people, and better feedback.[33] Second, and perhaps more important, Wang insisted that political reform is part of a complex process of change and that "[a] given political structure must fit the given historical, social, and cultural conditions."[34] This implied a lengthy period of transition. As Wang wrote: "In China, the construction of democratic politics implies overcoming the feudal political tradition and political consciousness that extended for more than 2,000 years since the Zhou–Qin period; it implies changing the undemocratic political traditions formed under semi-colonialism and semi-feudalism; it implies solving the contradiction between establishing an advanced political system on the basis of backward forces of production; and it implies enriching our thinking through practice." Such a process must take, as Wang put it, a "rather long time" (*jiaochang de shijian*).[35] Moreover, unless one develops democracy "scientifically," the results will be the opposite.[36]

In general, Wang's essays combine an almost Parsonian understanding of the way in which everything is linked to everything else with a Huntingtonian understanding of the need to build institutions and maintain stability through a strong government over a long period of transition. Hence, Wang is interested in political culture: how the turbulent history of twentieth-century China has led to an uneasy overlapping of traditional, modern, and post-1949 cultural concerns; and how the political system might play a role in shaping a modern political culture that will support reform. At the same time, Wang sees China as evolving slowly from what he calls

---

[32] Wang Huning, "Zhongguo zhengzhi tizhi gaige de beijing yu qianjing," pp. 5–6.
[33] Ibid., p. 10. See also Wang Huning, "Chuji jieduan yu zhengzhi tizhi gaige"; Wang Huning, "Juece gongneng de shehuihua ji qi tiaojian"; and Wang Huning, "Zhiwei fenlei yu ganbu guanli tizhi."
[34] Wang Huning, "Zhongguo zhengzhi tizhi gaige de beijing yu qianjing," p. 10.
[35] Wang Huning, "Lun minzhu zhengzhi jianshe," p. 34.   [36] Ibid., p. 36.

a "culture-centered political culture" to an "institution-centered political culture." The key is to strengthen the cadre force and other elements that can support institutionalization while China's political culture completes its long and painful transition.

Whereas the focus in Wang's *Collected Writings* is on political reform and democratization, his concerns are quite different in a number of articles published in the late 1980s and early 1990s that were not included in this volume. In these other essays, Wang took up the issue of public, particularly central, authority under the conditions of reform and limited resources. In Wang's view, devolving greater authority to China's industrial enterprises during the 1980s took place at a time when the level of economic development was low and markets were far from perfect. The role of local government therefore expanded to fill the gap; local government took over economic regulation and helped enterprises secure supplies of materials and markets for their products – functions that would normally be fulfilled by the market. As he put it, as the central government began to "wean" enterprises, local governments took up "breast feeding."[37]

The decrease in the functions of the central government and corresponding increase in the functions of local government resulted in a system in which the power to redistribute resources and satisfy interests was divided; in other words, local governments began to have the political power and economic resources to pursue their own interests at the expense of the central government. Wang argued that local governments had previously passed all resources on to the central government, which then redistributed them to the localities. Reform was greatly changing the relationship between central and local governments by diminishing the role of the central government in redistribution and by encouraging localities to satisfy their own interests.

At the same time, economic reform was stimulating a rapid increase in the number of interests and demands in society. Such demands were focused on local government, forcing the localities to concentrate ever more attention on their own needs. Accordingly, local governments increasingly concentrated on expanding their fiscal resources, and the fiscal contract responsibility system – under which governments promised to remit specific revenue targets to the central government while retaining any excess – provided the resources to pursue those interests. In Wang's view, the restructuring of incentives seriously undermined the ability of the central government to

---

[37] Wang Huning, "Zhongguo bianhua zhong de zhongyang he difang zhengfu de guanxi: Zhengzhi de hanyi," p. 4.

define and implement a policy that took the long-term best interests of the nation into account. As he put it: "Because the central government depends on the local government to guarantee its fiscal revenue and also depends on the local policies to satisfy localized interests (*difanghua de liyi*), it must make concessions to regional protectionism."[38]

The political implications of such trends were potentially ominous. Wang pointed to the rise of regional inequality in China and to the weakness of the Yugoslav Federal government (then still in existence) as consequences of localism. He also cited the 1988 elections, in which a number of candidates favored by the Party failed to be elected, to show that local interests were reducing the central government's prerogatives with regard to the appointment of local personnel.[39]

Wang's interest in the rise of a multiplicity of demands and interests was the focus of yet another article, one that appears to have been heavily influenced by Samuel Huntington's (1968) *Political Order in Changing Societies*. Like Huntington, Wang is concerned with the relationship between social demands and institutions, though he views them in somewhat different terms from Huntington. For Wang, the emphasis is on "social aggregate resources" (*shehui ziyuan zongliang*), which he views broadly to encompass not only material resources but cultural, value, educational, and religious resources as well. Like Huntington,[40] Wang sees a public authority that cannot extract sufficient resources from the society as being sharply constrained by social demands and hence ineffective. A paucity of social resources makes the creation of effective public authority more difficult even as it gives rise to greater social tension, so it is important in such societies to maintain and strengthen public authority. Wang sees China's socialist system as contributing to the strengthening of public authority and to the concentration of resources needed to maintain social equilibrium; without such authority, there would be an "anarchic struggle for resources among individuals, groups, and regions" leading to general social instability.[41] It should be noted that Wang's prescription for strong public authority was not necessarily a plea for authoritarian rule. In his writings, Wang sees the changes in Chinese society and the growth of the economy as demanding corresponding adjustments on the part of government,

---

[38] Ibid., p. 7. For a positive interpretation of these trends, see Jean Oi, *Rural China Takes Off*.

[39] Wang Huning, "Zhongguo bianhua zhong de zhongyang he difang zhengfu de guanxi: Zhengzhi de hanyi," p. 8.

[40] Samuel Huntington, *Political Order in Changing Societies*.

[41] Wang Huning, "Shehui ziyuan zongliang yu shehui tiaokong: Zhongguo yiyi," p. 11. See also Wang Huning, "Jifen pingheng: Zhongyang yu difang de xietong guanxi."

including greater efficiency and more democracy, though he also sees the development of democracy as a process that would take an extended period of time.[42]

Wang was also interested in the role of public values in forging political unity. As he put it: "The political life of a society must seek a fair degree of unity and homogeneity; otherwise, contradictions will appear everywhere and political development will be unstable."[43] In order to promote such unity, Wang advocated cultivating what he called "political aesthetics" (*zhengzhi shenmei*), a vague term that appears to mean the ability to apprehend and appreciate the political values and ideals appropriate for the time. In a passage reminiscent of Sun Yat-sen's discussion of "thinker-inventors" (*xianzhizhe*, those who were able to comprehend the trends of their time), their disciples (*houzhizhe*), and the unconscious performers (*buzhizhe*), Wang noted the elitism inherent in his concept: "Advanced elements in a society first apprehend (*tiren*) the aesthetic ideals that represent the direction in which history is developing, and then they energetically propagate these aesthetic ideals so that they spread to every member of society, creating an atmosphere conducive to the realization of these aesthetic ideals."[44] In short, the creation and maintenance of political values and ideals, like the extraction of resources and the development of strong and efficient public authority, were a necessary part of maintaining social order in the course of modernization.

Xiao Gongqin is a more historically minded thinker than Wang Huning. Born in Hunan in 1946, Xiao spent the Cultural Revolution as a worker in Shanghai's suburbs. In 1978, he tested into the history department at Nanjing University as a graduate student, receiving his master's degree in 1981. The following year, he was assigned to Shanghai Normal University and was promoted to associate professor in 1987 – highly unusual for someone without a Ph.D.[45] Although originally interested in the Yuan Dynasty, in the mid-1980s Xiao turned his attention to the late Qing–early Republican period and has concentrated on the problems of modernization and political transformation ever since. In his early work, Xiao focused on Yan Fu (1853–1921), the famed translator of Adam Smith's *The Wealth of Nations* and other major works of Western intellectual history. Yan's translations and commentaries marked a new stage in China's understanding of the West. Whereas China's efforts to introduce knowledge from abroad had previously been limited mostly to technology, particularly weapons and

---

[42] Wang Huning, "Zhongguo zhengzhi – Xingzheng tizhi gaige de jingji fenxi."
[43] Ibid., p. 139.   [44] Ibid., p. 140.
[45] See the biographical note in Xiao Gongqin, *Xiao Gongqin ji*.

later light manufacturing, Yan's translations served to make the point that Western technology was part of a complex culture; it would be impossible, as Yan's contemporary Zhang Zhidong was advising, to "take Chinese culture as the essence and Western learning for practical use" (*Zhongti xiyong*) – culture and technology were not separable. Yan is usually understood as introducing Western learning as a means to make China "wealthy and powerful" (*fuqiang*).[46] Following the revolution of 1911 and particularly in his support of Yuan Shikai's monarchical efforts, Yan is usually depicted as a tired and conservative old man who had fallen behind the spirit of his times.

Xiao argued that Yan's thinking should not be dichotomized into early reformism and later conservatism but instead should be seen as a whole. What unified Yan's thinking, in Xiao's opinion, was his understanding that societies were complex and organic wholes that could not be cut apart or transplanted lock, stock, and barrel; they had to evolve. Thus, Yan argued that modernization must be based on preserving the "national spirit" (*guoqing*), that is, on Confucianism. Western culture or technology could not simply be grafted onto China but had to find resonance within China's tradition; the task of modernization had to be based on the growth, development, and maturation of factors present in China's original culture.[47] Yan was consistent as a "neoconservative." Prior to the 1911 revolution, Yan was critical of "radicals" (*jijin zhuyizhe*), such as Kang Youwei and Liang Qichao in the 1898 Reform Movement, who wanted to accomplish everything at once; following the 1911 revolution, Yan continued to look to Confucianism as the essence of China's "national spirit." It was in this way that he allowed himself to be swept into Yuan Shikai's ill-fated monarchical movement and thus fall into personal tragedy.

What defined Yan as a neoconservative, in Xiao's opinion, was that he was not opposed to modernization – indeed, he harshly criticized the old autocratic system – but at the same time he was not a radical modernizer. Yan believed that radicals viewed the problems of modernization too simply and naively and ended up making matters worse; this explained Yan's disappointment with China's situation following the 1911 revolution. What Yan advocated was combining the old and the new, neither clinging stubbornly to an ossified understanding of the national essence (*guocui*), and therefore not modernizing, nor discarding the national essence and turning the culture into an empty shell incapable of digesting the Western

---

[46] Benjamin Schwartz, *In Search of Wealth and Power.*
[47] Xiao Gongqin, "'Yan Fu beilun' yu jindai xinbaoshou zhuyi biange guan," p. 32.

elements it was importing.[48] As Yan put it, "[w]ithout renewal there will be no progress; without the old there would be nothing to hold on to."[49] The trick was to modernize the national spirit while maintaining the culture as an organic whole.

Consistent with this view, in separate studies Xiao blamed the failure of the 1898 Reform Movement not on the obstinacy of the Empress Dowager or the treachery of Yuan Shikai – the usual suspects – but rather on the impatience and "radicalism" (*jijin zhuyi*) of Kang Youwei and other reformers. In Xiao's opinion, the Empress Dowager Ci Xi was not completely opposed to reform, but the reformers (led by Kang) believed that reform had to rapidly make a sharp break with tradition. There was a pan-moralistic (*fan daode zhuyi*) view holding that the new and the old, like fire and water, could not coexist. The reformers had simplistic and optimistic expectations, with the result that they misjudged the situation and the reform failed completely. As Xiao concluded: "When China most needed its political elites to use their wisdom and abilities to carry out reform, those extreme (*jizhixing*) elements in traditional culture stimulated the factors in those early Chinese reform elites that were most disadvantageous to reform and most advantageous to revolution."[50]

Xiao's interest was perhaps not so much in understanding the past as in prescribing for the present. Indeed, Xiao first presented his ideas on neo-conservatism to a conference on "China's Traditional Culture and Socialist Modernization" in December 1990. He Xin attended that conference, as did a number of "princes" (those whose parents were high-ranking cadres).[51] This conference was part of an increasingly heated debate between advocates of "incremental" change and those who favored "radical" change; indeed, Xiao's work was very much a part of this debate. However, Tiananmen greatly changed the terms of debate. Those who had doubts about the course of reform, or who quickly developed them following that tragedy, came to see Tiananmen not so much as a case of repression as another instance of romantic radicalism bringing about its own defeat. This conclusion was part analysis, part opportunism, and part reconciliation with a regime that had shown no tolerance for being challenged. In fact, most reformers had seen themselves as incrementalists trying to patch together a reform ("feeling the stones while crossing the river") in uncharted territory, though it is also true that, as reform developed in the late 1980s, the tensions

---

[48] Ibid., p. 35.   [49] Ibid.

[50] Xiao Gongqin, "Wuxu bianfa de zai fanxing," p. 20. See also Xiao's full-length treatment, *Weijizhong de biange*.

[51] Gu Xin and David Kelly, "New Conservatism," p. 221.

between "reformers" and "conservatives" mounted as the gap between their visions increased and as the problems generated by reform became more apparent. Deng's ill-fated effort to introduce comprehensive price reform in 1988 by "storming the pass" was one expression of such tension, as were the debates between democrats and new authoritarians – both of whom wanted to break the tension, albeit by different means.

It should be noted that although Xiao became one of the best-known articulators of neoconservatism in the early 1990s, he remained true to the new authoritarian faith of the 1980s: namely, that the point of incremental-ism was to build a political and economic system that could support liberal democracy. In this way Xiao, like Sheng Hong, was quite different from neoconservatives who simply sought to strengthen the central state as well as from the New Left thinkers (examined in the next chapter) who rejected economic and political liberalism in a search for a new path.

HE XIN AND STATE-CENTERED NATIONALISM

Nationalism was another force propelling changes in the way Chinese intel-lectuals and policy-makers viewed the world in the period following Tiananmen. Nationalism is hardly a new force in China; indeed it is the *leitmotif* underlying twentieth-century Chinese politics. In the 1980s, China had adopted a cosmopolitan orientation, linking domestic reform with open-ing to the outside world. This did not mean that China was not nationalistic in this period, but rather that its nationalism was directed toward economic development and a critique of traditional socialism (which impeded that development).[52] Following Tiananmen, however, the West (and the US in particular) seemed threatening and subversive. Disregarding those extreme voices associated with the Old Left, a new nationalism began to emerge.[53] Through the 1990s it has taken on many guises, ranging from *realpolitik* to discussions of post-colonialism. One of the first (and certainly one of the loudest) voices of the new nationalism was that of He Xin, an erstwhile literary critic who turned his attention to economics, politics, and interna-tional relations in the late 1980s. As perhaps the only intellectual to support the government in the days following Tiananmen, He quickly became a very public, and often reviled, figure.

Although more extreme – particularly with regard to his nationalism – than other neoconservatives, He shared many of the basic orientations of

---

[52] For a discussion of Chinese nationalism see Fewsmith and Rosen, "The Domestic Context of Chinese Foreign Policy."
[53] Suisheng Zhao, *A Nation-State by Construction*; and Peter Hays Gries, *China's New Nationalism*.

this approach. Although he publicly identified himself with the regime, his writings and interviews reveal little knowledge of or interest in Marxism; what concerned He was the power of the central government vis-à-vis the localities, the stability of society, and China's position in the world. In this way, He became identified as a exemplar of what might be called a "muscular" or assertive neoconservatism.

Nationalism, particularly anti-Americanism, was central to He Xin's views. Like many writers in this period, He contradictorily depicted the United States both as a power in decline and as one bent on world domination. In late 1988, he wrote that the United States had entered a period of inevitable decline and that, by the early part of the twenty-first century, it would be reduced to a large regional power without the strength to bother the East.[54] Perhaps more concerned about Japan's global ambitions,[55] He recommended changing China's coastal development strategy, opting instead for an economic alliance with the Soviet Union. Such an alliance would not only have the advantage of strengthening China, but just as importantly it would pre-empt Japan from allying with the Soviet Union and establishing a neocolonial dominance over China.[56] Similarly, the strengthening of the Chinese economy was necessary to prevent Japan from dominating the world in the next century.[57]

A year or so later, He seemed less certain of the inevitable decline of the United States and more worried about the failure of reform in the Soviet Union.[58] The breakup of the Soviet Union would cause China to lose its last strategic shield against the United States, so China should make use of any conflict between other countries and the United States. Evidently viewing America as the more serious strategic threat (despite insisting repeatedly that it was in decline), He dropped his previous fears of Japan and urged allying with Japan (indeed, to become like "lips and teeth").[59] He also urged supporting Germany in any disputes with the United States (suggesting that China should urge Germany to withdraw

---

[54] He Xin, "Dangqian Zhongguo neiwai xingshi fenxi ji ruogan zhengce jianyi (zhaiyao)," p. 1.
[55] As He wrote: "At present there is no other country more desirous of replacing a declining US as global hegemon than Japan." See He Xin, "Lun Zhongguo xiandaihua de guoji huanjing yu waijiao zhanlüe," p. 9.
[56] He Xin, "Dangqian Zhongguo neiwai xingshi fenxi ji ruogan zhengce jianyi (zhaiyao)," pp. 2–3.
[57] He Xin, "Lun Zhongguo xiandaihua de guoji huanjing yu waijiao zhanlüe," p. 14
[58] Nevertheless, in a 1990 interview with Japanese economist Yabuki Susumu, He said that "during the next 10–20 years the entire capitalist world economic system will experience the most profound and serious overall crisis since the dawn of history." See "Current World Economic Situation" (I), p. 11.
[59] He Xin, "Lun ZhongMeiRi guanxi de zhanlüe beijing yu duice," pp. 40–2.

from NATO) and supporting Southeast Asia, lest America return to that region of the world and threaten China.[60]

He argued that the world was headed toward unity,[61] but that it could be united either under US domination or be integrated on the basis of "fairness, equal sovereignty, common interest, and cooperation."[62] If America succeeds in its global ambitions, he warned, "the world will enter into a dark and chaotic age."[63] The biggest obstacle to the realization of US ambitions is China.[64] In his opinion, it does not matter what type of policy China adopts internally (i.e., whether it supports human rights or becomes a democracy), since US policy will not change; the United States simply does not want to see a "strong, unified, prosperous, and industrialized modern China."[65] In He's view, American demands for human rights and democracy were merely a part of its strategy to weaken and hopefully divide China.[66] It was to weaken China that the United States aggravated the political crisis of Tiananmen, using the Voice of America and other means to try to split China apart.[67] China should "comprehensively" adjust its foreign policy approach over the next decade so that it no longer facilitates US designs for global hegemony.[68]

Reflecting on the decade of reform prior to Tiananmen, He regarded the 1984–8 period as one of "romanticism." In his opinion, reform in this period not only shifted from the countryside to the cities but also branched out from economics into other spheres of activity, creating an atmosphere that disregarded the difficulty and length of time that reform would take.[69] Most people have viewed this period as one of great creativity and cultural flourishing, but He expressed dismay at the decline of ideology, national spirit, values, state consciousness, and social order.[70] The film *River Elegy* epitomized the tendency in the 1980s for cultural criticism to lead to an all-round criticism of politics and social reality and then to "complete Westernization." This led to a "new dogmatism" of worshipping Western values.[71] "For a while," He said, "American culture became the main current

---

[60] Ibid., pp. 45–6.   [61] Ibid., p. 32.   [62] Ibid., p. 31.
[63] Ibid., p. 47.   [64] Ibid., p. 34.   [65] Ibid., pp. 35–6.
[66] He Xin, "Wo xiang nimen de liangzhi huhuan," p. 481. In an interesting case of mirror-image thinking, He insisted that ideology played no role in US foreign policy; the United States saw the world in terms of a zero-sum game (*nisi wohuo* – literally, "you die, I live"). See He Xin, "Lun Zhongguo xiandaihua de guoji huanjing yu waijiao zhanlüe," p. 18; He Xin, "Dangdai shijie jingji xingshi fenxi," p. 57; and He Xin, "Wo xiang nimen liangzhi huhuan," p. 495.
[67] He Xin, "Wo xiang nimen liangzhi huhuan," pp. 484, 494.
[68] He Xin, "Lun ZhongMeiRi guanxi de zhanlüe beijing yu duice," p. 40.
[69] He Xin, "Dui woguo shinian gaige de fansi," p. 402.   [70] Ibid., p. 403.
[71] He Xin, "Aiguo de Qu Yuan yu ruguo de 'He Shang'."

and major tone of literature. This was a very bad development for China."[72] Tiananmen, He argued, was the result of such trends. As stability was re-established following Tiananmen, He argued that people came to realize that Western thought really could not solve China's problems.[73] It was on that basis that He argued for a return to Chinese values and an emphasis on nationalism and restoration of political authority.

As this argument suggests, He Xin expressed repeated concern about cultural imperialism, which he regarded as the essence of "peaceful evolution" and which, as we will see, would become a major concern of many intellectuals in the 1990s.[74] One form of "cultural imperialism" that He repeatedly railed against was neoclassical economics. Exporting neoclassical economics was one of the tools by which the United States sought to dominate the world, as was so vividly demonstrated by the results of radical price reform in the Soviet Union; shock therapy, He said, was simply "economic suicide." Chinese intellectuals were susceptible to the influence of neoclassical economics, particularly after 1984, because of their anxiety for quick success – another manifestation of the "romantic" mood that swept China in the late 1980s.[75] Accepting neoclassical economics would lead to China's further integration in the world economy; He argued that this would benefit US interests, not Chinese interests, because the United States was able to dominate international trade through its monopoly position. Obviously, joining the General Agreement on Trade and Tariffs (GATT, later the WTO) could be dangerous.[76] This was an argument that would be reprised in the early twenty-first century as opposition to "neoliberal" economics (see Chapter 8).

THE TURN AWAY FROM CULTURAL LIBERALISM

He's criticism of late 1980s cultural liberalism was part of a broader turn against the "cultural fever" that had dominated the latter part of that decade. In the 1980s, impatient intellectuals, wondering why reforms had not developed more quickly than they had, turned increasingly to dissecting their own culture. In many ways, these intellectuals picked up where the May

---

[72] "Current World Economic Situation" (III), p. 12.
[73] He Xin, "Aiguo de Qu Yuan yu ruguo de 'He Shang'," pp. 406–7. See also He Xin, "Wode kunhuo yu youlu," pp. 427–8.
[74] He Xin, "Tan dangdai ziben zhuyi," p. 70.
[75] Xin, "Lun woguo jingji gaige zhidao lilun de shiwu," p. 508.
[76] Ibid., p. 503. See also He Xin, "Dangqian jingji xingshi pinglun (zhi yi)," p. 544; He Xin, "Lun woguo jingji gaige zhidao lilun de shiwu," p. 506; and He Xin, "Woguo duiwai kaifang zhanlüe de yizhong shexiang," p. 83.

Fourth generation of intellectuals had left off. Indeed, one of the primary intellectual influences at the time was the work of Li Zehou, a philosopher at CASS, who argued that China's "enlightenment" project, inaugurated by the New Culture Movement (1915–20), had been constantly interrupted and deferred by "national salvation" movements that had grown up in response to foreign threat and war. It was time to get back to the enlightenment project.[77]

Enlightenment, in the view of many intellectuals, entailed a remaking of Chinese culture, exorcising the "feudal" elements of tradition, and opening up to influences from the West. This mood was well captured by Gan Yang, editor of the influential *Culture: China and the World* (*Wenhua: Zhongguo yu shijie congshu*) book series, who pleaded for cosmopolitanism and cultural renovation: "China must enter the world, so naturally its culture must also enter the world; China must modernize, so naturally we must realize the 'modernization of Chinese culture' – this is the common faith of every person of foresight in the 1980s, this is the logical necessity of the great historical take-off of contemporary China."[78]

This "cultural fever" culminated in the 1988 television series *River Elegy*. In this film, the dry, arid, exhausted soil – and culture – of the northwest (the cradle of Chinese civilization) is contrasted with the fertility, dynamism, and openness of the blue sea. If China hoped to revitalize its ancient civilization, the program suggested, it must look to the outside world, and particularly to the West. The film captured the confidence and optimism of many at the time that reform could be accomplished relatively quickly and easily if only the country would rally behind an enlightened leader, turn its back firmly on its "feudal" past, and embrace the outside world wholeheartedly.[79]

Although cosmopolitan in its orientation, it is important to recognize that *River Elegy* was quite nationalistic. The film asks pointedly such questions as, "Why did China fail to maintain the *great lead it used to have . . .*? Why did China fail to maintain its *cultural and political domination* over the world?"[80] As Jing Wang remarked, "[t]he modern elite are, after all, dreaming the same dream as their forebears of the dynastic past: wealth, power, and hegemony."[81] *River Elegy*, like other efforts to renovate China's culture, was clearly rooted in a nationalistic response to China's problems,

---

[77] See Li Zehou, *Zhongguo xiandai sixiangshi lun*; and Vera Schwarcz's masterful study, *The Chinese Enlightenment*.

[78] Quoted in Meng Fanhua, *Zhongshen kuanghuan*, p. 10.

[79] Su Xiaokang and Wang Luxiang, *He Shang* (*River Elegy*).

[80] Cited in Jing Wang, *High Culture Fever*, p. 123; emphasis in original. See also Frederic Wakeman, "All the Rage in China."

[81] Jing Wang, *High Culture Fever*.

but this nationalism sought to modernize China by remaking it in the image of the outside world.[82]

Although it was enthusiastically supported by reform-minded intellectuals and by then-General Secretary Zhao Ziyang (who ironically presented a copy of the series to visiting Singapore senior minister Lee Kuan Yew, an outspoken champion of traditional Chinese values), *River Elegy* aroused a storm of criticism from different points along the ideological spectrum. Conservative critics of the film blasted it as a prime example of "national nihilism" and bourgeois liberalization. Most vociferous in this regard was Party elder Wang Zhen, who accused it of "completely negating" the Chinese tradition and adopting a "Euro-centric" view of history.[83] Wang's criticism represented the ideological views of the Old Left, but people quite unsympathetic to the sort of leftism Wang Zhen represented also had serious reservations about the film.

In contrast to Wang Zhen's emphasis on "national nihilism," He Xin's criticism focused on what he regarded as the misplaced romanticism of the intellectual elite's cultural project.[84] A similar sort of criticism came from Wang Xiaodong, a young intellectual affiliated with the Communist Youth League, who would emerge in the 1990s as one of the main voices of popular nationalism. Born in 1955, Wang studied mathematics at Beijing University and then went to Japan for further study. Tiring of mathematical study, Wang went on to Canada before returning to China. He returned to find the "cultural fever" of the 1980s in full bloom, and found himself deeply opposed to the cultural cosmopolitanism it expressed.

Wang was neither part of the Old Left nor a cultural conservative, yet he was as harshly critical as others in his condemnation of *River Elegy*. What bothered Wang was what he perceived as the elitism of the authors of *River Elegy* and the cultural elite of which they were a part. These people, Wang believed, identified themselves with the West and denigrated the Chinese people on the basis of Western standards – what he would later dub a "reverse racism."[85] As he put it, the authors "ridiculed the Chinese peasants' dull-witted love of the yellow soil and praised highly

---

[82] Chen Fong-ching and Jin Guantao, *From Youthful Manuscripts to River Elegy*. Perhaps the word "cosmopolitanism" does not convey the complexity of China's emotional response to the outside world. As Jing Wang commented, "Chinese [enlightenment] intellectuals [are] at once proud of and hostile toward their own cultural and national heritage, while defiant toward and subservient to the imported Western culture at the same time." See Jing Wang, *High Culture Fever*, p. 124.

[83] Yi jia yan [pseud.], "'He Shang' xuanyangle shenma?" It quickly became known that this article was by Wang Zhen. An "editor's note" prefacing the article states that Zhao Ziyang had refused to run the article.

[84] He Xin, "'He Shang' de piping."

[85] Wang Xiaodong [Shi Zhong], "Zhongguo de minzu zhuyi he Zhongguo de weilai."

the courage and insight of Westerners in throwing themselves into myriad difficulties."[86] In a later article, Wang argued that, in the 1980s (and even in the 1990s), "Chinese intellectuals were swept up by the thinking that the Chinese culture was an inferior culture and the Chinese people an inferior race" – a trend of thinking that, in his opinion, the government had actually encouraged.[87] Wang argued that China needed nationalism and believed that the nationalism emerging in the 1990s, of which he was a tireless promoter, was a "normal nationalism" that corrected the abnormal situation that had prevailed in the 1980s and was not threatening to the outside world.

Wang's critique was not rooted in a Marxist–Leninist world view. Like many younger intellectuals, Wang evinced no faith in socialist values and yet rejected the Western capitalist and cultural tropes that had dominated discourse in the 1980s. Wang reflected a visceral nationalism that reacted against the cosmopolitanism of *River Elegy*; at the same time, he reflected a populist sentiment that rejected the elitism of those who had dominated discussions of Chinese culture in the 1980s. What differentiated Wang's critique from that of the Old Left (as reflected in Wang Zhen's article) and foreshadowed trends in the 1990s was the combination of populism, nationalism, and disregard of communist values.

"REALISTIC RESPONSES"

As noted in the previous chapter, the abortive August 1991 coup in the Soviet Union marked a watershed in Chinese elite politics. At first overjoyed by news of the coup, conservative critics of Deng Xiaoping began celebrating and holding meetings. With the collapse of the coup, Deng moved quickly to reassert his vision of reform, leading to his trip to the south and the Fourteenth Party Congress. The coup proved to be a watershed in another way as well. Within days of the failure of the coup, a number of young intellectuals associated with the theoretical department of *China Youth Daily* circulated a paper entitled "Realistic Responses and Strategic Options for China after the Soviet Upheaval." This paper drew heavily on the ideas that have been discussed in the preceding pages, and indeed it marked the first systematic attempt to draw together the diverse strains into a reasonably coherent program of neoconservatism (a term used in the document). Although circulated internally, the document was soon leaked

---

[86] Wang Xiaodong and Qiu Tiancao, "Jiqing de yinying: Ping dianshi xiliepian 'He shang'."
[87] Wang Xiaodong [Shi Zhong], "Zhongguo de minzu zhuyi he Zhongguo de weilai."

to the outside world, quickly becoming the subject of much commentary and sharp criticism.[88]

The document was written by Yang Ping, then the leading manager of the ideological and theoretical section at *China Youth Daily* and a close friend of Wang Xiaodong.[89] Yang and Wang called together perhaps a dozen young people, and "Realistic Responses" was a summary of their discussions. The article is sometimes referred to as a "manifesto of the princes' party" (*taizidang*), but no "princes" were at the meeting that evening. That does not mean, however, that Yang and Wang were unfamiliar with the thinking of some people at higher levels. One of those at the discussion meeting was Jiang Hong, who later became deputy head of the State Asset Management Bureau. Jiang reflected the sometimes erratic paths, in careers and thinking, taken by young people between the late 1970s and the 1990s. A key player in the democracy wall movement of 1978–9, Jiang shifted his thinking after Tiananmen and became deeply involved in the still shadowy maneuvers of neoconservatives in the government. Jiang was a close friend of Chen Yuan, Chen Yun's son, and Pan Yue, the son-in-law of Liu Huaqing, the PLA general promoted to the Politburo Standing Committee and vice-chairmanship of the CMC at the Fourteenth Party Congress. Pan clearly had political ambitions and fostered neoconservative discussions among young intellectuals. To a certain extent, "Realistic Responses" was a result of such efforts.[90]

"Realistic Responses" tried to place itself between two ideological extremes. On the one hand, it criticized "utopian socialism" – the Old Left – for continually relying on mass movements, which (the authors believed) would end up destroying the very socialism that it purportedly wanted to save. The "ossified" thinking of such socialism only caused "resentment" among the people. On the other hand, it criticized "utopian capitalism" – liberal reformers – for advocating a type of "radical reformism" that was ultimately unwilling to stop short of destroying the entire present order.[91] Instead of these two extremes, the authors called for a program of "social stability and gradual reform" that drew on both Western rationalism (Bertrand Russell, Karl Popper, and Frederick von Hayek are cited as examples of rational thinkers) and Chinese tradition. The new ideological orientation of the regime, the authors hoped, would fight against "ideological superstition" while maintaining control; sufficient space would be allowed for theoretical

[88] Gu Xin and David Kelly, "New Conservatism."   [89] Ibid., p. 231.
[90] Ling Zhen, "Zugepai de xingdong xinhao"; author interviews.
[91] *China Youth Daily* Ideology and Theory Department, "Realistic Responses and Strategic Options for China after the Soviet Upheaval," pp. 18–19.

exploration.[92] Neoconservatism, the article said, converged with Western rationalism in its opposition to radicalism and emphasis on gradualism.

The central concern of the article was how the CCP had to change from a revolutionary party to a ruling party. Although the authors did not elaborate in detail, obviously they were exploring, however tentatively, efforts to establish viable political institutions. They were not abandoning the ruling role of the CCP but rather were trying to figure out institutional arrangements through which it might be able to preserve political stability. The authors reflected great awareness of the CCP's fragile legitimacy. As they noted, there were historically two bases for the CCP's legitimacy, the October Revolution in Russia and the "Marxism of the mountains and valleys" of Mao Zedong. With the first pillar severely shaken (and indeed about to disappear), it was all the more necessary to emphasize the "Chineseness" of the Chinese revolution. As the authors put it, it was necessary to emphasize "uniting Marxism with Chinese reality . . . with emphasis on China's national condition."[93] In the Yan'an days of the revolution, Mao had de-emphasized the specifically Marxist aspects of his evolving ideological system by demanding that Marxism be combined with Chinese reality. Deng had carried this process further by emphasizing "seek truth from facts" and by calling for building "socialism with Chinese characteristics." Now the authors of "Realistic Responses" were calling for taking this process another step forward. Just how big a step they had in mind was suggested by their call to emphasize the "rational elements" of China's traditional culture. Considering that China's revolution had been made to destroy China's "feudal" culture, reincorporating Chinese tradition into the ideology of the CCP would not be an easy or uncontested process. But the authors argued that, unless they could do so, "we will establish the Chinese value system on a dry stream-bed, on a trunkless tree."[94]

The desire to reincorporate elements of China's Confucian past into its current ideology was one aspect of a plainly expressed nationalism. In opposing "peaceful evolution," the state should emphasize nationalism and patriotism as well as the national interest and China's unique "national characteristics" (*guoqing*). In this regard, the article called for jettisoning the remaining ideological elements from China's foreign policy and focusing exclusively on China's national interest. Almost heretically – given the strong Chinese approval of the coup in the Soviet Union and the equally strong sense of despair after it failed – the authors argued that it would not necessarily have been to China's advantage had the coup succeeded. The

---

[92] Ibid., p. 29.   [93] Ibid., p. 20.   [94] Ibid., p. 22.

result might well have been a stronger, more nationalistic Soviet Union on China's northern border.[95]

Finally, "Realistic Responses" emphasized the importance of stability, which in terms of economic policy meant that the emphasis should be on "digesting" previous reforms rather than on making new breakthroughs. The authors argued for "steady reform" and continued "experiments," particularly in smaller enterprises, but called for "attack[ing] and contain[ing] radical reformism" such as the continued "devolution of authority and granting of benefits" (*fangquan rangli*) and the rapid implementation of price reform and the shareholding system.[96] Thus, it combined the incrementalism called for by people like Sheng Hong with the criticism of the feudal-lord economy called for by Chen Yuan.

---

[95] Ibid., p. 27.   [96] Ibid., pp. 23–4.

CHAPTER 4

The enlightenment tradition under challenge

Prior to 1993, neoconservatism consisted primarily of the ruminations of a handful of intellectuals. It was a diverse and not very coherent movement, drawing on people with distinctly different attitudes and statuses within the Chinese system. Although well connected with some conservative leaders, there was an unmistakable opportunism in He Xin's xenophobic defenses of the government, which contrasted with Chen Yuan's politically more important efforts to articulate an alternative economic agenda. Wang Huning, who had set off internal arguments about new authoritarianism, wrote nothing about the subject as public debate unfolded in 1989, but he would emerge as a politically important adviser to Jiang Zemin in the mid- and late 1990s and then to Hu Jintao in the new century. People like Sheng Hong and Xiao Gongqin wrote frequently but were intellectuals with limited policy impact, not to mention a different intellectual agenda from others. Yang Ping and Wang Xiaodong can perhaps be regarded as intellectual entrepreneurs who worked, with considerable success, to inject previously marginal ideas into the mainstream, though their connections with parts of the political system should not be underestimated.

The appearance of "Realistic Responses" in 1991 marked a certain coming of age of these ideas, not so much a political manifesto of the "princeling faction" (*taizidang*) – though that element was present – as an argument that China's future lay in pioneering a "third way," rejecting both Marxism–Leninism (as traditionally understood) and Western capitalism.[1] Such a third way would include an assertion of nationalism, but it was not clear what such a nationalism would espouse since it somewhat paradoxically incorporated both an assertion of Chinese identity and an adoption of "Western rationalism." There were also hints of populism that coexisted uneasily with implicit assumptions of elite control. Although "Realistic

---

[1] The use of the term "third way" to describe these intellectual efforts should not be confused with the articulation of a liberal "third way" (or "third force") in China in the 1930s and 1940s. See Carson Chang, *The Third Force in China*.

Responses" called for readjusting central–local relations in favor of the center and rejected blind faith in market forces as "utopian capitalism," it did not reconcile that agenda with either its acceptance of market forces (shy of blind faith) or with the continuing poor performance of state-owned enterprises and the rapid growth of the non-state sector that had accompanied the growth of market forces. In short, although "Realistic Responses" marked a certain maturation of neoconservative thought, it was really more of a starting point for further exploration than a full-blown political agenda.

By the 1992–3 period, China was emerging from the shock caused by Tiananmen and the heavy-handed propaganda campaign waged by the government against bourgeois liberalization. The economy had picked up and indeed had nearly careened out of control, as loose monetary policies were adopted to support Deng Xiaoping's call for a renewed period of reform. An orgy of real estate and stock speculation stimulated new income inequalities, between classes as well as between regions.

Because of these trends, Deng's call for renewed reform and economic development in 1992 did not cause many intellectuals simply to pick up where they had left off before and continue on the trajectory of liberal economic thought and Western-oriented reform that had dominated pre-1989 discussions. On the contrary, much of the discourse that emerged in the mid-1990s was affected by new concerns and new intellectual trends. First and foremost, the end of socialism in Eastern Europe and the subsequent disintegration of the Soviet Union not only set off ruminations about why those events had taken place and how China could avoid a similar fate (the concern among most intellectuals was not saving socialism but rather avoiding the economic decline and political disintegration that had accompanied the democratization of those countries, particularly Russia) but also about globalization. Despite divergent perspectives, intellectuals across the ideological spectrum believed that the demise of socialism in Eastern Europe and the former Soviet Union heralded a new global order, one dominated by international capital. What they disagreed about were the consequences of this new global order for China.

Second, with the upsurge of the economy and a loosening of the old rules governing economic activity, China was swept by a wave of commercialism that continues to the present day. Previously marginalized groups – individual entrepreneurs, joint venture employees, and entertainers – began to create a new urban consumer culture.[2] With the passing of Tiananmen,

---

[2] Geremie R. Barmé, *In the Red*, especially chapters 6, 8, and 9.

Marxist ideology lost whatever residual hold it had maintained on people, and the state implicitly but strongly reaffirmed the social contract that had emerged in the 1980s: economic prosperity in exchange for political quiescence. On the one hand, the wave of consumerism contributed to social stability by refocusing urban residents' attention from politics to material comforts,[3] but on the other hand it created resentments and marginalized those left behind. Unlike the 1980s, in which the vast majority of people benefited from reform, by the 1990s there was an increasing sense of "winners" and "losers," both economically and psychologically.[4]

Such changes set off a very different social dynamic, one that had implications for intellectuals not only in the way they thought about society but also in the way they related to it in material terms. Previously, intellectuals had thrown themselves into reform efforts without thought of material reward; now they began to find that their values were no longer society's values. In the Maoist period, intellectuals had been treated well materially, and even the campaigns that targeted them were a backhanded acknowledgment of their importance. As the 1980s gave way to the 1990s, however, intellectuals found their income shrinking relative to other groups and that their ideas and ethos were no longer esteemed.[5] One might argue, as Yu Yingshi has, that intellectuals have been increasingly marginalized throughout the twentieth century, yet intellectuals have been slow to give up the traditional notion that they are the bearers of the highest cultural values of society. Nonetheless, the 1990s presented very strong evidence that intellectuals as a group were not valued by Chinese society.

This change in status came about quickly. In 1988, as noted in Chapter 3, the television miniseries *River Elegy* epitomized the intellectual project of a cultural elite (indeed, that is what Wang Xiaodong found so repellant about it), one that conceived of itself as carrying on an intellectual and cultural mission that stems from the May Fourth Movement. Only two years later, another television series, China's first domestically produced soap opera, would reflect an extraordinarily different ethos. *Yearnings* (*Kewang*), which began broadcasting in November 1990, was put together hastily by a group of writers, including Wang Shuo and the respected author Zheng Wanlong, in a self-conscious effort to create a commercial success, something that does not come naturally to Chinese intellectuals. Starting with stock

---

[3] Yunxiang Yan, "The Politics of Consumerism in Chinese Society."
[4] Actually, this change can be dated from the late 1980s, when inflation eroded the incomes of many people; this trend contributed to the resentments that were displayed so clearly in Tiananmen Square in spring 1989. Li Ping, *Zhongguo xiayibu zenyang zou*, pp. 67–70.
[5] Ibid.

characters – the kindly, filial daughter, the "sappy intellectual," the "shrew," and so forth – the scriptwriters added flesh and blood and created a television drama that drew huge audiences.[6] In her brilliant portrait of the intellectual scene in the 1990s, Jianying Zha quotes Li Xiaoming, the chief scriptwriter, as saying: "If you're a television writer, and you know that the majority of your Chinese audience had to save up for years to buy a TV set, then you'd better come to terms with them."[7] Commercialism had come to the Chinese intellectual scene, and it was a painful transition for many. Commercialism destroyed the "feeling that a writer is the beloved and needed spokesman of the people and the conscience of society."[8]

One reflection of this commercialization of culture was the rates that top performers could charge. In the late 1980s, a headline performer might earn as much as 2,000 yuan for a performance; by 1992, such fees had risen to between 5,000 and 7,000 yuan, and by the mid-1990s top performers could earn tens of thousands of yuan for a single performance.[9] This commercialization of culture was also reflected in such popular writings as Jia Pingwa's *Abandoned Capital*, which depicts seamy sex and crass cynicism in a society that has lost its ideals.[10] As literary critic Xiao Xialin put it: "Ours is the world of the abandoned capital. Everywhere you look, the basic values of civilization – justice, truth, ideals, and the sublime – are in a state of alienation. Morality itself has nothing more than a utilitarian value. All we dream of now and hope for in the future are sex and money."[11]

Reviewing the intellectual scene, the Shanghai-based critic Xu Jilin commented that intellectuals in the latter part of the 1980s really were "intellectual heroes," treated as celebrities on college campuses and urban streets. However, by the 1990s this was no longer the case, as intellectuals became marginalized by the changes in social values that accompanied the growth of the economy.[12] Similarly, Wang Hui, editor of the country's most influential intellectual journal *Dushu* (*Reading*), wrote that "[i]ntellectuals in the 1980s thought of themselves as cultural heroes and persons of foresight (*xianzhi*), but intellectuals in the 1990s are struggling to find a new way of adapting. Facing a commercial culture that has penetrated everywhere, they have painfully recognized that they are no longer cultural heroes and the molders of values."[13]

---

[6] Jianying Zha, *China Pop*, pp. 38–9.   [7] Ibid., p. 38.   [8] Ibid., p. 46.

[9] Meng Fanhua, *Zhongshen kuanghuan.*

[10] Jia Pingwa, *Fei du*; Jianying Zha, *China Pop*, pp. 129–64.

[11] Quoted in Barmé, *In the Red*, p. 184.   [12] Xu Jilin, *Ling yizhong qimeng*, p. 10.

[13] Wang Hui, "Dangdai Zhongguo de sixiang zhuangkuang yu xiandaixing wenti," p. 134. This has been translated as "Contemporary Chinese Thought and the Question of the Modern."

It was not just that commercialization presented intellectuals with a profound crisis of identity but also that intellectuals began to disintegrate as an identifiable social group. Despite deep divisions among intellectuals throughout China's modern history, there was never any doubt about intellectuals as a distinct social category with a sense of self-identity and group ethos. As Xu Jilin put it:[14]

The difference in intellectual mode between the 1990s and the 1980s is that in the 1980s, even though there were all sorts of debates and ideological differences, the intellectual background, assumptions of thought [*sixiang yushe*], and value tendencies that lay behind these various divisions were fundamentally the same. Behind [the divisions] there still existed a common ideological platform [*sixiang pingtai*], namely enlightenment discourse. However, with the 1990s, that commonality no longer exists. A unified ideological platform has completely disintegrated.

Even as commercialization undermined the role of intellectuals as the conscience of society, professionalization also drove some intellectuals into their ivory towers to undertake the sort of specialized research typical of their counterparts elsewhere in the world. Others joined the government as members of "think-tanks." This was certainly a trend that had started in the 1980s, but by the 1990s intellectuals in government had become increasingly professionalized; they had become "policy wonks," not generalists. Increasingly they talked mainly to those university-based intellectuals who shared their specialties rather than to intellectuals in general.

Finally, by the 1990s, the Chinese intellectual community was far more international than it had been a decade earlier. Not only had professional contacts with overseas Chinese and Western academics grown substantially, but significant numbers of Chinese intellectuals had studied for prolonged periods in the West. These intellectuals either stayed in the West, taking up university or other positions, or returned to China. In either case, they spoke more with Chinese outside of China and were more aware of intellectual and academic trends in the West. The phenomenal growth of the Internet greatly facilitated this internationalization of Chinese discourse. In many ways, these trends simply reflect the growth and internationalization of Chinese society and economy, but they also mark the profound difference between China in the 1980s and China as it enters the twenty-first century.

If globalization and commercialization were two major economic and social phenomena sweeping across the landscape in the early 1990s, a new willingness (some might say eagerness) to reflect on the failings of reform

---

[14] Xu Jilin, *Ling yizhong qimeng*, p. 15.

was another. In the 1980s, criticism of reform came mostly from "conservatives," primarily those ideologues with ties to the propaganda system, the planned economy, and parts of the military who tried to uphold "socialism" in the face of reform. Reformers had consistently pushed for more reform, worrying that conservative forces would stop reform but not that reform itself might create new problems. Yet by the 1990s a considerable number of intellectuals began to worry about the consequences of declining central revenues (in relative terms), increasing income gaps between both classes and regions, corruption, and other problems. In part these new reflections marked a certain maturation of economic and social thought as problems began to be conceived less in terms of "reform" versus "conservatism" and more in terms of solutions to specific problems. There was more of a sense that China should concentrate less on "isms" and more on "problems." Nevertheless, these reflections on the problems China faced raised new questions about where reform was going. Whereas reformers in the 1980s could look to the old system as the negative image they wanted to escape and to the West as holding out solutions they wanted to move toward, by the 1990s there was less certainty about the goal of reform. Even as marketization increased apace, the problems associated with it made people ask new questions about the role of the state and social fairness. And the rise of such questions meant that "isms," or (more accurately) broad intellectual orientation, could not be dissolved completely into analysis of "problems"; indeed, by the end of the 1990s and into the new century there was a new concern with "isms" even as concern with solving "problems" continued.

These questions were further related to wide-ranging reflections on what had gone wrong in the 1980s. The question of reform had seemed so easy then; no one thought about reform as a decades-long process. A sense of optimism had prevailed. Tiananmen burst that optimism. Whereas reform and maintaining the old system had seemed the only alternatives in the 1980s, after Tiananmen the alternative of social and political collapse had to be considered as well. Tiananmen thus had a sobering effect; even the most reform-minded intellectuals had to stop and ask questions about system building, not just (as in the 1980s) about destroying the institutions of the old order.

This reaction, it should be noted, differed greatly both from views widely held in the West and by democracy activists in both China and the West. Democracy activists and their supporters in the West continued to see issues largely as they had in the 1980s, hoping that a democratic movement would bring down the old order and bring forth a new democratic order. The possibility of such a scenario ending in social chaos was rarely discussed, and this is why democratic activists found themselves isolated not only from the Chinese government but also from many of the same intellectuals who had supported them in the heady days of spring 1989. The intellectual atmosphere in China had changed dramatically.

Finally, one must consider the very changed relationship with the United States. As the collapse of socialism in Eastern Europe and the Soviet Union defined one pole in intellectual thinking about the international environment, the United States formed the other. Intellectuals held overwhelmingly favorable views of the United States in the 1980s; many initially supported the sanctions imposed by the Bush administration on the Chinese government in the wake of Tiananmen. But by the early 1990s, that positive image began to be replaced by suspicion and sometimes hostility. The triumphalism apparent in America following the demise of socialism did not help. It was widely believed after the Soviet Union had done everything that the United States had asked, including getting rid of socialism, that the United States had done little to help the peoples of the former Soviet Union. It was widely believed that America was perfectly happy to watch Russia and the other republics of the former Soviet Union fall into a position from which they would never be able to challenge the United States again. The subsequent decision to expand the North Atlantic Treaty Organization (NATO) only served to confirm these suspicions. More directly, by the early 1990s, many Chinese – intellectuals and ordinary people alike – came to believe that America was not against government repression or even socialism but against China itself. The belief that the United States wanted to "hold China down," as many put it, grew quickly and took hold. The opposition of the United States to China's bid to host the 2000 Olympics was a major turning point for many people in this regard. The bid to host the Olympics was a point of pride for many people; opposition to it could only be seen as hostility toward the Chinese people.[15]

The failure of socialism in Eastern Europe and the Soviet Union, the new awareness of globalization that that collapse brought about, the commercialization of Chinese society and culture, the changing status of

---

[15] There is no question, as Perry Link points out, that the normally ham-handed propaganda machine performed brilliantly in building up popular expectations and then allowing the United States to take the fall for the subsequent disappointment. Nevertheless, it would be wrong to see the changed popular perceptions as simply the product of government manipulation. This was a period in which many statements perceived as hostile to China (not just to the Chinese government) were made. It was also followed up by the ill-advised decision to stop and inspect the *Milky Way*, a Chinese ship that was incorrectly thought to be carrying precursor chemicals for the manufacture of chemical weapons. See Perry Link, "The Old Man's New China."

intellectuals, the changed perceptions of the United States, the raising of new questions about the effects and goals of reform, heightened concerns about social and political stability, and nuts and bolts questions about how one might successfully carry out reform all pointed to an intellectual atmosphere that was vastly different from that in the 1980s.

Merely to list this range of changes is to suggest the variety of responses that began to emerge in the early 1990s. For instance, Wang Shuo, the popular novelist and champion of the underside of Chinese life, embraced the new commercialization and flaunted the opportunity to throw off the constraints imposed by the cultural elite.[16] To the surprise of many, Wang Meng, a liberal writer and Minister of Culture in the late 1980s, came out in defense of Wang Shuo. For both Wangs, the commercialization of culture was liberating, a way of burying "leftism" forever.[17]

In contrast, other intellectuals began to express concern over the decline in their traditional ethos. This was apparent in the 1993 debate, touched off by Wang Xiaoming and several colleagues, about the decline of China's "humanistic spirit" (*renwen jingshen*). Wang's essay started with a dramatic statement: "Today, the crisis of literature is very obvious. Literary magazines are changing direction in great numbers, there is a universal decline in the quality of new literature, the number of readers with an ability to appreciate [what they are reading] is declining steadily, and the number of writers and critics discovering that they have chosen the wrong career and leaping 'into the sea' [of business] is growing larger and larger."[18] Trying to uphold the ethos of a cultural elite in the face of commercial pressures was an increasingly thankless task, and even those determined to pursue such an ideal found it necessary to redefine their role in society. But the psychological pressures behind such a debate can be imagined.

It was not only the pressures of commercialization but also the loss of values in general that drove many intellectuals to search for meaning.[19] Some, such as Liu Xiaofeng, turned to Christianity. Working in Hong Kong since completing his dissertation in theology in Switzerland in 1993, Liu has indefatigably probed Christianity for an absolute truth that transcends sociohistorical and cultural–ethnic boundaries.

A contrary response to the same search for values has been the revival of interest in "national studies" (*guoxue*). The rise of national studies in the

---

[16] Wang Shuo, *Playing for Thrills*; Wang Shuo, *Please Don't Call Me Human*. On Wang Shuo, see Geremie R. Barmé, "The Apotheosis of the *Liumang*," in Barmé, *In the Red*, pp. 62–144.

[17] "Wang Shuo zibai"; Xu Jilin, *Ling yizhong qimeng*, p. 264; Barmé, *In the Red*, pp. 298–301.

[18] Wang Xiaoming, "Kuangyeshang de feixu," p. 1.

[19] Ding Xueliang, "Dangdai Zhongguo de daode kongbai."

1990s marked an assertion of cultural nationalism, but it was not without a certain amount of official sponsorship. Cultural nationalism arose in response both to the perceived decline in values in China and to the belief that Western values could not solve the problems of the modern world.[20] As noted in the previous chapter, interest in China's tradition had been stimulated by the efforts of several well-known overseas Chinese scholars in the mid-1980s, and this had resulted in the establishment of one of the major popular (*minjian*) cultural groups of that era: the Academy of Chinese Culture, formed by a number of Beijing University professors.[21] Despite the interest the lectures and writings of the academy attracted, revival of traditional Chinese culture and studies on Confucianism were not viewed as being on the intellectual cutting edge in the 1980s. By the early to mid-1990s, however, "national studies" had not only achieved intellectual respectability but had become an intellectual fad (*guoxuere*), standing in counterpoint to the cosmopolitan cultural fever that had swept China only a decade before.

By the early 1990s, many believed that there had been a woeful loss of moral values in contemporary China – as reflected in corruption, commercialism, crime, and hedonistic lifestyles – and that there was much in China's tradition that was still of great value in the contemporary world. The deepening cultural and moral crises suggested that the problem lay not in China's traditional culture, as adherents of the May Fourth tradition believed, but rather in the decline of traditional values.[22] This understanding was bolstered by the rapid development of Japan and the "four small dragons" with attendant discussions of "Confucian capitalism," as Western social scientists and Asian commentators alike rediscovered the positive aspects of Confucianism for economic development: the frugality, work ethic, probity, respect for family and education, and acceptance of authority were all seen as reinforcing economic development and even as defining a uniquely Asian path to development.[23] In 1991, Ji Xianlin, a well-known scholar of Chinese literature at Beijing University, published an article that looked at the cyclical rise and fall of civilizations and concluded that Chinese civilization would rise again. As he put it epigrammatically, "[t]he river flows east for thirty years and [then] flows west for thirty years."[24] He followed this with other articles arguing that Western civilization was based

[20] Min Lin, *The Search for Modernity*, p. 147; Liu Xiaofeng, *Geti xinyang yu wenhua lilun*.
[21] See, for instance, Jiang Qing, *Gongyangxue yinlun*.
[22] Wang Hui, "Dangdai Zhongguo de sixiang zhuangkuang yu xiandaixing wenti," p. 134.
[23] Peter L. Berger and Hsin-Huang Michael Hsiao (eds.), *The Search for an East Asian Development Model*.
[24] Ji Xianlin, "Dongxifang wenhua de zhuanzhedian."

on an antagonistic relationship with nature and thus could not solve the ecological and environmental problems of the modern age. Chinese civilization, with its belief in harmony between humanity and nature, could provide a way out.[25]

In the late 1970s and early 1980s, as China emerged from the Cultural Revolution, intellectuals were obsessed by a desire to understand where the revolution had gone wrong and with a profound wish to prevent anything resembling the Cultural Revolution from ever happening again.[26] Intellectuals placed the blame squarely on "leftism." The enormous excesses of the Chinese revolution – from the "socialist transformation" of the mid-1950s to the anti-rightist movement of 1957, the Great Leap Forward of 1958–60, and finally the Cultural Revolution of 1966–76 – were attributed to a "leftism" that accepted uncritically a (contradictory) mix of Stalinist economic planning and Maoist mobilization, that rejected the importance of rationality and hence of intellectuals, that emphasized the "class nature" of human beings to the detriment of their humanity, and that turned the nation inward, rejecting the importance of learning from the West. These trends were also encompassed by the term "feudalism," a term of opprobrium that had nothing to do with its meaning for the economic and political history of the West or even its traditional meaning of local self-rule in China; instead, it connoted everything negative that had been attributed to Chinese traditional society through the long course of China's revolution: patriarchalism, authoritarianism, bureaucratism, anti-intellectualism, and fanaticism, to name a few. As China's revolution had increasingly criticized "capitalism," trying desperately in the course of the Cultural Revolution to "cut off the tail of capitalism" and to criticize "bourgeois rights," feudalism had flourished. "Leftism" was thus rooted in "feudalism," and the task of intellectuals and reform-minded Party people was to expunge these evils and thus set China on a course toward "modernity."

Given this basic (if somewhat oversimplified) diagnosis of what was wrong with China, it was natural that intellectuals turned to the May Fourth tradition for inspiration and moral sustenance. The May Fourth tradition had always contained contradictory elements: a radical critique of traditional Chinese culture and a demand to learn from the West combined with a nationalism that rejected cosmopolitanism in favor of nativism. Li Zehou, a member of the CASS Philosophy Institute, articulated for his

---

[25] Ji Xianlin, "'Tianren heyi' fang neng chengjiu renlei"; Ji Xianlin, "'Tianren heyi' xinjie."

[26] This and the following two paragraphs are drawn from my article, "Historical Echoes and Chinese Politics: Can China Leave the Twentieth Century Behind?"

generation of 1980s scholars the need to disentangle the "liberal" elements of the May Fourth tradition – those that emphasized "enlightenment" – from those that were caught up in nationalistic efforts to "save the nation." Li argued that every time the cultural critique seemed to offer hope of introducing new, enlightenment values into Chinese culture, it was overwhelmed by nationalism ("national salvation") as China faced one crisis after another.[27] Now, in the 1980s, it was finally time to take up the task of enlightenment and carry it through to fruition.

This enlightenment project dominated intellectual discourse in the 1980s. Whether it was discussions of "alienation" in socialism,[28] efforts to bring an end to "life-long tenure" and create a rational civil service,[29] policy proposals to marketize the Chinese economy,[30] translations of Western thinkers,[31] nascent writings about human rights and democracy,[32] or "reconceptualizations" of capitalism and socialism to emphasize their similarities, the task was to expunge "leftism" from Chinese social, economic, and political life. This focus on the dangers of leftism and feudalism assigned a lofty position to the West – particularly the United States, which took on an aura of modernity that provided a mirror opposite to the leftism that intellectuals sought to root out. Western culture provided fuel for ongoing critiques of Chinese culture, thus continuing the May Fourth rejection of traditional values, while the Western economic and political systems served as foils to criticize the planned economy and authoritarian political system of China. If discussions of the United States and other Western countries in the 1980s were superficial, it was because the point was not to understand how those systems actually worked but instead to provide a fulcrum from which faults in the Chinese system could be criticized. However superficial these discussions may have been, they clearly saw themselves as lying within the May Fourth enlightenment tradition, and they provided a cosmopolitanism that helped support the political relationship being forged with the West as well as reformers within the Party.

[27] Li Zehou, *Zhongguo xiandai sixiangshi lun*; Vera Schwarcz, *The Chinese Enlightenment*. See also Woei Lien Chong (ed.), *Li Zehou*.

[28] Wang Ruoshui's *Wei rendao zhuyi bianhu* is the classic work in this regard.

[29] Yan Jiaqi was one of the first and best-known advocates of instituting a civil service system. See Yan Jiaqi, *Toward a Democratic China*.

[30] Wu Jinglian was probably the best known of the early advocates, but there were many others. See Fewsmith, *Dilemmas of Reform*.

[31] Gan Yang edited a famous series of translations under the general title *Culture: China and the World*. See Chen Fong-ching and Jin Guantao, *From Youthful Manuscripts to River Elegy*, pp. 159–85.

[32] Su Shaozhi was an early and consistent advocate of democratization. See Su Shaozhi (ed.), *Marxism in China*; see also Su's memoirs, *Shinian fengyu*.

CRITIQUE OF THE MAY FOURTH ENLIGHTENMENT PROJECT

Although the May Fourth enlightenment project dominated intellectual endeavors in the 1980s, it was badly shaken by the end of the 1990s. Wang Hui, the editor of *Reading* mentioned previously, has argued that enlightenment thought lost its vitality because it was predicated on a fundamental acceptance of Western categories of thought – including liberal democracy,[33] neoclassical economics, individualism, and law – and because it relied on such dichotomies as China versus the West and tradition versus modernity to analyze China's problems. Such values and categories proved powerful when reflecting on the failings of socialism in the 1980s, but they lost their vigor, Wang argued, as globalization and marketization changed the relationships between state and society in China and between China and the outside world.

The basic problem was that globalization and marketization did not lead to the "good society." China's reform had indeed marketized the economy and linked it to the world, as enlightenment intellectuals had urged, but the result was not fairness and social justice – much less political democracy – but rather polarization, corruption, and a mutual penetration between political and economic power; indeed "the process of marketization itself had manifested new contradictions that were, in a certain sense, even more difficult to overcome" than those of the 1980s.[34] Enlightenment intellectuals had not changed their focus on state autocracy to the analysis of the "complicated relations between state and society that were developing in the course of the formation of the capitalist market," which in Wang's view was the central issue of the 1990s.[35]

In response to the changed circumstances of the 1990s, a number of young scholars, including Wang Hui, adopted a variety of postmodernist and critical methodologies by which they hoped to move beyond the enlightenment critique of the previous decade. In China, this group is usually referred to as the "New Left" – "new" to distinguish them from old Marxist–Leninist ideologues like Hu Qiaomu and Deng Liqun (who became known as the "Old Left") and "left" to suggest that their thought remains on the left side of the political spectrum, which in China is identified with "socialism"

---

[33] Wang notes that conceptions of democracy were restricted to reform programs designed by the highest levels and that they neglected political participation. There is some truth in his criticism – Chinese intellectuals have generally been wary of the lesser-educated rural population – but it is also true that they were working in an environment in which even limited "formalistic" democracy (as Wang calls it) marked progress. Wang's criticism appears in "Dangdai Zhongguo de sixiang zhuangkuang yu xiandaixing wenti."

[34] Wang Hui, ibid., pp. 16 and 8.   [35] Ibid., p. 20.

broadly (and ambiguously) defined. The opposite trend of thought (the "right") is liberalism. The term New Left is one that identifies aspects of the intellectual stance of this group, but like most labels it is also of polemical value. Because the term "left" has negative connotations for intellectuals, calling this group the New Left is intended to discredit them. Those who are generally identified with this group would prefer to think of themselves as "critical" intellectuals – in the sense of that term as used in literary criticism in the West.

These critical or New Left intellectuals are composed primarily of scholars who have been educated extensively in the United States, some of whom have taken up jobs in American universities and others of whom have returned to China to take up prestigious university and research positions. Becoming familiar with the variety of the critiques of capitalism and capitalist society that abound in academia and reflecting on the situation in China, these scholars began to doubt whether China could, or should, follow the "Western route."[36] This made the goal of reform more obscure than it had seemed only a few years earlier. In part, as Suisheng Zhao commented, the "demythification" of the West that is central to this critique was the product of wider and more frequent exchanges with the United States. As intellectuals have come to know the United States better, they have acquired the knowledge and the boldness to become more critical.[37] As works by such influential scholars as Edward Said, Michel Foucault, and Fredric Jameson were introduced into China, there was a growing interest in and acceptance of postmodernism and deconstructionism.[38] The introduction of such critical methodologies marked a new turn in the old debate about the relative merits of "Eastern" (meaning Chinese) culture and "Western" (mostly US) culture. In the wake of Tiananmen, the development of postmodernism, deconstructionism, studies of neocolonialism, and other critical methodologies – like the revival of interest in traditional culture – began to mark a major departure from the May Fourth tradition.

---

[36] Wang Hui, "Dangdai Zhongguo de sixiang zhuangkuang yu xiandaixing wenti," p. 2.
[37] Suisheng Zhao, *In Search of a Right Place?*, p. 13.
[38] The introduction of postmodernism is usually dated from the lectures given by Fredric Jameson at Beijing University in the mid-1980s. Many of Jameson's works have since been translated into Chinese and have become virtually required reading for Chinese intellectuals, particularly those in literary criticism. Despite the introduction of postmodernist thought in the mid-1980s, it was only with the Tiananmen incident and the subsequent changes in Chinese society that postmodernism really caught on. See "Bianzhe qianyan" (Editors' introduction) in Wang Hui and Yu Guoliang (eds.), *90 niandai de "houxue" lunzheng*; Edward Said, *Orientalism*; Edward Said, *Culture and Imperialism*; Michel Foucault, *The Order of Things*; and Fredric Jameson, *The Cultural Turn*. For a useful introduction, see Perry Anderson, *The Origins of Postmodernism*.

While such methodologies can provide valuable insights by uncovering forgotten voices and offering new explanations, there has been a marked tendency in recent years to deconstruct Western narratives of Chinese history. These narratives, it is said, have not only been projected by those serving Western interests but have also been accepted by Chinese intellectuals. This line of thinking became prominent with a 1993 article by Zhang Kuan, then a literature student at Stanford University, that discussed Edward Said's books *Orientalism* and *Culture and Imperialism*. Besides giving an overview of Said's argument that Westerners have distorted and uglified the reality of the Orient for their own purposes, Zhang argued that Western images of China changed from quite favorable (indeed, idealized) views held by early Jesuit missionaries and enlightenment intellectuals to decidedly negative images as the West began to oppress and exploit China. He stated further that many contemporary American scholars of China were trained by the military in order to "understand the enemy," ignoring the many China scholars who courageously opposed US policy toward China in the years after World War Two.[39]

The brunt of Zhang's argument, however, is not his critique of Western distortions of China but rather the acceptance by Chinese intellectuals of these Western portrayals. In this regard, Zhang is critical both of contemporary manifestations of Orientalism in China and of the broader enlightenment tradition in modern Chinese thinking. An example of the former is Chinese artists whose works have become popular in the West, such as the film director Zhang Yimou, Zheng Nian (Cheng Nien, the author of *Life and Death in Shanghai*), and Zhang Rong (Chang Jung, author of *Wild Swans* and, more recently, co-author of *The Unknown Story of Mao*). Zhang argues that their success is built on pandering to Western images of China; they have, he says, "used some fantastic and unreasonable things to make Westerners feel stimulated, intoxicated, or nauseated, to make Western audiences or readers feel what aesthetics call 'sublime' [*chonggaogan*] and compassionate and to have a sense of racial and cultural superiority

---

[39] In his later article "Zaitan Sayide," Zhang ties this influence directly to John King Fairbank and his students. The theme that Western views of China have changed from idealizing it to condemning it as Western colonialism developed has become widespread in recent years. In a review of the book series *Xifang shiyeli de Zhongguo xingxiang* (The Image of China in Western Eyes) edited by Huang Xingtao and Yang Nianqun, the liberal scholar Qin Hui argues that Western images of China vary according to profession and interest rather than historical period. Thus, business people take a more optimistic view of China whereas "missionaries" (including contemporary human rights advocates) take a more negative view. See Qin Hui, "Bainian zhuanhuan – 'Shangren' yu 'jiaoshi' de Zhongguoguan."

[*zhongzu wenhua shangde youyuegan*]. Thus, their works are popular and sell well."[40]

In examining the broader question of Chinese images of the West, Zhang adopts the term "Occidentalism" as the opposite of Orientalism to indicate distorted presentations of Western reality. Although the concept of Occidentalism includes denigration of Western culture, Zhang is more concerned with the idealizations of the West that he believes have been prevalent in China since the May Fourth Movement. It was, of course, the May Fourth Movement that introduced and popularized many concepts of the European enlightenment to China; Zhang is so wary of enlightenment values that he takes Said to task for basing his criticisms of the West on those values. Zhang argues that humanism contains within it the anti-humanist values that became the basis of colonialism and culminated in the Holocaust: "The evil perpetuated on the Jews under German fascism was the inevitable [result] of the logical development of enlightenment discourse; it returned the anti-humanist practice hidden in the humanist faith from the colonies back to Europe."[41]

Zhang's rejection of enlightenment values is clearly intertwined with an affirmation of Chinese values – though he is vague about precisely what those values are. Zhang does not share the New Confucian agenda of resurrecting a revivified Confucian tradition, but he does share the New Confucian belief that the May Fourth Movement went too far in its criticism of Chinese traditional values, with the result that, "[f]or a fairly long period of time, we have diluted [*danhua*] our own cultural identity, excessively taking Western [views] of right and wrong to be right and wrong."[42] Elsewhere Zhang declares that it is the duty of Chinese intellectuals to build up a "discourse of resistance" so that the country can better counter Western demands regarding such issues as human rights and intellectual property rights.[43]

---

[40] Zhang Kuan, "OuMeiren yanzhong de 'feiwo zulei'," pp. 7 and 9. This sort of attack on Zhang Yimou and others has become a staple in criticism of "colonial culture" in recent years. For instance, the leftist journal *Mainstream* declared, "Zhang Yimou, Chen Kaige, and their ilk make use of the textual form of 'pop culture' – cinema – to offer the barbarous and ugly aspects of our nation's former-day habits and customs to the West so as to gratify the hegemonic 'the West-is-the-center' mentality and to seek postcolonial rewards." See Cheng Zhi'ang, "Beware of So-Called Popular Culture," p. 52. The convergence of views between a postmodernist literary critic like Zhang Kuan and an Old Leftist journal like *Zhongliu* exemplifies why liberal intellectuals consider postmodernists the "New Left" and see the New Left as working in tandem with the Old Left.

[41] Zhang Kuan, "Wenhua xinzhimin de keneng," p. 20.

[42] Zhang Kuan, "Zaiyan Sayide," p. 12; see also Zhang Kuan, "Wenhua xinzhimin de keneng."

[43] Zhang Kuan, "Sayide de 'dongfang zhuyi' yu xifang de hanxue yanjiu," p. 37.

Zhang Kuan was one of the earliest and most influential participants in discussions on Orientalism and colonial culture, but he was by no means alone. For instance, Qian Jun recalls Edward Said writing about being invited to an Arab country to teach English literature – only to find the English department so dominated by colonial culture that they would only permit him to teach in the traditional English manner and not say anything critical. "I think," adds Qian, "that if Said were to come to China the situation would probably be about the same." For Qian, like Wang Xiaodong (whose views on culture were discussed in the previous chapter), the cultural fever of the 1980s demonstrated the enduring influence of imperialism in China, with *River Elegy* exemplifying this tendency.[44]

Wang Hui, one of the leading intellectuals in contemporary China, has argued that they continue to accept Western understandings of modernity; the narrative or the developmental model may differ from that of the West, but the goal remains the same.[45] Wang believes that Chinese socialism, and modern Chinese thought in general, has sought a way to modernize that avoids the pitfalls of Western capitalist development. Marxism in China is a modernizing ideology, and Mao Zedong's socialist thought was a type of "modernist theory that was opposed to capitalist modernity."[46] Elsewhere, Wang goes further, pointing out the contradictions within the modernist project and arguing that "a modernity opposed to modernity is not only a special manifestation of Chinese thinkers but a reflection of the structural contradictions within modernity itself."[47] Arguing that the categories of "socialism" and "capitalism" are no longer meaningful in a marketized and globalized China, Wang has tried to develop an approach that transcends not only those categories but also such dichotomies as Western versus Chinese and modern versus traditional. In doing so, Wang argues that the problem of socialism in China is part of a worldwide "crisis of modernity," so any answer to China's problems cannot be based solely on Western concepts of modernity but must respond also to the problems in Western capitalism. As Wang's comments about capitalism and "complex relations" between state and society suggest, he is deeply suspicious of market forces, constantly seeing the hand of power influencing and distorting social and economic outcomes. As he puts it, it is simply "utopic" to think that "fairness, justice,

---

[44] Qian Jun, "Saiyide tan wenhua," pp. 14–15. See also Liu Kang, "Quanqiuhua 'peilun' yu xiandaixing 'qitu'."

[45] Wang Hui, "Dangdai Zhongguo de sixiang zhuangkuang yu xiandaixing wenti," pp. 20–2.

[46] Ibid., p. 10.　　[47] Wang Hui, "Guanyu xiandaixing wenti dawen," p. 24.

and democracy can be achieved in the domestic and international arenas naturally out of the market."[48]

Given the debates that have emerged in recent years over China's integration into the world economy, it is important to note that Wang also sees globalization not as the extension of free markets but as the growth of multinational corporations that collude with domestic political forces to undermine both market forces and political democracy.[49] Hence Wang is not content with calling for political democracy (in which capitalist relations predominate) but argues further that political democracy must be coupled with economic democracy and cultural democracy.[50] Only in such a way can social fairness and justice prevail.

In surveying contemporary intellectual efforts to come to grips with the problem of modernity, Wang reserves his highest praise for Cui Zhiyuan. Cui, who received his Ph.D. from the University of Chicago and then taught at the Massachusetts Institute of Technology before going to Qinghua University, has probably worked harder than anyone else to develop a Chinese social science that is both informed by Western social science and at the same time critical of mainstream Western thinking. Cui is one of a large number of scholars who were quite young when the Cultural Revolution ended. Having no direct personal experience of Maoism, they tend to be more sympathetic toward (some would say they romanticize) the Maoist era, if not in its details then in some of the goals and social experiments.[51] Liberal thinkers in China react strongly and negatively to Cui's suggestions that Maoist practices can be shorn of their radicalism and thence provide a basis for economic democracy in contemporary China; for instance, no

---

[48] Wang Hui, "Dangdai Zhongguo de sixiang zhuangkuang yu xiandaixing wenti," p. 20.

[49] Wang Hui, "Guanyu xiandaixing wenti dawen," pp. 28–9.

[50] Wang Hui, "Dangdai Zhongguo de sixiang zhuangkuang yu xiandaixing wenti," p. 18.

[51] Although generational differences are important, one must be careful not to assume that generalizations are universals. The Red Guard generation (often called *laosanjie*), drawing on their experience in the countryside during the Cultural Revolution, contributed greatly to the implementation of rural reform and the breakup of the communes. Nevertheless, even friends who worked together on the early rural reforms have diverged over the years: some have tried to tackle the problems remaining in the rural areas by pursuing further property rights reform – essentially privatization – while others have advocated a type of return to socialism. The problem that these and other scholars have faced in dealing with the countryside is essentially one of public goods. The communes provided public goods (e.g., welfare and health care) to rural residents, and their breakup left a vacuum that has not been effectively filled to date. Deng Yingtao, Deng Liqun's son, was a prominent participant in the rural reforms in the 1980s, but in the 1990s he has embraced socialist solutions; he has also worked closely with Cui Zhiyuan in this regard. See Cui Zhiyuan, Deng Yingtao, and Miao Zhuang, *Nanjiecun*. Nevertheless, in general, young scholars of Cui's generation seem more inclined to embrace "collectivist" solutions than do those who are older.

liberal would accept Cui's assertion that "[t]here are really quite a few positive factors in Mao's thought waiting to be excavated."[52] Similarly, liberals bridle at the notion that the Anshan Iron and Steel Factory Constitution, held up by Mao during the Cultural Revolution as a model of worker participation, really foreshadowed "quality circles" and can be resurrected as a model of economic democracy in the present era. Nonetheless, Cui has drawn on neo-evolutionary biology to argue that just as animals in the course of evolution might lose a characteristic while retaining the gene – and thus the ability to regain the lost characteristic at some later point in evolutionary history – contemporary Chinese society can draw on some of the practices of the Mao era, including that of Anshan, to create a more just and humane society in the future.[53] Cui argues strongly that only by acknowledging workers as "stakeholders" in enterprises can China create a society that is both economically efficient and socially fair.

Cui draws heavily on analytic Marxism (especially the work of John Roemer), neo-evolutionary biology, and critical legal studies (particularly Roberto Unger) to derive what are basically social democratic solutions to China's problems.[54] For instance, in rejecting intellectual trends in China that accept the neoclassical paradigm of Western economics, including calls for the "clarification of property rights" and for privatization,[55] Cui argues that many people in the United States and other advanced capitalist nations are changing significantly their understandings of private property.[56] Indeed, Cui notes that critical legal studies have shown that there is no such thing as "absolute private property."[57] "Property rights" are not unified and exclusive but rather a "bundle of rights" that can be dissolved and recombined in a variety of ways. He cites changes in US laws that recognize the rights not just of shareholders but also of stakeholders as

---

[52] Cui Zhiyuan, "Zailun zhidu chuangxin yu di'erci sixiang jiefang," p. 26.

[53] Cui Zhiyuan, "Angang xianfa yu houfute zhuyi." Interestingly enough, even such a liberal official as Hu Ping (head of the Special Zones Office of the State Council) referred favorably to the Angang Constitution in a speech defending the Special Economic Zones. See Hu Ping, "Special Zone Construction and Opening to the Outside," p. 25.

[54] John Roemer (ed.), *Property Relations, Incentives, and Welfare*; Roberto Mangabeira Unger, *Democratic Experimentalism*.

[55] Zhang Weiying has been particularly forceful in this regard. See *Qiye de qiyejia*.

[56] See in particular Cui Zhiyuan, "Zhidu chuangxin yu di'erci sixiang jiefang." In his article "Meiguo ershiji zhou gongsifa biange de lilun beijing," Cui argues that the recognition of stakeholder rights marks an important change in the understanding of the property rights of shareholders. For a refutation by liberal economist Zhang Weiying, see "Suoyouzhi, zhili jiegou ji weituo."

[57] Cui Zhiyuan, "Zhidu chuangxin yu di'erci sixiang jiefang," p. 10. It should be noted that critical legal studies have played an important role in the ongoing development of legal thinking, but they are hardly as widely accepted within legal circles as Cui's footnotes might lead one to believe. See Nicholas Mercuro and Steven G. Medema, *Economics and the Law*.

one important instance of this. Thus, Cui argues against the permanence (*yongdongji*, "inertia") of institutions, saying that they can be altered and renewed in a variety of ways over time to make them more democratic. He believes that reformers who want to move quickly to clarify property rights are engaged in a type of "institutional fetishism" that will prematurely close off important institutional innovations and curtail economic democracy. Cui places great weight on the role of institutions both in changing individual behavior and in supporting ideals: "Human nature is not immutable."[58]

Put in more general terms, Cui's work argues that China should not pursue single-mindedly the neoliberal economic model of the West – not only because significant questions about the validity of that model have been raised in the West[59] but also because China can build on its own legacies (and here he means the legacies of socialism) to avoid some of the problems of the West.[60] In so arguing, Cui seems to be combining a moral revulsion at the concentration of wealth and abuse of power that have occurred in the reform years with an idealism that socialist and economic democracy can be implemented in China despite the lack of stable social, economic, and legal institutions to build upon. Although Cui would deny any nationalist intent, his critiques of Western neoliberalism and his evocation of China's Maoist heritage are very much a part of the 1990s' turn away from the new enlightenment problematique of the 1980s and an effort to build a China-centered social science in contradistinction to Western traditions.

LIBERAL THOUGHT IN CONTEMPORARY CHINA

This overview of New Left or critical approaches to the problems of contemporary China suggests the outlines of a major cleavage between these intellectuals and those who identify themselves as "liberals." Although there are

---

[58] Cui Zhiyuan, "Zailun zhidu chuangxin yu di'erci sixiang jiefang," p. 26.
[59] Cui often cites the work of Joseph E. Stiglitz, who has been a leading critic of the standard neoclassical model; see, for instance, his *Whither Socialism?*
[60] In this sense, Cui's work is very different from those who look to China's Confucian heritage for solutions to its present problems. It should be noted that there is an important but unarticulated argument going on between those of the New Left and at least some of their critics about the value of the Chinese revolution. Although those of the New Left reject both the mass mobilizations of the Maoist era and the rigid, bureaucratic apparatus associated with the planned economy, they nevertheless see the revolution as overwhelmingly positive. For instance, in their discussion of state capacity, Hu Angang and Wang Shaoguang note the very rapid increase in state capacity following the revolution and argue that "such an accomplishment was indeed rare in the annals of the world" (*Wang Shaoguang Proposal* [I], p. 47). Liberals and traditionalists, while willing to work within the framework bequeathed by the revolution, seem much less enamored of the revolution itself.

many streams of thought in contemporary China, the difference between the New Left and liberals is perhaps the deepest and most politically salient (we will discuss nationalists separately, though, as their thinking overlaps significantly with that of the New Left). Like the term "New Left," the term "liberal" should probably not be accepted uncritically, even though there has been less controversy over its use within China – either by liberals or their critics – than there has been of the term "New Left." Moreover, contemporary Chinese liberalism shares the broad outlines of classical Western liberalism, though the Western tradition's complexity and diversity make direct comparisons difficult. Nevertheless, it is important to keep in mind that Chinese liberalism is also informed by Chinese tradition, particularly the *minben* (people as the foundation) tradition associated with Mencius, as well as by the liberals' understanding of modern Chinese history and the nature of the problems facing contemporary China.

As we have outlined, contemporary Chinese liberals identify themselves with the May Fourth enlightenment tradition. In the 1980s, they championed reform, which meant not only marketization and political liberalization (and eventual democratization) but also opposing the people, ideas, and forces that they saw as upholding the old order. These included orthodox understandings of Marxism–Leninism, the bureaucracies that lay at the core of the "planned economy," and those ideologues who wielded the "big stick" against people like themselves and who maneuvered to uphold and take advantage of the old system. For liberals, Tiananmen did not change their understanding of the forces that needed to be opposed; indeed, it only reinforced that understanding.

This understanding of the problems facing China points to a fundamental difference between liberals and the New Left, namely, their very deep disagreement over the nature of the problems facing China. For intellectuals like Wang Hui and Cui Zhiyuan, the Old Left of orthodox Marxist–Leninists has lost its power and influence as marketization and globalization have destroyed the old planned economy and opened (entangled) China to (with) the outside world; the problem for them is what type of China will be built upon the ruins of the old system, whether a "fair" society can emerge or whether economic and social disparities will be locked into place. As will become apparent, liberals share many of these concerns (though their approach to solving them is quite different), but they also see the Old Left as continuing to wield considerable power in China. Thus, liberals often speak in terms of "left" and "right" or "conservatives" and "reformers," while the New Left dismiss such formulations as passé, and reflective of a "Cold War mentality."

The community of liberal intellectuals was badly damaged by Tiananmen and its aftermath; many lost their voice and influence as they either took up residence overseas or were forced to remain silent in China. Nevertheless, there are several important liberal thinkers, both older and younger scholars, who have remained active or have become active again. The best-known of these include Li Rui, Mao's former secretary, who has written a series of works excoriating the leftist past;[61] Hu Jiwei, former editor-in-chief and director of *People's Daily*, who has published his memoirs and some articles in Hong Kong;[62] and Wang Ruoshui, former deputy editor-in-chief of *People's Daily*, who similarly published a memoir in Hong Kong and wrote a number of articles, mostly on Mao Zedong, before his death in 2002.[63] Such voices, quite influential in the 1980s, no longer carry the weight they once did, in part because the government is no longer sympathetic to their views and generally denies them access to mainland media, and in part because younger academics see them as not well trained (in contemporary academic terms) and hence "out of date." Nevertheless, their writings carry weight in some circles and stand in constant counterpoint to revisionist views of history. Whereas some younger scholars, such as Cui Zhiyuan, suggest that there are positive aspects of the Maoist era, these and other scholars of the older generation remind those who will listen that the Maoist era really was bad.

In general, these scholars of the older generation restrict themselves to writing about the past rather than engaging in polemics with their post-modernist colleagues. One exception was Li Shenzhi, the former head of the Institute of American Studies at CASS, who emerged as the dean of liberal thought between the mid-1990s and his death in 2003. Born in 1923, Li graduated from the Sichuan campus of Yanjing College during the war against Japan and was one of several young, talented people recruited by Zhou Enlai to serve as secretaries and speech writers. Li accompanied Zhou Enlai to the Geneva and Bandung conferences but was then attacked during the anti-rightist movement of 1957. Although he was allowed to return to the Xinhua News Service in the 1960s, it was only in the late 1970s – when he was selected to head the newly established Institute of American Studies – that he became an influential voice in foreign policy.[64] In the aftermath of Tiananmen, Li was retired because of his liberal views. Although he maintained a low profile in the early 1990s, by the middle

---

[61] Li Rui, *Li Rui fan "zuo" wenxuan.*
[62] Hu Jiwei, *Cong Hua Guofeng xiatai dao Hu Yaobang xiatai.*
[63] Wang Ruoshui, *Hu Yaobang xiatai de beijing.*
[64] On Li's background, see A. Doak Barnett, *The Making of Foreign Policy in China*, pp. 88–9, 129.

part of the decade he began writing prolifically. Well known for his understanding both of China's tradition and the West, Li was one of the most
respected intellectuals in China. Moreover, his age and retirement from
official responsibilities, as well as his concerns about political trends in
China and intellectual trends among younger Chinese, made him willing
to speak out in a way that few people dared.

Li was an unapologetic and unreconstructed May Fourth enlightenment
intellectual. He calls himself a true son of the Chinese enlightenment,[65]
believing that China lacked the scientific tradition that informed Western
philosophy and the democratic tradition that regulated state–society relations in the West.[66] In direct contrast to the New Left, Li argued that the
goals of the May Fourth Movement, laid down 80 years ago, were never
reached, so the spirit of the May Fourth Movement remains as important
as ever.[67] Moreover, he argued that the essence of the May Fourth enlightenment tradition was liberalism and individualism. He quoted Hu Shi,
one of the founders of the May Fourth Movement, as follows: "Now, there
are some people who tell you, 'Sacrifice your individual freedom and strive
for the freedom of the country!' I say to them, 'Fighting for your individual freedom is fighting for freedom for the country! Struggling for your
individual dignity (*renge*) is struggling for the dignity of the country! A
country of freedom and equality cannot be created by a group of slaves'."[68]
Li quoted to similar effect other heroes of the May Fourth Movement –
including Chen Duxiu, Cai Yuanpei, and Lu Xun – thus making clear that
the values of individualism, human rights, and tolerance were embedded
in the very fabric of the May Fourth Movement. This restatement of May
Fourth values not only stood as a rejoinder to the New Left (who tend
to look more to collective solutions than to individualism), but also to
the Communist Party, which perennially tries to subsume the May Fourth
spirit under the rubric of "patriotism."

Li Shenzhi argued that the thinking of the founders of the May Fourth
Movement was really "the liberalism and individualism of mainstream,
orthodox world thought over the past three centuries."[69] It was, in other
words, a conjoining of Chinese thought and Western liberalism, a manifestation of China's joining the world. This suggested a very different
attitude toward globalization than that held by postmodernist thinkers. In
contrast to the New Left views already described, Li took a positive view
of recent trends. Not unlike Wang Hui, Li took 1989–92 as marking a

---

[65] Li Shenzhi, "Bian tongyi, hedongxi," p. 822.
[66] Li Shenzhi, "Zhongguo chuantong wenhuazhong jiwu minzhu yewu kexue."
[67] Li Shenzhi, "Chongxin dianran qimeng de huoju," p. 2.   [68] Ibid., p. 5.   [69] Ibid., p. 6.

watershed in the acceleration of globalization (a process he traces back to Columbus' landing in the Americas), one that was brought about by global capitalism – as symbolized not only by the collapse of socialism in Eastern Europe and the breakup of the Soviet Union but also by the CCP's acknowledgment, at the Fourteenth Party Congress in 1992, of the need to continue reform in the direction of further marketization. Rather than exhibit the shock shown by conservative politicians or the sense of threat exhibited by New Left intellectuals, Li stated simply and boldly that "[t]he events that happened between 1989 and 1991 can in fact be understood as the force of information destroying the fortress of isolation."[70]

What was different in the globalization of recent years when compared with that of the past five centuries, and which gave symbolic import to the date 1992, was that the pace of globalization had increased exponentially and its nature had changed. By emphasizing "globalization," as opposed to the clash of national interests, Li and others were able to depict a process that transcended the nation-state system and hence threatened Western culture as much as it did Eastern culture. The proper response to globalization was not nationalism but modernization.

Like all Chinese intellectuals, Li was certainly nationalistic; it is impossible to read his essays without sensing the pride he has in Chinese culture and in the accomplishments of China.[71] But Li was critical, even contemptuous, of the rising voices of the new nationalists. For instance, in one article he noted that as China's economy developed and a small number of people finally had some money in their pockets, a mood of pompous arrogance (*xuqiao*) emerged, but "[t]his sort of crude nationalism is completely contrary to the spirit and trend of globalization."[72] In another article, Li wrote:

What is strange is that there are at the moment not a few students who have studied overseas who are quite different from their elders. They cannot see the good points in others and frequently develop a mood of what I call, "an attitude of pompous arrogance" (*xuqiao zhi qi*). Perhaps this precisely reflects China's progress, but it lacks the attitude of "knowing shame approaches courage" (*zhichi jinhu yong*) possessed by the generation of Sun Yat-sen, Kang Youwei, Wang Guowei, Chen Yinke, and Hu Shi.[73]

What worried Li about the attitude of these young nationalists (who will be discussed in the following chapter) is that they overestimated the progress

---

[70] Li Shenzhi, "Quanqiuhua yu Zhongguo wenhua."
[71] See, for instance, Li Shenzhi, "Zhongguo zhexue de jingshen."
[72] Li Shenzhi, "Quanqiuhua yu Zhongguo wenhua," p. 7.
[73] Li Shenzhi, "Guanyu wenhua wenti de yixie sikao," p. 1132.

that China had made in the previous few years and that their nationalism would prevent China from continuing to learn from the rest of the world. As he put it at one point, those who declared that we should "rely on Chinese culture to save the world" are "arrogant and conceited" (*kuangwang*); not only will this approach not push forward China's modernization, it runs directly counter to China's cultural tradition.[74]

Li's understanding of the strengths and weaknesses of China's cultural and social traditions informed his response to globalization; Li was not naive about its impact but welcomed it nonetheless. He hoped that globalization would foster economic development and that economic development would eventually bring about a middle class – a genuinely revolutionary change in China's social structure. Moreover, only such a social revolution could root out the sources of radicalism in Chinese culture and prepare the ground for law and democracy.[75] In this sense, globalization could enrich Chinese culture through social change.

In meeting the challenge of globalization, Li evinced greater confidence than many of his younger colleagues. Acknowledging that China's core problem was the loss of identity,[76] Li argued that there were many values in China's traditional culture that remained important for re-establishing a moral order, values that were not only compatible with globalization but could also contribute to global civilization. Nationalism, he argued, was stimulated in China by the pressure of the foreign powers; once China has gained a position of equality with other countries in the world, Chinese culture would, Li predicted, return to its roots in culturalism and cosmopolitanism (*tianxia zhuyi*) – which in the present world would be globalism.[77] Summing up, he stated: "The modernization of China's culture must take tradition as its foundation and globalization as its goal."[78] There was, no doubt, a genuine idealism in Li's vision of the future,[79] one that clashed not only with the cynical view of global capitalism and cultural imperialism held by young critics but also with the hard realism of many in the foreign policy establishment.

Finally, Li made clear that political reform was part of cultural modernization and China's joining the world. In early 1998, as China entered one of its periods of political relaxation, Li published a short essay arguing that

[74] Li Shenzhi, "Zhongguo yingqu shenmayang de fengfan?," p. 955.
[75] Li Shenzhi, "Faxian lingyige Zhongguo," p. 1249.
[76] Here Li references Perry Link's article, "China's 'Core' Problem."
[77] Li Shenzhi, "Quanqiuhua yu Zhongguo wenhua," p. 8.   [78] Ibid., p. 9.
[79] See, for instance, his observation that the human species had a common starting point and then spread out to the far reaches of the globe but now is coming together again. Li Shenzhi, "Bian tongyi, hedongxi," p. 826.

the time had come for political reform to catch up to economic reform. Li's essay was pegged to the just-completed Fifteenth Party Congress, the most liberal in Party history, which had endorsed the "continued promotion of political reform." Jiang's report to the Party Congress had called for a "country with rule of law" (*fazhi guojia*), as Jiang was trying to promote his campaign to strengthen the legal institutions of the country. However, Li's essay interpreted Jiang's report as going further than Jiang apparently intended. Li argued that whereas Party documents normally called for "rule by law" (*fazhi*), the Fifteenth Party Congress had introduced the term "rule of law."[80] Li, no doubt with the hope of pushing the Party further in this direction, praised this breakthrough. But returning to the theme of China's culture, he noted that "[t]he greatest defect in China's cultural tradition is that it lacks human rights."[81] Implementing "rule of law" would bring about fundamental political change, improve human rights in China, and let China join the world and earn the respect of other countries.[82] Thus, the only way to meet the challenge of globalization was to establish institutions that were compatible with it – democracy and rule of law – and not to try to rely on market forces alone.[83]

The differences between New Left intellectuals and liberals revolved primarily around their very different understandings of the relationship between capitalism (both domestic and international) and power. As we have suggested, New Left thinking was highly suspicious of the power relationships embedded in capitalism and distrustful that liberal democracy is capable of restraining such relations sufficiently to bring about a fair society. This perspective was natural given the domestic and international situation in which China found itself. Internationally, there was a dramatic increase in foreign investment, stimulating the discussions of postcolonialism noted previously, but there was also the dramatic failure of Russia to implement successful economic or political reforms after listening – too eagerly, in the eyes of many Chinese – to the advice of Westerners. It is little wonder, then, that the New Left drew heavily on Immanuel Wallerstein's world system theory, which emphasizes the hierarchical nature of international

---

[80] Unfortunately, this term is also pronounced *fazhi*, but the character for *zhi* in this expression differs from the character for *zhi* in the first expression. Whereas the character *zhi* in "rule by law" carries the meaning "control or restrain," that for *zhi* in "rule of law" means "govern," giving the expression a less authoritarian connotation.

[81] Li notes that this phrase was coined by Mao Yushi, Hu Yaobang's former secretary (who was speaking at the same conference), but that he (Li) fully endorsed it.

[82] Li Shenzhi, "Yeyao tuidong zhengzhi gaige."

[83] Li Shenzhi, "Quanqiuhua yu Zhongguo wenhua," p. 5.

capitalism.[84] The state of Sino–US relations throughout much of the 1990s played into this dynamic, exacerbating these tendencies.

Although the intellectual trends just described are understandable given China's circumstances, it is not difficult to detect a utopic element, influenced by nationalism, in the writings of New Left writers. As in Cui Zhiyuan's writings, the New Left is suspicious of efforts to prematurely define property rights and to implement political democracy in the absence of economic democracy (and of cultural democracy, in the view of Wang Hui). When the New Left wrote of democracy, they tended to cite Rousseau and his support of direct democracy.[85] In making such arguments, China's New Left was clearly drawing on a tradition of populism in modern China. Perhaps they turned toward China's populist tradition because they suspect – with good reason – that privatization, clarification of property rights, and even political democracy would institutionalize the privileges of the *nouveau riche* who have emerged in recent years. These people often had (and have) substantial political backing and managed to take advantage of their positions to benefit from economic reform; they are, in the words of sociologist Sun Liping, the "never left-out class" (*bu luokong jieji*).[86] Indeed, perhaps the most potent charge that the New Left made against liberals was that they ignored social justice in their championing of private property.[87]

In contrast, liberals believed that the New Left turned their backs on precisely those enlightenment values needed for economic and political reform; for this reason, liberals often accused them of collaborating (directly or indirectly) with the government. Thus, Zhao Yiheng believed that New Left thinking was merely a continuation of the neoconservative thinking examined in Chapter 3,[88] Xu Ben has argued that the New Left are "cultural explicators of official nationalism and authoritative domestic policies,"[89] and Zhang Longxi goes so far as to accuse the New Left of being "spokespersons for the Ministry of Foreign Affairs."[90] Lei Yi, a well-known historian at the Institute of Modern History, pointed out the irony of a Third-World scholar using the postmodernist discourse developed in the West to criticize the cultural hegemony of the West (which many New Left scholars did). Even in trying to escape the dominant discourse of the West, one was almost inevitably captured by Western discourse; true escape is difficult, if

---

[84] Immanuel Wallerstein, *The Modern World System.*   [85] Cui Zhiyuan, "Lusuo xin lun."
[86] Sun, Liping, "Zhongguo shehui jiegou zhuanxing de zhongjinqi qushi yu yinhuan."
[87] Xu, Jilin, "Xunqiu 'disantiao daolu' – guanyu 'ziyouzhuyi' yu 'xinzuopai' de duihua."
[88] Zhao Yiheng, "'Houxue' yu Zhongguo xinbaoshou zhuyi."
[89] Xu Ben, "Shenma shi Zhongguo de 'houxin shiqi'?"
[90] Zhang Longxi, "Duoyuan shehui zhongde wenhua piping."

not impossible. More importantly, Lei Yi argued that if Chinese scholars were going to import postmodernist discourse, they should "sinify" it by carrying out an archaeology of dominant discourses in China.[91]

Just as the New Left and the liberals differed in their understandings of capitalism and power, they had sharply different understandings of Chinese history. Indeed, although they cannot fully lay out their different interpretations of modern history because of its political sensitivity, this is the area in which some of their most profound differences lie. As noted before, they disagreed most about the relevance of the May Fourth tradition. The New Left saw it as largely irrelevant to the problems of contemporary China; if it was once a vital tradition, it was not so anymore. This attitude toward the May Fourth tradition was clearly related to their understanding of the value of the communist revolution. Although the New Left can be quite critical of the government, it nevertheless saw much that it believed to be worthwhile in the communist revolution, in terms both of accomplishments and moral values. For Western observers who have long since dismissed the communist revolution as a mistake – or at least as something whose time has come and gone – this is the area of greatest disconnect, the place where the change in intellectual outlook was so unexpected that it has gone largely unnoticed or been dismissed as an atavistic trend of "neoconservatism." But when Wang Hui looked at Mao Zedong as exploring a path to modernity that is critical of Western modernity, and when Cui Zhiyuan resurrected the "good" aspects of Maoism (as in the Anshan Constitution), there is something more profound going on.

In contrast – as our discussion of Li Shenzhi makes clear – liberals had profound reservations about the value of the Chinese revolution. Although few were willing to say (or perhaps believe) that it was unnecessary, they were intent on bringing a liberal economic and political order out of the society that the revolution wrought. Their disagreement about the value of the May Fourth tradition had much to do with their assessments of the worth of the Chinese revolution. This is why liberals are a greater threat to the CCP's legitimacy and why they have borne the brunt of political criticism.

[91] Lei Yi, "Beijing yu cuowei."

CHAPTER 5

The emergence of neostatism and popular nationalism

Although the previous chapter laid out the major differences between the New Left and liberals, attention was focused primarily on differences in their world views. To that extent, the discussion was fairly abstract, as are many of the writings in this genre. This chapter focuses on more specifically political issues that have arisen parallel to the discussions described in Chapter 4. In particular, we focus on two issues that at first glance appear to be contradictory: the emergence of a body of neostatist thought that has revolved around the issue of "state capacity" on the one hand, and the emergence of populist nationalism on the other. Chapter 3 discussed the nationalism of people like He Xin and the recentralizing impulses of people like Chen Yuan. However, even though He Xin's tone was populist, he was so obviously directing his views upward (toward the leadership) that he never tested the popular basis for his views. Similarly, although Chen Yuan sought ways to combine market economics with a stronger central government, he never developed a systematic conceptual approach. These limitations condemned the neoconservatism of the 1989–92 period to the margins of Chinese intellectual life, even as it expressed a prevalent mood within a segment of the political leadership.

By 1992–3, however, as noted in the previous chapter, the economic and social bases had developed for a broader intellectual acceptance of New Left ideas that would have been considered "conservative" only a few years earlier. Yet as social thinkers like Wang Hui, Cui Zhiyuan, and others began to explore new understandings of "modernity" and different development paths, other scholars – particularly Hu Angang and Wang Shaoguang, whose ideas are discussed shortly – turned their attention to the issue of "state capacity." State capacity is an old issue in American political science that received an infusion of new intellectual vitality in the 1980s as

Joel Migdal, John Zysman, and others began to look at how strong states could bring about social change and economic development.[1]

Although the neostatist desire to increase state capacity appears at first glance to move in the opposite direction from popular nationalism and its criticisms of the existing government – and both of these seem distant from the New Left concerns discussed in Chapter 4 – in fact, all three of these trends share a basic intellectual orientation, and personal relations across them tend to be quite close. At least three concerns cross-cut these otherwise different approaches and bind them together. First, there is a common nationalism directed primarily against the United States, both in terms of its presumed desire to control China internationally and in terms of the American model of liberal democracy and neoclassical economics. Second, the approaches share a concern with social justice, though they differ somewhat in their preferred solutions. Finally, all three approaches share a populist orientation, although the neostatist is characterized by a concern for state building that popular nationalists like Wang Xiaodong do not display.

The greatest tension across these different groups of thinkers is centered on the figure of Zhu Rongji. At least prior to China's final push to join the World Trade Organization (WTO), neostatists like Hu Angang and Wang Shaoguang were interested in influencing state policy and in appealing to Zhu. They saw Zhu as someone who could both centralize state power and marketize the economy. In contrast, the New Leftists worried about "premature" institutionalization, the clarification of property rights, the power relations hidden behind capitalist relations, and the integration of China's economy into the international economy. Hence, they opposed much of what Zhu was trying to do. Nationalists share the neostatists' desire to strengthen the state but are skeptical of the present political leadership's ability to govern successfully, to articulate China's national interests forcefully, or to use state power to bring about social justice. Keeping in mind these commonalities and differences, we turn first to the issue of state capacity and the work of Hu Angang and Wang Shaoguang.

Wang Shaoguang was among a cohort of bright young Chinese students who came to study in the United States in the 1980s; he went on to teach at Yale University before moving to the Chinese University of Hong Kong. Although his graduate work focused on the Cultural Revolution, he quickly

---

[1] Joel Migdal, *Strong Societies and Weak States*; John Zysman, *Government, Markets, and Growth*.

developed an interest in the issue of state capacity and how that might relate to China's economic and political development.

While Wang came to the United States for advanced study, Hu stayed in China. Graduating from the Tangshan Institute of Technology, Hu got a job at the Chinese Academy of Sciences (CAS). The first book on which he was a major collaborator was *Survival and Development*. This book was published internally in 1989 but not openly until 1996. It stressed China's "national conditions" and how they prevented China from following the West's developmental path. In particular, China's large population and consequent low per-capita resource base meant that China would need a strong government that could "coordinate" (*xietiao*) the various demands on resources. China could not simply follow the Western model of allowing some people to become very affluent.[2] Fortunately for Hu, the book was passed to Deng Nan, Deng Xiaoping's daughter, who then passed it (or a summary) on to her father. Deng Xiaoping praised the work, and – not surprisingly – state resources were then lavished on the "national conditions research group" at CAS that Hu worked with.[3]

In 1991, Hu came to Yale as a visiting scholar and met Wang Shaoguang. Together they worked on a research report entitled "Strengthen the Guiding Role of the Central Government during the Transition to a Market Economy: On China's State Capacity." In trying to "operationalize" the concept of state capacity, Hu and Wang focused on the state's extractive capacity, not only because it is easy to measure – making it easy to compare trends across both time and space – but also because, in their opinion, it was the pressing issue of the day. In focusing on extractive capacity, Hu and Wang chose to ignore other, more difficult (but nonetheless important) components of state capacity, such as legitimation capacity, corruption, and bureaucratic efficiency.

Hu and Wang argued that the extractive capacity of China's central government was quite weak. They cited statistics to show that central government revenues as a percentage of GNP had fallen from 31.2 percent in 1978 to 14.7 percent in 1992, and they projected that such revenues would fall to only 11.3 percent in the year 2000.[4] At least as serious, they argued, was the ratio between central government revenues and total government

---

[2] Zhongguo kexueyuan guoqing fenxi yanjiu xiaozu, *Shengcun yu fazhan*.   [3] Author interviews.

[4] Hu Angang and Wang Shaoguang, *Jiaqiang zhongyang zhengfu zai shichang jingji zhuanxing zhong de zhudao zuoyong*. (Hereafter cited as *Wang Shaoguang Proposal (I)* or *(II)*.) *Wang Shaoguang Proposal (I)*, p. 60. It should be noted that because of the tax reform adopted in 1994, central revenues began to climb. Instead of being 11.3 percent of GNP in 2000, as Hu and Wang predicted, they were about 14.3 percent. I appreciate Barry Naughton sharing his data with me.

revenues. In the period of the Seventh Five-Year Plan (1986–90), central government revenues accounted for only 40 percent of all government revenues, and Wang and Hu estimated that this figure would fall to only 34 percent by the year 2000.[5] In contrast, the comparable figure in France was 88 percent, in Brazil 84 percent, in India 69 percent, and in the United States – the lowest of all industrialized countries – it was still 59 percent.[6]

The growing wealth of the localities and the declining capacity of the central state had clear and negative political ramifications, in the opinion of Hu and Wang. The result was a "weak center and strong localities";[7] the relationship between center and localities had become one of "negotiation and bargaining between equals."[8] The consequences of such a situation were said to be quite severe. Not only would macroeconomic stability and economic growth be undermined, but even China's political unity would be threatened. China's weakened state capacity put China at risk of disintegrating, just as Yugoslavia had. As they put it: "If we were permitted to take another step here and speculate on the worst case scenario, it seems possible that once the 'political strong man' at the center (for example, Deng Xiaoping) passes away, a situation like that in Yugoslavia after the death of Tito could take place in China . . . *we could go from economic disintegration to political fragmentation, and, in the end, fall into national disintegration.*"[9]

Wang and Hu argued that the relative decline in central state revenues was fundamentally due to the fiscal reforms introduced in the 1980s, reforms that gave localities incentives to build up their local economies but not necessarily to pass on increased revenue to the central government. Local revenues were not remitted to the central government not only because many were designated as extrabudgetary and thus earmarked for local purposes but also because the central government did not have tax offices in the localities. Provincial governments were supposed to pass up part of the revenues they collected, but the localities had an interest in retaining as much revenue as possible, so there was much "slippage" between what was collected and what was remitted.

Decrying the decline of central government revenues – the "two ratios" (the ratio of all government revenues as a percentage of GNP and the ratio of central government revenues as a percentage of all government revenues), as they were known – had been a staple of conservative political rhetoric

---

[5] Ibid., p. 64. In fact, central revenues as a percentage of GDP reached a low in 1995 and, in part because of the tax reforms implemented in 1994, began to increase thereafter.
[6] Ibid., p. 63.   [7] Ibid., p. 24.   [8] *Wang Shaoguang Proposal (II)*, p. 5
[9] *Wang Shaoguang Proposal (I)*, pp. 66–7; emphasis in original.

throughout the 1980s. During that period, however, those who worried about Beijing's declining share of the wealth were primarily such bureaucracies as the Ministry of Finance and the State Planning Commission, organs that had a vested interest in strengthening the role of the planned economy and maintaining their own bureaucratic power.

In contrast to such old conservatives who argued for centralization and against marketization, Hu and Wang argued in favor of centralization *and* marketization. As they put it, "reform does not necessarily mean weakening state capacity, and a market economy does not necessarily connote the elimination of state intervention; modernization certainly does not need a weak central government."[10] In making this case, Hu and Wang drew on the tradition in American political science that argues that "strong states" are important in establishing stable societies and bringing about rapid economic development.[11]

Hu and Wang's use of this political science literature stood the mainstream Chinese intellectual perspective of the 1980s on its head. In that decade, those who viewed themselves as reformers generally argued that it was necessary to break down the "overconcentration" of power in the central government on the grounds that the government stifled the development of market forces. For many, anything that undermined the power of the Stalinist state was *ipso facto* reform-oriented and marketizing. There were market-oriented reformers who dissented from this view – the best known of whom was economist Wu Jinglian – but both the realities of political contestation and the understanding of reform-minded economists led the Dengist state to adopt the decentralizing strategy known as "devolving authority and granting benefits" (*fangquan rangli*).[12]

Shortly after the publication of their report on state capacity, Hu Angang and Wang Shaoguang shifted their focus to the problem of regional inequalities, which had begun to draw increasing attention. From the beginning of the reform period, the central government had encouraged the provinces along the eastern seaboard to carry out reforms that were more far-ranging than those in the inland areas. This policy was reflected in the establishment of the first four Special Economic Zones (Shenzhen, Zhuhai, Shantou, and Xiamen) and the generous fiscal contracts given to Guangdong and Fujian

---

[10] Ibid., p. 54; emphasis in original.
[11] In addition to Migdal's and Zysman's works cited in note 1, other influential works in this tradition include Frederic C. Deyo (ed.), *The Political Economy of the New Asian Industrialization*; Peter Evans, *Embedded Autonomy*; Gary Gereffi and Donald L. Wyman (eds.), *Manufacturing Miracles*; Chalmers Johnson, *MITI and the Japanese Miracle*; and Peter Katzenstein (ed.), *Between Power and Plenty*.
[12] Wu Jinglian, "Guanyu gaige zhanlüe xuanze de ruogan sikao."

provinces. The Seventh Five-Year Plan (1986–90) formalized the strategy, and the policy of integrating the east coast into the international economy by putting "both ends on the outside" (*liangtou zaiwai* – i.e., importing raw materials and exporting finished products) further extended the policy. These policies clearly helped China's economic development, but they also brought about increasing inequalities as the eastern seaboard began to develop more quickly.

Following Tiananmen, the grievances of interior provinces were given greater voice, and the central government announced that it would adopt a "biased" or "slanting" (*qingxiang*) policy that would favor the interior. At the same time, the number of rural workers seeking employment in coastal cities grew significantly, drawing increased attention as rail lines were clogged (particularly around the lunar new year), shanty towns grew up, and crime rates increased.[13] Nevertheless, when Deng Xiaoping visited Shenzhen in 1992, he argued that the problem of regional differences need not be addressed too quickly: "Of course, it will not do to adopt this method [of the developed regions supporting the interior] too early. Now, we cannot weaken the vitality of the developed regions, and we cannot encourage 'eating from the common pot'."[14]

Hu Angang disagreed with this assessment and regarded growing regional inequalities as one of China's most important problems. Though regional differences raised questions of fairness, it is apparent that the more urgent problem in Hu's mind was that of social order.[15] Thus, he reported that a questionnaire given to provincial officials attending the Central Party School in 1994 showed that 84 percent identified social instability as the greatest problem generated by regional gaps; 16 percent feared such gaps could lead to national division.[16] As in their report on state capacity, Hu and Wang argued that regional inequalities cannot be left to the market, since the market alone might well increase rather than reduce income disparities. The government had an indispensable role to play.[17] A state could take effective action only if it had both a strong desire to address regional inequalities and a strong capacity to do so.[18] Thus, their research on regional inequalities reinforced their conclusions in the report on state capacity – namely, that the fiscal strength of the state needed to be increased and the

---

[13] Dorothy Solinger, *Contesting Citizenship in Urban China.*
[14] Deng Xiaoping, "Zai Wuchang, Shenzhen, Zhuhai, Shanghai dengdi de tanhua yaodian," p. 374.
[15] For their argument on fairness, see Hu Angang, Wang Shaoguang, and Kang Xiaoguang, *Zhongguo diqu chaju baogao*, pp. 292–303.
[16] Ibid., p. 542.   [17] Ibid., pp. 312–17, 337.   [18] Ibid., pp. 318–25.

strength of the state used to address the moral, social, and political problems presented by regional inequality.

Hu Angang and Wang Shaoguang opposed the negotiated relationship between the central government and the provinces (devolving authority and establishing fiscal contracts) because it had led, in their opinion, to the creation of privileged enclaves and vested interests with special privileges. The need to strengthen the state, implement a universal and centralized tax system, and establish the principle of "fair competition" among the various regions of China led them to argue that the most privileged of all enclaves – the Special Economic Zones – should be abolished. Hu Angang raised this issue in an internal report in early 1994. This argument was then picked up by the press, with the *Economic Daily* writing a series of articles from July 2 to July 6 under the title, "How Will the Special Zones Continue to Be Special?" In August, Hu expanded on the views he had previously expressed internally by writing in the Hong Kong paper *Ming pao*. According to Hu, no local authorities should have the right to reduce or waive central tax levies or to enjoy any extralegal, extrasystemic economic privileges. He also expounded his views in a lecture to provincial governors at the Central Party School in June.[19]

Hu's arguments touched off a major debate. The *Shenzhen Special Zone Journal* responded with a series of highly vitriolic and personal attacks on Hu, and the *Enlightenment Daily* ran an article arguing that the zones should be made even more special.[20] The crux of the responses was (1) that the SEZs were still necessary to introduce and experiment with various forms of management and government–enterprise relations and (2) that Hu's arguments did not take the realities of China into account, that to eliminate the SEZ's special role would amount to "contemporary egalitarianism": "The special zones' development does not hinder other regions. Their development and the development of other regions can only promote one another; they do not negate one another."[21] In June 1994 Jiang Zemin visited Shenzhen and tried to dampen the debate by declaring that the Party's and state's policies toward the SEZs had not changed. Nevertheless, Hu felt partial vindication when Zhu Rongji told Lee Hsien Loong (son of Singapore senior minister Lee Kuan Yew and later prime minister) in October of that year that, although the basic policies would remain unchanged, "some readjustment and improvement" was needed in specific measures.[22] The change in official

---

[19] Ibid., p. 541. See also Wang Shaoguang and Hu Angang, *The Political Economy of Uneven Development*.
[20] *Guangming ribao*, October 7, 1994.
[21] Cited in Zhu Tao, "A Brief Introduction to the Special Zones Debate," p. 44.
[22] Ibid., p. 46.

policy on regional differences was more palpable: the 1994 NPC meeting drew considerable attention to regional inequalities, Jiang Zemin explicitly called for reducing regional gaps in his speech to the Fifth Plenum in September 1995, and in 2000 the development of western China was made a major theme of the NPC meeting.[23]

Hu and Wang's criticisms of "devolving authority and granting benefits" and of regional inequalities were clearly intended as critiques of the Deng Xiaoping reform program, and in this sense their views were clearly a part of the broader intellectual reflection on the "failings" of the 1980s and particularly of the 1990s. Like other New Left intellectuals, Hu and Wang focused on the problem of social fairness, which was both a moral and a political issue. Social fairness was a moral issue in the general sense that reforms creating winners and losers also created a moral obligation to help those who lost from reform – as well as in the specific sense that growing income inequalities undermined the egalitarian commitments that underlay much of the Communist Party's claim to legitimacy. Social fairness was a political issue because, as Hu Angang argued, the sense of injustice was fueling social tensions and outbreaks of violence.[24]

The neostatist approach touted by Hu and Wang clearly resonates within the halls of government. Although influence is a notoriously difficult force to measure, there is reason to believe that their advocacy of tax reform played an important role in the reform of 1994. It is not that people in the government, particularly the Ministry of Finance, had not thought of implementing tax reform – indeed, Lou Jiwei was appointed vice-minister of finance largely to draft a reform of the tax system – but that Hu and Wang's report on state capacity packaged the idea in a compelling fashion that helped persuade political elites outside the ministry to accept ideas they had previously rejected. Hu has said that the report was first published in excerpted form by an internal publication of the Xinhua News Agency, *Domestic Trends, First Draft* (*Guonei dongtai qingyang*) in June 1993. This is a publication directed at provincial- and ministerial-level cadres. The report was subsequently reprinted in the Central Policy Research Office's publication *Internal Information* (*Neibu xinxi*), which is directed at the top leadership, and then, in a longer version, in the *People's Daily's* internal publication, *Internal Reference Reading* (*Neibu canyue*), which has a much wider circulation. Thus, Hu tried to influence government opinion at different levels by circulating his ideas through various internal publications, and these efforts certainly fed into the government's decision (in the summer

---

[23] *Xibu dakaifa zhanlüe juece ruogan wenti.*   [24] Cheng Li, "Promises and Pitfalls of Reform."

of 1993) to revamp the tax system.[25] Certainly the constant attention Hu and Wang have drawn to the problems of regional inequality and political instability have similarly influenced the government's willingness to address such issues, most recently in the decision to develop the west.

THE RESPONSE TO HUNTINGTON

Early neoconservative articles tried to explore a path that differed both in economic and political terms from the 1980s discourse of orthodoxy versus reform and centralization versus decentralization; likewise, the revival of interest in national studies and New Left critiques tried to carve out a path between "socialism" and "Westernization." This was a question both of political legitimacy – was the Chinese revolution wrong from the very start? – as well as of Chinese identity: did modernization mean Westernization?

Although many of these issues were implicit in much Chinese writing of the early 1990s, it was, ironically, Samuel Huntington's 1993 article in *Foreign Affairs*, "The Clash of Civilizations?," that really jelled the discussion and gave it focus. Of course, Huntington's article (and later book) did not fall on barren ground.[26] In Asia, as the region prospered economically, there was a growing consciousness of "Asian values" and their distinctiveness from – and sometimes opposition to – Western values. The book that heralded the debate over Asian values was Shintaro Ishihara's *The Japan That Can Say No*, published in 1989.[27]

Although Ishihara's book can be seen as the opening shot in this debate, the debate over Asian values accelerated following the end of the Cold War. Barely had the Cold War ended when Francis Fukuyama published his controversial 1989 article (and later book), "The End of History."[28] Fukuyama argued that, with the disintegration of the Soviet Union and collapse of Marxism–Leninism, the last great ideological debate of modern history had come to a close: the West had won. The post-Cold War world would be unified ideologically under Western neoclassical liberalism.

Not long after Fukuyama (a former member of the Policy Planning Staff at the Department of State) pronounced ideological victory, Anthony Lake, National Security Adviser in the first Clinton administration, gave his

---

[25] Hu Angang, "Background to Writing the Report on State Capacity," pp. 15–18.
[26] Samuel Huntington, "The Clash of Civilizations?"; Samuel Huntington, *The Clash of Civilizations*.
[27] Shintaro Ishihara, *The Japan That Can Say No*.
[28] Francis Fukuyama, "The End of History?"; Francis Fukuyama, *The End of History and the Last Man*. See also Francis Fukuyama, "A Reply to My Critics."

well-known speech on "democratic enlargement" at the School of Advanced International Studies of Johns Hopkins University. Building on the academic literature on "democratic peace," Lake turned theory into practice, arguing that the world would be a safer place if American policy could help foster democracies around the world.[29] At the same time, as the Cold War came to a close and as images of Tiananmen remained vivid in people's minds, human rights came to have a greater importance in US foreign policy. This was particularly the case when President Bush and National Security Adviser Brent Scowcroft, both schooled in realpolitik, left Washington to be replaced by people with a much more activist approach to human rights, including Anthony Lake, Secretary of State Warren Christopher, and Undersecretary of State for East Asian and Pacific Affairs Winston Lord. President Clinton endorsed this approach not only in his acceptance speech (not "coddl[ing] dictators, from Baghdad to Beijing") but also in his 1993 trip to Japan and South Korea.[30]

For many in Asia, these trends suggested an American triumphalism, even arrogance. Asian critics saw a very different world than Fukuyama and other exponents of American triumphalism. The United States had won the Cold War, but it appeared to have expended itself in the effort.[31] Crime rates were high, as were drug use, divorce, pornography, and other indicators of social malaise. The US economy appeared to be on the ropes, as growth rates declined and productivity stagnated. In 1988, the United States went from being the world's largest creditor nation to the world's largest debtor nation.

In contrast, Asia was at that time a study of economic prosperity and social order. Growth rates were high. Books in Western academe began to relate these high growth rates to Asian culture. "Confucian capitalism" became a hot topic, both in Asia and the West.[32] There was constant talk of Asia as the most dynamic region in the world, and there was great confidence that the twenty-first century would be the Pacific century, and particularly the Asian century. China, growing at double-digit rates, shared in this confidence. When the International Monetary Fund (IMF) in 1993 announced that China's economy, when measured in terms of purchasing price parity (PPP), was already the third largest economy in the world

---

[29] Anthony Lake, "From Containment to Engagement."
[30] William Jefferson Clinton, "Remarks to Students and Faculty of Waseda University"; William Jefferson Clinton, "Address to the National Assembly of the Republic of Korea."
[31] Asian critics approvingly cited Paul Kennedy's *The Rise and Fall of the Great Powers*, which suggested that the United States was engaged in "imperial overreach."
[32] Peter L. Berger and Hsin-Huang Michael Hsiao (eds.), *In Search of an East Asian Development Model.*

and would likely become the largest economy in the world by 2025, pride swelled.[33]

The curious incident of Michael Fay brought these various feelings together. The West loudly objected to the court-decreed caning of Michael Fay, an expatriate accused of vandalism, saying that such corporal punishment was a violation of human rights. Singapore senior minister Lee Kuan Yew relished the moment and lectured the United States. If only the United States would cane a few people, he suggested, US society would not be in such disarray.[34] Soon Malaysian Prime Minister Mohamad Mahathir joined with Shintaro Ishihara to write *The Voice of Asia*,[35] and the debate over Asian values was in full swing. It was into this atmosphere that Huntington launched his article.

Chinese responses to Huntington's article varied, but many took umbrage – seeing the article as a declaration of Western (and specifically American) superiority, or worse as racially tinged. As reviewed by Wang Hui, the editor of *Reading* whose views were discussed in the previous chapter, Huntington's essay reflected a "strong tendency toward Western cultural centrism" that "stimulated cultural nationalism" in China because it led many Chinese intellectuals to think "they were alien to Western cultures."[36]

The young nationalist Wang Xiaodong, writing under his pen name Shi Zhong, was one of those who expressed resentment. Like many contemporary Chinese who have come to view all ideological expressions as a cover for underlying interests, Wang argued that any clash between nations would be based not on civilization but on economic interest. Huntington's article was, Wang believed, an American defense of the status quo and a declaration that the West would not let China into the developed world.[37] In another article, Wang expressed the same thought more bluntly:

I have never believed that the US is really all that concerned with the human rights of the Chinese people . . . I also find it hard to believe that the pragmatic American people are willing to spend that much capital to surround us because we believe in Marxism. The reason that the US does not like us is because we are strong; we have the possibility of developing and then could be an obstacle to America's special place in the world.[38]

---

[33] International Monetary Fund, *World Economic Outlook*, 1993.
[34] Alejandro Reyes, "A Caning in Singapore Stirs Up a Fierce Debate about Crime and Punishment."
[35] Mohamad Mahathir and Shintaro Ishihara, *The Voice of Asia*.
[36] Wang Hui, "Wenhua pipan lilun yu dangdai Zhongguo minzu zhuyi wenti." In conversation, several people expressed to me the same view (albeit more bluntly), saying that Huntington's views "proved" that the West would never admit Asians – and particularly Chinese – as equals.
[37] Wang Xiaodong [Shi Zhong], "Weilai de chongtu."
[38] Wang Xiaodong [Shi Zhong], "Ping liangzhong butong de gaige guan."

More recently, Wang declared, "I think that Mr. Samuel P. Huntington is a racist, whose 'clash of civilizations' is nothing but a euphemism used instead of the politically incorrect 'clash of races'."[39]

Wang Huning, then about to move to Beijing to work with Jiang Zemin, offered a more subtle critique, one that reflected the cultural concerns taken up in New Left critiques. Wang connected Huntington's discussion of culture and cultural conflict to the notion of "soft power" discussed by Joseph Nye and others. Wang agreed with Nye that, with the end of the Cold War, the importance of "hard power" has declined while that of "soft power" has increased – but this did not necessarily make the world a less threatening place. Cultural arguments, Wang said, often reflected political interests and sometimes expanded into armed conflict (as in Bosnia–Herzegovina). Moreover, cultural influence was directly related to political and economic strength, so developed countries were often comfortable talking in terms of an "erosion of sovereignty" while developing countries found that such "cultural expansionism" often ended up threatening political stability and national sovereignty. Furthermore, cultural influence was directly related to the construction of international norms and regimes, which were not always in the best interest of the developing nations. As Wang put it in a passage that suggests his familiarity with postcolonial criticism:

If one nation-state is able to make its power appear reasonable in the eyes of another people, then its desires will encounter less resistance. If the culture and ideology of one nation-state is attractive, other people will voluntarily follow it. If one nation is able to establish international norms [*guifan*] that are consistent with its domestic society, there is no need for it to change itself. If one nation-state is able to support an international regime, and other nation-states are all willing to go through this regime to coordinate their activities, then it [the first nation-state] has no need to pay the high price of hard power.

Cultural imperialism, in short, is a cheap way of achieving the goals that states formerly employed hard power to attain.[40]

As Wang Huning's argument suggests, many in China saw Huntington's thesis from the perspective of ongoing discussions of "Orientalism," believing that there was a need to strengthen Chinese culture in order to meet the challenge of the clash of civilizations.[41] Others sought to meet this challenge by bolstering Chinese culture with nationalism. Jiang Yihua, a senior scholar at Fudan University in Shanghai, viewed Huntington's argument

[39] Wang Xiaodong [Shi Zhong], "The West in the Eyes of a Chinese Nationalist," p. 20.
[40] Wang Huning, "Wenhua guozhang yu wenhua zhuquan," p. 356.
[41] Zhang Kuan, "Zaitan Sayide."

through the lens of China's past: "The bitter history of Asian countries over more than a century shows that the countries of the West that came to Asia established a bloody colonial ruling order or semi-colonial ruling order. They never really supported the nations of Asia to 'enter the West' economically, politically, or culturally . . . [W]hat they brought to Asia was primarily colonial culture." Jiang viewed Huntington's argument about the clash of civilizations and his extolling of Western values as universal values[42] as a continuation of this imperialist past. Having escaped the "cultural hegemonism" of the West, China would not now accept Western values as its own.[43]

WANG SHAN AND EMERGENCE OF POPULIST NATIONALISM

The previous discussion dealt with the way in which a number of influential intellectuals responded to China's domestic and international situation in the 1990s. Some of these responses, such as the neostatism of Hu Angang and Wang Shaoguang, had a palpable influence on the political system, but most were explorations among an intellectual elite with no direct connection to politics. Nevertheless, as we have suggested, many of these discussions contained a populist element – whether it was Wang Xiaodong's excoriation of the cultural elite who authored and directed *River Elegy*, He Xin's efforts to rally support for a beleaguered government, or the economic democracy touted by Cui Zhiyuan and many others. If populism was in the air, no one had yet tapped this vein to show that their ideas actually had popular support.

That changed in 1994 with the publication of *Looking at China through a Third Eye*. The author turned out to be Wang Shan, a young writer whose persona is reminiscent of that of Wang Shuo, the popular chronicler of the underbelly of urban life. Like Wang Shuo, Wang Shan had already written a first novel, *Tian Shang* (*Heaven's Elegy*), that depicted a world of hooliganism, incorporating traditional notions that there was a code of honor among that underclass that contrasted favorably with values of their social betters. When an interviewer suggested to Wang that his novels give people the impression that he is a sort of hooligan from the lower classes and that he hates the upper classes, Wang replied that Chinese society has always been divided into an upper class (*shangliu*) and a lower

---

[42] It should be noted that Huntington denies this. It is not clear whether Jiang misread Huntington or rather (more likely) supplied this interpretation despite Huntington's actual words.

[43] Jiang Yihua, "Lun dongya xiandaihua jinchengzhong de xinlixing zhuyi wenhua."

class (*xialiu*); elsewhere he comments that he represents the lower ranks of officialdom.[44]

Born in 1952, Wang was the youngest of those known as *laosanjie*, the three classes (which "graduated" from high school in 1966, 1967, and 1968) who made up the Red Guard generation and were sent to the country-side when Mao had seen enough of the chaos they had generated. Wang went to Shanxi province in 1968, where he labored in the fields for a year before going to work in a coal mine. In 1970, perhaps using his father's connections (his father was a military cadre), Wang joined the PLA, where he served for seven years. In the 1980s, he became director of the Great Wall Social Research Institute (*Changcheng shehui yanjiusuo*). Wang seems to be an unsatisfied and intemperate person; his literary agent noted that Wang switched jobs frequently, and "always inexplicably ended by being fired."[45]

Wang declared that the greatest influences on his thinking were a "sense of responsibility" bequeathed by his father's generation to carry on the task of the revolution and the "heroic thought" (*yingxiong zhuyi sichao*) of tempering oneself through struggle, something he apparently cultivated during the Cultural Revolution.[46] Unlike most of those older than himself, Wang obviously retained a romantic attachment to the Cultural Revolution and to the figure of Mao Zedong, a passion that flared up with Deng's trip to the south in 1992 and the resulting wave of speculation. Wang saw 1992 as a dividing line. Before then, all strata of Chinese society had gained from reform; after that, power and the market merged so that one stratum exploited another.[47] As Wang's friend and literary agent Xu Bing put it, prior to 1992, Wang was a "determined and wildly enthusiastic supporter of reform," but by the spring and summer of that year "his support became rational and conditional."[48]

Wang was not alone in his doubts about the course of reform. We have cited the views of many people who had begun to reconsider the course of reform beginning in the 1990s, but such doubts – even the discussions of the new authoritarianism – were carried out in intellectual and political circles. Wang was not an intellectual, at least not in the sense of belonging to those in government, think-tanks, and universities who thought and wrote for each other. Wang was an outsider who claimed few friends in intellectual circles.[49] What Wang Shan did was to make his doubts public

---

[44] Liu Zhifeng, "Disizhi yanjing kan Zhongguo," pp. 302, 304.
[45] Xu Bing, "Wang Shan qi ren," p. 61.   [46] Liu Zhifeng (ed.), *Jieshi Zhongguo*, pp. 298–9.
[47] Xu Bing, "Wang Shan qi ren," p. 38.   [48] Ibid., pp. 50–1.
[49] Liu Zhifeng, "Disizhi yanjing kan Zhongguo," p. 303.

by writing what became an instant best seller; in so doing, Wang showed that his doubts were widely shared among the urban population.

The cover of *Looking at China through a Third Eye* identifies one "Luo yi ning ge er" as the author. In the preface, "Luo yi ning ge er" is identified as a German and as Europe's most famous Sinologist. Wang had chosen the name from a dictionary that transliterated foreign names. Germany had the attraction of having produced well-known intellectuals over the years, thus providing an air of *gravitas*, and was also neutral regarding Chinese affairs and hence capable of seeing China's situation "objectively" as a bystander (the implication that "a third eye" was supposed to convey). Attributing authorship to a foreigner may also have permitted the book to be published more easily; it certainly aroused interest and curiosity, much as Joe Klein's attribution of his book *Primary Colors* to "Anonymous" did in the United States. Most important, it attracted buyers and made the book the object of conversation and speculation for months.[50]

What made *Looking at China through a Third Eye* a powerful polemic, however, was its linking of urban anxieties to a systematic critique of the Dengist reforms. Wang strikes hard at urban anxieties by talking in ominous terms about the growing tide of peasants entering the cities. Anyone who flips through Chinese history, Wang declares, will discover that without exception all of China's dynasties have been destroyed by peasants who left the land. They are a "powder keg" and a "living volcano" that have unleashed a wave of criminal activity in the cities and present a serious danger to the political stability of China.[51]

Having raised the specter of peasant violence, Wang unfolds a sympathetic picture of Mao Zedong, contrasting Mao's policies favorably with those of Deng. As unbelievable as it is, Wang pictures Mao – the person who unleashed the Great Leap Forward and brought about the death of perhaps 30 million Chinese – as the only leader who truly understood the peasants. Wang argues that Mao was basically sympathetic to the peasants, but the task of modernization forced Mao to sacrifice their interests in favor of industrialization. By keeping peasants (described as "lacking in education and full of traditional rebelliousness") "locked docilely" on the land and by "squeezing the peasants' stomachs," Mao was able to pursue industrialization for three decades and was able to turn China into a nuclear power. Had he not done so, says Wang derisively, "today China would

[50] See Yang Ping, "The Third Eye – Commenting on *Seeing China through a Third Eye*"; Sha Feng, "Ultraleftists within CCP Launch Comeback by Criticizing Five New Rightists"; and Tseng Hui-yen, "*Looking at China with a Third Eye* Reportedly Written by Pan Yue."

[51] Wang Shan [Luo yi ning ge er], *Disanzhi yanjing kan Zhongguo*, pp. 28, 62–3.

look like India."[52] Mao tried to transform the peasants, but after the Great Leap Forward they revealed their "spontaneous capitalist tendencies" and challenged the Party through their laziness, migration, and black markets, confirming Mao's fears that rural society was a "hotbed of spontaneous disease and germs." In the end, Wang suggests, it was the peasants who betrayed Mao and not the other way around, but then "we often find that Chinese simply do not understand or love their leader, Mao Zedong."[53]

Reflecting the same resentment of China's cultural elite as Wang Xiaodong, Wang Shan declares in *A Third Eye* that intellectuals lack the "knowledge, experience, ability, character, and prestige" to participate effectively in government and push forward the democratization of the country.[54] The history of China's various democratic movements, beginning with the Hundred Flowers Movement in 1957, shows that owing to the lack of maturity of China's intellectuals, their struggles have failed to promote the causes for which they strove. In 1957, Wang declares, intellectuals went too far. Mao wanted an "open door" rectification campaign in order to check the unbridled power of the bureaucrats. When accusations were raised against people in the Party, they apologized for their wrongdoing, "but this only whetted the ambitions of intellectuals. Students in Beijing and Shanghai started to leave their campuses. An incident had the possibility of evolving into a destructive riot. Thereupon, Mao could not but take action."[55] The intellectuals, like the peasants, were not worthy of Mao. The "tragic history of 1957," Wang writes, proved that "the intellectuals created by China's old culture and civilization . . . are born with faults that they cannot overcome. Because of this, they cannot unite with the ruling Party, the state power, and the primary forces that are leading the people forward and thereby bring their great ability to bear."[56]

Wang also casts a sympathetic eye on the Cultural Revolution, particularly on Mao's motivations in initiating it. In striking contrast to the Mao who is known to the West and older intellectuals in China, Wang depicts him as a benevolent, idealistic leader, one even given at times to sentimentalism. Wang describes Mao as having been "like a good and patient family head, thinking of the whole country as a 'large family'." He also declares that "Mao was a god, and people are perhaps only beginning to understand him several years later."[57] Mao's initiation of the Cultural Revolution is depicted as the effort of an idealist to overcome the gap between the common people and officials; his motive was to pre-empt the political crises

---

[52] Ibid., pp. 34, 37, 40.   [53] Ibid., pp. 39, 40, 45.   [54] Ibid., p. 88.
[55] Ibid., p. 92.   [56] Ibid., pp. 93–4.   [57] Ibid., pp. 78, 167.

that certainly would have erupted from such an elitist system by bringing about a non-bureaucratic, classless, and democratic society. The tragedy of Mao was that Chinese society did not have the conditions for such a democratic society and thus his effort failed.[58] But Mao, the author argues, was not wrong in his initial motivation; the mistakes that resulted in tragedy occurred later (and were largely the fault of Jiang Qing and Lin Biao). Indeed, Wang suggests that "people may discover that some ideas from the Cultural Revolution are wise and prescient."[59]

Wang's assessment of Mao is certainly related to (one is tempted to say derived from) his evaluation of contemporary China. *A Third Eye* argues that the reform period eroded faith in Marxism–Leninism, undermined the power and authority of the Party and state, and unleashed a host of social problems – including corruption, crime, economic polarization, and moral decay – that the government, given its weakened authority, is increasingly unable to deal with. Unless something is done to reverse the erosion of state authority, the author maintains, China will find itself beset by political and social turmoil. Ideology is important for Wang. He declares that "[a] society without faith is in danger"[60] and argues that the Dengist reforms have progressively eroded Maoist ideology until there is nothing left to inspire people and unify the nation:[61]

As soon as one problem is solved, another emerges. As soon as the traditional ideology of Mao Zedong's idealism begins to be broken, then the government's defense line must retreat step by step. Local governments continuously extend their hands asking for new "policies" and the central government has no choice but to compromise in the face of solving new problems. China's economic structural reform was really created in this way. Now, when we look back, what is left of Mao's inheritance? How much is left? Deng Xiaoping has repeatedly said that the four cardinal principles must be upheld, but how much has really been upheld?

For all of Wang Shan's disdain of officialdom and intellectuals (whom he accuses of being destructive), he is clearly in favor of autocracy. In an interview, writer Liu Zhifeng says, "[y]ou hint that China needs a god like Mao Zedong, a great idol"; Wang replies, "[y]es, but I can't easily say this." Liu continues: "My understanding is that you are saying that China needs a period of rule by man, of elite rule, and cannot very quickly institute rule by law." Wang's response: "Yes, elite rule. Rule by law is unreliable."[62]

Wang's desire for elite rule is rooted in his passion for stability. For all of his expressed sympathy for the Cultural Revolution, Wang declares that he wants China to "improve" (*gailiang*) rather than "reform" (*gaige*) for

---

[58] Ibid., pp. 100, 106, 150.   [59] Ibid., p. 176.   [60] Ibid., p. 211.   [61] Ibid., p. 61.
[62] Liu Zhifeng, "Disizhi yanjing kan Zhongguo," p. 312.

fear that reform will be too destabilizing.[63] As he puts it: "What I fear most is that as soon as revolutionary thought or theories are imported into China they will stimulate the division of strata, which has already started, and bring about a destructive revolution. China needs stability."[64] In order to enhance stability and stop the decline in morals in society, Wang unabashedly favors raising high the banner of communism, "so that it becomes the banner flying above our heads and becomes our common faith (*xinyang*) and religion (*zongjiao*)."[65]

Wang's diagnosis of China's social ills and his hope that the CCP could provide stability in a period of transition is related to an unabashed nationalism. Wang makes clear his belief that the student demonstrations of spring 1989 were encouraged and supported (if not instigated) by the United States and were aimed at overthrowing the CCP because America feared China's nuclear power.[66] Like other nationalists, he asserts not only that the United States is in moral and social decline but also that the cure to the ills generated by an "economic mechanism flooded with liberalism" could only lie in the East.[67]

STRATEGY AND MANAGEMENT

In late 1993, a new journal called *Strategy and Management* (*Zhanlüe yu guanli*) started publication and quickly became a forum for new and often critical ideas, including nationalism and populism. Even the physical appearance of *Strategy and Management* suggested a journal that differed significantly from the hundreds of academic journals normally circulating in China. It is printed on far better paper than the average journal, indicating its substantial financial backing – reputedly contributed by a wealthy overseas Chinese from Thailand but also suggesting its support from the military. The "honorary director" was former PLA Chief of Staff Xiao Ke, the director was former Secretariat member Gu Mu, and the "senior advisers" included such luminaries as retired general Zhang Aiping, former *People's Daily* editor-in-chief Qin Chuan, former State Economic Commission head Yuan Baohua, and former Secretariat member Yan Mingfu.[68] The editor of *Strategy and Management* was Qin Chaoying, son of the

---

[63] Ibid., p. 316.   [64] Ibid., p. 318.   [65] Ibid., p. 330.
[66] Wang Shan [Lo yi ning ge er], *Disanzhi yanjing kan Zhongguo*, pp. 7–8, 24.   [67] Ibid., p. 25.
[68] It is not clear whether – and, if so, to what extent – *Strategy and Management* is supported by the military. Some say it does have military backing; others maintain that it does not. In any event, it seems that the journal enjoys substantial editorial freedom and thus has the character of a non-official (*minjian*) publication. It was assigned a new editor in the summer of 1998 and became more liberal in orientation. Some say that its nationalism was too far out of line with official policy, triggering the editorial change. The journal was shut down in 2004.

former editor-in-chief of the *People's Daily*, Qin Chuan, but the editorial direction came primarily from Yang Ping and Wang Xiaodong. As noted in Chapter 3, Yang Ping was the chief drafter of "Realistic Responses" in 1991 and had served as an editor of *China Youth Daily*, one of the most popular papers in the country. Yang Ping was interested in exploring various nationalist and neoconservative ideas as a way for China to overcome what he and many others saw as the problems generated by the reforms of the 1980s. As "Realistic Responses" and the editorial board of *Strategy and Management* suggested, this was a group of youth who were well connected with higher-ups in the Party but who were also frustrated by what they regarded as the lack of new ideas and forceful leadership of the Party. The different perspective of this group stemmed in part from generational differences and in part from their self-identification with the common people. Yang Ping and Wang Xiaodong brought to their editorial direction a strong sense of nationalism, a desire to see a strong state that expressed that nationalism, and a sense of populism that made them sometimes quite critical of the existing government. Although many outside observers label them "neoconservatives," they reject that label and instead see themselves as "true liberals" or as part of the New Left (*xin zuopai*).

Although by 1993 there were many articles that expressed nationalistic sentiments, few journals took on the topic of nationalism directly and openly. *Strategy and Management* did just that in a symposium in the June 1994 issue. The articles were not particularly inflammatory – certainly much less so than Wang Shan's book *Looking at China through a Third Eye*, published later the same year – but they did raise some important issues.[69] For instance, Pi Mingyong (from the Academy of Military Sciences) argued that nationalism had been a difficult issue in twentieth-century China because it was necessarily compromised. The "great nationalism" of the Han Chinese conflicted with the "small nationalism" of the minority nationalities, Pi wrote, while the anti-traditionalism of the nationalistic May Fourth Movement denigrated the history of the very people it hoped to lift up. Therefore, the Chinese government had always adopted an ambiguous policy that tried to use the strengths of nationalism without incurring its weaknesses.[70] Yin Baoyun (from Beijing University) argued that nationalism was a vital component of economic development but that many Third-World countries had encountered difficulties because they emphasized culturalism, racism,

---

[69] For instance, Wang Yizhou's article, "Minzu zhuyi gainian de xiandai sikao" (Contemporary reflections on the concept of nationalism) is a solid academic discussion of nationalism without any effort to tout Chinese nationalism.

[70] Pi Mingyong, "Zhongguo jindai minzu zhuyi de duozhong jiagou."

or localism, neglecting the pride and progressive spirit of nationalism. Korea's Park Chung Hee provided a positive example of how nationalism could be used to bolster economic development.[71]

Another major theme in the pages of *Strategy and Management* was populism. Like nationalism, populism was not something that was widely discussed in the open press in the early 1990s. Thus, a symposium on populism in late 1994 gave high-profile attention to this important topic. Sun Liping, a professor in the Sociology Department of Beijing University, made the point that much of Maoist rhetoric and practice was populist. The rhetorical status given to peasants and workers, the egalitarian distribution system, the effort to eliminate income differences across regions, the commune movement during the Great Leap Forward, and the criticism of Soviet "revisionism" and of "bourgeois rights" during the Cultural Revolution all reflected populist values. So even though the political system was hierarchical and authoritarian, populism was very much a part of the CCP's tradition.[72] Hu Weixi (of Qinghua University) pushed this analysis back further, noting that the "national essence" movement (*guocui yundong*), the anarchist movement, and the rural reconstruction movement in the first half of the twentieth century – despite all their differences – shared a populist orientation.[73] Although discussed in a historical vein, their concerns were clearly contemporary.

CHINA CAN SAY NO

The growing sense of popular nationalism reflected in the publication of *Looking at China through a Third Eye* was confirmed with a vengeance by the 1996 publication of *China Can Say No*. Whereas *A Third Eye* focused primarily on domestic social and political issues with a nationalistic slant, *China Can Say No* was an unabashed outpouring of nationalistic feeling with little attention to domestic issues. Hastily written and published, the five young authors were taking advantage of the anti-American sentiment that had welled up in the wake of the 1995–6 Taiwan Straits crisis and the dispatch of two American carrier task forces to the area. In writing a nationalistic best seller, the authors of *China Can Say No* demonstrated

---

[71] Yin Baoyun, "Minzu zhuyi yu xiandai jingji fazhan."

[72] Sun Liping, "Pingmin zhuyi yu Zhongguo gaige." It should be noted that "populism" can be translated into Chinese several ways; *pingmin zhuyi* ("common people-ism") and *mincui zhuyi* ("people essence-ism") are most common. The former captures the sense of class conflict while the latter invokes a sense of *volk*.

[73] Hu Weixi, "Zhongguo jinxiandai de shehui zhuanxing yu mincui zhuyi."

that the same broadening of mass culture that had previously been evident in popular literature, television, and the entertainment industry was also available for political mobilization.

China Can Say No was striking not just because of its highly emotional tone but also because the authors all claimed to have been strongly influenced by the United States, only to have become disillusioned in the 1990s. They cited US efforts to block China's bid to host the 2000 Olympics, the *Yin He* incident, opposition to China's GATT/WTO bid, the Taiwan issue (especially Lee Teng-hui's visit to the US), American support for Tibet, and alleged CIA activity in China to account for their changed attitudes.[74] They had come to realize, they claimed, that the United States was not the bastion of idealism that it claimed to be; "human rights" was merely a façade behind which America pursued its national interests. In fact, far from championing ideals in the world, the United States was an arrogant, narcissistic, hegemonic power that acted as a world policeman; now it was doing everything in its power to keep China from emerging as a powerful and wealthy country.[75]

There is no doubting the support for publishing *China Can Say No* within government circles: Yu Quanyu, then the very conservative deputy head of China's Human Rights Commission and a frequent contributor to China's left-wing journals, endorsed the book in an afterword. But it is equally evident, and perhaps more important, that there was a mass audience for such works.

Although many intellectuals pointed out that the book was shallow, poorly written, and overly emotional, it is also apparent that many read it and perhaps even enjoyed the venting of the frustration that they shared (though perhaps not to the same degree). The book quickly sold almost two million copies. The authors soon followed with a sequel,[76] and imitators sprouted up "like bamboo shoots after a spring rain."[77] Within government circles, it appears that there was at first a sense that someone had finally expressed their frustrations with the United States. One reason was that many government officials share – even if on a more sophisticated level – the authors' view that US actions are guided by national interest, that concern with human rights is a smoke screen for opposing China, and that US

---

[74] Song Qiang, Zhang Zangzang, and Qiao Bian, *Zhongguo keyi shuobu*, pp. 36, 62, 71, 77, 143, 147, 186, 243.

[75] Ibid., pp. 34, 140, 312, 316, 322, 326.   [76] Song Qiang et al., *Zhongguo haishi neng shuobu*.

[77] See Liu Kang and Li Xiguang, *Yaomo Zhongguo de beihou*; Peng Qian, Yang Mingjie, and Xu Deren, *Zhongguo weishenma shuobu?*; Zhang Xueli, *Zhongguo heyi shuobu*; Li Shuyi and Yong Jianxiong (eds.), *Ershiyi shiji Zhongguo jueqi*; He Jie, Wang Baoling, and Wang Jianji (eds.), *Wo xiangxin Zhongguo*; and He Degong, Pu Weizhong, and Jin Yong, *Qingxiang Zhongguo*.

policy is based on containment and/or subversion. Moreover, government officials had endured years of abuse at the hands of US columnists. "Let the United States taste some of its own medicine" seems to have been a fairly common sentiment.

That anti-American sentiments were widespread at the time is supported not only by sales figures but also by survey research. Public opinion on foreign policy questions is a politically sensitive topic, and few surveys are allowed (or allowed to be published). One exception was the well-known survey done by Wang Xiaodong, Fang Ning, and others at *China Youth Daily*, which has been conducting investigations of youth attitudes since the mid-1990s.[78] Taking advantage of the fiftieth anniversary of the end of the war against Japan, *China Youth Daily* conducted a large-scale public opinion poll in May of 1995; it found that 87.1 percent of respondents believed the United States was the country "least friendly" to China, while 57.2 percent indicated that the United States was the country toward which they felt most negative. Reflecting cynicism about American motives, 85.4 percent believed that the United States engaged in the Gulf War "out of its own interests."[79] A concluding essay argued that the nationalism reflected in the survey showed that China "still has hope." Setting the results of the survey against recent discussions of globalization, the author (or authors) declared – in the best realist tradition – that the world was still divided into nation-states; the dividing line separating nation-states was far stronger than any other, including (with reference to Huntington) culture. However, the article concluded that one division did not fall neatly into the realist paradigm: that between the "haves" and the "have-nots." The West, the article explained, is guided by self-interest; it fears both that the rest of the world is too poor, which might induce those in poorer nations to immigrate to the West, and that the rest of the world is too prosperous, which would "threaten their [the West's] superiority." Those in the "have-not" camp, the article asserted, "love our camp, love our China." China should have no illusions about the West.[80]

---

[78] See *Zhongguo qingnian bao*, February 1, 1997, for a five-part series on survey research and its uses.

[79] *Beijing qingnian bao*, July 14, 1995, p. 8. The United States was not the only target of Chinese popular opprobrium. One survey of Chinese attitudes toward Japan, conducted at the end of 1996, surprised even the surveyors. For example, the word "Japan" "most easily" made 83.9 percent of the youth surveyed think of the Nanjing massacre and made 81.3 percent think of "Japanese denial" and the "war of resistance against Japanese aggression." When asked which Japanese in the twentieth century is most representative of Japan, first place (28.7 percent) went to Tojo Hideki, of World War Two fame. When asked to place a label on the Japanese, 56.1 percent chose "cruel" – the most frequently chosen personality trait. See *Zhongguo qingnian bao*, March 18, 1997, trans. FBIS-CHI-97-094, May 16, 1997.

[80] "Miandui 'shengtu de yingdi'."

China Can Say No was widely popular and influential. Reviewing the results of a survey of reading habits, researchers concluded: "It is worth paying attention to the great influence on readers of the thinly veiled (*lugu*) discussion of nationalist sentiment (*minzu zhuyi qingxu*) with regard to international relations in this popular literature"; they also noted that *China Can Say No* "unexpectedly" (*juran*) was the most influential book in the post-1993 period.[81] It is important to observe another side to *China Can Say No* that was apparent to Chinese readers but has been largely ignored in the United States: the populism of the book had a distinctly anti-government tone to it as well. The authors charged that the Chinese government had been naive and soft in its dealings with the United States, that it should be more forthright in just saying "no," and that the government was neither confident enough nor competent enough – it was too wrapped up in the past and insufficiently bold in engineering China's modernization.[82] *China Can Say No* had a populist edge that was highly skeptical of the government. Government officials may have welcomed an expression of nationalism, but they also realized that it was something that could be turned against them, as it had been so many times in the twentieth century.

[81] See Kang Xiaoguang, Wu Yulun, Liu Dehuan, and Sun Hui, *Zhongguoren dushu toushi*, pp. 52–9.
[82] Song et al., *Zhongguo keyi shuobu*, pp. 64, 90, 165.

PART III

Elite politics and popular nationalism

CHAPTER 6

Jiang Zemin's rise to power

The Introduction addressed the issue of the state and intellectuals in broad terms; we are now in a position to consider the issue more specifically. As we saw in the first two chapters, elite politics in the immediate aftermath of Tiananmen was an inside game. This was a period in which a relatively small number of political elites sharply contested the basic issues of the day: the definition (in terms of policy) of reform and opening up, and the relative balance of power between Deng Xiaoping and likeminded reformers on the one hand and Chen Yun and ideological and economic conservatives on the other. Intellectuals had an extremely limited role in this period. Economists could and did advise the government to "increase the weight of reform," but a fundamental re-evaluation of the importance of the market economy had to wait for Deng Xiaoping's trip to the south in 1992 and the subsequent convocation of the Fourteenth Party Congress.

If intellectuals were excluded from meaningful political participation in this period, they nevertheless began a painful process of re-evaluating the course of reform, what had led to the tragedy of Tiananmen, and the role of intellectuals in contemporary China. As a result, a very different intellectual atmosphere began to emerge in the 1990s. This new intellectual discourse was largely independent of politics, a genuinely societal discourse. However, unlike the discourse that grew up in the late 1980s whose participants came to confront the government, many intellectuals in the 1990s found themselves implicitly or explicitly more supportive of the government than they or their counterparts had been only a few years before. The prospect of governmental collapse and social chaos, the object lesson provided by the economic decline in Eastern Europe and the subsequent disintegration of the Soviet Union, a newfound respect for the complexity of reform and state building, and (especially after 1993) a new sense of nationalism – as well as the costs of continuing opposition – inclined many intellectuals to be more tolerant and even supportive of government efforts.

Disillusionment with radical reform (indeed with radicalism in general), consternation with the inequalities that reform had brought to China, and a growing frustration with American triumphalism – not to mention American actions – supported new efforts to rethink the course of reform. Could there be a model of reform that preserved China's identity, avoided the economic and political inequalities associated with capitalism, and yet developed the economy? As we have seen, much of this reflection was rooted in discussions of the new authoritarianism in the 1980s, and found expression in many forms: the neoconservatism of Wang Huning, Xiao Gongqin, Chen Yuan, and He Xin; the New Left writings of Wang Hui and Cui Zhiyuan; the neostatism of Hu Angang and Wang Shaoguang; and the populist nationalism of Wang Shan, Wang Xiaodong, and the authors of *China Can Say No*.

This new atmosphere tended to push democratic activists to the margins of Chinese intellectual and social life. Whereas Western commentators continued to view the image of the lone person standing in front of a column of tanks as emblematic of the aspirations of the Chinese people, more and more Chinese saw that person as symbolizing the excessive romanticism of the 1980s reform movement. A new sobriety came to the fore, and the economic progress and social stability of the early and mid-1990s seemed to vindicate a new authoritarian or neoconservative approach to reform – especially in view of the problems the Russian Republic continued to experience. Although the more conservative intellectual atmosphere associated with neoconservatism, the New Left, and nationalism developed largely independently of government direction (though the government certainly permitted the development of such discourse), government officials – particularly from the mid-1990s onward – frequently shared many, though not all, of the attitudes of such intellectuals. This was, after all, a government that believed it had to forge ahead with economic reform without questioning the official judgment on Tiananmen, a government that needed to deal with many of the social, economic, and political problems that had given rise to the more conservative intellectual atmosphere in the first place: growing regional inequality, income polarization, central–provincial relations, corruption, internal migration, crime, tense Sino–US relations, and so on. To the extent that there was a common interest in problem solving, intellectuals could, by the mid-1990s, take up roles as advisers. The roles of Hu Angang and Wang Shaoguang are illustrative in this regard.

The interests of critical intellectuals and mainstream government officials, however, diverged on at least two major issues. First, the government continued to back marketizing reforms, a growing role for the private sector, and increasing integration into the global economic order. Whether because of the semireformed nature of the system or the specific interests of the people involved, these reforms often contributed to the corruption, abuse of power, and income inequality that made so many intellectuals skeptical of capitalist solutions. Even as the government pushed forward with what most outside observers believed to be necessary, if painful, reforms, intellectuals decried the social injustices created.

Second, although the government shared and encouraged the nationalism of many intellectuals, it did not share the populism. Populism, as we have noted, was inevitably directed against the government elite, and as the critical perspectives of New Left intellectuals blended with the popular nationalism of people like Wang Xiaodong, a powerful critique emerged of a weak and corrupt government selling out the Chinese people in the interests of the government and international corporations. This was a critique that mostly festered in intellectual circles, but it could on occasion – most notably, following the US bombing of the Chinese Embassy in Belgrade – burst into full view.

Increasingly, the Chinese government has been forced to take this critical public opinion into account – not only because of the mobilizing potential inherent in it but also because there are political leaders and interests that support these views. Thus, intellectual critique plays into "oppositional politics." The result is that the government has increasingly had to engage its critics in the public arena. This is not (or at least not yet) the long-hoped-for emergence of a "public sphere" in China, but it does suggest that the days of government pronouncements and media "education" of public opinion have passed. Not only is there now a more obvious dialogue between state and society, but the scope of this dialogue has widened significantly. Only a few years ago, no public discussion of foreign policy was allowed. Wang Shan's *Looking at China through a Third Eye* smashed that taboo, and now books and journals are filled with critiques of official policy. It was only natural – given the role that concern with globalization played in stimulating the discussions of the New Left examined in Chapter 4 – that China's participation in the WTO became a major point of intellectual dissension.

We will examine in this and the following chapters some of the ways in which intellectual concerns have intersected with elite politics. Here, we turn our attention back to high politics and particularly to the process through which Jiang Zemin consolidated his authority. It will be recalled that, in looking at the period immediately following Tiananmen, Jiang Zemin was not much of a factor; although general secretary, the main fight was taking place well above his head. To the extent that he did speak out, he was extremely cautious – and thus incurred the wrath of Deng Xiaoping. By 1994, however, the situation had changed significantly. Deng's trip to the south had set off a new round of rapid economic growth and reform, while Zhu Rongji's appointment as vice-premier had placed a solid reformer in charge of the economy, effectively eclipsing Premier Li Peng. Moreover, the actuarial tables were beginning to have an important impact on elite politics. Jiang's closest political supporter, former president Li Xiannian, died in June 1992, followed soon thereafter by the Party's most authoritative ideologue, Hu Qiaomu, in September 1992. Chen Yun was apparently quite ill in 1994 and finally died in April 1995. Deng Xiaoping's health was also failing; when he was shown on television watching fireworks during the October 1 National Day celebration in 1995, the Chinese public was shocked to see an old man staring out blankly. Everyone knew the end could not be far away. Thus, by 1994, it was apparent that a political transition of enormous importance was unfolding.

THE FOURTH PLENUM: EMERGENCE OF THE "THIRD GENERATION"

The Fourth Plenary Session of the Fourteenth Central Committee convened in Beijing on September 25–28, 1994. The session was devoted to issues of Party building, particularly "democratic centralism." Previously, the plenum had been scheduled to discuss the economy as well; however, in what may well have been his last intervention in politics, Deng suggested that economic issues be dropped from the agenda.[1] It was not that there were no economic issues worth discussing. On the contrary, the economy took a serious turn for the worse in 1994. In the spring, the NPC had approved a commitment to keep inflation under 10 percent (down somewhat from the 13 percent registered in 1993). By the summer, it was obvious that the goal could not be attained, and in August the NPC Standing Committee announced that inflation would be kept under 15 percent. The year would end with a yearly inflation rate of 21.7 percent.[2]

If inflation was disturbing, the performance of the state-owned economy was even more so. By September, some 44 percent of SOEs were losing money, "triangular debts" had ballooned to 400 billion yuan, and about

---

[1] Reportedly, Deng in September instructed that the plenum concentrate on democratic centralism. See Jen Hui-wen, "What Is the 'Bottom Line' of CCP Political Reform?"
[2] Ling Zhijun, *Chenfu*, pp. 388–428.

80 percent of SOE income went to debt service.[3] In mid-September, the State Statistical Bureau issued a report in which it said that China's economy was on the verge of entering the "red zone," indicating severe trouble. This was only the third time such a report had been issued; previous reports had come in the summer of 1988 and the spring of 1993.[4]

The decision to focus the plenum on democratic centralism thus reflected Deng Xiaoping's declining health and a decision to declare openly the passing of leadership to a new generation, and particularly to Jiang Zemin. Deng and other top leaders were most worried about three interrelated problems: the authority of the CCP vis-à-vis society, the authority of the center vis-à-vis the localities, and the authority of Jiang Zemin vis-à-vis his colleagues in the leadership. All three problems revolved around the question of whether Jiang could become the "core" of the Party in reality as well as name. The term *core* can perhaps best be understood as that combination of informal and formal authority that makes a leader the final arbiter of Party issues – the ability, as the Chinese put it, to "strike the table" (*pai banzi*) and end discussion. Five years after Deng had made Jiang general secretary and declared that he was the "core" of the Party, Jiang still lacked that authority.

The Fourth Plenum was a major victory for Jiang, the point at which it can be said that Jiang began to come into his own as a political leader. The *People's Daily* editorial hailing the close of the plenum stated that "the second-generation central leading collective has been successfully relieved by its third-generation central leading collective" – a point reiterated by Li Peng during his November trip to Korea and again by Jiang Zemin a few days later during his trip to Malaysia.[5] The plenum adopted the "Decision on Some Major Issues on Strengthening Party Building," which on the one hand excoriated negative trends such as corruption and weakness of grass-roots Party organizations and, on the other hand, urged renewed attention to democratic centralism – emphasizing the subordination of lower levels to higher levels, the part to the whole, and everything to the Party center. As the decision put it, "there must be a firm central leading body . . . and there must be a leading core in this leading group." And that core, the plenum reiterated, was Jiang Zemin.[6]

Moreover, Jiang's effective power was enhanced when three of his protégés were promoted to the center. Huang Ju, mayor of Shanghai, was

---

[3] *South China Morning Post*, October 27, 1994, p. 11, in FBIS-CHI, October 27, 1994, pp. 52–3.
[4] Ling Zhijun, *Chenfu*, p. 416.   [5] Hsu Szu-min, "On the Political Situation in Post-Deng China."
[6] "Decision of the Central Committee of the Communist Party of China Concerning Some Major Issues on Strengthening Party Building."

promoted to the Politburo; while Wu Bangguo, Party secretary of Shanghai and already a member of the Politburo, and Jiang Chunyun, Party secretary of Shandong province, were added to the Party Secretariat. The promotion of Wu Bangguo and Jiang Chunyun served not only to shore up Jiang Zemin's personal support at the center but also apparently to check the authority of Zhu Rongji, a potential rival. With the economy performing poorly in 1994, Zhu began to come under fire from both the right and the left.

Leftists criticized efforts to "privatize" the economy, and Zhu lashed out at liberal economists who urged him to undertake more radical reforms.[7] Jiang began to parcel out bits of Zhu's portfolio. Wu Bangguo was named deputy head of the Central Finance and Economic Leading Group (replacing Li Peng) and thus would share leadership of that critical body with Zhu, under the general supervision of Jiang, who remained head of the group. More importantly, Wu was placed in charge of the reform of state-owned enterprises, which was designated as the focus of economic reform in 1995. It is not surprising that the personal relationship between Wu Bangguo and Zhu Rongji in the following years was frosty at best.[8] At the same time, Jiang Chunyun was given the task of overseeing agriculture, another task for which Zhu Rongji had previously been responsible.

Although the plenum decision stressed the presumably conservative theme of democratic centralism, it sounded several "liberal" themes that had been associated with NPC chairman Qiao Shi but would later – at the Fifteenth Party Congress in 1997 – be taken over by Jiang Zemin. For instance, the plenum declared that democratic centralism and "system construction" were necessary so that the Party's policies "will not change with a change in leaders or with a change in their ideas and their focus of attention."[9] Previously, when Qiao Shi had taken over as chairman of the NPC, he had declared that "democracy must be institutionalized and codified into laws so that this system and its laws will not change with a change in leadership, nor with changes in [individual leaders'] viewpoints and attention."[10] Moreover, the decision called for inner-Party democracy,

---

[7] Zhu said "some people in economists' circles have advocated the role of the invisible hand in guiding the economy [and] blindly worshipped spontaneous forces . . . " *Zhongguo tongxun she*, December 1, 1994, trans. FBIS-CHI, December 2, 1994, pp. 24–5.

[8] Author interviews.

[9] "Decision of the Central Committee of the Communist Party of China Concerning Some Major Issues on Strengthening Party Building," p. 16.

[10] Xinhua, March 31, 1993, in FBIS-CHI, March 31, 1993, p. 34.

declaring that "[i]f there is no democracy, there will be no socialism, nor socialist modernization."[11]

The sounding of such themes is no doubt partly attributable to the drafting process in which different views within the Party needed to be balanced against each other. But it also suggests that, even as he was making a bid for personal power, Jiang was conscious of both a demand and a need to stress democratization and institutionalization. Deng Xiaoping had sounded these themes in his justly famous 1980 speech "On the Reform of the Party and State Leadership System," but Deng's own status as a revolutionary elder, the repeated conflicts over policy, and doubtless also Deng's reflexive resort to personal decision-making prevented implementation of his ideas.[12] As a member of the post-revolutionary generation, Jiang could never possess Deng's personal authority; he would have to find ways to build institutions even as he augmented his personal power.

FIGHTING CORRUPTION

Even as Jiang tried to reinforce his personal strength through the strategic promotion of protégés, to rein in centrifugal tendencies by re-emphasizing democratic centralism, and to steer a course of "stability and unity" by curbing inflation and slowing the pace of economic reform, he also made a dramatic bid to win public support by finally swatting some tigers in the ongoing campaign against corruption. Public anger at Party corruption had fed the 1989 protest movement as well as the subsequent "Mao craze" that surfaced in late 1989 and the early 1990s,[13] but corruption had been difficult to tackle because of the political clout protecting some of the worst offenders. Hu Yaobang discovered this in 1986 when his hard-hitting campaign against corruption aroused the anger of Party elders and contributed to his own downfall the following January.[14]

The Party had launched a campaign against corruption in the immediate aftermath of Tiananmen, but that had faded away like its predecessors. Finally, in the summer of 1993 and amid evidence that corruption was spreading uncontrollably, the Party launched another campaign. For the first year of this campaign, it seemed to go pretty much as its predecessors

[11] "Decision of the Central Committee of the Communist Party of China Concerning Some Major Issues on Strengthening Party Building," p. 16.
[12] Deng Xiaoping, "On the Reform of the System of Party and State Leadership."
[13] Geremie Barmé, *Shades of Mao.*   [14] Joseph Fewsmith, *Dilemmas of Reform,* pp. 194–7.

had – catching many flies but few tigers.[15] In the winter of 1994–5, however, the campaign shifted into high gear. The first major casualty was Yan Jian-hong, the wife of former Guizhou provincial Party secretary Liu Zhengwei, who was executed in January for taking advantage of her connections in order to embezzle and misappropriate millions of yuan.[16]

Then, in February 1995, Zhou Beifang was arrested. Zhou, the head of Shougang (Capital Iron and Steel) International in Hong Kong, is the son of Zhou Guanwu, who was then not only head of the model enterprise Shougang but was well connected to such senior leaders as Wan Li, Peng Zhen, and perhaps Deng Xiaoping himself. It will be recalled that Deng visited Shougang in May 1992 as part of his campaign to reinstitute his vision of reform. The day after Zhou Beifang was arrested, the elder Zhou retired as head of Shougang. In addition, Deng Xiaoping's son, Deng Zhifang (a manager with Shougang International), was apparently detained and questioned with regard to the case, though no charges were filed against him.[17]

At the same time, an ongoing investigation into corruption in Beijing Municipality apparently resulted in the detention of some sixty cadres in the city, including the secretaries of Party chief Chen Xitong and mayor Li Qiyan. Then, in early April, Vice-Mayor Wang Baosen, who had been implicated by the investigation, committed suicide. The upheaval in the city came to a climax in late April when CCP secretary Chen Xitong, a member of the Politburo and ally of Deng Xiaoping, was removed from office and subsequently placed under investigation. At the Party's Fifth Plenary Session in September 1995, Chen was officially removed as a member of the Politburo and in 1998 was sentenced to sixteen years in jail, though he was later released on medical parole.[18]

With the removal of Chen Xitong, it seemed apparent that the effort to strengthen "democratic centralism," the campaign against corruption, and the power struggle among the leadership had come together. Chen had clearly disdained Jiang, and his removal was critical to the consolidation of Jiang's power, but Jiang had invoked the campaign against corruption rather than the older tactic of ideological deviance to rid himself of Chen.

---

[15] The slow pace of the campaign against corruption in 1993 might be due to Deng Xiaoping's apparent statement, during an inspection trip around Beijing on October 31 of that year, that the campaign should not be allowed to undermine the "reform enthusiasm" of cadres and citizens (see *South China Morning Post*, November 30, 1993). This comment makes it all the clearer that Jiang Zemin's stepping up of the campaign in late 1994 really was intended to distance himself from his erstwhile patron – as his actions against Deng protégés would strongly suggest.

[16] "Crimes behind the Power."   [17] Zhang Weiguo, "Chen Xitong an yu quanli douzheng."

[18] "Communiqué of the Fifth Plenary Session of the Fourteenth Central Committee of the CCP."

In a single stroke, Jiang Zemin moved against one of the most entrenched local leaders in the country, made a bid for popular support in the campaign against corruption, and acted against powerful people who might oppose him in the future – including the Deng family and Party elder Wan Li (Wan was a longtime supporter of Shougang and, as a former vice-mayor of Beijing, had close ties to the city's leadership).

The ouster and investigation of Chen Xitong reflected old-style politics, as one powerful politician defeated another and increased his hold on power, but it was also part of Jiang's popular campaign against corruption and was used to burnish the leader's reputation with the public. It was additionally a stroke, even if a selective one, in a continuing effort to move toward the rule of law in China. Jiang hardly had the power of his predecessors Mao and Deng; he had to invoke general rules in order to move against personal political antagonists. In this, the resolution of the Fourth Plenum appears to have played a significant role. That resolution declared: "The principle of everybody being equal before discipline should be upheld and those Party members who violate discipline should be investigated and dealt with severely."[19] It is not known whether this and other strictures were written into the resolution with the Chen Xitong case in mind.

One other aspect of the Chen Xitong case should be mentioned, and that is Chen's role in Tiananmen. Chen and then-Beijing Party secretary Li Ximing had played a very active role in urging the Party to adopt a hardline stance in the face of popular demonstrations, apparently writing reports that were biased and inflammatory. As a result, they were widely disliked in Beijing. Li Ximing had been forced to step down following Deng Xiaoping's trip to the south, during which Deng had specifically named Li as a "leftist."[20] Now, Chen was forced to step down because of corruption. It seems that in removing Chen, Jiang was indirectly addressing the still angry citizens of Beijing – but doing so in a way that did not call for a direct reversal of the verdict on Tiananmen.

Jiang's ouster of Chen Xitong was his most significant move on the chessboard of elite politics since the 1992 removal of Yang Baibing, and the first that could be attributed to Jiang alone. Chen's arrest hardly brought consensus within the political elite, for the same interests and currents that had clashed in the years following Tiananmen remained. These divergent

---

[19] "Decision of the Central Committee of the Communist Party of China Concerning Some Major Issues on Strengthening Party Building."

[20] The official version of Deng's talks that are contained in the third volume of his *Selected Works* names no names, but that he identified Li Ximing, Wang Renzhi, Gao Di, and others as "leftists" was widely reported at the time and confirmed by interviews.

interests were reflected both in the Party leadership and in those that Jiang gathered around him for policy advice. Within Jiang's own entourage were conservative officials such as Teng Wensheng (Deng Liqun's protégé), who headed the Policy Research Office of the Central Committee, and Ding Guan'gen (the conservative head of the Propaganda Department), whom Jiang continued to employ despite his being widely disliked within the Party, not to mention among intellectuals. At the same time, there were more "liberal" advisers, such as former Shanghai mayor and all-round political mentor Wang Daohan. Wang played a critical role in helping Jiang navigate the hidden shoals of elite politics, shaped much of Jiang's approach to foreign affairs, and was invaluable as a liaison with the intellectual community. There was also Liu Ji, Jiang's close friend from Shanghai who served as vice-president of CASS from 1993 to 1998, then played an active though much lower-profile role in Beijing, and finally was exiled back to Shanghai to take up a deanship in an MBA program.[21] In between these conservative and liberal advisers, were a number of people who have worked to further Jiang's interests bureaucratically. The most important of these was Zeng Qinghong, who served as head of the Central Committee's General Office from 1993 to 1998 and then moved over to head the important Organization Department. Zeng was promoted to be an alternate member of the Politburo at the Fifteenth Party Congress in 1997, and then to the number five position on the Politburo Standing Committee in 2002.[22]

In the course of the next few years, Jiang tried to navigate between the conflicting demands of the "left" and "right," and the tensions between these poles were sometimes reflected in friction within the group around Jiang. As we shall see, Jiang's response was to try to carve out a "middle course" that would allow him to maneuver between conflicting pressures while not becoming overly tied to any particular interest. But first he had to deal with pressures from the Old Left.

THE LEFTIST CRITIQUE OF REFORM

As Jiang moved to consolidate power at the Fourth Plenum, the question was: which way would Jiang lead China? From 1989 until 1992, Jiang had steered a cautious path, one that no doubt gave conservatives cause to believe that he was "one of them." In 1992, Jiang had then switched gears, as he certainly had to, by endorsing Deng's talks during his southern

---

[21] It should be noted that the influence of Wang Daohan and even more so of Liu Ji appears to have waned in 1999 and 2000.

[22] On Zeng, see Gao Xin, *Jiang Zemin de muliao*, pp. 71–196.

tour and supporting the Fourteenth Party Congress report that strongly endorsed Deng Xiaoping's reform line and warned against the danger on the left. Following the Fourteenth Party Congress, however, Jiang shifted back toward the center; he showed no inclination to allow the critiques of leftism appearing in the wake of Deng's southern sojourn to continue. This shift back to the center appears to have been part of a broad compromise between different forces in the Party. Deng won a major endorsement of his policies and significant personnel victories. But Deng stopped short of removing leftists from a number of major positions.

In the wake of the Fourteenth Party Congress, Jiang struck a course that might be broadly considered neoconservative, albeit without the explicit nationalistic or populist appeals that some neoconservatives called for. The ideological atmosphere that grew up in the wake of Tiananmen probably facilitated Jiang's policy direction, just as Jiang's cautious political direction encouraged a more conservative intellectual atmosphere. Although Jiang tolerated the *de facto* privatization of much economic activity in the wake of Deng's southern trip and Zhu Rongji's efforts to squeeze inflation out of the economy, his statements remained ideologically cautious or conservative. Moreover, although Jiang's power had increased, he was not in a position to alienate powerful figures in the Party – and many of those figures were on the left. Thus, conservatives seem to have calculated that a well-aimed critique of the effects of the Dengist program would either convince or force Jiang to identify himself with leftist causes.

In August 1994, leftists convened a meeting in Xiangshan, northwest of Beijing. Attended by such people as Deng Liqun, Xu Weicheng, Shao Huaze, Wang Renzhi, He Jingzhi, Li Ximing, Gao Di, and Yuan Mu, the meeting reportedly declared that the collapse of socialism in Eastern Europe and the former Soviet Union was due to "revisionism," the old Maoist term for heterodox understandings of Marxism–Leninism. Deng Liqun allegedly went so far as to suggest that Deng's views were themselves revisionist: "Deng Xiaoping's theories must be tested in practice to show whether they are correct or wrong. Any attempt to advocate using Comrade Deng Xiaoping's theories to negate or replace Marxism as the guiding principle for revolution and construction in China is idealist and goes against the 'Communist Manifesto.' No doctrine or theory, now or in the future, can replace Marxist truth and science."[23] In September, more or less the same cast of characters convened a meeting in Shijiazhuang, the capital of Hebei province. Speeches were delivered on such themes as "Revisionism and

[23] Lo Ping, "The Anti-Deng Meeting Incident in Hebei."

Right-Deviationist Thinking Are the Traitors of Marxism," "The Line We Are Pushing Now Is One Which Practices Capitalism under the Leadership of the Communist Party," "The Turmoil of 1989 Was the Product of the Party's Right-Deviationist Line," and "The Damage Done to the Country by the Pro-US Line."[24]

Leftist criticism accelerated in early 1995 when a sharply worded document entitled "Several Factors Influencing China's National Security" was anonymously forwarded to the Central Committee and circulated internally. Although no name was attached to the document, it was reportedly written by a researcher at CASS and endorsed by conservative ideologue Deng Liqun. The article, which became known as the first "10,000 character manifesto" (in reference to its length and political character), warned that the proportion of state-owned enterprises in China's aggregate industrial output value had fallen from 76 percent in 1980 to 48.3 percent in June 1994, that there were already 328,000 registered private enterprises with over five million employees and 100 billion yuan of capital, and that a "new bourgeoisie" had already taken shape as a class in itself.[25] As if this were not enough, the document warned that the nature of the Party was changing as more and more technically trained specialists were promoted to leadership positions, that the sovereignty of the country was being undermined by increasing economic dependence on the West, and that "bourgeois liberal" thinking was once again on the rise and linking up with private entrepreneurs to form a threat to the Party. Although the document explicitly or implicitly questioned the whole reform enterprise since the Third Plenum of 1978, it reserved special venom for Deng Xiaoping's 1992 trip to Shenzhen. Not only did it state that bourgeois liberalization has gained the upper hand "since 1992," it also argued that bourgeois liberalization had "spread unchecked under the 'anti-left' signboard" – an apparent reference to Deng's statement during his trip to Shenzhen that the left was the "main danger."

In the late summer or early fall of 1995, as tensions in the Taiwan Straits mounted, a second "10,000 character manifesto" was circulated. Entitled "A Preliminary Exploration of the Shape of China's Domestic and Foreign National Security in the Next Ten or Twenty Years and the Primary Threats to It," this second document maintained that China faced a hostile international environment made up of "monopoly capitalists" who view China as

---

[24] Ibid.
[25] In Marxist terminology, "class in itself" indicates a class that has formed sociologically but has not yet articulated a distinct class ideology. When the latter state is reached, Marxists speak of a "class for itself."

an enemy and that domestically China was undergoing a number of social changes that were threatening its national security and social stability.[26] Unlike the first manifesto, which concentrated on domestic trends, this second document focused on the reasons for the disintegration of the Soviet Union and the collapse of socialism in Eastern Europe – issues that had been central in the 1991–2 period but had since calmed down in the wake of the Fourteenth Party Congress and the efforts to rebuild diplomatic ties with the new Russia. This second manifesto argued that the threat of "peaceful evolution" was the critical issue and that China's reliance on the international economy had weakened China's "national" (domestic) industries, thus making China more vulnerable to Western pressures. The document went on to warn that the ideological confusion in the Party – particularly the belief that it is not necessary to determine whether a given policy is "capitalist" or "socialist," an agnostic approach that derived directly from Deng's trip to the south – might lead to the appearance of a Gorbachev-type leader within the CCP in the next ten to twenty years, though presumably the author was concerned about a much shorter time frame.[27]

SOCIOECONOMIC CHANGES

This resurgence of leftist criticism, which had receded in the period following the Fourteenth Party Congress in 1992, reflected the tensions generated by the rapid socioeconomic changes that occurred after Deng's trip to the south, just as did the various New Left criticisms considered in Chapter 4. Deng's criticism of leftism and his call for faster economic growth not only brought the usual expansion of investment but also stimulated, for the first time, a lively and speculative real estate market. In 1992, some 73 billion yuan was invested in real estate, 117 percent more than the previous year.[28] By the end of the year, there were over 12,000 real estate companies, a 2.4-fold increase over the year before. These companies leased some 3,000 pieces of land with a total area of 22,000 hectares, marking an 11-fold increase over 1991. In addition, 428,886 million square meters of housing were sold, a 40 percent increase over the previous year.[29] At the same time, local areas continued to open up "developmental zones" in the hope of attracting

---

[26] "Weilai yi, ershinian woguo guojia anquan de neiwai xingshi ji zhuyao weixie de chubu tantao."
[27] Ibid., pp. 139, 141, 143. Since Zhu Rongji has often been called a Gorbachev-type figure, the barb was presumably aimed at him.
[28] He Qinglian, *Xiandaihua de xianjing*, p. 52.
[29] Xinhua, May 21, 1993, in FBIS-CHI, May 21, 1993, pp. 28–9. See also Zhu Jianhong and Jiang Yaping, "Development and Standardization Are Necessary."

foreign capital and taking advantage of loopholes in the financial regulations. By the end of 1992, there were said to be some 8,000 developmental
zones.[30]

According to He Qinglian, the crusading economic journalist who published a best seller in 1998 entitled *The Pitfalls of Modernization*, Deng's
southern journey prompted the formation of hundreds of "joint stock companies." In Jiangsu province alone, over 200 such enterprises were established in the 18 months following Deng's trip, and in Hebei province the
number of joint stock enterprises jumped from a mere 23 at the beginning
of 1992 to 133 a year later.[31] He Qinglian argued that the local enthusiasm for
forming such enterprises resulted from local officials and enterprise managers who saw the joint stock system as a way to drain off state-owned assets
for their own benefit.[32] State-owned assets were not only lost to domestic
enterprises; joint ventures shared the bounty as well. Already by 1992, she
argued, some 46 billion yuan had been lost to joint ventures.[33]

He Qinglian dubbed the selling of land (most of which had previously
been an unvalued asset) as China's "enclosure movement," a reference to
the seventeenth-century English movement of the same name. According
to He, the boom in the real estate market enriched those with connections
at the expense of the common people, obstructed the formation of a fair
competitive mechanism, and fostered rampant corruption. Such real estate
speculation drove up land prices and put housing out of reach of most
people – and caused much resentment.[34]

One problem of the booming real estate market was that it was fueled
by a speculative fever that created a bubble economy that could, as one
researcher put it, "vanish without warning."[35] Much of the money invested
came from inland units using money allocated for grain purchases, giving
the peasants IOUs instead. According to one report, at least 57 billion yuan
was diverted in early 1993 through interbank loans to the coastal areas,
where it was used to speculate in real estate and the stock market. As a well-
known researcher in the State Council's Development Research Center put
it: "Local authorities and banks are ripping off billions of yuan to fund real
estate projects. That's why they have no money to pay the peasants."[36] Thus,
the speculation in coastal real estate exacerbated tensions in the countryside
even as it fueled the growing gap between the coast and the hinterland.

[30] Xiang Jingquan, "Review and Prospects of China's Economic Development."
[31] He Qinglian, *Xiandaihua de xianjing*, p. 23.
[32] Ibid., p. 29.   [33] Ibid., p. 30.   [34] Ibid., p. 65.
[35] "Central Authorities Urge Banks to Draw Bank Loans and Stop Promoting the Bubble Economy."
[36] *South China Morning Post*, July 4, 1993, in FBIS-CHI, July 7, 1993, p. 33.

The Maoist period had exerted great efforts to equalize regional differences by large transfer payments to the hinterland and through massive and unwise investments in the "third front" military industries that were built in the hinterland in case the United States or the Soviet Union invaded.[37] The Dengist era reversed these policies by stopping large-scale investments in the third front and by curtailing transfer payments, thus allowing China's "natural economy" to reassert itself. The natural tendency for the east coast – where human talent, technology, communications, and transportation are disproportionately concentrated – to move ahead was obscured at first both by the rural reforms, which increased the incomes of the large numbers of farmers who live inland, and by the slow start of urban reform, particularly in Shanghai (where large numbers of SOEs were concentrated). After the mid-1980s, however, rural incomes began to stagnate, the massive investments in inland areas were curtailed, and TVEs along the east coast began to play an increasingly important role in the economy. In 1992, as just noted, much money flowed to the east coast from inland areas in the hopes of higher returns, thus fueling the speculative bubble. At the same time, foreign investment began growing by a large amount. Seemingly all of a sudden, the east coast began to move ahead quickly, and the gap between the coast and the hinterland began to widen noticeably.[38]

Much of the gap that developed between regions and among citizens was due to the explosive growth of the private economy in this period. Figures on the size of China's private sector are notoriously difficult to pin down because of the propensity of private entrepreneurs to claim to be collectives or to underreport the size of their business. Nevertheless, even if one looks only at the official figures, it is apparent that China has experienced very rapid growth in this sector in recent years. One might date the growth of a significant private sector from 1987, when the Thirteenth Party Congress declared that the private sector should be "permitted to exist," and from the revision of the state constitution in March 1988 to legalize the conduct of private business. The number of registered private enterprises more than doubled between 1991 (before Deng's trip) and 1993 (after the Fourteenth Party Congress), and the amount of registered capital soared from about 12 billion yuan to over 68 billion yuan – more than a 5-fold increase.

The rapid expansion of private enterprise, real estate speculation, and stock transactions that followed Deng Xiaoping's 1992 journey to the south were paralleled by an equally rapid growth of foreign investment in China.

---

[37] Barry Naughton, "The Third Front."
[38] Barry Naughton, "Causes et conséquences des disparités dans la croissance économique des provinces chinoises."

Direct foreign investment more than doubled, from $4.6 billion to $11.3 billion, between 1991 and 1992; it then doubled again, to $27.8 billion, in 1993.[39] By the summer of 1996, as elite tensions remained high because of the Taiwan Straits crisis and domestic criticism of reform, a new wave of criticism – this one focusing on the impact of foreign investment – began in the pages of *Economic Daily (Jingji ribao)*, the country's most authoritative economic paper, which is supervised by the State Council. On June 20, *Economic Daily* ran a commentator article introducing a series of fifteen articles that in the coming days would take an unusually critical look at the impact of foreign capital on Chinese enterprises. The commentator article argued that the role of foreign investment in China's economy was growing rapidly: imported capital then accounted for about 20 percent of all investment in fixed assets in China, foreign-invested enterprises (*sanzi qiye*) accounted for 39 percent of China's exports, and foreign trade equaled some 40 percent of domestic production; all this suggested a high degree of dependence. Opening up to the outside world was good, the commentator said, "but looking across the various countries of the world, [we see] that opening up definitely cannot be without certain principles and certain limits." It is important to "pay attention to protecting national industries."[40] As an accompanying report on joint ventures in China's beer industry asked, "Must Chinese beer [companies] form so many joint ventures? How much longer can Chinese-produced beer last?"[41]

The articles in *Economic Daily* were undertaken at the paper's own initiative but with the intention of appealing to Li Peng, who headed the State Council to which the paper was subordinate. Feeling that the assault on China's policy of opening to the outside could not go unrefuted, economic reformers – including Zhu Rongji – urged *People's Daily* to issue an authoritative rebuttal.[42] Thus, on July 16, about a month after *Economic Daily* launched its series of columns, *People's Daily* published a major commentary implicitly refuting the series. The placement of the *People's Daily* commentary in the upper left-hand "lead article" space of the front page, endorsed by an "editor's note," conveyed the sense of importance that *People's Daily* attached to this rebuttal.[43]

The obvious – and unusual – public disagreement between *Economic Daily* and *People's Daily* suggests high-level leadership disputes regarding the issue of foreign capital, disputes that would burst into public view

---

[39] *Zhongguo jingji nianjian, 1995*, p. 766.
[40] Commentator, "Dajia lai taolun zhege zhongda keti – Cong pijiu hezi yinqi de sikao."
[41] Jiang Po, "Guochan pijiu you biyao gao zhema duo hezi ma?"   [42] Author interview.
[43] Ma Licheng and Ling Zhijun, *Jiao feng*, pp. 282–3.

three years later when the Chinese leadership finally decided to make the commitments necessary to reach agreement with the United States and other trading partners over China's accession to the World Trade Organization (see Chapter 7). The dispute in the pages of these two leading dailies clearly reflected the intersection of ideological concerns (as expressed in the various "10,000 character" manifestos and other documents), societal concerns (as expressed by the economic nationalism of various enterprises), and elite politics (as reflected in the differing opinions of the two papers). The incident further confirmed the economic and social bases of contemporary Chinese nationalism and the differing responses of the Chinese leadership to international economic forces and the social changes in China.

These dramatic socioeconomic changes have had the effect of producing a *nouveau riche* class. In the mid-1980s, there was fevered talk in the Chinese press, which turned out to be exaggerated, of the emergence of "ten-thousand-yuan households" (*wanyuanhu*) – an almost unimaginable amount of income in a period in which the average rural resident earned only about 350 yuan per year. A decade or so later, there were at least one million households with annual incomes exceeding one million yuan. This was an enormous change with profound social, psychological, and political implications. In many ways, of course, this was a long overdue and healthy change that seemingly marked the appearance of a middle class, albeit one that was still quite small in terms of China's population, or even its urban population. Nevertheless, the new middle class, including the much more prosperous *nouveau riche*, drove the new consumerism of the 1990s and so changed the nature and role of culture in Chinese society by commercializing it and diversifying it.

The seamy side of this story is that those who did the best in this new economy – and some did very well indeed – almost always seemed to have strong political connections. Sometimes they were bureaucrats who tired of the office routine and jumped into the sea of business but retained their connections to colleagues who could offer all-important approvals or access to scarce resources. Sometimes they were family members of officials still in office. Sometimes they were enterprise heads who used their positions to siphon off large amounts of state-owned assets to private firms that they controlled directly or indirectly. Often they were the offspring of high cadres who used their family connections to amass large sums of money. In other words, corruption – massive corruption – was a major part of the story of income redistribution in the 1990s.

A well-known study calls this *nouveau riche* group the "never-left-out class" (*bu luokong jieji*) because every time Chinese society entered a new round of adjustment in which resources were reallocated, this group has benefited the most. The same study argues that this group possesses "comprehensive" (*zongtixing*) capital resources, meaning that it is able to mobilize its multidimensional economic and political contacts to monopolize the best opportunities.[44] This is the same group of people that He Qinglian described when she argued that, through the "marketization of politics," officials – or those with close relations to officials – have directed millions of dollars worth of assets into private hands, bringing about a form of "primitive socialist accumulation" that rivals anything Marx and Engels observed about "primitive capitalist accumulation." The result, He argued, has been income inequality surpassing that in either Japan or the United States (keeping in mind that China had a much more equal distribution of income than either of those countries less than a decade before), the rise of secret societies, and mass resentment. China, she argued, seems to be heading not toward liberal democracy and capitalism but toward a "government and mafia alliance."[45]

These socioeconomic trends quickly became a source of popular discontent, and political and intellectual leaders from across the spectrum – the left, the New Left, neostatists, populist nationalists, and liberals – all responded with diagnoses and prescriptions. The leftist articles (the "10,000 character manifestos") cited previously were clearly intended to exert pressure on Jiang primarily from within elite circles. Although foreign commentators rarely take leftist pronouncements seriously, the evidence strongly suggests that at various times the left has been an important force in elite politics. Even if it has not been able to set the political agenda, it has been able to obstruct the formulation and implementation of reforms. This is in part because the left positions itself as the upholder of Marxist orthodoxy and thus is able to accuse reformers of "deviating" from Marxism. Even after two decades of reform, such charges still have an impact because the Party cannot abandon Marxism without giving up all claims to legitimacy. It should be noted that many leftists come out of the propaganda system and hence are well versed in the language of Marxism–Leninism. As expert symbol manipulators, they can constrain the actions of the leadership. The left further derives influence from the age and long-term service of many of its leaders. As Party elders, they exert an influence out of proportion to their numbers. It should also be noted that the left champions the interests of many members at lower levels, people who oppose reform because they

[44] Sun Liping, "Zhongguo shehui jiegou zhuanxing de zhongjinqi qushi yu yinhuan."
[45] He Qinglian, *Xiandaihua de xianjing*.

fear it will hurt their interests. So the left is not devoid of a certain mass base; to the extent that it can tap into the fears of workers facing layoffs and a decline in their social status, it can extend that mass base to certain sectors of the population. Thus, after circulating the first 10,000 character manifesto, leftists went to the northeast – which was experiencing wide-scale layoffs – and called meetings in factories to explain the content of the article.[46] This pushed the bounds of acceptable political behavior and was soon curtailed. But the threat to Jiang Zemin was real.

THE FIFTH PLENUM: TRYING TO SHAPE AN AGENDA

When the Fourteenth Central Committee convened its Fifth Plenum on September 25–28, 1996, there were two items at the top of the agenda. The first was the Ninth Five-Year Plan that was to be formally approved by the Fourth session of the Eighth NPC meeting the following spring. As the leadership of the CCP was clearly aware, the inauguration of a new plan presented them with an opportunity to lay out an agenda for where this "third generation" of leadership intended to take China. In other words, if the Fourth Plenary Session the preceding year was marked by political succession, the Fifth Plenum was defined by the effort to lay out, if only in preliminary terms, a program that would define the new generation as distinct from its predecessors.

It has often been remarked that Mao's era was defined by the concentration of power and Deng's by its dispersion; Mao's concentration of power is said to have brought to an end a period of domestic disorder and international war while Deng's devolution of authority unleashed the economic energy that brought a new level of prosperity to the country. The problem of the Jiang Zemin era, as the discussions on neostatism showed, was finding a way that combines centralization and decentralization – or, more precisely, building viable institutions without stifling economic growth.

As might be expected, the explanation of the proposal that Li Peng gave to the plenum split the differences among interests and presented a program that was as acceptable as it was vague. The crux of the proposal lay in its affirmation of the critical role played by a limited number of large-scale state-owned enterprises; these 1,000 enterprises, which accounted for over 70 percent of the profits and tax payments of all state-owned enterprises, would be strongly supported by the state and would embody the principle of "taking the publicly owned economy as the main component

---

[46] Author interviews.

and the state-owned economy as the guiding factor."[47] Smaller state-owned enterprises were given permission to proceed "more freely" with regard to developing new forms of organization and ownership. The tertiary economy was encouraged to develop freely. What was left vague, however, was an explanation of *how* large-scale SOEs were to be reformed successfully given that similar efforts over the preceding fifteen years had not been impressive, as well as – and perhaps more importantly – how smaller-scale industries should proceed to reshape themselves.

The second issue that dominated the agenda was political leadership. Jiang was trying to consolidate his authority but was obviously still facing considerable difficulty. The left had raised the issue of political direction by circulating the 10,000 character manifestos; the right, then led by NPC Chairman Qiao Shi, was challenging Jiang by emphasizing law and democracy (of the inner-Party sort) and by ignoring calls to support Jiang as the "core." At the Fifth Plenum, Jiang clearly tacked to the left, at least in ideological terms, by emphasizing the need to "talk politics," an admonition that seemed to include ideological considerations in the formulation of policy but also emphasized the need for Party discipline.[48] As Jiang told the plenum:[49]

I also want to underscore one issue here. Our senior cadres – especially provincial party committee secretaries, provincial governors, ministers, Central Committee members, and members of the CCP Central Committee Politburo – must pay attention to politics. By politics, I mean political direction, political stand, political viewpoints, political discipline, political perception, and political sensitivity . . . Can we afford not to pay attention to politics, or can we afford to lower our guard and stop fighting when hostile forces in the West want to "Westernize" (*xihua*) and "divide" (*fenhua*) us, and impose their "democracy" and "freedom" on us; and when Lee Teng-hui is bent on promoting "Taiwan independence."

This frank statement suggests the difficulty Jiang Zemin was having in securing the compliance of many of his colleagues as well as Jiang's need to play the nationalistic card in his warnings of foreign (primarily American) efforts to "Westernize" and "divide" China.

---

[47] Li Peng, "Explanations of the Proposal for the Formulation of the Ninth Five-Year Plan and the Long-Term Target for the Year 2010," p. 21.

[48] The call to "talk politics" was drawn from a remark Deng had made during an inspection tour of Tianjin. That speech is not included in the three-volume compendium of Deng's selected works, but it is contained in a volume published in conjunction with the Sixth Plenum of the Fourteenth Central Committee. The volume editors acknowledge that the selection is only an excerpt of Deng's remarks and that the title, "Always Talk Politics," had been selected by the editors. See Zhonggong zhongyang wenxuan yanjiushi (ed.), *Shehui zhuyi jingshen wenming jianshe wenxian xuanbian.*

[49] Jiang Zemin, "Leading Cadres Must Pay Attention to Politics."

CARVING OUT A MIDDLE PATH

Following the Fifth Plenum, in late 1995 and early 1996, Jiang made a series of internal speeches that tried to distinguish his own program from those of his critics on both the left and the right. Jiang called for drawing a line between Marxism and anti-Marxism in seven areas: between socialist democracy and Western parliamentary democracy, between developing a diverse economy with a predominant public sector and privatization, between studying what is advanced in the West and fawning on the West, and so forth. These distinctions were trumpeted in an important series of commentator articles carried by the PLA newspaper *Jiefangjun bao* between April 1 and May 6, 1996.

A major purpose of these articles was to warn against rightist tendencies. In this sense they were consistent with the conservative tendency in post-Tiananmen political commentary, and their conservative tone may explain their appearance in the PLA newspaper rather than in *People's Daily*. An editorial note accompanying the first of these eight articles stated that, "[i]n the course of opening to the outside world and economic structural reform, some trends of social thought have inevitably affected the troops, and the corrosive effect on cadres and troops of various sorts of corrupt thinking and culture should not be underestimated." That first article discussed drawing a line between "socialist democracy" and "Western parliamentary democracy," decrying the latter but nonetheless calling for new efforts to gradually perfect the former. "Democracy," the commentary stated in its opening line, "is one of the fundamental goals for which our Party has always struggled."[50]

Other articles, however, were more openly critical of the left, even as they defended Party policy against charges of rightism. For instance, in calling for patriotism in the context of opening to the outside world, one article stated – in an implicit but clear reference to Deng Liqun's well-known comment – that "some comrades even believe that every new bit [*fen*] of foreign investment that is brought in is another bit of capitalism."[51] At least two of the commentaries highlighted the thesis that China was in the "primary stage of socialism," a thesis that would become central at the Fifteenth Party Congress in 1997.[52] The most interesting of the commentaries was the final one, which more strongly than its predecessors

---

[50] "Jianchi he fazhan you Zhongguo tese de shehui zhuyi minzhu."
[51] "Zai duiwai kaifang zhong hongyang aiguo zhuyi jingshen."
[52] "Yongyuan baochi he fayang jianku fendou jingshen" and "Jianchi gongyouzhi de zhuti diwei buneng dongyao."

called for opposing "dogmatism" and "vulgar" Marxism. While Marxism must be upheld, it declared, "without being developed, Marxism would lose its vitality and energy." It was therefore necessary to "break through dogmatic interpretations of Marxism and erroneous viewpoints that are attributed to Marxism, and break through those judgments and conclusions that practice has already proven to be wrong and that are not appropriate to the new circumstances brought about by change."[53]

The most systematic effort to define a middle course and respond to the criticisms of the left came when Xing Bensi, vice-president of the Central Party School, published a long article in *People's Daily*. Apparently angered by the silence with which the *People's Daily* greeted his speeches – a silence induced perhaps by the inability of top leaders to agree on how to respond – Jiang arranged for the publication of Xing's article.[54]

In trying to define what constituted "real" Marxism (and thus refute the left that positioned itself as defender of the faith), Xing argued that a lot had changed since the birth of Marx 150 years ago. Although "some" of the "fundamental principles" (*jiben yuanli*) of Marxism are still applicable, he said, "indeed a considerable portion of the principles" of Marxism have changed. Xing claimed that there are parts of Marxism that contain universal truth and are still applicable, parts that need to be supplemented, and also parts that are "completely unsuitable for use, which should not be continued and upheld in the present day."[55] Thus, according to Xing: "The criterion for determining the border dividing Marxism and anti-Marxism has to rest on developed Marxism; in present day China the 'only correct' criterion for distinguishing Marxism and anti-Marxism is the 'theory of socialism with Chinese characteristics established by Deng Xiaoping' – most importantly upholding the 'one center [economic construction] and two basic points' [the four cardinal principles and emancipating the mind]." Xing thus juxtaposed "Deng Xiaoping theory" against leftist thought and referred explicitly to the first 10,000 character manifesto when he criticized those who declared that reform had brought about a "new bourgeoisie."

At the same time, Xing defined a "right" that was just as anti-Marxist as the left. Xing cited several manifestations of rightism, including "privatization" and revisionist interpretations of Chinese history that implied that China had taken the wrong road in pursuing the revolutionary path and that it was now necessary to say "farewell to revolution." This was a reference to the well-known book (discussed in Chapter 3) by prominent

---

[53] "Makesi zhuyi yongyuan shi women shengli de qizhi."   [54] Author interview.
[55] Xing Bensi, "Jianchi Makesi zhuyi bu dongyao."

philosopher Li Zehou and leading literary critic Liu Zaifu. Although Xing's criticism of Li and Liu's book illustrated the need for the Party to respond to intellectual discussions, Xing's motive here seems to have been to set up a "right" to juxtapose to the "left" of the manifestos. By doing so, Xing could define a "middle course" for Jiang. Xing's criticism of *Farewell to Revolution* also served the purpose of warning liberal thinkers to hold their peace as Jiang turned his primary attention to warding off the left.[56]

What Xing Bensi's long article in *Renmin ribao* did was to begin staking out a defensible middle ground in China's political spectrum. In trying to define a middle course, Jiang seemed at once to be taking a leaf from history and trying to sidestep his most serious political dilemma. Chinese politics since Tiananmen, as in many crisis situations, tended to be defined by polarities: one was either for "upholding socialism" or for "bourgeois liberalization." Taking heed of the fate of his predecessors, Hu Yaobang and Zhao Ziyang, Jiang spent much of his first six years making sure that no one could accuse him of being "lax" on bourgeois liberalization. Indeed, it was this proclivity for caution, if not conservatism, that roused Deng's ire in 1992. But cautiousness implied impotence. Without differentiating himself from the left, Jiang had neither the ability to tackle the serious problems that plagued the economy nor the freedom to define a "line" of his own. In short, cautiousness meant passivity; Jiang was general secretary, but it was the left that defined the limits to his actions.

In contrast, Deng had defined himself and had been able to carry out reform by carving out a "middle course." Indeed, Deng secured his authority in the post-Cultural Revolution context by abandoning the "struggle *between two lines*" in favor of a "struggle *on two fronts*" (that is, both left and right).[57] At least in some readings of history, Mao had done the same thing in his battles against "rightist opportunism" (represented by Chen Duxiu) and "leftism" (represented by Wang Ming).[58] As Chinese politics had polarized in the late 1980s, it had been increasingly difficult to prevent them from reverting to a struggle between two lines, as indeed the harsh criticism of Zhao Ziyang in the wake of Tiananmen suggested that, to a certain extent, it had. Now, after six years as general secretary and after being able slowly to build up his personal authority, Jiang began his attempt to define a new center.

Carving out a middle course, however, is not a simple matter. It needs to be articulated and defended against critics on both the left and the

---

[56] Shen Hongpei, "Ershi shijimo gongchan zhuyi dalunzhan," p. 9.
[57] Tang Tsou, "Political Change and Reform," p. 222.
[58] Xing Bensi, "Emphasis on Study, Politics, and Uprightness as Fine Party Traditions."

right. Although Xing's article was a step in this direction, Jiang was not yet prepared to confront directly the disputes wracking the Party. In the spring of 1996, Jiang was clearly tacking to the right, endorsing a new round of reform. In May, Jiang met with the enterprise heads and political leaders from seven provinces, telling them that reform had reached an "extremely critical moment."[59] This was Jiang's strongest affirmation of reform in the period since he took over as general secretary.[60] Nevertheless, by fall, he was again charting a conservative ideological direction.

SIXTH PLENUM: BUILDING SPIRITUAL CIVILIZATION

When the Sixth Plenary Session of the Fourteenth Central Committee convened on October 7–10, 1996, it adopted a 14,000-character decision entitled, "Resolution of the CCP Central Committee Concerning Several Important Issues on Strengthening the Building of Socialist Spiritual Civilization." In many ways, this resolution seems designed to respond to and defend Jiang from charges that the economic reforms he was presiding over – and those measures he was contemplating – would lead to bourgeois liberalization and privatization. The result was a tortuous document; the committee process by which it was drafted is visible in nearly every paragraph.

The plenum resolution defended reform, but it also warned that "[a]t no time should we achieve short-term economic growth at the expense of spiritual civilization."[61] This was a phrase authored by Teng Wensheng, the protégé of Deng Liqun's whom Jiang had brought over to head the Policy Research Office and, no doubt, to assure conservatives that their concerns would be heard.[62] Indeed, the document came perilously close to giving equal value to economic development and spiritual civilization, as leftists had long urged. It declared: "Economic development as the central link must be grasped firmly and unswervingly. But failure in the promotion of ethical and cultural progress will lead to damage to material progress and even change the nature of society."[63]

The Sixth Plenum resolution was a disappointment to many intellectuals as well as to some of Jiang's own policy advisers. People compared it unfavorably with the resolution on building spiritual civilization that had been

[59] Xinhua, May 5, 1996, in FBIS-CHI-96-088, May 5, 1996.   [60] Ling Zhijun, *Chenfu*, p. 512.
[61] "Resolution of the CPC Central Committee Regarding Important Questions on Promoting Socialist Ethical and Cultural Progress."
[62] Gao Xin, *Jiang Zemin de muliao*, pp. 237–76.
[63] "Resolution of the CPC Central Committee Regarding Important Questions on Promoting Socialist Ethical and Cultural Progress."

adopted a decade earlier under Hu Yaobang's auspices.[64] In language reminiscent of Mao Zedong's "Yenan Forum on Literature and Art," the 1996 document called on writers and artists to "immerse themselves among the masses" and to "earnestly and seriously consider what social effects [*shehui xiaoguo*] their works may produce." Similarly, it called for strengthening control over press and publishing circles and for keeping the propaganda front and public opinion "firmly" in the hands of "those comrades who are loyal to Marxism, Leninism, and Mao Zedong Thought."[65]

In short, despite Jiang's efforts over the preceding months to carve out a viable middle ground, the Sixth Plenum communiqué ignored these themes. In fact, it does not mention "drawing a line" between Marxism and anti-Marxism; there is neither criticism of dogmatic interpretations of Marxism nor any effort, such as in Xing Bensi's article, to define what constitutes "true" Marxism in the contemporary world. The conservative, cautious tone of the resolution reflected the tense atmosphere at the top of the Party in the months preceding Deng's death.

REVIVING REFORM

Although Jiang chose caution in the fall of 1996, he and his advisers were clearly exploring alternative approaches at the same time. Jiang's 1995–6 talks on distinguishing Marxism from anti-Marxism marked an initial effort, but in the fall of 1996 – almost at the very time that the Sixth Plenum was convening to consider the resolution on building spiritual civilization – a volume was published that showed a very different side of Jiang's thinking. This effort to define Jiang's program in more positive and systematic terms became visible with the October 1996 publication of *Heart-to-Heart Talks with the General Secretary.*

Fourteen young scholars, mostly based at the Chinese Academy of Social Sciences, wrote the book (others participated in discussions about its content), which was an extended gloss on Jiang's 1995 speech to the Fifth Plenum on twelve major problems facing China. Although Jiang's speech had been a reasonable and considered look at the difficulties facing China (drawing comparison to Mao's famous "Ten Great Relationships" speech), there had been little follow-up in policy terms. Indeed, the speech was so well balanced that the policy implications of it were not immediately clear, and the speech soon dropped from public view. A year later, these young intellectuals tried to flesh out Jiang's proposals, dropping some of

---

[64] Ibid.   [65] Ibid.

the balance from the original speech and developing a number of proposals that actually did have implications for the direction in which China was to develop.

The most eye-catching feature of the volume – apart from the picture of Jiang on the cover – was the preface and endorsement by Liu Ji, vice-president of CASS. Despite his background in natural science (he is a 1958 graduate of Qinghua University), Liu took up social science and emerged as a strong voice for reform in the 1980s. A frequent contributor to the reformist paper *World Economic Herald*, in 1982 Liu wrote an article entitled "Making the Decision-Making Process More Scientific," which was said to have been a major influence on Wan Li's 1986 speech, "Making the Decision-Making Process More Democratic and Scientific Is an Important Topic in Political Structural Reform."[66] After Jiang Zemin went to Shanghai in the mid-1980s, he became very close to Liu Ji, elevating Liu to deputy head of the municipal propaganda department. It was in this capacity that Liu was named to head the work group that took over the *World Economic Herald* after Jiang decided to close the controversial paper. Liu's role in this episode certainly exacerbated his relations with many reform-minded intellectuals, but it demonstrated his personal loyalty to Jiang.[67] In 1993, Jiang transferred Liu to Beijing, appointing him as vice-president of CASS.

As vice-president of the Chinese Academy of Social Sciences, one of Liu's jobs was to cultivate a new corps of intellectuals who could provide policy advice for Jiang. This was not an easy task, given the mutual suspicions separating the intellectual community from the political leadership in the years following Tiananmen and the ideological taboos that continued to restrict intellectual discussions – taboos that were personified in CASS by the leadership of Wang Renzhi and Teng Teng, both staunch conservatives. *Heart-to-Heart Talks with the General Secretary* was the most visible manifestation to date of Liu's efforts to bridge this gap and to begin improving the intellectual atmosphere.[68]

The decision to bring together a number of young intellectuals to write *Heart-to-Heart Talks with the General Secretary* was a self-conscious effort to rebut leftist criticisms made in the first and second "10,000 character manifestos" as well as the rising tide of nationalism. It was well recognized

[66] Liu Ji, "Lun juece kexuehua"; Wan Li, "Juece minzhuhua he kexuehua shi zhengzhi tizhi gaige de yige zhongyao keti"; Gao Xin, *Jiang Zemin de muliao*, pp. 197–233.

[67] For Liu's role in this complicated incident see Gao Xin, *Jiang Zemin de muliao*, pp. 208–14.

[68] *Heart-to-Heart Talks* was only the first in a series of books. It was followed quickly by a more substantive and systematic effort to discuss the various problems facing China. See Xu Ming (ed.), *Guanjian shike*. Note that the title, "the critical moment," comes from Jiang Zemin's remark in Shanghai on May 4, 1996.

that such trends would, if not refuted, severely constrain Jiang Zemin's range of policy choices and his effective power. The rapid improvement in Sino–US relations since March 1996 – fostered by exchanges between Liu Huaqiu, head of the Foreign Affairs Office of the State Council, and Anthony Lake, President Clinton's National Security Adviser – clearly facilitated this effort to respond to critics; Secretary of State Warren Christopher was due in Beijing in November, only weeks after the publication of *Heart-to-Heart Talks*, to finalize plans for Jiang Zemin and President Clinton to exchange summits.[69]

Perhaps the single most notable feature of *Heart-to-Heart Talks with the General Secretary* was its no-holds-barred defense of reform; the title of the second chapter put it as directly as Deng Xiaoping ever had: "Reform, Reform, Reform: There Is No Other Road for China." Recognizing that many problems had accompanied the development of reform, the authors – consistent with the idea of trying to carve out a middle course – argued that it was wrong to reject continued reform either by adopting all-out Westernization or by pulling back and adopting conservative policies. Their attention, however, was focused on the latter concern. Joining ongoing debates about the cause of socialism's collapse in the former Soviet Union, the authors placed the blame on Brezhnev and not on Gorbachev, as China's leftists were wont to do. Brezhnev-type leaders easily appear in difficult circumstances, the authors argued, but the result of Brezhnev was not eighteen years of "stability" but eighteen years of stagnation. The lesson to be drawn from the experience of Brezhnev is that, without reform, there will indeed be instability.[70] Those who advocate retreat whenever reform faces major difficulties, the authors wrote, always say that they are protecting socialism, but in the end they cause great losses to socialism.

Responding to the debate over the large influx of foreign funds, which we saw reflected in the public disagreement between *People's Daily* and *Economic Daily*, the book wholeheartedly endorsed opening to the outside world. Closing the door, it noted, was not really an option. Despite the increasingly fierce competition (between nations and within nations) as multinational corporations increasingly became a part of domestic economies, China had no choice but to face up to this competition. This choice required self-confidence, the adoption of favorable government policies (which were not specified, but protectionism was rejected as not very effective), and the retreat of government from enterprise operations.[71]

[69] Author interview.
[70] Weng Jieming, Zhang Ximing, Zhang Qiang, and Qu Kemin (eds.), *Yu zongshuji tanxin*, pp. 18–19.
[71] Ibid., pp. 16–19.

Heart-to-Heart Talks, like *The Critical Moment* that soon followed, also reinterpreted the relationship between China's Confucian tradition and socialism. It drew an analogy to a tree, arguing that China's traditional culture can be understood as the roots, Marxism–Leninism as the trunk, and the outstanding parts of various cultures from around the world as the branches. It should be noted that this analogy stood the orthodox CCP understanding of history on its head. Whereas the CCP had traditionally rooted itself in the May Fourth *rejection* of China's Confucian heritage, the tree analogy envisioned contemporary Marxism as growing out of Confucianism. Although this imagery drew harsh criticism from the left wing of the Party, it was perfectly consistent with what the Party had been trying to do over the past several years: somehow "square the circle" connecting China's traditional history and its modern revolution so that the latter can be viewed as a continuation, rather than a refutation, of the former.[72]

Heart-to-Heart Talks was deliberately written as a response to leftist criticisms of reform, to refute the growing tide of nationalism, and to set out a more positive agenda for Jiang Zemin.[73] As with trial balloons in American politics, the book was both identifiable with Jiang Zemin (given Liu Ji's role) and yet had a certain plausible deniability. *Heart-to-Heart Talks* anticipated the publication of a new series of books under the sponsorship of Liu Ji, called *Contemporary China's Problems*, that would eventually include more than twenty titles. The publication of these books, some of which will be discussed here, marked a fascinating attempt by a group of Jiang's advisers – sometimes referred to as the "enlightened" (*kaiming*) group within the leadership – to set out what they believed were the main problems facing China and to raise possible solutions. This book series was in many ways analogous to the books and articles written in the 1980s by members of Hu Yaobang's intellectual elite and Zhao Ziyang's think-tanks, but whereas those writings more clearly directed their policy advice upward to the leadership, these books engaged an emerging sphere of public opinion, refuting those they disagreed with and building support for views they favored. On the one hand, they reflected the greater role intellectuals play in policy formation in contemporary China; on the other hand, they suggested the increasing need to respond to, refute, and encourage views growing up independently among the intelligentsia and the broader public.

---

[72] The effort to base contemporary Marxism on Chinese traditional culture is a major thrust of efforts to reinvigorate the Party's legitimacy and give content to an otherwise hollow Marxism. See the chapter on ideology in Xu Ming (ed.), *Guanjian shike*, pp. 54–83.

[73] Author interviews.

The left reacted quickly and strongly to the expression of these more liberal views. For instance, in August 1996, Yuan Mu – the conservative ideologue who achieved fame, and infamy, as the public defender of the government in the days after Tiananmen in his role as spokesman of the State Council – gave a long speech at the national "Theoretical Symposium on the Question of Consolidating and Strengthening the Class Foundation of the Ruling Party." Yuan was clearly exercised by trends he had seen in theoretical discussions, in policy decisions, and in the attitudes of many Party members. He was anxious to emphasize the distinction Deng had drawn in 1989 between two types of reform, one that upheld the four cardinal principles and the other that "restored capitalism": the former was correct, whereas the latter is what had led to the collapse of socialism in Eastern Europe and the Soviet Union. Yuan lambasted liberal economists who refused to preface the term "market economy" with the all-important modifier "socialist" and who called for reducing the percentage of the state-owned economy to 20 or even 15 percent (an obvious reference to Cao Siyuan). Decrying trends toward privatization, Yuan declared bluntly: "Without state-owned enterprises and without public ownership of the means of production, there is no socialism." Yuan was also concerned about keeping private entrepreneurs out of the Party organization. As he said, the Party has repeatedly declared that private entrepreneurs, because they are capitalists engaged in exploitation, are not permitted to enter the Party. Nevertheless, he said, local Party organizations ignore this injunction.[74]

The leftist assault continued even as Deng Xiaoping lay dying. The leftist journal *Mainstream* (*Zhongliu*) published a long critique of *Heart-to-Heart Talks* by one Feng Baoxing (apparently a pseudonym). Feng mockingly derided *Heart-to-Heart Talks*, saying that the authors' desire to "modernize" Marxism meant diluting it as an ideological weapon for directing class struggle and also meant turning Marxism into nothing more substantive than a new version of Chiang Kai-shek's "New Life Movement" – the vapid conservative movement Chiang had sponsored in the 1930s in an attempt to instill a diluted Confucian morality.[75] Feng also criticized *Heart-to-Heart Talks* for putting out a "revisionist" interpretation of Deng Xiaoping's thinking (diluting Deng's admonition that socialism means "eliminating exploitation and avoiding polarization"), for arguing that individualism is compatible with Marxism, for desiring to mix Chinese culture with Western culture, and for advocating greater integration into

---

[74] Yuan Mu, "Zhongguo gongren jieji shi Zhongguo gongchandang bu ke dongyao de jieji jichu," pp. 11 and 5.
[75] Feng Baoxing, "Zhe shi yiben shenmayang de zhuzuo?" p. 233.

the world economy. "If we do as the authors propose," Feng wrote, "our policy of opening up to the outside world will inevitably be led onto the wrong road, our economy will lose its independence, and we will be thrown into the embrace of the 'great unity' of international monopoly capital."[76] Referring to Liu Ji's endorsement of the book, Feng wrote, "I don't understand why this book, which includes viewpoints directly opposite of our Party's consistent proposals, directly opposite the resolution of the Sixth Plenum, and directly opposite the general secretary's proposals regarding establishing socialist spiritual civilization, would receive such high praise from this leading comrade."[77]

At almost the same time, a third 10,000 character manifesto was circulated. Entitled "Several Theoretical and Policy Issues on Upholding the Dominant Position of Public Ownership," this article was written by the editorial office of the conservative journal *Contemporary Trends* and published in the fourth issue of 1996. This manifesto zeroed in on the ownership issue and particularly on the policy of "grasping the large and letting go of the small" that had been adopted in 1995. Citing Jiang Zemin's 1996 statement that China should "always maintain the dominant position of the public sector," the manifesto argued that "dominance" cannot be redefined to mean that the state could simply hold a predominant share of assets within the national economy. The manifesto went on to argue that, if small enterprises were privatized (the intention of the policy), then "the immense majority of the working class will become wage workers, and class polarization will become a general phenomenon."[78] The manifesto also took issue with the proposal that the state sector of the economy be reduced to around 20 percent, as well as with the notion that ownership does not determine economic development. It argued further against the proposition that the state should remove itself from competitive industries and adopt a role of supporting infrastructure and certain basic industries. As the manifesto put it, "people who uphold this view actually want the state to bear all the losses so that different types of capital can make their earnings." Doing so, the manifesto declared, would end up turning the state-owned economy into one that is "mainly in the service of foreign capital."[79]

Perhaps the most interesting of the manifestos published at that time, though not generally counted as one of the 10,000 character manifestos, was one titled "Reform and Economic Man." This essay reflected the thinking

[76] Ibid., p. 239.   [77] Ibid.

[78] *Dangdai sichao* editorial department, "Guanyu jianchi gongyouzhi zhuti diwei de ruogan lilun he zhengce wenti," p. 58.

[79] Ibid., p. 60.

of the New Left more than the Old Left, but it showed the overlap that had emerged between the two groups. The point of the essay was that any reform – whether in China, Eastern Europe, or the former Soviet Union – takes the concept of "economic man" (as conceived by Adam Smith) as central, and that the concept of "economic man" is fundamentally contradictory to the collectivism that is central to the socialist ethos. Indeed, the author argued that the richest villages in contemporary China, such as Henan's Nanjie Village, are all run as collectives with a leader acting wholeheartedly in the public interest.[80] The introduction of individualism, based on the concept of economic man, is not the solution to problems in socialism but on the contrary can only exacerbate those problems. Thus, the article argued, the more the notion of economic man has been introduced in state-owned enterprises, the worse they have done, and the more individualism has come to be accepted by society, the more social problems have developed.[81] Putting the issue in apocalyptic terms, the author declared that, if reform guided by the concept of economic man was not "decisively" (*guoduan*) turned around and the collectivist concept restored, then everything for which the Party had struggled for seventy years would be lost.[82]

TROUBLE FROM THE RIGHT

At the same time that Jiang felt pressured from the left, he was also being buffeted from the right. By the mid-1990s, Qiao Shi, then the third-ranked member of the Politburo Standing Committee and head of the NPC, had established himself as the standard-bearer of the liberal wing of the Party. When Qiao took over as head of the NPC in March 1993, he was stripped of his other positions as secretary of the powerful Central Political and Legal Committee and president of the Central Party School. But Qiao apparently continued to have much influence in the security apparatus in which he had built his career. Ren Jianxin, who replaced Qiao as head of the Central Political and Legal Committee, had been promoted by Qiao, and Wei Jianxing, who had become secretary of the Central Discipline Inspection Commission (CDIC) and subsequently replaced Chen Xitong as Beijing Party secretary (before being replaced in turn by Jia Qinglin), had strong ties to Qiao.[83] Meanwhile, Qiao turned the NPC into a base

---

[80] Xin Mao, "Gaige yu jingjiren," p. 216.   [81] Ibid., pp. 213–14, 221.
[82] Ibid., p. 227.   [83] Gao Xin and He Pin, "Tightrope Act of Wei Jianxing."

of support, much as Peng Zhen (who headed that body from 1983 to 1988) had used it as a base from which to oppose reform.

Qiao, who ranked higher than Jiang Zemin in the Shanghai underground in the late 1940s, frequently challenged Jiang by being out in front of him on reform issues. As noted earlier, he beat the drums for Deng's reform campaign in the spring of 1992 long before Jiang Zemin came out in support of it. In January 1995, even as Jiang Zemin was stressing democratic centralism and the role of the core, Qiao chose to stress political reform and democratization.[84] At the same time, Qiao stepped up the pace of legislation and incorporated greater expertise into its formulation; he also gave greater weight to provincial initiative and to the speed of economic reform than did Jiang Zemin or Li Peng.[85]

Aiding Qiao in this effort was Tian Jiyun, the Politburo member whose withering criticism of leftism in April 1992 may have cost him a seat on the Politburo Standing Committee. During the March 1995 session of the NPC, Tian listened sympathetically to Guangdong delegates, who complained that China's rulers were not allowing the NPC to function as the "highest administrative organ" as called for by the constitution. The day after this raucous meeting, 36 percent of NPC delegates either abstained or voted against Jiang Chunyun, Jiang Zemin's handpicked nominee as vice-premier. Never before had China's legislature registered such a large protest.

---

[84] Xinhua, January 5, 1995, in FBIS-CHI, January 6, 1995, pp. 11–13.
[85] Xinhua, October 13, 1994, in FBIS-CHI, October 20, 1994, pp. 35–7.

CHAPTER 7

Elite politics in an era of globalization and nationalism

Between the Fourth Plenum in 1994 and the Fifteenth Party Congress in 1997, "public opinion" played a limited but not insignificant role. As discussed in Part II, the intellectual atmosphere became considerably more conservative and nationalistic in this period, which helped the government preserve the social stability that it prized so highly. Moreover, there was greater interaction between government and intellectual circles as each tried to influence the other (a trend that coexisted with its opposite, as some intellectuals oriented their activities toward society – ignoring the government – while others withdrew into scholarly endeavors or developed new critiques of government). We have seen how intellectuals such as Hu Angang and Wang Shaoguang influenced government policy, at least to some extent, on such issues as tax reform and regional disparities, and how the government tried to organize and solicit new, but acceptable, ideas through such books as *Heart-to-Heart Talks with the General Secretary*. We have also seen how the Old Left tried to influence both elite politics and public opinion through the various 10,000 character manifestos. There were also clear connections between elements of the elite and expressions of nationalistic opinion, whether through journals such as *Strategy and Management* or books such as *China Can Say No*.

These conflicting trends of elite and popular opinion reached a new level of intensity in 1997 as Jiang tried to put his imprint on the post-Deng era, only to face another powerful wave of nationalism that grew up around the issues of China's entry into the WTO and, more importantly, the tragic bombing of the Chinese Embassy in Belgrade. As one century yielded to the next, nationalism, corruption, globalization, elite conflict, and new intellectual controversies suggested an important reshaping of the Chinese polity.

DENG'S DEATH AND JIANG'S MOVE TO CONSOLIDATE POWER

Facing challenges from the left and right, one might think that Jiang hoped Deng Xiaoping would survive long enough to see Jiang through the critical Fifteenth Party Congress. Indeed, on the eve of Deng's death, the left circulated the fourth 10,000 character manifesto.[1] Despite this challenge, Deng's passing in February 1997 proved a blessing for the general secretary. Because Deng's demise was long anticipated and activities surrounding the events occurred with orchestrated smoothness, its impact has been obscured. Stability and continuity seemed to be the order of the day, but – in his eulogy at Deng's funeral – Jiang dropped a hint that he had something more than mere continuity in mind. Jiang quoted Deng as saying (when he returned to power in the late 1970s) that there are two possible attitudes: "One is to act as a bureaucrat, the other is to work."[2]

It seemed a risky quote for Jiang to cite, given his reputation for caution. But Jiang was using Deng's words to make his own personal declaration – that he, too, was determined to "work."

Jiang's intimation of important changes to come was perhaps as much a reflection of the dilemmas facing the Party as it was of personal ambition. As Deng entered his final decline, the Party fought vigorously over his legacy; with Deng's passing the Party would have to make choices. The first and arguably most critical point of decision came in March, when a draft of Jiang's report to the Fifteenth Party Congress was circulated among officials for comment. Reportedly it met with a barrage of criticism from the left. Jiang either had to water down his proposals extensively or break with the left, something he had refrained from doing in the years since his arrival in Beijing. Indeed, Jiang had drawn much support from the left wing of the Party in his early years. As late as 1996, Jiang had reached out to the left with his statement in the Sixth Plenum resolution cited previously that "spiritual civilization would not be sacrificed to material civilization."

However, the political situation had changed notably since Jiang had arrived in the capital. Many conservative Party elders – including Li Xiannian, Hu Qiaomu, Wang Renzhong, and Chen Yun – had died. Such generational change did not end opposition to more thoroughgoing reform, as there seemed to be a limitless supply of central officials whose careers and interests are tied to the preservation of the old state-run economy, but it certainly weakened political resistance at the highest reaches of the Party. What is more, the mounting problems of state-owned enterprises were becoming

[1] Wei Ming, "Yijiu jiu'er nian yilai zichan jieji ziyouhua de dongtai he tedian."
[2] Jiang Zemin, "Memorial Speech at Deng Xiaoping's Memorial Meeting."

increasingly difficult to deny. In 1996, for the first time, subsidies to SOEs actually outweighed their contributions to the state budget. Leftists, for all their ability to obstruct reform, had never been able to present a viable alternative; Li Peng's efforts in the wake of Tiananmen had been their last, best hope.

Given the possibilities presented by the changed political landscape, the crisis facing the economy, and Jiang's own need to put his stamp on the post-Deng era, Jiang went to the Central Party School in late May to give the most important political speech of his career. In a thinly veiled jab at the left, Jiang declared that "[t]here is no way out if we study Marxism in isolation and separate and set it against vivid development in real life." In the unpublicized portion of the speech, Jiang reportedly went further, explicitly criticizing the left and laying out his rationale for reform of the ownership structure.[3] Deng had raised the slogan "guard against the right, but guard primarily against the left" in his 1992 trip to the south, but it had been largely dropped from the official media (except for inclusion in formal Party resolutions) following the Fourteenth Party Congress later that year. Now Jiang was reviving it and identifying himself with Deng's reforms. For a leader often criticized as bland, cautious, and technocratic, Jiang was beginning to reveal a degree of decisiveness previously visible only in his deft maneuvers against political enemies.

Although Jiang had previewed some of his major themes in his speech to the Central Party School, it was not until the Fifteenth Party Congress convened in Beijing on September 12–18 that the full scope of Jiang's program and his personnel arrangements for carrying it out were unveiled. The theme of the congress, as Jiang's report declared, was to "hold high the banner of Deng Xiaoping theory," and Deng Xiaoping theory was subsequently incorporated into both the Party and state constitutions. Jiang had evidently considered a variety of ideological themes in his efforts to consolidate his own authority; it certainly would have been more satisfying to enunciate a doctrine that could reasonably have been considered "Jiang Zemin theory" rather than to tie his fortunes to the "theory" of the deceased Deng. Praising Deng, however, had two distinct virtues: no one could openly disagree; and, the more Deng was praised, the more the leftists who looked to Mao's legacy were disparaged. Jiang's report, then, was a highly authoritative response to the 10,000 character manifestos and other expressions of leftist discontent. Thus, Jiang declared in his report to the congress that Deng Xiaoping theory "breaks with outmoded conventions

---

[3] Xinhua, May 29, 1997, in FBIS-CHI-97-105, May 29, 1997; author interview.

on the basis of new practice" and that "[d]iscussing Marxism without regard to our actual situation and development of the times is misleading."[4]

This effort to break with leftist interpretations of Marxism–Leninism was also apparent in Jiang's unexpected decision to feature the thesis that China is in the "primary stage of socialism," an argument that had been developed by then-General Secretary Zhao Ziyang at the Thirteenth Party Congress in 1987 in order to justify further reform but then quietly dropped after 1989. Jiang revived the thesis in 1997 to legitimize reforming SOEs through the widespread adoption of the shareholding system, a theme anticipated in *Heart-to-Heart Talks with the General Secretary* and Liu Ji's writings.[5] "The shareholding system," Jiang declared, "can be used both under capitalism and socialism." Large and medium-sized state-owned enterprises would be reorganized into "standard corporations" with "clear ownership" that would be genuinely independent of government control. The largest of them (frequently proposed as some 500–1,000 SOEs) would be reorganized into large enterprise groups that were to function like *chaebol*, while smaller enterprises could be reorganized, merged, leased, contracted out, or sold off – a policy known as "grasp the large and let go of the small" (*zhuada fangxiao*).[6] Jiang also called for the development of diverse forms of ownership, a formulation that would permit the continued rapid development of the private economy. Together these reforms would allow room for a massive restructuring of the Chinese economy in the years ahead.

One of the most interesting aspects of Jiang's report to the congress was that even as he touted Deng's reputation and legacy, he hinted that he himself would push that legacy forward, which he tried to do in the years since. Jiang cited Deng's 1978 battle with Party Chairman Hua Guofeng's "two whatevers" ("whatever decisions Chairman Mao made, we resolutely support; whatever instructions Chairman Mao made, we will steadfastly abide by") as a period of "emancipating the mind"; he said Deng's 1992 trip to the south was a second such period. Intimating that he would continue this process, Jiang called for an "emancipation of the mind in the new period."[7] Conservative Premier Li Peng, of all people, made this implication clear when he reiterated to a group of delegates that the present was the third of three periods of emancipating the mind.[8] This theme would

---

[4] Jiang Zemin, "Text of Political Report by General Secretary Jiang Zemin at the 15th CPC National Congress."

[5] Liu Ji (ed.), *Shehui zhuyi gaige lun*, pp. 190–217.

[6] Richard Baum, "The Fifteenth National Party Congress: Jiang Takes Command?"

[7] Jiang Zemin, "Text of Political Report by General Secretary Jiang Zemin at the 15th CPC National Congress."

[8] Xinhua, September 13, 1997, in FBIS-CHI-97-260, September 17, 1997.

be picked up and expanded upon in the months that followed during the limited political opening that became known as the "Beijing spring."

The other news that caught the Western headlines was that Qiao Shi had been dropped from the Central Committee. Qiao, as noted before, had repeatedly challenged Jiang Zemin's authority by calling for greater attention to law and by ignoring Jiang's call to rally around the "core" of the Party (i.e., Jiang). Qiao certainly presented a political problem for Jiang, and Jiang responded by lining up support for Qiao's ouster. Although Jiang apparently surprised Qiao by calling for all those over age 70 to step down (only to have Party elder Bo Yibo say that the rule should not apply to Jiang himself), the real work had been done behind the scenes. Qiao supporters Wan Li and Yang Shangkun reportedly sat mute through the meeting, realizing that they had been out-maneuvered.[9]

Many interpreted Qiao's removal as a pulling back from the liberal themes that he had touted, but in fact Qiao's ouster facilitated Jiang's move to the "right." With Qiao in place, any movement to relax political control and emphasize the rule of law would have been taken advantage of by Qiao to increase the role of the National People's Congress at Jiang's expense. By getting rid of Qiao, Jiang was free to adopt much of Qiao's program.

In his report to the Party congress, Jiang devoted considerable space to political and legal reform; he stated: "Without democracy, there can be no socialism and no socialist modernization." Although Jiang stopped well short of endorsing anything resembling Western-style democracy, his repeated use of the word "democracy" (some 32 times) prompted hopes of greater opening up. More important for many listeners was his use of the term "rule of law" instead of the standard formula "rule by law."[10] This formulation seemed to presage a new era in institution building and an acceptance of limitations on the arbitrary use of power.

Personnel arrangements made at the congress (see Table 2) supported the fresh image Jiang was cultivating, while the removal of many older personnel enhanced Jiang's ability to control the Party. Overall, 60 percent

---

[9] Author interviews.

[10] Richard Baum, "The Fifteenth National Party Congress: Jiang Takes Command?" In Chinese, "rule by law" is rendered *yifa zhiguo*, the *zhi* meaning "to rule," whereas "rule of law" is phonetically the same but a different character, meaning "system," is used for *zhi*. It is probably a hopeful exaggeration to render the latter phrase "rule of law" since the Chinese phrase carries more a sense of institutionalization than of law having a independent status, as the English phrase suggests. Jiang probably meant to convey a sense of regularization, already a step forward, whereas liberal intellectuals have tried to push the interpretation a step farther. See Li Shenzhi, "Yeyao tuidong zhengzhi gaige."

Table 2: *Leadership of the Chinese
Communist Party Following the 15th
Party Congress*

Politburo Standing Committee

Jiang Zemin (age 71)	Hu Jintao (55)
Li Peng (69)	Wei Jianxing (66)
Zhu Rongji (69)	Li Lanqing (65)
Li Ruihuan (64)	

Politburo – Other Full Members

Ding Guan'gen (64)	Qian Qiqian (69)
Huang Ju (59)	Chi Haotian (68)
Jia Qinglin (57)	Wen Jiabao (55)
Jiang Chunyun (67)	Wu Bangguo (56)
Li Changchun (53)	Wu Guanzheng (59)
Li Tieying (61)	Xie Fei (64)*
Luo Gan (62)	Zhang Wannian (69)
Tian Jiyun (68)	

Secretariat

Hu Jintao (55)	Wen Jiabao (55)
Ding Guan'gen (64)	Zhang Wannian (69)
Luo Gan (62)	Zeng Qinghong (58)
Wei Jianxing (66)	

*Died October 1999.

of the 193 people selected as full members of the latest Central Committee were new. The newly elected Central Committee was younger, better educated, and more professionally capable than any of its predecessors. Military representation on the Central Committee also declined from five years previous and, more importantly, no PLA representatives sat on the powerful Politburo Standing Committee. This, combined with Jiang's call to reduce military staffing by 500,000 – with 100,000 to be shorn from the officer corps – marked a clear effort to make China's military smaller, better equipped, more professional, and less political.[11]

One aspect of the Fifteenth Party Congress that is particularly illuminating in terms of institutionalization is the way Li Peng was handled. Having served two terms as premier, Li was constitutionally barred from continuing in office, but no Party head or premier had ever left office voluntarily. The obvious friction between the newly instituted formal rules and the long-standing informal rules was clearly a delicate issue, especially given

[11] Cheng Li and Lynn White, "The 15th Central Committee of the Chinese Communist Party."

Li's role in Tiananmen. His complete removal from office would have been viewed as a repudiation of the crackdown, and there would no doubt have been new calls to "reverse the verdict" on the Tiananmen demonstrations. Such a possibility was actually suggested by a letter – calling for such a reappraisal – that Zhao Ziyang sent to the Central Committee on the eve of the Fifteenth Party Congress.[12] Several scenarios for dealing with Li Peng were bruited during the summer, but in the end Jiang decided to give Qiao Shi's NPC position to Li but allow Li to retain the number-two ranking on the Politburo Standing Committee. Qiao Shi was angered by his dismissal (though apparently able to secure the appointment of some of his followers as a price), and Zhu Rongji was similarly upset by not being named as the second-ranking member of the Politburo Standing Committee (the usual ranking of the premier, which Zhu was slated to become the following spring). Nevertheless, Jiang was able to move Li to a distinctly less power-ful position without a major political upheaval, an effort to blend informal and formal politics.

In short, the Fifteenth Party Congress was an important milestone in the Party's development: the first time power had passed fully from the revolutionary generation to a post-revolutionary generation. Moreover, it had done so smoothly. Jiang had survived from an improbable beginning to become "core" of the Party in reality. As important as securing personal power was, Jiang was not – and could not become – the sort of pre-eminent leader Deng had been. Jiang lacked the revolutionary legitimacy, the author-ity within the military and other key Party components, and perhaps the personality to dominate the Party the way Deng had. Although intensely conscious of his role as Party leader and hence sensitive to perceived slights, Jiang was nevertheless a consensus builder. He preferred to meet challenges by maneuvering rather than by confrontation. And he realized that both his own personal authority and the legitimacy of the Party required greater attention to institution building. Thus, whether ousting political threats like Chen Xitong and Qiao Shi, diminishing the political clout of the PLA, or laying out a program for reform, Jiang sought to base his legitimacy in institutional procedure. The transformation to a more authoritarian and less Leninist political system was underway. But such transformations are delicate at best. Jiang hoped for tranquillity to solidify his own rule and create a more stable political system. Such tranquillity would prove elusive.

---

[12] Zhao's letter was not circulated to the delegates at the time of the congress, so they had no chance to discuss it. The text is reproduced in *Beijing zhi chun*, no. 54 (November 1997), p. 105.

BEIJING SPRING

As Jiang moved to secure power, promote his scheme for enterprise reform, and create a better atmosphere for Sino–US relations, he began to allow greater space for political expression, at least among intellectuals.[13] In the summer of 1997, the press was filled with reform-minded articles as the Party prepared public opinion for the upcoming congress and intellectuals tried to push the limits of acceptable discussion. Proposals for the establishment of a "socialist market economy," soon to be endorsed by the congress, appeared regularly; more sensitive was that some intellectuals again began raising demands for political reform. After several years of relative quiescence, liberal thought was making itself heard in broader circles.

The first to openly raise the issue of political reform was Shang Dewen, then a 65-year-old economics professor at Beijing University. In August 1997, he penned a letter to Jiang Zemin in which he said the disjuncture between economic reform and political reform was causing "contradictions, frictions, and conflict." He then proceeded to outline a program of democratization, including direct election of the presidency and checks and balances among three branches of government, that might take a quarter century to implement – but needed to be inaugurated immediately.[14] A gentle person, Shang's letter was extremely circumspect but also unmistakable in its demand for democratization. His initial letter was followed up by two similar appeals.[15]

China's intellectuals, as Shang Dewen's inaugural letter suggests, were quick to sense the changing mood and pick up the themes articulated at the Party congress. In November (two months after the congress), Fang Jue, then a 44-year-old former deputy director of the planning commission of Fuzhou city, distributed a statement calling for political reform. Fang, who had previously been a researcher in the Institute of Politics at CASS and later had left government to go into business in 1995, called for multiparty democracy, direct elections of legislative bodies at all levels, the acceptance of international economic and political norms, respect for human rights, and an improvement in China's international relations, especially with the United States and Japan. It was the most direct and farthest-ranging proposal for political reform since Tiananmen – and Fang remained free until the crackdown on democratic activists a year later.[16]

---

[13] This section is adapted from my article, "Jiang Zemin Takes Command." Permission of *Current History* to use this material is gratefully acknowledged.

[14] Shang Dewen, "Guanyu Zhongguo zhengzhi tizhi gaige de ruogan wenti yu jiben duice."

[15] Shang Dewen, "Cong eryuan jiegou kan Zhongguo."

[16] Fang Jue, "Zhongguo xuyao xinde zhuanbian"; see also Steven Mufson, "Former Chinese Official Advocates Democracy."

In December, Hu Jiwei, the crusading former editor-in-chief of *People's Daily*, published a series of articles calling for political reform in a major Hong Kong daily. Scathing in its criticism of Deng Xiaoping and his handling of the June 4 incident, Hu decried the fact that Zhao Ziyang had been under house arrest and "deprived of his minimal rights as a Party member and citizen" ever since. Hu asked pointedly, "[o]ne can well imagine that if a ruling Party can wantonly deprive its leaders of their minimal human rights, is it not more difficult for this Party to respect the human rights of dissidents in general?"[17]

In March the journal *Methods* (*Fangfa*), whose editorial board was stocked with liberal intellectuals, ran a series of articles that would have been risky only a short time before. Picking up Jiang Zemin's call for "rule of law" and political reform at the Fifteenth Party Congress, China's liberal intelligentsia tried to push for greater political reform. Zhang Ximing, a young journalist at CASS who had been involved in the writing of *Heart-to-Heart Talks with the General Secretary*, opened by calling for a press law (something that had been widely discussed in the 1980s before being abandoned after Tiananmen) that would protect freedom of the press.[18] Ma Licheng, then a journalist in the editorial department of *People's Daily* who would soon become famous for co-authoring a controversial book called *Crossed Swords*, followed with a short article arguing that press supervision of public authority would benefit, not detract from, social order. Press supervision, Ma said in adapting a line from Deng Xiaoping, "could be used by capitalism, and could be used as well by socialism."[19] Liu Junning, a political theorist at CASS, argued that political reform should start by protecting individual property rights. Historian Lei Yi argued that, with the task of national independence accomplished by the 1949 revolution and with the people's livelihood basically guaranteed by the economic reforms, it was time to move on to the third of Sun Yat-sen's three principles: democracy.[20]

In striking contrast to the mood of only a couple of years before – when *China Can Say No* topped the best-seller list and spawned a whole cottage industry of imitators – books depicting the United States in a more

---

[17] Hu Jiwei, "If the Party Is Correct, Bad Things Can Be Turned into Good Things; If the Party Is Wrong, Good Things Can Be Turned into Bad Things"; Hu Jiwei, "Despotic Dictatorship Lingers On"; Hu Jiwei, "Given a Good Central Committee, We Will Have a Good Party; Given a Good Party, We Will Have a Good State." The citation is from part three. Shao Huaze, head of *People's Daily*, reportedly went to Hu's house to serve him with a warning that he had violated Party discipline. See Yin Yen, "Hu Jiwei Served with Warning after Releasing Articles Criticizing CCP Autocracy and Exposing Its Errors in June 4 Incident."

[18] Zhang Ximing, "Xinwen fazhi yu shehui fazhan."   [19] Ma Licheng, "Xinwen jiandu buxing 'zi'."

[20] Liu Junning, "Caichanquan de baozhang yu youxian zhengfu"; Lei Yi, "Minzu, minsheng, minquan."

favorable light began to appear on the market. One notable work was *China Will Not Be "Mr. No"* by Shen Jiru, a senior intellectual in the Institute of World Economics and Politics at CASS, which was published in the *China's Contemporary Problems* book series under the general editorship of Liu Ji. Like *Heart-to-Heart Talks*, Shen's book joined the long-standing debate over the causes of the Soviet Union's collapse. Whereas the earlier book had concentrated on domestic causes, Shen extended the argument to international relations by arguing that it had been the steadfast refusal of Soviet leaders to cooperate with other countries and open up their country (which had earned Soviet Foreign Minister Andrei Gromyko the nickname of "Mr. No") that had brought about its demise. In opposition to conservatives' argument that it was reform that led to collapse, Shen and others argued that it was the *lack* of reform that brought about the failure of socialism in the Soviet Union and Eastern Europe.[21]

Like *Heart-to-Heart Talks*, the publication of Shen's book was tacit recognition that public opinion had become important, even in the realm of foreign policy. In the face of nationalistic books like *China Can Say No*, reformers within the government needed to justify publicly the policy of rapprochement that Jiang was pursuing vis-à-vis the United States. An even more outstanding instance of using public opinion both to justify accelerating reform and to advance policy battles within the upper reaches of the Party was the publication of *Crossed Swords*, easily the most controversial book of the spring.

Written by Ma Licheng of the theoretical department of *People's Daily* and *People's Daily* senior reporter Ling Zhijun, the book starts by tracing the history of the emergence of the Dengist reforms – particularly the opening up of intellectual freedom – against the opposition of Mao's successor, Hua Guofeng, and goes on to link this early period of relaxation to the heated debates surrounding Deng Xiaoping's trip to the south in 1992. Finally, and most controversially, the book details the sharp political debates of 1995–7, specifically the efforts of the Old Left to hamstring reform through the circulation of the 10,000 character manifestos. Ignoring certain historical realities, particularly that much of Deng's animus in his 1992 trip was directed against Jiang Zemin, the book portrays Jiang as inheriting and pushing forward the "emancipation of the mind" begun in 1978.[22] *Crossed Swords* was even more controversial than other works published during the spring because, like Shen Jiru's book, it was included in the *China's Contemporary Problems* series and because it publicly criticized the leftist

---

[21] Shen Jiru, *Zhongguo bu dang "bu xiansheng."*   [22] Ma Licheng and Ling Zhijun, *Jiao feng.*

manifestos, which had been widely circulated but not published (except for the one in *Mainstream*). Despite Liu Ji's close relationship with Jiang Zemin, it was apparent that the publication of *Crossed Swords* was part of the ongoing conduct of "court politics" surrounding the Party leader rather than a direct reflection of his views. In an effort to conciliate (or at least mediate among) different wings of the Party, Jiang had surrounded himself with a variety of advisers, ranging from the conservative Teng Wensheng to the neoconservative Wang Huning to the more liberal Liu Ji. Inevitably there were controversies among such people, and the personal animosities among some of them were quite deep. For instance, Wang Renzhi, the former head of the Propaganda Department who was forced to step down (following Deng's trip to the south) and take a position as Party secretary of CASS, was angry about the publication of *Heart-to-Heart Talks* and quarreled on more than one occasion with Liu Ji, then a vice-president of CASS.[23] This may well have made Liu even more willing to allow the publication of *Crossed Swords*. In any event, it was clear that the publication of *Crossed Swords* set off a political maelstrom. Ding Guan'gen, the conservative head of the Propaganda Department who was widely disliked by intellectuals, quickly condemned the book. Wang Renzhi was predictably outraged, as was conservative elder Song Ping. Leftists, who were angered by the *Crossed Swords'* wholesale criticism of them, organized a meeting in April to attack the book, to which they invited communist ideologues from Russia (provoking liberals to mock the gathering as one of the "Communist International"). Eventually, the editors of the conservative journal *Mainstream*, which had published one of the 10,000 character manifestos, took the authors of *Crossed Swords* to court, charging copyright violation. The court eventually dismissed the charges, but not without some dramatic political theater.[24]

With this clash of criticism and countercriticism swirling around him, Jiang decided to go to Beijing University on May 4 to participate in the university's centennial ceremonies. Jiang made this decision on his own and against the counsel of some of his advisers; they feared that the trip would be too controversial and perhaps even stir up a new student movement. Beijing University has been the fount of liberal thinking in modern China and, more specifically, the leading force in the 1989 Tiananmen demonstrations. Wang Dan, the student leader released to the United States in April 1998, was a Beijing University student.

---

[23] Author interviews.   [24] "Zhongliu Loses Lawsuit against 'Jiaofeng'."

Critics have argued that Jiang's visit to Beijing University paid too much attention to patriotism and the university's role in the development of the CCP (the co-founders of the party, Li Dazhao and Chen Duxiu, were both Beijing University faculty). Nevertheless, what seems important was Jiang's personal gesture in reaching out to intellectuals. According to some professors at the school, the president's visit was highly successful. Jiang spent a whole morning there, addressing faculty in French, English, Russian, and Japanese (which he said he would speak better if he had not been forced to learn it under the Japanese occupation) and exchanging couplets of Tang poetry with students.[25]

Jiang's visit to Beijing University appears to have been part of a strategy to assuage the anger left by Tiananmen without formally revising the Party's judgment on that event. Like the removal of the Yang brothers from the military in 1992, the ouster of the widely disliked Beijing Party secretary Chen Xitong in 1995, the various campaigns against corruption, and the easing of Li Peng out of the premiership, Jiang's visit to Beijing University was an important gesture that tried to put Tiananmen behind him and reach out to the intellectual community at the same time.

RESTRUCTURING GOVERNMENT AND THE ECONOMY: THE NINTH NPC

In the year following Deng Xiaoping's death, Jiang was remarkably successful in putting his own mark on Chinese politics. He rejected pressure exerted by the Old Left, opened up the intellectual and political atmosphere modestly but significantly, and dealt skillfully with personnel issues at the Fifteenth Party Congress. These moves were necessary if Jiang was going to handle successfully the paramount issue of the day, economic reform.

The biggest problem was that of the state-owned enterprises. In some ways, China had sidestepped the problem of SOEs in the 1980s and early 1990s as the TVE sector grew dramatically. The SOE sector, however, did not fade away. In some ways, it actually increased in importance as the number of workers employed by SOEs rose by 40 million between 1978 and 1994.[26] Despite the decreasing importance of SOEs in the overall economy, they continued to dominate important sectors, particularly heavy industry, and their failure to reform was increasingly a drag on economic growth. By the late 1990s, it was apparent that SOE reform could not be avoided.[27]

---

[25] Author interviews.   [26] Nicholas Lardy, *China's Unfinished Economic Revolution*, p. 3.
[27] Edward Steinfeld, *Forging Reform in China*.

One of the central obstacles in SOE reform had always been the relationship between the enterprises and the state. It was not only that the enterprises sought help from their supervising administrators but also that the various ministries had an incentive to support even weak SOEs and to encourage production even if it was not economically efficient. Unless the apron strings that bound SOEs to state ministries could be severed, there was no way that SOEs, however their ownership structure might be changed, could truly make their way in the market economy. This issue cut to the heart of the debates about socialism and also involved major interests in Chinese society. Ministries had no real desire to force their subordinate industries onto the market, just as industries had no incentive to compete when administrative support was available.

Furthermore, there was the question of how and to what extent China's economy should be linked to the international economy. Since China had begun to open its doors in the late 1970s, its trade with the outside world had expanded rapidly. In the mid-1990s, in an effort to increase foreign investment, China had relaxed its rules on foreign ownership. This had brought a huge increase in the amount of foreign funds invested, but it had also stimulated economic nationalism in response. Should the rules on foreign investment be relaxed even further? If they were not, would foreign enterprises continue to invest large sums in the Chinese economy? Without the pressures of foreign investment, how could enterprises behind a wall of protection be expected to reform? Such questions were, of course, linked to China's bid to join the WTO – to what extent should China compromise in order to join the world trade body?

This last question was closely related to China's international relations. China's isolation following Tiananmen put the government under a great deal of pressure. China initially concentrated its efforts on Asia and managed to gain diplomatic recognition from Indonesia and Singapore, from which China had long been estranged. At the same time, it was able to persuade Saudi Arabia to extend diplomatic relations, followed by South Africa. Such diplomatic successes put Taiwan under greater pressure but did little to normalize China's relations with the United States. Indeed, there is reason to believe that conservatives in China had scant interest in improving relations with the United States, at least past a certain point. Tension with the leading capitalist nation in the world had the effect of legitimizing continued efforts to oppose "bourgeois liberalization" at home and to delegitimize the private economy.

Coming into his own as a political leader, Jiang Zemin recognized the importance of improving relations with the United States for both domestic reform and his own legitimacy. Gaining China's international acceptance as one of the great powers of the world would diminish the lingering effects of post-Tiananmen isolation; it would also realize the century-old desire of Chinese patriots to no longer be treated as a second-rate power but instead to be regarded as an equal in world affairs. This was an issue of status that would clearly enhance Jiang Zemin's political prestige, but it was also an economic issue with profound implications for domestic reform.

In March 1998, the Ninth Session of the NPC formally named Zhu Rongji premier, replacing Li Peng. Luo Gan, secretary general of the State Council, presented a proposal for a massive restructuring of the government. Pointing to the costs of bloated administration, to the demands posed by the reform of state-owned enterprises, and to the challenges presented by the Asian financial crisis, he outlined a sweeping plan to reduce the number of government ministries from 40 to 29. Although Jiang had called for administrative restructuring at the Fifteenth Party Congress the previous fall and Luo Gan had presented the plan to the NPC, this was clearly Zhu's program.

The plan to reorganize the government marked the biggest readjustment of the government–enterprise relationship since the beginning of reform. Combined with the "grasping the large and letting go of the small" policy adopted in 1995, the elimination of so many of China's line ministries opened up the possibility of a radical retreat of the government from the economy. The idea appears to have been to centralize the supervision of a limited number (500–1,000) of large enterprise groups in the State Economic and Trade Commission (SETC). Zhu established a number of inspection groups, each headed by a person of vice-ministerial rank, that were to keep tabs on the enterprise groups and report directly back to the SETC. Because they were no longer ministerially based, they were expected to provide the government with more objective information on the state of industry. At the same time, numerous enterprises at the local level were reorganized as shareholding enterprises or simply sold off.

The impact of the South Korean model on this reorganization plan was apparent. Just as the Korean economy was dominated by a small number of large-scale *chaebol*, so too would a relatively small number of enterprise groups dominate the Chinese economy. Moreover, just as management of the Korean economy was highly centralized, the Chinese plan eliminated the multiplicity of bureaucratic interests, centralizing control in the SETC. Finally, just as small-scale enterprise was left to the market in Korea, so the central state would retreat from ownership and management of most industry in China. Private enterprise would be given room to expand;

indeed, the government hoped it would expand rapidly because the pressure of unemployment was perhaps the most serious problem China faced. Not only would people laid off from state-owned enterprises need to find new jobs, there was still a large number of underemployed people in the rural areas – frequently estimated to be at least 150 million – who needed to switch to non-agricultural employment. Only private enterprise, with its small investment of capital and labor-intensive production, could hope to provide sufficient employment.

Along with the plan to reorganize government and streamline industry, there was also an intent to wed the Chinese economy more closely to the global economy. It was at this time – in the spring of 1998, as details of President Clinton's forthcoming trip to China were being planned – that China expressed renewed interest in joining the World Trade Organization (WTO). China had first applied to join the trade body, then known as the General Agreement on Trade and Tariffs (GATT), in 1986 but negotiations to complete China's entry were interrupted by Tiananmen.[28] There was a period of renewed interest and possibility in 1994, prior to the formal establishment of the WTO at the beginning of 1995, but by then the bar to admission had been raised significantly. This was not simply a matter of political bias against China (though, given the image of China in the US, tougher conditions were certainly needed to convince a skeptical Congress); primarily it reflected a new image of China as a potential economic jugger-naut that might overwhelm the United States with cheap exports. In any case, Chinese negotiators were not yet willing to make the sort of com-mitments that would secure their entry, so the opportunity passed. Trade negotiations were suspended during the tensions in the Taiwan Straits fol-lowing President Lee Teng-hui's visit to Cornell University, and it was only after Sino–US relations improved in the wake of that incident that serious trade negotiations could be resumed.

Jiang Zemin had long been a supporter of China's entry into the WTO, as a way both of tying China's economy more closely to the world's and of demonstrating his ability to enhance China's status as a world power. However, many bureaucracies in China feared the impact of joining the trade organization, and Li Peng had effectively blocked serious negotia-tions.[29] But by the spring of 1998, the time was ripe to reopen negotiations.

---

[28] The history of China's GATT/WTO bid is traced in Harold K. Jacobson and Michel Oksenberg, *China's Participation in the IMF, World Bank and GATT*; Susan Shirk, *How China Opened Its Door*; Margaret M. Pearson, "China's Integration into the International Trade and Investment Regime"; and Margaret M. Pearson, "The Case of China's Accession to GATT/WTO."

[29] Author interviews.

Sino–US relations were significantly improved, deflating opposition on nationalist grounds, and Li Peng was stepping down as premier. Thus, on March 8, Jiang Zemin stated: "We have to gain a complete and correct understanding of the issue of economic 'globalization' and properly deal with it. Economic globalization is an objective trend of world economic development, from which none can escape and in which everyone has to participate."[30] The direction in which Jiang hoped to move the country was quite apparent.

NATIONALISM, ELITE POLITICS, AND THE WTO

Given the economic nationalism in 1995, the precarious economic situation facing China in 1996–8, and the concern with its economic security and potential vulnerability to the Asian financial crisis, it is almost surprising that China continued to express interest in the WTO.[31] Whereas the period following Tiananmen had been marked by a new suspicion of the outside world and a resurgence of nativist thinking, the WTO challenged China to engage – and be engaged by – the world in the best cosmopolitan tradition. In the 1980s this thinking came naturally, if somewhat naively; in the 1990s China's sophistication regarding the outside world had leaped ahead, but cosmopolitan thinking was under fire in many circles. In terms of elite politics, this posture of "half-in, half-out" of the world was highlighted by both rhetoric and conflict. In 1989, Jiang Zemin had stressed the difference between "socialist" reform and opening up versus "capitalist" reform and opening up; in 1991, he had stressed the danger of "peaceful evolution." Jiang had only slowly relaxed his concern with being accused, like his predecessors, of being "lax on bourgeois liberalization," and he was quick to retreat if domestic stability seemed threatened. Aside from (or perhaps lurking behind) such ideological concerns were very different interests, both political and economic. A certain degree of international tension was good for those who liked to raise the nationalist banner; it also provided a good excuse to continue to protect the interests of enterprises and bureaucracies that were threatened by international competition. Conversely, other enterprises and bureaucracies benefited from opening up internationally. To a degree, policy oscillations reflected these competing interests.

[30] *Renmin ribao*, March 9, 1998, p. 1.
[31] This section is adapted from my article "The Impact of the Kosovo Conflict on China's Political Leaders and Prospects for WTO Accession," which was prepared for and published by the National Bureau of Asian Research, Seattle, WA.

As we have seen in looking at the sub-elite level, the enlightenment project and globalization had come under considerable criticism by many intellectuals in the 1990s. Lurking behind much of this criticism, as with similar criticism in the West, was a deep-seated suspicion of multinational firms and capitalism. But whereas such criticisms in the West tend to be fueled more by concerns with the environment and labor standards, in China they are fueled by nationalism – the fear that China will be entrapped by global capital and by US "hegemony" in particular. This was the point at which the nationalistic concerns of the New Left intellectual elite slid very easily into the rawer, more populist nationalism typified by *China Can Say No*.

China's proposed entrance into the WTO thus struck an uneasy balance between the desire of Chinese leaders to demonstrate China's "great power" status and to further economic development by joining the international economy on one side, and, on the other, the protectionist instincts of some regions and bureaucracies, the ideological and political concerns that such integration might prove socially disruptive, the concerns of New Left intellectuals, and the populist nationalism of a large segment of the public.

Following China's failed bid to become an inaugural member of the WTO, the 1995–6 Taiwan Straits crisis further delayed negotiations. Nevertheless, the very seriousness of that crisis prompted new efforts to improve relations. As a result, Jiang Zemin traveled to the United States in October 1997, the first Chinese president to do so since Li Xiannian visited in 1986, and President Clinton returned the visit by going to China in June 1998 – the first presidential visit since President Bush's ill-fated trip in February 1989. As the relationship warmed, discussions on China's accession to the WTO were renewed. In the months leading up to President Clinton's visit, China evinced considerable interest in joining the WTO, but US negotiators were convinced that China was still hoping for a "political pass" – that is, an agreement allowing them into the WTO out of consideration for Sino–US relations rather than an offer requiring serious economic commitments.

There were clearly domestic political factors in China that were blocking progress toward a WTO agreement in this period. Jiang Zemin's support for China's entry into the GATT/WTO can be traced back to the 1993–4 period. China's efforts to join the WTO were coordinated by Vice-Premier Li Lanqing, who was known to be close to Jiang (as well as to Li Peng) and enjoyed a reputation as a strong supporter of China's bid. But Li Lanqing's efforts were constrained by Li Peng, who continued to serve as premier until March 1998. Li Peng opposed China's efforts to join the WTO – at least on terms that came close to being "commercially viable" – on both foreign policy and protectionist grounds. Li was always a major voice within the Chinese government against close ties with the United States. Not only did he move slowly and reluctantly in the period following Tiananmen to improve bilateral relations (e.g., by ending martial law and allowing astrophysicist Fang Lizhi to leave the US Embassy for exile), he also used his position as head of the Foreign Affairs Leadership Small Group to undercut efforts by the Ministry of Foreign Affairs to improve Sino–US relations.[32] Given the division of labor on the Politburo Standing Committee, it was easy for Li to set a tone on foreign policy that made it difficult for Jiang Zemin to improve relations. At the same time, as premier and as a product of ministerial culture, Li consistently supported the interests of China's bureaucracy – making him a popular figure within influential circles. Indeed, one could argue that Li's greatest (negative) effect on China's government was his willingness to let things drift. Lacking vision and unwilling to ride roughshod over inefficient bureaucrats, Li allowed China's SOEs to become ever more inefficient and eventually to threaten the solvency of the banking system.

In March 1998, Zhu Rongji replaced Li Peng as premier. At first, this seemed to make little difference. Zhu focused primarily on domestic reform, particularly the plight of SOEs, and seems to have worried that international competition would make his task harder, not easier. There may also have been an element of bureaucratic competition involved. Zhu is clearly someone who is very possessive of his power as premier, and he moved vigorously to centralize control over the economy in his office. As we have seen, he quickly elevated the SETC above other bureaucratic interests; he also undercut the authority of the various vice-premiers – including Li Lanqing, who had good relations with both Jiang Zemin and Li Peng and had been touted as a possible candidate for premier.

In any event, the opportunity to move forward on the WTO issue in the run-up to President Clinton's visit to China was missed. It was only in the fall of 1998 that the issue moved back onto the agenda, and it seems to have done so largely at the initiative of the American government. At the time, a number of issues were once again roiling the bilateral relationship: China was cracking down on the China Democracy Party; there were reports of illegal contributions to the Democratic Party; and,

---

[32] Li's efforts to hamper relations, even in petty ways, were visible when George Bush, as former president, traveled to China on two occasions, both times asking to see Wan Li, an old friend and tennis partner. Li Peng blocked Bush's request both times, perhaps afraid their conversation would turn to the last time the two had met – in May 1989, as the Tiananmen demonstrations were nearing their climax. Author interviews.

most sensational of all, Congressman Christopher Cox began investigating allegations that China had engaged in extensive nuclear spying. Indeed, it was startling that within six months of Clinton's highly successful trip to China, Sino–US relations were once again caught in a downward spiral. The WTO was seen as an issue that could provide ballast to the relationship. It would recognize China's full membership in the global economy, remove the annual ritual of renewing China's MFN status, and underscore important interests that the two nations have in common.

According to Chinese sources, President Clinton wrote Jiang Zemin a letter on November 6, 1998, expressing hope that the WTO issue could be resolved in the first quarter of 1999. On February 8, 1999, Clinton is said to have written a second letter to Jiang Zemin stating that he hoped that WTO negotiations could be concluded during Premier Zhu Rongji's visit to the United States. A third letter, on February 12, expressed hope that a package deal could be reached.[33]

By January 1999, the Chinese position on the WTO had changed enough that Premier Zhu was able to tell Alan Greenspan, chairman of the US Federal Reserve, that China was prepared to offer substantial concessions. Nevertheless, a clear-cut leadership decision on concessions was apparently made only in February, after receipt of President Clinton's letters. Sometime in the latter part of the month there seems to have been an enlarged Politburo meeting that approved broad-gauged concessions in an effort to achieve WTO membership. All major bureaucracies would have been represented at such a meeting and would have had an opportunity to present their views – although the expression of those views would have been constrained by the obvious support of the top leadership, and particularly of Jiang Zemin, for joining the WTO.

To argue that there was, at least formally, full bureaucratic consultation does not mean that there was consensus. Although support for China's entry into the WTO appears to have grown over the preceding years, the same divisions that had plagued China's previous efforts continued to exist. The difference now was that Jiang Zemin's own resolve seems to have grown and the reorganization of the government in spring 1998 had enhanced Zhu Rongji's leverage. Zhu's own support for China's entry into the WTO apparently increased over the preceding months. From Zhu's perspective, China's economy faced three major problems. First, in the wake of the Asian financial crisis, China's exports were suffering. With the Chinese economy entering a period of deflation, a weakening of exports

---

[33] Author interviews.

would have serious adverse consequences for the country's overall economic performance. Second, foreign investment in China was beginning to slow, and entry into the WTO and permanent MFN status were seen as ways to reassure investors. Third, and most important, foreign competition was widely seen as a means to force otherwise reluctant SOEs to carry out painful restructurings. Protectionism was beginning to cost China plenty as SOEs, supported by bureaucratic interests and high tariffs, continued their inefficient ways. Zhu wanted to carry out a restructuring plan that would force the more efficient industries to become competitive on the world market, thus becoming pillars of a leaner state-owned economy, and simultaneously force less efficient industries to be sold off or shut down.

Even as Zhu prepared for his departure to the United States, however, opposition came from an unexpected source. On March 24, 1999, frustrated by its inability to persuade Serbian leader Milosovic to accept the Rambouillet agreement, NATO began to bomb targets in Serbia. Originally intended as a short campaign to intimidate Milosovic into compliance, it encountered unexpectedly stiff resistance, including the expulsion of many Kosovars from their homeland, and thus had to be extended – ultimately for 78 days until Milosovic capitulated. Because the Yugoslav campaign was initially seen as a purely local issue of limited duration, there appears to have been no consideration of the campaign's effects on other countries, particularly Russia and China. Yet this impact soon proved to be tremendous.

For years, the thrust of US policy vis-à-vis China across a whole range of issues – including trade, human rights, and arms control – was to accept "international norms." There were, or so the line went, certain universally accepted norms that were embodied in various conventions and treaties; China, if it wanted to be accepted as a full member of the international community, would have to accept those norms and "play by the rules." Doing so would assure it equal treatment, a chance to "sit at the table" and influence the future evolution of rules governing the international system. It was a powerful appeal, backed as it was by positive incentives for compliance and penalties for non-compliance. It even appealed to many in China who both desired China to be recognized as a great power and hoped that China would fully join the international system.

However, the issue of bombing Serbia to protect the rights of Kosovars was never taken to the United Nations Security Council. American officials were probably correct when they claimed that doing so would have been ineffective and that the Chinese government would use such a forum to constrain US actions; nevertheless, unilateral NATO action touched the deepest fears of many Chinese officials. It seemed that the United States and NATO could join in any action, at any time and any place, without international consultation. Moreover, the NATO meeting in May declared that the organization's mission would include "out of area" concerns, yet "out of area" was not defined.[34] Worse, from the Chinese government's perspective, was the NATO declaration that "human rights" transcended "sovereign rights." Chinese officials immediately began envisioning the use of US and/or NATO forces in or around China itself – North Korea, Taiwan, Xinjiang, and Tibet were the places most frequently named. Even had there never been a bombing of the Chinese Embassy in Belgrade, there would have been long-term consequences of the NATO actions in Yugoslavia.

Because of such concerns over US actions in Serbia, conservatives in China suggested that Zhu Rongji's trip to the United States be postponed. But these suggestions were overruled, indicating the weight that Jiang Zemin put on Sino–US relations and the WTO issue.

Most of the negotiating on the WTO issue had taken place in Beijing in March, and a deal appeared pretty much complete. On the eve of Zhu's departure, however, President Clinton met with his advisers over the weekend of April 4–5. His foreign policy advisers – National Security Adviser Samuel Berger and Secretary of State Madeline Albright, along with United States Trade Representative (USTR) Charlene Barshefsky – favored clinching a deal that was better for American business than any had dared hope for only a few months earlier. However, Clinton's domestic advisers – Treasury Secretary Robert Rubin, National Economic Council head Gene Sperling, and domestic political adviser John Podesta – argued that if there were no guaranteed protections for labor unions and industries that competed directly with their Chinese counterparts then Congress would vote to kill the deal, and that would be worse for US–China relations than no agreement at all. President Clinton sided with his domestic advisers and requested that the USTR go back to the negotiating table to ask for both extended protection for textiles and added assurances against large-scale increases in imports.[35] Thus it was that, when Zhu Rongji's plane touched down on April 6, the stage was set for one of the most conspicuous foreign policy failures of recent years.

On the morning of April 7, President Clinton declared that it would be an "inexplicable mistake" to walk away from a good agreement with

---

[34] "The Defense Capabilities Initiative and NATO's Strategic Concept."
[35] Helene Cooper and Bob Davis, "Overruling Some Staff, Clinton Denies Zhu What He Came For."

China. Then, in a two and a half-hour meeting with Premier Zhu at the White House that evening, he did exactly that. Although an agricultural agreement was quickly signed the next morning, Zhu was sent back to China almost empty-handed.[36]

Shortly after President Clinton turned his back on the WTO deal, details of China's concessions appeared in a 17-page document posted on the USTR website. The decision to post such details – without informing the Chinese – apparently came from the White House. Oddly, White House officials did not feel that the US business community had been vocal enough in supporting China's accession. This unilateral posting was a breach of faith that was insulting to the Chinese side, and it quickly compounded the political difficulties of those Chinese in favor of WTO membership.[37]

The reaction in China to the failed WTO agreement and to the publication of details was both strong and immediate. Wu Jichuan, Minister of Information Industries (which includes telecommunications), reportedly tendered his resignation (which was not accepted).[38] Wu's apparent resignation offer and his subsequent actions, particularly his curious announcement on September 13 that it was illegal for foreign firms to buy into China's Internet business (something that was already happening), indicates the ferocity of high-level opposition.[39] Wu Jichuan himself has a reputation as a mild-mannered person – not the sort to defy his boss, particularly one with a reputation for a bad temper like Zhu Rongji. The fact that Wu played such a public role in the domestic controversy indicates that he had strong political backing, backing that could only have come from former premier Li Peng. It also indicates that criticism of Zhu was immediate and harsh.

Thus, there had already been a strong reaction in China when, on the morning of May 8, news was received that the United States had bombed the Chinese Embassy in Belgrade. Beijing's initial reaction was one of shock and confusion. There were clearly expressions of outrage within the Chinese government, but it appears that the top leadership quickly came to the conclusion that the bombing was either accidental, as the United States claimed, or that it reflected a low-level conspiracy within the depths of some bureaucracy and not government policy. But the bombing came on

---

[36] Ibid. See also Helene Cooper and Bob Davis, "Barshefsky Drove Hard Bargain." For a vivid description of President Clinton's meeting with Premier Zhu Rongji, see Steven Mufson and Robert G. Kaiser, "Missed US–China Deal Looms Large."

[37] Yong Wang, "China's Accession to WTO."

[38] *Shijie ribao*, May 5, 1999; *Wall Street Journal*, May 3, 1999, p. A16.

[39] "China Warns off Foreign Investment in Internet."

the heels of many events that were seen as "anti-China": accusations of illegal campaign contributions and nuclear spying, new denunciations of China's human rights record in the wake of arrests of democracy activists, the bombing campaign in Serbia, and now the failure to reach an agreement on the WTO. Nationalistic sentiment within the government reached a new peak, and there was real and deep anger among the broader population, especially students.

In the wake of the WTO failure and the embassy bombing, Zhu Rongji was abused mercilessly by public opinion. Articles on the Internet and student demonstrators labeled him a "traitor" (*maiguozei*) following the embassy bombing. At the same time, some old cadres were heard to mutter that the government's readiness to accept globalization was like Wang Jing-wei's willingness to serve as head of Japan's puppet government in occupied China during World War Two. Others called Zhu Rongji's compromises in Washington the "new 21 demands selling out the country" – a reference to Japan's infamous demands of 1915 that sought to reduce China to a colony.

Jiang Zemin's own position was very delicate. Within the government, Jiang was widely seen as "soft" on the United States and as a strong advocate of WTO membership. There were rumblings that the real "traitor" was not Zhu Rongji but rather Jiang Zemin. In the face of this rising tide of hostility, Jiang Zemin told an internal meeting that China had waited thirteen years to join the WTO (GATT) and it could wait another thirteen years.[40] But Jiang and other top leaders also recognized the importance of the US relationship: without the trade benefits it provides, developing the economy would be impossible to continue; and without a reasonably good political relationship, many resources would have to be devoted to building up the military. Thus, the relationship was considered just too valuable to sacrifice to the emotion of the moment. Jiang therefore had to preserve the US relationship as well as demonstrate to his critics his toughness.

This dual need was quickly reflected in the divided messages sent by the *People's Daily*. On the one hand, Jiang Zemin's public statements and the authoritative editorials issued by the *People's Daily* underscored continuity in policy even while expressing outrage over the bombing. For instance, in Jiang's May 13 speech welcoming the return of embassy staff from Yugoslavia, he reiterated that China "must continue to unswervingly take economic construction as the central task."[41] A series of editorials in the *People's Daily* emphasized that policy would not change and concluded with the declaration that China wants to "develop amity and cooperation

---

[40] Author interviews.   [41] Xinhua, May 13, 1999.

with developed countries in the West, including the United States."[42] On June 12, Vice Prime Minister Qian Qichen declared, "China does not want confrontation with the United States."[43]

At the same time, the *People's Daily* also published a series of very harsh articles signed "observer" (*guanchajia*). Such observer articles are published rarely, which indicates their importance, but they are not as authoritative as editorials, which are approved by the top leadership. Observer articles thus express views that are highly important but that do not carry the endorsement of the Party and so cannot be said to reflect official policy. A pair of critical "observer" articles published in the *People's Daily* on May 16 and May 27 suggested deep anti-US sentiment.[44] These articles were followed by a particularly strident observer article on June 22, which pushed rhetoric well beyond the bounds of diplomatic discourse by comparing – at length – the United States to Nazi Germany.[45]

Rather than express a point of view different from that of Jiang Zemin, these articles were intended to show the military and other critics that his government could be just as harsh on the United States as they were. These articles, which were evidently approved by Ding Guan'gen, head of the Propaganda Department, suggest the degree of threat that Jiang felt in the immediate aftermath of the embassy bombing. This interpretation jibes with reports of Jiang adopting harsh rhetoric in internal meetings – saying, for instance, that US imperialism will not die (*wangwozhixin busi*, an evocative expression used by Mao Zedong) and calling for "biding time while nurturing grievances" (*woxin changtan*).[46]

Given the delicacy of Jiang's position and the genuine anger felt in student circles, the Party quickly made the decision to channel public opinion by providing buses for students to go into the embassy district from the universities in the Haidian district (in northwestern Beijing). Students got off the buses and walked past the US ambassador's residence, throwing stones as they went, and then on to the embassy building and chancellery – throwing more bricks, stones, ink bottles, and occasionally feces. It was certainly better, from the Party's point of view, to have such public anger directed at the United States than to have students throw stones at Zhongnanhai (the compound in which the leadership lives), which they certainly would have done had the Party's reaction been perceived as weak.

---

[42] "Firmly Implement the Independent Foreign Policy of Peace."   [43] Xinhua, June 12, 1999.
[44] Observer, "Humanitarianism or Hegemonism?"; Observer, "On the New Development of US Hegemonism."
[45] Observer, "We Urge Hegemon Today to Take a Look at the Mirror of History."
[46] Author interviews.

That this explosion of anti-American anger came a month before the tenth anniversary of the Tiananmen crackdown was certainly a plus from the Party's point of view.

The reaction in China was extraordinary because it was the first time since 1949 that elite politics, bureaucratic interests, intellectual opinion, and broader (but still urban) public opinion came together to oppose the official position on an important foreign policy issue. Indeed, more than any other issues, China's proposed membership in the WTO and the reaction to the embassy bombing demonstrate the coming together – at least temporarily – of elite politics and public opinion. Without understanding the change in political atmosphere and public opinion described in the previous chapters, neither the actions of the government nor those of the students in the spring of 1999 makes sense.

THE NEW LEFT CRITICS AND THE WTO

The WTO issue brought together bureaucratic and elite politics with popular concerns. With the deepening of economic reform, the improvement of Sino–US relations, and the replacement of Li Peng with Zhu Rongji as premier, bureaucratic resistance was muted and elite opposition finessed. However, the failure of the WTO agreement in April – and especially the bombing of the Chinese Embassy in May – raised again all the old issues and embroiled the WTO issue in the most important rift in elite politics since the death of Deng. Because it affected real interests throughout the country, because it was a direct expression of the globalization that had been at the center of intellectual discussions since 1992, and because – with the bombing of the embassy – it engaged the nationalistic emotions that had built up in the course of the 1990s, the WTO became an issue that engaged public opinion like none other since Tiananmen. The merging of popular concerns over globalization, sovereignty, and national identity with elite struggles over power and the course of reform gave the WTO opposition a scope and power that left Zhu Rongji vulnerable, put Jiang Zemin on the defensive, and threatened to end China's bid for admission. Restarting negotiations and reaching a last-minute agreement in mid-November was a difficult and fragile process; it could easily have gone awry.

Recalling the discussion in Chapter 4 of the New Left and liberals and how their different responses to globalization marked one of the fundamental points separating these very different schools of thought, it is not surprising that the New Left almost uniformly opposed China's entry into the WTO (at least on the terms being offered), while liberals came down in support of it. At the same time, the issue of nationalism – exacerbated greatly by the bombing of the Chinese Embassy – sharply divided the New Left from the liberals. The former, not to mention those already identified as populists, took a strongly nationalistic stance, while liberals worried openly and deeply about the impact of a rising nationalism.

New Left commentary was led by Gan Yang, who quickly criticized Zhu Rongji and the Chinese leadership for focusing too much on gaining entry to the WTO during Zhu's trip to the United States, thus giving away their negotiating advantage. This effort, Gan said, reflected the "pro-US, pro-West" (*qinMei qinxifang*) stance of the Chinese leadership. Regarding Zhu's comment that he allowed the United States to vent its anger (*xiaoxiaoqi*), Gan said: "Unless China collapses and becomes like present-day Russia, Americans will always have anger. This sort of deep-rooted anger cannot be vented [*xiaobuliao*]."[47]

Similarly, Cui Zhiyuan (whose views were also discussed in Chapter 4) argued that the benefits of joining the WTO at this time were uncertain but the costs very real. For example, he argued that WTO membership, by protecting the intellectual property rights of the United States and other advanced capitalist nations, would hurt the development of China's high-tech sector. His argument was based on the need to protect infant industries from foreign competition; if China agreed to the provisions on trade-related property rights, China's high-tech industries would not have time to develop. Cui also argued that the WTO provisions (as summarized in the outline of Chinese commitments that the USTR posted in April 1999) would force China's financial markets open, preventing China from using capital controls to protect itself from events like the Asian financial crisis. Moreover, as with many other young intellectuals, there is more than a whiff of nationalism in his thinking. He quotes former UN Secretary General Boutros Boutros-Ghali, a person who had more than a few disagreements with the US government, as stating that "[t]he US sees hardly any need for diplomacy; power is enough. Only weak nations need diplomacy."[48]

One Beijing-based scholar, in a fairly typical expression of New Left opinion regarding international capital and the WTO, argued that the only reason the United States had changed its mind and had become eager for China to join the WTO was because the US strategy of globalization had encountered difficulties in 1998 (Japan unilaterally announced economic aid for countries hurt by the Asian financial crisis, Hong Kong

---

[47] Gan Yang, "Ping Zhu Rongji fangMei de shiwu yu wenti."
[48] Cui Zhiyuan, "Jiaru shijie maoyi zuzhi bushi Zhongguo dangwu zhiji."

interfered in its stock market and fought off international speculators, Malaysia announced capital controls, and so forth) and because China had announced a policy of expanding domestic demand, thus threatening to pull away from the international economic order.[49] Clearly this scholar saw the WTO as part of a broader web of institutions designed to enhance the control of Western capitalist states, particularly the United States, over the developing world. As he wrote:[50]

The US controls the regulations that have been formulated by the international economic organizations; all are designed to accord with the interests and needs of the institutional model of the strong capitalist states. As soon as China joins the WTO, the US can at any time find an excuse to interfere in, sanction, and intimidate our country into accepting so-called "international norms" that do not accord with our national characteristics. And to help the multinational companies to control China's industrial and financial lifelines, it [the US] will usurp our economic sovereignty and force us to carry out suicidal reforms just as it has in Latin America, Russia, Southeast Asia, and elsewhere.

Another fairly typical expression of this line of thinking returned to the issue of globalization. According to the authors, "globalization is really Americanization and incorporation into multinational corporations." Its purpose is to force governments around the world to take orders from the "multinational corporations and international financial chieftains who control the world's economy" and from the "IMF, World Bank, WTO, UN, and other organs controlled by the US government and Federal Reserve Bank" – all of which is to serve the interests of the United States.[51] The same authors warned that entering the WTO presented a greater risk than any other reform undertaken by China, that it could destabilize society, and that "as soon as China enters the WTO, the US will be able to find an excuse at any time to interfere in our country and sanction us."[52]

In contrast, liberals were far more welcoming of the WTO, as they had been of globalization in the debates earlier in the decade. For instance, Liu Junning argued that China's accession to the WTO would force a separation between politics and economics, increase the transparency of policy-making, increase pressure to implement rule of law, and undermine the structural basis of corruption. In short, "China's entry into the WTO implies that China will start to formally [*zhengshi*] integrate itself into the

---

[49] Shao Ren, "Zhongguo: Ruguan buru tao," p. 6.   [50] Ibid., p. 14.
[51] Di Yinqing and Guan Gang, "Meiguo wei shenma jiyu yu Zhongguo chongkai ruguan tanpan."
[52] Di Yinqing and Guan Gang, "Guanjian shi yao zhangwo jingji fazhan de zhudongquan." See also Di Yinqing and Guan Gang, "Ruguan dui Zhongguo changyuan liyi jiujing yiweizhe shenma."

world capitalist economic and political system, the basic characteristics of which are market economics and democratic politics."[53]

The gulf between the New Left and liberals was already quite great before the Chinese Embassy in Belgrade was bombed; with the explosion of nationalistic emotion following that event, the rhetoric became more heated and more personal – and the gap between the two sides less bridgeable. We have already noted the public condemnations many made of Zhu Rongji (and the more private questions raised about Jiang Zemin), but soon the Internet and later the bookstores were filled with expressions of nationalism.

Liberals were concerned about this new outburst of nationalism. The most interesting expression of concern came from Xiao Gongqin, the intellectual who had embraced neoconservatism more openly than any other. As noted in Chapter 3, Xiao – consistent with his original neoauthoritarian approach – had always hoped to use the power of the state to bring about a liberal, democratic polity; this approach distinguished him from other neoconservatives, New Left critics, and nationalists. In that quest, he had seen nationalism as a positive force, something that could rally people and provide stability during a difficult transition period. In 1999, however, Xiao was taken aback by the emotion displayed by students marching on the US Embassy, and he came to believe that nationalism could quickly and easily become irrational and that "opportunists" could easily fish in troubled waters. As he pointed out, the greatest danger of such emotional discourse was that it could easily exclude more rational ideas. As he put it: "Any insufficiently radical or insufficiently extreme voices could be attacked and suppressed as 'capitulationism,' 'assisting the enemy,' 'fifth columnist,' or 'traitor'."[54]

Wang Xiaodong wrote a short but heated response, reflecting the deepening gap between different positions on the ideological spectrum. "No matter how others hit us," Wang asked, "would it be better for us to very 'understandingly' respond without anger?"[55] Wang quickly wrote a number

[53] Liu Junning, "Zhongguo jiaru WTO de zhengzhi yiyi."
[54] Xiao Gongqin, "Jingti jiduan minzu zhuyi." Xiao's whole approach was distinguished by his deep-seated aversion to emotionalism and extremism, which he saw as the root of China's failure to modernize. Thus, in his discussions of the 1898 reform, Xiao blamed Kang Youwei and other reformers for their radicalism, which caused moderates and conservatives to join together in opposition to the reform. In 1999, Xiao saw Wang Xiaodong and other nationalists as displaying the same lack of moderation.
[55] Wang Xiaodong [Shi Zhong], posting under "Guanyu Zhongguo minzu zhuyi de taolun (er)."

of articles, which were brought together with some of his earlier writings to form the first book of a new wave of nationalistic writings, *China's Road under the Shadow of Globalization*.

Wang co-authored this book with (among others) Fang Ning, then a professor at Capital Normal University and later deputy head of the Politics Institute at CASS, and Song Qiang, the lead writer of *China Can Say No*. Like that earlier volume, *China's Road* was endorsed by Yu Quanyu, the former deputy head of China's Human Rights Commission (under the equally conservative Zhu Muzhi), who has allied himself with leftist causes in recent years. According to Yu, "[t]he attack of America's bombs brought a conclusion to the debate among our intellectuals in recent years; who is right and who is wrong is now clear to all."[56] Yu also touted *China's Road* as the third major expression of nationalism after *China Can Say No* and *Behind the Demonization of China*; like the other works, *China's Road* quickly hit the best-seller list. This self-professed genealogy is interesting because in previous years Wang Xiaodong had kept his distance from the authors of *China Can Say No*, believing them shallow and extreme, as well as from such Old Leftists as Yu Quanyu. Perhaps his removal from *Strategy and Management* in 1998 made him more willing to associate himself with these people, but perhaps also the impact of the bombing had caused different groups to coalesce.

Wang, who contributed the bulk of the book, gives his most extended expression of nationalism. He takes every opportunity to denigrate and mock the political and intellectual elite of China, especially so-called liberals. He depicts them as lapdogs, saying they "support the US, support everything about the US," whereas the reality is that the interests of China and the United States clash.[57] The United States, fearing China's growing strength, simply will not let China join the world; indeed, it has made clear its intention of using NATO to control the world in the twenty-first century.[58] Against this unsentimental view of power politics, Wang sees China's elite as selling out the interests of China for their own selfish purposes. The foreign policy elite have long cherished excessively high hopes for Sino–US relations,[59] Wang writes, but in fact the United States simply does not care about Sino–US relations, the United States pursues its own interests selfishly, and it is simply laughable to believe that Americans

---

[56] Yu Quanyu, "Qianyan: Women de guojia dayou xiwang," p. 2.
[57] Fang Ning, Wang Xiaodong, and Song Qiang (eds.), *Quanqiuhua yinyingxia de Zhongguo zhilu*, p. 21.
[58] Ibid., p. 22.   [59] Ibid., pp. 7, 11.

have a higher sense of morality.[60] Like Wang Shan in *Looking at China through a Third Eye*, Wang Xiaodong laments the lack of spirit (*yanggang zhi qi*) among Chinese leaders and intellectuals.[61] The Serbs, through their stubborn resistance to the overwhelming force of NATO, demonstrated that they – unlike many in China – still have self-respect.[62] According to Wang, India's elite shows more panache than China's (a reference to India's defying Western norms by conducting a nuclear test).[63]

Wang's contempt for China's intellectual and political elite explains much of his self-announced democratic thought. Wang declares that he wants to see China democratized and that he favors "one man, one vote." But clearly Wang believes that the Chinese people, given a chance, would throw the pro-American (*qinMei*) foreign policy elite out and reject the liberal intelligentsia. As he puts it, "[w]ithout individual rights, the people will not believe that they are the masters of the nation, will not exert themselves on behalf of the nation, and will have no way to stop the ruling clique (*shangceng jituan*) from selling out the country for its own self interest."[64] Nationalism is driving Wang's "liberalism"; the commitment to democracy is secondary.

Whereas Wang Xiaodong rarely invokes the language of Marxism (he is too focused on national power to care much about Marxist theory), his primary co-author Fang Ning wallows in the vocabulary of dependency theory. According to Fang, colonialism was replaced following World War Two by neocolonialism – the use of foreign capital to bind and exploit the Third World. But neocolonialism was losing its grip as some nations escaped dependency and others carried out revolutions. Thus, the world was moving toward postcolonialism (*houzhiminzhuyi*), which requires more military force to shore up the position of the Western "core" nations.[65] The US actions in Iraq and Yugoslavia, Fang declared, reflected this logic.

The Party's official theoretical journal, *Seeking Truth*, which tends to be conservative but nevertheless represents a mainstream government point of view, has similarly explored Western "cultural imperialism." For instance, one article lamented US cultural dominance (US movies, it said, accounted

---

[60] Wang states that, contrary to intellectual opinion in China, American opposition to the war in Vietnam did not derive from moral concerns but simply from the fact that the United States was losing the war; ibid., p. 26.

[61] Ibid., p. 15.   [62] Ibid., p. 147.   [63] Ibid., p. 49.

[64] Ibid., p. 31. Elsewhere he writes, "in China, 'nationalism' stems from the lower and middle classes, while 'reverse racism', pro-American and pro-Western attitudes, are common in the upper class of dignitaries, many of whom are corrupt officials hated by the people." See Wang Xiaodong, "The West in the Eyes of a Chinese Nationalist," p. 25.

[65] Fang Ning, "Ershiyi shiji de liangzhong qushi."

for only 6–7 percent of world production but over half of total projection time) and claimed that the reason "international monopoly capital groups" promoted colonial culture was to turn those living in the Third World "into slaves without their knowing it." With such a slave mentality would come economic and political domination.[66]

Shortly after the embassy bombing, Fang Li, a bureau chief in the Policy Research Office of the Central Committee (of which Wang Huning was then deputy head), published an article in the Central Party School's internal journal *Theoretical Trends* (*Lilun dongtai*) arguing that the "cultural diplomacy" of the United States had become a very important tool for "dividing" (*fenhua*) and "Westernizing" (*xihua*) socialist countries. In trade negotiations the United States tries anything it can to induce other nations, "especially developing nations," to open their cultural markets. The result, Fang concluded, was that "whether from a macro-perspective or a micro-perspective, the United States' cultural expansion is bound tightly with its economic expansion, so that in the course of economic exchange it [cultural expansion] can achieve the effect of 'politics in command' [*zhengzhi guashuai*]."[67]

---

[66] Liu Runwei, "Zhimin wenhua lun."
[67] Fang Li, "Meiguo quanqiu zhanlüe zhong de wenhua kuozhang yu cantuo."

PART IV

A new era in Chinese politics

CHAPTER 8

Hu Jintao takes over: a turn to the left?

In the Chinese political system, Party congresses provide an occasion for the gathering and analysis of the sort of information that allows the system to take stock of itself. Most of these analyses are internal, and thus are never viewed by the public, but as the Sixteenth Party Congress approached, one such analysis, compiled under the auspices of the Central Organization Department, was published openly.[1] Unfortunately, when the *New York Times* wrote about the publication, it was quickly withdrawn, shutting down this tentative move in the direction of greater openness.[2] Nevertheless, this publication, which deals with the growing social order problems facing China, provides a vivid picture of Chinese society as seen from the perspective of the organization system.

"Mass disturbances" numbered some 58,000 in 2003, and would rise to 74,000 in 2004 and 87,000 in 2005. Most such incidents – some 70–80 percent, according to one county in Shandong province, and 90 percent according to a survey in Sichuan – were caused by tensions between cadres and masses, and most of the violence was initiated by cadres.[3] The Organization Department attributed these disturbances largely to growing income inequalities, saying that "if income inequalities cannot be controlled within certain limits, the broad masses of the people will inevitably lose faith in socialism and their faith in the Party will be shaken. It is even possible that reform could be broken off and social chaos [ensue]."[4] But the problem was not just income inequalities; it was also a matter of local cadres seizing economic opportunities by force, preventing people under their control from the chance to prosper. Incidents were often large – sometimes involving thousands and even tens of thousands of people – and occasionally violent.

[1] Zhonggong zhongyang zuzhibu ketizu (ed.), *Zhongguo diaocha baogao: 2000–2001 xin xingshi xia renmin neibu maodun yanjiu.*
[2] Erik Eckholm, "China's Inner Circle Reveals Big Unrest, and Lists Causes."
[3] Zhonggong zhongyang zuzhibu ketizu (ed.), *Zhongguo diaocha baogao*, pp. 66, 83, and 84.
[4] Ibid., p. 79.

One deputy Party secretary in Hunan's Xinning county had an ear cut off as he tried to collect taxes; in Hunan's Longshan county two cadres were killed in clashes.[5]

Academic writings were, if anything, more vivid. In a well-researched article in *Strategy and Management*, Yu Jianrong, a rural researcher at CASS, describes the increasing level of organization of peasants in a county in inland Hunan province (the same county where Mao, 80 years earlier, had organized peasants). The peasants in Hunan began organizing in 1992 to protest the high level of taxation (higher than central policies allowed). Most of the peasant leaders were somewhat better educated (middle-school level) and had spent time out of the village as soldiers or workers; some were elderly school teachers who sympathized with the peasants. By 1998, the loose organizations of peasants began to coalesce into stronger organizations with tighter linkages among villages. Local cadres, trying to crush the "burden-relieving and complaint representatives," seized several leaders, tied them up, hung sign-boards around their necks, and held a criticism and denunciation meeting. The son of one of those being denounced charged the platform to rescue his father, as many other villagers took the cue and began to assault local cadres (and the thugs they had hired), driving them away. The result of an investigation by provincial and city leaders basically affirmed the views of the peasants; the local Party secretary was removed and others were dealt with administratively. Thereafter, peasant organizations, although not formally recognized, became a part of the *de facto* reality in this part of Hunan.[6]

In a follow-up article published a few months later, Yu argues that there was a crisis of governance at the local level; the legitimacy of grassroots administration was failing and the ability to control society was declining. Particularly worrisome was the merging of "evil forces" and local administration. As Yu puts it:[7]

By right, township officials should be the agents of the central government, but instead it was they who criticized the report detailing how the central government would lighten the burdens on peasants as an "evil document," even contemptuously deriding it as "dog crap." In order to extort the blood and sweat of the peasants to fatten themselves, township officials do not care about the country being ruled in peace for a long time; instead they aid and abet the growth of evil forces in society and let these forces clothe themselves in the apparel of "squadrons that are upholding the law" or "work squads." These evil forces despise discipline, act unreasonably and arbitrarily, commit crimes and break the law, and oppress the people.

---

[5] Ibid., p. 83.   [6] Yu Jianrong, "Nongmin you zuzhi kangzheng jiqi zhengzhi fengxian."
[7] Yu Jianrong, "Nongcun hei'e shili he jiceng zhengquan tuihua." See also Yu Jianrong, *Yuecun zhengzhi*.

Zhao Shukai, a researcher at the State Council's Development Research Center, took a similarly negative view of township governance. Many townships were in debt – some two-thirds by Zhao's estimate – and that indebtedness, including the difficulty townships had paying their employees, changed the nature of governance at the local level. In the 1980s, many townships had invested in enterprises, but many of those had gone bankrupt, which was a major cause of the debt.[8] Moreover, the number of cadres at the township level had tripled since the 1980s; altogether, county and township governments took in approximately 20 percent of China's governmental revenue, but they supported 71 percent of China's public employees.[9]

There was also intense pressure on townships to collect taxes. Cadres who did not fulfill their revenue collection assignments were not paid their wages, and cadre performance evaluations were based largely on their ability to collect taxes and fees. Such pressures rewarded rough behavior on the part of cadres and even became a criterion for cadre selection. As Zhao puts it, "the logic for choosing village cadres has become 'whoever can collect money will become a cadre, even a good cadre.' Thus, the 'tough guys' in the rural society, and even the ruffians, would naturally become the wielders of public authority." The purpose of local government was to serve itself, not the public.[10]

This picture of deteriorating rural governance is vividly depicted in Cao Jinqing's book, *China along the Yellow River*, and perhaps even more tellingly by Li Changping, a former township Party secretary in Hubei province, whose letter to Premier Zhu Rongji describing the poverty of local peasants, set off a storm in China.[11] Later, two writers, Chen Guidi and Chun Tao, ignited a firestorm with their *Investigation into China's Peasants*, which quickly became a best-seller and nearly as quickly was banned by the government (though it continued to sell briskly in pirated editions sold in private bookstalls).[12] Such books brought the issue of rural poverty to the attention of an urban population that had largely ignored the problems of the hinterland as they tried to forge a life for themselves in the cities, while at the same time the more scholarly work, including the survey mentioned above by the Central Organization Department, forced the issue onto the government agenda.

---

[8] Zhao Shukai, "Lishixing tiaozhan," p. 217.
[9] Li Peilin, "Zhongguo jingji shehui fazhan de wenti he qushi," p. 76.
[10] Zhao Shukai, "Nongcun zhili."
[11] Cao Jinqing, *Huanghe bian de Zhongguo*; Li Changping, *Wo xiang zongli shuo shihua*. Cao Jinqing's book has been translated as *China along the Yellow River*.
[12] Chen Guidi and Chun Tao, *Zhongguo nongmin diaocha*. This book has been translated into English as *Will the Boat Sink the Water?*

Soon the subject of social stability was on everyone's lips. Hu Angang and Wang Shaoguang, who had raised the topic of declining central revenues in the 1990s, raised this issue sharply in a widely read article in *Strategy and Management*. Just as they had raised the specter of national disintegration in their report on state capacity, they suggested that, left unaddressed, social tensions in China could lead to the collapse of the system, as it had in Indonesia. They pointed to the more than 48 million workers dismissed from state-owned and collective enterprises as one source of instability (they state that 100–200 million people report being dissatisfied with their living conditions), and a combination of dissatisfaction with living conditions and complaints about corruption, income inequality, and employment as another potential cause of popular anger. Unfortunately, in their view, economic growth, in and of itself, would not bring social stability – the gap between rich and poor was growing, and the pattern of economic development in China was one of "growth without employment" or "unfair growth." If China confronted a slowdown in economic development, social instability could destroy the system.[13]

Systematically testing the degree of social tensions was the premise behind a large-scale (n = 11,094) nationwide survey carried out in 2002 by Li Peilin and others at CASS. They were interested not only in the degree of tension in society, but how that tension was distributed by region and by social class, especially by one's perceived position in society. Their findings were quite sobering. For instance, when urban residents were asked who the primary beneficiaries of reform were, more people (59.2 percent) selected "Party and state cadres" than any other category (though private entrepreneurs and entertainers were not far behind at 55.4 percent and 43 percent respectively).[14] But, when responses were arranged by social class, the results were even more disturbing. Whereas "only" 50 percent of the wealthiest elements in society believed that Party and state cadres were the chief beneficiaries of reform, over 77 percent of the lowest-income respondents cited cadres as the primary beneficiaries.[15] Not surprisingly, attitudes toward increasing the salaries of cadres and the seriousness of corruption also varied by income.[16]

Li's results were confirmed by other surveys. For instance, the survey research Lu Xueyi and others conducted in 1999 in Hubei's Hanchuan city showed that 69.2 percent of the respondents believed that as a group officials most easily attained high income – but only 13.6 percent believed

---

[13] Hu Angang, Wang Shaoguang, and Ding Yuanchu, "Jingji fangrong beihou de shehui bu wending."
[14] Li Peilin, Zhan Yi, Zhao Tingdong, and Liang Dong (eds.), *Shehui chongtu yu jieji yishi*, p. 203.
[15] Ibid., p. 207.   [16] Ibid., pp. 212–14.

that officials should receive high incomes.[17] Respondents believed that those with technical skills, better education, and a willingness to work hard should receive the highest incomes but they perceived that those in these three groups in fact had incomes far below what they should have. Lu concludes that income inequality itself was not as much of a problem as the perceived unfairness of income distribution. In contrast, cadres tended to see the issues differently. They pointed to private entrepreneurs and entertainers rather than themselves as the chief beneficiaries of reform.[18] Indeed, according to a survey of cadres attending a training program at the Central Party School, *not one* respondent identified cadres as being the chief beneficiaries of reform.[19]

Survey results also revealed that many people saw conflict as prevalent in society and likely to get worse in the future. Only 4.7 percent of the respondents declared that there was no conflict in Chinese society; nearly a third said that there was "a comparatively large amount of conflict" or "serious conflict."[20] Over 80 percent believed that social conflict was likely to get worse to some degree in the future, which, as the authors state, was an "extremely dangerous expectation."[21] When asked what they would do if a co-worker or neighbor were to ask them to participate in a collective action or petition, only 9.3 percent said they would try to persuade them not to undertake such an action, whereas a third of the respondents said they would participate.[22]

The social mood that generated these results also lay behind the pessimistic views of 100 experts surveyed by CASS sociologist Lu Jianhua. When he asked if there would be a "comprehensive social crisis" in China, 45.9 percent said "there was some possibility" and another 11 percent thought it was "very likely."[23]

In the wake of Tiananmen, conservative commentators derided the notion that China was developing, or ever would develop, a middle class, a social phenomenon that was thought would threaten the CCP, the vanguard of the proletariat. That perceived threat lay behind the Party's 1989 resolution barring private entrepreneurs from joining the Party. A decade later, however, Chinese intellectuals and the Party alike were re-evaluating that position; the advantages of a middle class in securing social stability had become apparent, and even the Central Organization Department's study mentioned above argued that China should develop a middle class.

[17] Lu Xueyi (ed.), *Dangdai Zhongguo shehui yanjiu baogao*, p. 77.
[18] Li Peilin et al. (eds.), *Shehui chongtu yu jieji yishi*, p. 203.
[19] Ibid., p. 204   [20] Ibid., p. 91.   [21] Ibid., pp. 92–3.   [22] Ibid., p. 106.
[23] Lu Jianhua, "Zhuanjia yanli de shehui xingshi jiqi qianjing," p. 20.

But how close was China to developing a middle class? Lu Xueyi's 2001 study on China's social strata is a major contribution to our understanding of social differentiation in China. Based on large-scale surveys in four places – the Shenzhen Special Economic Zone in southeast China, Anhui provincial capital of Hefei, the county-level city of Hanchuan in central Hubei province, and Zhenning county in southwestern Guizhou province – Lu and his colleagues argue that the economic development of the reform years indeed expanded the size of the Chinese middle class, but it remained far from the size necessary to bring about an "olive-shaped" society that sociologists identify with stable societies. As Lu puts it, those segments of the population that should have increased (that is, the middle class), did not, or at least not sufficiently, while those segments that should have decreased in size (the lower income groups), did not.[24] The result was a distorted, and to some extent illegitimate, social structure that left social stability – and future economic growth – very much in doubt.

Although the number of agricultural workers had decreased from 70 percent of China's working population to 44 percent, the number of peasants remained extremely large and unlikely to be absorbed into a middle class any time soon. Because of the weight of this and other lower-income strata, the average person in most areas of China continued to have a below-average income. For instance, in Hanchuan, reflective of much of central China, over 65 percent of the population had incomes *below* the average monthly family income of 141 yuan.

At the same time, the middle class could not expand significantly. Lu and his colleagues calculated that only 10.3 percent of Hanchuan's population fell into the "middle-middle" income group, while a whopping 86.6 percent fell into the "lower-middle" and low-income groups. Structurally, much of China remained traditional (that is, overwhelmingly agricultural), even though the east coast economy was modern and integrated into the global economy. Although the number of private entrepreneurs had increased greatly in recent years, they still only accounted for 0.6 percent of the population – less than that in Japan in 1950.[25]

Lu was particularly concerned that economic growth in and of itself would not change the social structure. There were too many obstacles left over from the planned economy that continued to hinder social mobility. A major obstacle was the household registration system. Although restrictions on movement have been loosened considerably in recent years, it was still difficult for peasants to move into cities and become integrated into

[24] Lu Xueyi (ed.), *Dangdai Zhongguo shehui yanjiu baogao*, p. 69.   [25] Ibid., p. 52.

urban society. They were not allowed to take up certain jobs, their household registrations remained rural, and their access to schools and other urban facilities remained limited at best. The educational system, which concentrated investment in urban areas and in tertiary education, worked to the disadvantage of the rural population. And the cadre system, which was increasingly linked to education, was also preventing lower-income people, whether in urban or rural areas, from ascending the social ladder.[26] Lu's 2004 book on social mobility further documents these trends, showing that social mobility rates were slowing. It was particularly difficult for those who had reached the middle class to climb further into the highest social strata; middle class status itself was very precarious.[27]

The combination of a distorted social structure and the perception of illegitimate income distribution was bad for future economic and social development as well as for social stability. The large mass of relatively poor people in China's interior simply did not have the money for consumption that would drive economic development, without which it would be impossible for those areas to develop a middle class. For instance, in 1999, per capita consumption expenditure of agricultural workers was only 85 yuan, 73.9 percent of their monthly income.[28] With such small demand, it was difficult for an entrepreneurial class to develop. And those with talent and ambition tended to migrate from the rural areas, leaving large areas of the country with little hope of developing a modern social structure.

The result, as Lu and others argue, was that China was developing a social structure not unlike Latin America where a promising beginning for economic development had stalled because a small, internationalized urban sector had not absorbed the large, poor population into an urban middle class. It is possible, but highly undesirable, to combine a modern economy with a traditional social structure. That outcome, Lu suggests, would breed social instability and slow economic growth.[29]

Focused on the need for a fairer distribution of income, Lu expresses frustration with policies that concentrate solely on economic growth. As he puts it, "for some years we have drawn up this or that policy to bring about the rapid growth of the market economy . . . but we have not focused on appropriate social policies to cultivate a modern structure of social strata."[30] Expressing similar concerns, Li Peilin states that for years China thought it could grow its way out of problems, but "a new round of economic growth would, on the contrary, exacerbate things, even to

---

[26] Ibid., pp. 95–7.   [27] Lu Xueyi (ed.), *Dangdai Zhongguo shehui liudong*, p. 164.
[28] Lu Xueyi (ed.), *Dangdai Zhongguo shehui yanjiu baogao*, p. 71.
[29] Ibid., pp. 72–5.   [30] Ibid., p. 92.

the extent of severely threatening the sustainability and stability of contin-ued growth." Has the time come, he asks, when China should adjust its development strategy from "taking economic development as the center" to "taking the coordinated development of the economy *and* society as the center" (emphasis added)?[31] Such concerns were soon to find expression in the new administration of Hu Jintao and Wen Jiabao, but they were nearly absent from the Sixteenth Party Congress when it met in November 2002.

SIXTEENTH PARTY CONGRESS

When the Sixteenth Party Congress convened in Beijing in early November 2002, there were two major issues on the agenda, both of which would extend at least through the Seventeenth Party Congress in 2007. The first was the degree to which China's policies would change to reflect the social challenges discussed above, and the second was the degree to which power could be transferred smoothly. Given the degree to which policy and power have been interrelated in China, these two issues were inevitably linked to one another.

The issues of policy and power were underscored by the very differ-ent backgrounds of the major players. Jiang Zemin, of course, was from Yangzhou, in the lower Yangtze River valley, and had spent most of his career in Shanghai. Jiang's protégé, Zeng Qinghong, to whom Jiang often seemed to want to transfer power, had also spent his career in Shanghai, though his youth was spent in his ancestral home of Jiangxi. Hu Jintao had been raised in Anhui, not far from Yangzhou, but had spent most of his professional career in the poor inland provinces of Gansu, Guizhou, and Tibet. Wen Jiabao, who would emerge as premier, was born in Tianjin, but similarly spent much of his career in Gansu province as a geologist. There was no question that Hu and Wen had far more intimate knowledge of the poor hinterland, and their inland concerns were often juxtaposed with the coastal orientation of Jiang and Zeng's "Shanghai faction." Similarly, Hu's base of support in the Communist Youth League, which he once headed, contrasted with Zeng's extensive network among the *gaogan zidi*, the sons and daughters of high-level cadres, of which Zeng was one (his father, Zeng Shan, had joined Mao during the Jiangxi period and eventually rose to head the Interior Ministry).

Contrary to the hopes of scholars like Li Peilin and Lu Xueyi, the report to the Sixteenth Party Congress, delivered by Jiang Zemin, gave little

---

[31] Li Peilin et al. (eds.), *Shehui chongtu yu jieji yishi*, pp. 10 and 24.

indication of a shift in policy. It celebrated the Three Represents (*sange daibiao*), called for "keeping pace with the times" (*yushi jujin*), and declared that the "strategic adjustment of the economic structure has been crowned with success" and that "it is of vital importance to take economic development as the main task." The report recognized that there were problems in society. It noted, for instance, that income in rural areas had increased slowly, that unemployment was up, and that a variety of environmental issues had emerged. Nevertheless, the report called for a quadrupling of the GDP by the year 2020 and emphasized science and technology as drivers of economic growth. Science and technology, of course, would help upgrade industry along the coast – areas that already had a basis for adopting newer technologies – but likely would not drive job creation, particularly in the interior. Despite the urging of sociologists such as Li and Lu, the report firmly endorsed continuing along the developmental path the country had been following: "Keep economic development as the central task," it urged, "and solve problems cropping up on our way forward through development. Development is the fundamental principle."[32]

Understandably, eyes were focused more on personnel issues rather than on policy questions. China has not had a good track record in peacefully transferring power: Mao Zedong's designated successors – Liu Shaoqi, Lin Biao, and Hua Guofeng – all failed to attain sustainable power, and Deng Xiaoping's first two choices – Zhao Ziyang and Hu Yaobang – had likewise fallen amidst political struggle. Jiang Zemin, contrary to early expectations, succeeded in consolidating power despite the very complicated politics of the post-Tiananmen period and his relative lack of experience at the highest level of China's political system. Now, the question was whether he was willing and able to transfer power to a younger set of leaders.

The question was complicated by the fact that Jiang Zemin was clearly closer to Zeng Qinghong than to Hu Jintao. Jiang had tried to elevate Zeng Qinghong to Politburo Standing Committee (PBSC) status in the years before the Sixteenth Party Congress, but this had been rejected by his colleagues, suggesting that Jiang's power had limits and that Zeng was not popular among the upper echelons of the CCP. Hu had been added to the Politburo Standing Committee in 1992 by Deng Xiaoping, who had taken a liking to the young leader and had put him in charge of personnel arrangements for the Fourteenth Party Congress. Given his inability to promote Zeng Qinghong, Jiang acquiesced to Deng's choice; he did, after

---

[32] Jiang Zemin, "Quanmian jianshe xiaokang shehui, kaichuang Zhongguo tese shehui zhuyi shiye xin jumian."

all, name Hu as vice-chairman of the CMC in 1997 and elevated him to be vice-president of the PRC in 1998. These appointments, both made following Deng's death, clearly put Hu in line to succeed Jiang as head of the Party, but Jiang never brought Hu into his inner circle. Although Jiang accepted Hu's heir-apparent status, he never seemed comfortable with it.

Nevertheless, as the Sixteenth Party Congress approached, "institutionalization" became the buzzword in media reports. The Chinese media touted Hu's elevation to Party head as the first peaceful transfer of power in CCP history. Although the transition was peaceful, it was hardly without tensions. As will be seen, Hu was able to consolidate considerable power in a remarkably short period of time, but tensions remained throughout his first term as general secretary. Hu's succession was more the result of a balance of power in the Party, Hu's own talents as a political leader, and the weight of Deng Xiaoping's arrangements than it was an indication of institutionalization. The days of Maoist rule are indeed gone, but political institutions are less constraining than they often appear from the outside. Succession in Leninist systems remains difficult.

The first clear sign of extra-institutional maneuvering appeared when the Xinhua News Agency announced that Jia Qinglin, the Party secretary of Beijing, and Huang Ju, the Party secretary of Shanghai, both close to Jiang Zemin, would be "transferred to the center."[33] These two important personnel changes meant that Liu Qi, who was named to succeed Jia Qinglin as Beijing Party secretary, and Chen Liangyu, who took over as Shanghai Party secretary, would join the Politburo since the Party leaders of those two major cities are routinely seated on the Party's highest policy-making body. It became apparent when the Sixteenth Party Congress met that not only would these two sit on the Politburo, but that Jia's and Huang's "transfer to the center" indicated that both would sit on the PBSC – the core of China's power structure. At the NPC meeting the following spring, Jia Qinglin was named to head the CPPCC and Huang Ju took over as vice-premier in charge of finance. Jiang was able to arrange this by taking the extraordinary measure of expanding the PBSC from seven to nine members. Table 3 shows the Politburo lineup following the Sixteenth Party Congress.

When one looks at this list, it is apparent that Zhu Rongji had succeeded in promoting Wen Jiabao as his replacement, Li Peng had succeeded in having his chosen replacement, Luo Gan, take over as head of the Political and

---

[33] Xinhua, October 22, 2002, reported the next day in "Beijing Shanghai Chongqing shiwei zhuyao fuze tongzhi zhiwu tiaozheng."

Table 3: *Leadership of the Chinese
Communist Party following the
16th Party Congress*

Politburo Standing Committee
(ages in 2002 in parentheses)

Hu Jintao (60)	Huang Ju (64)
Wu Bangguo (61)	Wu Guanzheng (64)
Wen Jiabao (60)	Li Changchun (58)
Jia Qinglin (62)	Luo Gan (67)
Zeng Qinghong (63)	

Politburo – Full Members

Cao Gangchuan (67)	Wang Zhaoguo (61)
Chen Liangyu (56)	Wu Yi (64)
Guo Boxiong (60)	Yu Zhengsheng (57)
He Guoqiang (59)	Zeng Peiyan (64)
Hui Liangyu (58)	Zhang Dejiang (61)
Liu Qi (60)	Zhang Lichang (63)
Liu Yunshan (55)	Zhou Yongkang (60)
Wang Lequan (57)	

Politburo – Alternate

Wang Gang (60)

Secretariat

Zeng Qinghong (63)	Wang Gang (60)
Liu Yunshan (55)	Xu Caihou (59)
Zhou Yongkang (60)	He Yong (58)
He Guoqiang (59)	

Legal Affairs Committee, and Jiang Zemin had succeeded in having five or six of his closest political associates join the Politburo Standing Committee. Hu Jintao had indeed replaced Jiang Zemin as general secretary of the Party, but it was evident that Jiang intended to retain political influence through his protégés. Jiang's desire to follow the Deng model of slow withdrawal from the political scene was even more evident when it was announced that Jiang would stay on as head of the powerful CMC. Traditionally, the highest leader in China has been the person who linked the PLA and the Party by concurrently holding the highest position in both systems. But, when Deng had retired from the PBSC in 1987, he had the Party constitution rewritten so that the head of the CMC would not have to be a member of the PBSC, thus paving the way for Deng to retain control over the military. The division between the PBSC, headed by Zhao Ziyang, and the CMC, headed by Deng, had contributed to the tragedy of Tiananmen. Now Jiang was replicating this pattern.

The composition of the rest of the Politburo did not change the impression of Hu Jintao being surrounded by others whose political allegiances lay elsewhere. It had been widely predicted that at least one or two of Hu Jintao's close allies from his CYL days, such as Li Keqiang or Li Yuanchao, would be promoted to the Politburo both to support the new general secretary and as possible candidates to replace Hu in 2011 at the Eighteenth Party Congress (assuming Hu will serve two terms). But this did not happen. And Zeng Qinghong, Jiang's closest associate, not only joined the PBSC but was also named to head the Secretariat, the body that oversees the implementation of Politburo decisions.

Hu's position was obviously delicate. When Zeng Qinghong spoke at the Central Party School in late November 2002, he talked of cadres being "under the firm leadership of the Party center with Hu Jintao as general secretary," a formulation that conspicuously denied Hu the designation of "core," a term that had been used to signal Jiang Zemin's paramount status.[34] When the *People's Daily* listed China's leadership, it listed Jiang Zemin first, ahead of Hu.[35] And when Hu gave an inner-Party acceptance speech, he promised to "seek instruction and listen to the views of Jiang Zemin."[36]

As the designated successor to a politician still very much alive, Hu Jintao needed to follow two contradictory imperatives: first, he had to demonstrate loyalty, and second, he had to establish independent authority, a task that included promoting people loyal to him, building coalitions, and articulating his own political program. This classic conundrum, often called the "successor's dilemma," applied to Hu after he took the formal reins of power just as it did when he was waiting in the wings. Only by continuing to show fealty to Jiang could he take advantage of the natural trajectory of incumbency to consolidate power, but only by moving away from Jiang could he establish power in his own right. Hu has played this delicate game with great skill.

Hu's first public appearance after being named general secretary was to deliver a speech on the twentieth anniversary of the promulgation of China's 1982 constitution (which had been drawn up in the wake of the Cultural Revolution). Stressing the need to "rule the country through law" (the theme of the Fifteenth Party Congress in 1997), Hu declared that "no organization or individual can be permitted the special privilege of going

---

[34] Zheng Hongfan. "Zeng Qinghong zai zhongyang dangxiao shengbuji ganbu jinxiuban biye dianli shang qiangdiao wei shixian shiliuda queding de mubiao renwu nuli fendou."

[35] "Zhongguo gongchandang dishiliuci quanguo daibiao dahui zai Jing bimu."

[36] Erik Eckholm, "China's New Leader Promises Not to Sever Tether to Jiang."

outside the constitution and the law" and that "all Party organizations at various levels and all Party members must act as models in upholding the constitution, strictly manage affairs in accordance with the constitution, and conscientiously operate within the scope of the constitution and law." Hu's emphasis on law not only continued a policy enunciated by Jiang Zemin (and, before him, Deng Xiaoping), but also marked good strategy for someone still in a precarious position politically. Advancing institution-alization would redound to Hu's personal benefit. And it would not, as a first reading might indicate, erode the Party's position in the polity. After all, as Hu stated, the constitution was the "unified expression of the Party's proposals and the people's will." The Party would operate within the scope of the constitution, but the constitution was the legal expression of the Party's will.[37]

The very next day, Hu headed to Xibaipo, the sleepy central Hebei town that served as the CCP's last revolutionary capital before Mao and his comrades entered Beijing in 1949. Hu had obviously thought hard about the image he sought to project. In going to Xibaipo, Hu sought to ally himself with the good traditions of the CCP; it was at Xibaipo that Mao Zedong had warned against succumbing to the sugar bullets of the urban bourgeoisie. Hu reminded the Party – especially leading cadres – to bear in mind Mao's "two musts," namely, that they "must remain modest, prudent, and without arrogance or rashness" and they "must uphold the spirit of plain living and hard struggle." Giving deference to Jiang Zemin's Three Represents, which had just been endorsed by the Sixteenth Party Congress, Hu nevertheless emphasized the third of those three tenets, namely the "fundamental interests of the vast majority of the people" – whereas Jiang had given greater prominence to the first tenet, the advanced forces of production.[38]

Given Hu's experience in the interior of China, it had long been expected that he would pay greater attention to the needs of China's hinterland and those left behind in the country's headlong rush to develop. Indeed, not long after returning from Xibaipo, Hu presided over a Politburo meeting that discussed rural issues in anticipation of the rural work conference that would convene in early January. The meeting noted the need for "compre-hensive planning" (*tongchou*) of urban and rural economic development, introducing a concept that would become a major theme of the Party's Third Plenary Session in 2003. At the rural work conference, Wen Jiabao,

[37] "Hu Jintao zai xianfa shixing ershi zhounian dahui shang de jianghua."
[38] "Hu Jintao he zhongyang shujichu tongzhi dao Xibaipo xue kaocha."

who would be named premier at the National People's Congress meeting in March 2003, said that "The level of relative affluence that China has now attained is not comprehensive or balanced, and the main discrepancy is in the rural areas." He went on to call for increasing rural incomes, in part by eliminating the agricultural tax, and urged that contractual rights be stabilized. The arbitrary requisitioning of agricultural land, he noted, a major cause of social tensions in the countryside, should be ended.[39] Unfortunately, this problem would only become more severe in the coming years.

The attention that Hu Jintao and Wen Jiabao paid (and would continue to pay) to rural issues reflected China's development needs – the increasing gap between the wealthy east coast and the poorer inland areas (and more specifically between the rural areas and the cities) was a constant theme in social commentary – but it also set up an implicit contrast with Jiang Zemin, whose personal style seemed increasingly detached from the concerns of ordinary citizens and whose economic development efforts had sparked the phenomenal growth of Shanghai and other east coast metropolises but had opened up the tremendous gap with the agricultural interior. Hu was careful to give credit to his predecessor, but his personal behavior and attention to the "fundamental interests of the vast majority of the people" nevertheless differed significantly from the behavior of Jiang. At New Year's, Hu Jintao went to Inner Mongolia to join peasants in a yurt; the previous year, Jiang was pictured on the front page of the *People's Daily* wearing a Western suit and giving a formal address.[40]

The tensions evident at the Sixteenth Party Congress continued the following spring as the annual meeting of the NPC convened. The *People's Daily* pictured Jiang leading the Politburo into the NPC session. Jiang, although no longer on the Politburo, was nevertheless shown in the center of the picture, a full step ahead of Hu Jintao and others. Of course, Jiang was still president of the PRC at the time, but this visual eclipsing of Hu suggested a leader unwilling to give up his pride of place in the political system. On April 6, 2003, China's Arbor Day, following the closing of the NPC, Jiang was again prominently displayed in the center of a picture in the *People's Daily*. By this time, of course, Jiang was no longer president of the PRC or even a member of the Central Committee, although he was still head of the CMC. But there was no obvious reason why the head of the

---

[39] Wen Jiabao, "Renzhen guanche shiliuda jingshen, wei tuijin nongcun xiaokang jianshe er fendou."
[40] "Hu Jintao zai Neimenggu kaocha shi qiangdiao shenke renshi zhizheng weimin de zhongda yiyi qieshi jiejue hao qunzhong shengchan shenghuo wenti"; Jiang Zemin, "Gongtong zujin shijie de heping yu fazhan."

CMC should be included in the picture, other than to emphasize Jiang's "helmsman" role.

CONFRONTING SARS

Given the delicate nature of the relationship between Jiang and Hu, it is perhaps understandable – if not forgivable – that the leadership did not confront the new disease that had been discovered in Guangdong province the previous November and would subsequently be known to the world as Severe Acute Respiratory Syndrome (SARS). Whether because of the leadership transition that was to take place at the NPC or the usual impulse of the CCP not to report difficulties openly, the leadership decided not to report the development of SARS honestly. And it is clear that this was a decision, not an absence of knowledge; Guangdong health authorities had reported the new virus to Beijing in November, and one bold Guangdong newspaper, *Nanfang dushibao*, had reported on the disease in December. It was not until April 2, 2003, however, that the newly named premier, Wen Jiabao, presided over a State Council meeting that discussed the SARS issue. The meeting, based on a briefing by the Ministry of Health (no doubt presented by its minister, Zhang Wenkang), declared that SARS had "already been brought under effective control."[41] The following day, Zhang told a news conference that Beijing had had twelve cases of SARS and three deaths. On April 9, the Vice Minister of Health, Ma Xiaowei, declared that there had been twenty-two cases of SARS in the city and four deaths. "Today, the numbers I report are correct," he stated baldly but falsely. Indeed, even as Ma was reporting these numbers, Jiang Yanyong, the retired head of China's premier military hospital, Number 301, declared publicly that he knew of at least 120 cases of SARS at Number 301 Hospital and two other military hospitals.[42]

On April 17, Hu Jintao presided over a PBSC meeting, the very convening of which stood in contrast to the April 2 meeting's declaration that the work of prevention and cure had obtained "obvious results." This meeting warned officials not to delay reports and not to cover up the situation.[43] There was no indication at this time that a decision had been made to remove Zhang Wenkang or Meng Xuenong (the mayor of Beijing) from office; indeed, foreign reporters were told on the morning of April 20 that

---

[41] "Wen Jiabao zhuchi zhaokai Guowuyuan changwei huiyi."
[42] John Pomfret, "Doctor Says Health Ministry Lied about Disease."
[43] "Zhonggong zhongyang zhengzhiju changwei weiyuanhui zhaokai huiyi yanjiu jinyibu jiaqiang feidianxing feiyan fangzhi gongzuo."

Zhang and Meng would be at a press conference that day to report on the SARS situation. They never made it; they were fired instead.

It is thus apparent that the startling decision to remove Zhang and Meng from their positions was made at the last minute. The decision may have come late, but the frustration had apparently been mounting for some time. According to *Washington Post* correspondent John Pomfret, as early as April 7 – two days before Jiang Yanyong spoke publicly about the cover-up – Wen Jiabao visited China's Center for Disease Control and talked about the failure of the military to report on the situation. City officials similarly covered up the situation. Zhang Wenkang apparently knew what was happening, but could not control it.[44]

In sacking Zhang and Meng, Hu was clearly trying to make a point about accountability that would become one of the hallmarks of his administration. Indeed, Zhang and Meng were not the only ones fired during the SARS crisis. In May, the Xinhua News Agency reported that at least 120 officials had been sacked for dereliction of duty.[45] As many people have noted, there was a political dimension as well. Zhang Wenkang was closely aligned with Jiang Zemin, and Meng Xuenong was an ally of Hu Jintao. It was apparently impossible to fire one of Jiang's supporters without sacrificing one of Hu's as well.

There was also a need to restore foreign confidence, which had been badly eroded by the handling of the crisis. Hu turned to Wu Yi to act concurrently as minister of health (she was already a vice-premier), and transferred Wang Qishan from Hainan to replace Meng as mayor of Beijing. Wu and Wang were both very well known to the foreign community. As head of the Ministry of Foreign Trade and Economic Cooperation (MOFTEC, later renamed MOFCOM, Ministry of Commerce), Wu had been instrumental in negotiating China's accession to the WTO. Wang, who was senior economic policy-maker, was also the son-in-law of the conservative Yao Yilin, who had died in 1994. Wang had emerged in the early 1980s to play a critical role in China's rural reforms. Later, in 1989, he became deputy head of the Construction Bank of China, and in 1998 became vice-governor of Guangdong province. In 2000, he moved to the State Economic Reform Commission. In these various capacities, he had extensive interaction with the foreign business community. And both Wu and Wang were known as officials who could get things done. Their appointments thus promised to bring the SARS crisis under control and to restore foreign confidence.

[44] John Pomfret, "China's Crisis Has a Political Edge."
[45] "More than 120 Government Officials Punished over SARS in China"; Erik Eckholm, "The SARs Epidemic: China," p. 13.

One of the most remarkable aspects of the SARS crisis is that it did not lead to widespread questioning of government authorities or demands for political reform. It did not turn out to be, as some believed it would at the time, China's Chernobyl. On the contrary, on April 25, Li Changchun, the Politburo Standing Committee member in charge of propaganda, presided over a Propaganda Department meeting that elaborated on the line that Hu Jintao had been adopting, namely, "uniting the will of the masses into a fortress, dedicating ourselves in unity, seeking truth in a scientific way, overcoming difficulties, and winning victories" (this was Hu's "24-character" instruction, which was originally included in an April 15 article in the *People's Daily*).[46] A Propaganda Department notice the following day emphasized the importance of the Three Represents and demanded that propaganda units emphasize the "great national spirit" in the struggle against and victory over SARS.[47] Following this meeting and notice, there were numerous "commentator articles" in the *People's Daily* calling for strengthening the national spirit, and on May 1, these propaganda efforts culminated in Hu Jintao's call to launch a "people's war" against SARS.[48] In this media campaign, the role of the military was emphasized, nicely obscuring the inglorious role the PLA had played in exacerbating the crisis in the first place.

This propaganda campaign shows that in an era when modern technology makes covering up events more difficult (but not impossible), the Propaganda Department still has enormous leverage in framing an issue and influencing people's perceptions. The call for a "people's war," the mobilization of the military to build a special SARS hospital in Beijing (known as *Xiaotangshan*), and the mobilization of the cellular structure of the CCP to control population movements (for instance, by using street committees to check who is entering and leaving housing units) had a populist edge and displayed the Party as unified in fighting the disease. Given the genuinely frightening circumstances of the SARS crisis, these efforts won plaudits for Hu Jintao, even on the Internet, and enhanced the credibility of the Party. They also contrasted with Jiang Zemin's absence from the media.

---

[46] "Li Changchun zai zhongyang xinwen xuanchuan bumen fuzeren huiyi shang qiangdiao zhongzhi chengcheng tuanjie fengxian kexue qiushi zhansheng kunnan duoqu shengli"; Yang Jian and Liu Siyang, "Hu Jintao tong Guangdong yiwu gongzuozhe zuotan, qiangdiao yao shizhong ba renmin qunzhong anwei leng nuan fang zai xin shang, quanli yifu zuohao feidianxing feiyan fangzhi gongzuo."

[47] "Zhongxuan bu fachu tongzhi yaoqiu dali hongyang he peiyu minzu jingshen, qieshi jiaqiang fangzhi feidian xuanchuan sixiang gongzuo."

[48] "Guangfan dongyuan henzhua luoshi chunfang chunkong da yichang fangzhi yibing de renmin zhanzheng."

Jiang was living in Shanghai, which was spared the SARS crisis, and his "running away" was widely noted on the Internet. There was even an effort to spin the foreign media, as associates of Hu Jintao spread the word that Hu's efforts were effective, whereas the cover-up had been the fault of Jiang Zemin.[49]

STUDYING – AND REDEFINING – THE THREE REPRESENTS

The Sixteenth Party Congress had approved a campaign to study the Three Represents, and Li Changchun had called for the same during a national meeting of propaganda department heads in January.[50] It is likely that the launch of the campaign was delayed by the SARS crisis, but by June the Party felt able to move ahead with the promised ideological campaign. On June 11, the *People's Daily* published an authoritative editorial that called for a "new high tide" in the study of the Three Represents, and on June 22, the Party issued a circular demanding that cadres study Jiang's speeches "On the 'Three Represents'" and "On Party Construction" as well as selections from *Jiang Zemin on Socialism with Chinese Characteristics*. A 125-page pamphlet, *Study Guide to the Important Thinking of the "Three Represents,"* was also issued.[51]

The new campaign increased speculation that Jiang Zemin was "reasserting" himself after being eclipsed during the SARS crisis. There no doubt was tension between the two leaders, but it is too simplistic to describe their relationship as a "power struggle." Whatever the new general secretary felt about Jiang packing the Politburo with his close associates, Hu was always careful to show deference to his predecessor. Even as he moved to introduce new and more populist themes into CCP rhetoric, Hu always wrapped them in the cloak of the Three Represents. For his part, Jiang had given Hu a strong vote of confidence when meeting with delegates to the NPC, stating:

Since the Sixteenth Party Congress, the new leadership collective with Comrade Hu Jintao as general secretary has worked in a down-to-earth manner, opened new advances, has emphasized studying and implementing the important thinking of the "Three Represents" and the spirit of the Sixteenth Party Congress. They have grasped development – this most important task in this ruling Party and in making

---

[49] Discussions with foreign journalists covering the SARS crisis in Beijing.

[50] Li Changchun, "Zai quanguo xuanchuan buzhang huiyi shang de jianghua," p. 6.

[51] "Zhonggong zhongyang guanyu zai quandang xingqi xuexi guanche 'sange daibiao' zhongyao sixiang xin gaochao de tongzhi"; CCP Central Propaganda Department, *"Sange daibiao" zhongyao sixiang xuexi gangyao*.

the country prosperous. They have strengthened and improved Party building, been concerned with the masses' production lives, especially in demanding that comrades throughout the Party firmly keep in mind the "two musts" and continue in hard struggle. We should say that these tasks have been grasped accurately and effectively; they are a good start in implementing the spirit of the Sixteenth Party Congress.[52]

This strong endorsement, however, did not mean that there were no tensions. As noted above, Jiang's shadow loomed large over the political scene as reflected in the photographs of Jiang in the *People's Daily* – Jiang's pictures were often given central placement and were cut to the same size as those of Hu Jintao when pictures of both leaders appeared. But the SARS crisis seems to have added tension to an already delicate situation. The contrast between Hu's concern for the people, including his meeting with doctors and his traveling to Guangzhou – the epicenter of the crisis – contrasted sharply with Jiang Zemin's extremely low profile as he stayed in Shanghai. Indeed, Jiang's only comment during the crisis came on April 26, just days after the cover-up was exposed and as the number of reported cases was still increasing, when he curiously told visiting Indian defense minister George Fernandes, "After arduous efforts, we have achieved obvious results in controlling SARS."[53]

It was against this background that the campaign to study the Three Represents took on more of a political edge than it would have had in the absence of the SARS crisis. And it was at this time that Hu Jintao recast Jiang's Three Represents to better fit his (Hu's) ideological needs by giving an unusual speech on July 1, the eighty-second anniversary of the founding of the CCP. CCP observances of Party Day, as the anniversary has come to be known, follow a clear pattern. Decennial anniversaries are marked by major leadership speeches, while non-decennial anniversaries are commemorated more quietly with the *People's Daily* running a front-page editorial. Thus, it was not unusual for Jiang to commemorate the eightieth anniversary of the Party with a major address – his July 1, 2001, speech – but it was highly unusual for Hu Jintao to give a major speech on the eighty-second anniversary. It was also unusual for Hu to present his views in the address as his "personal understandings." Leadership speeches are expressions of the Party's ideological views, so for Hu to present his personal views of the Three Represents was out of the ordinary. But doing so allowed him to expand on the content of the Three Represents without challenging Jiang Zemin directly.

[52] "Jiang Zemin: Shizhong jianchi yushi jujin shizhong jianchi jianku fendou."
[53] "Jiang Zemin huijian Yindu guofang buzhang."

After giving due deference to Jiang Zemin, Hu elaborated his ideas around the theme of "building a Party that serves the interests of the public and governs for the people" (*lidang weigong, zhizheng weimin*), a phrase originally introduced by Jiang in his July 1, 2001 speech, but which Hu emphasized by repeating ten times. Drawing on traditional Confucian language and ideas, Hu stated: "People's support or non-support is the fundamental element that determines whether a political Party or government will rise or decline." Building on Jiang's language, Hu went beyond his predecessor by asserting that in "building a Party that serves the interests of the public and governs for the people, and insisting on appraising our policy decisions on the basis of whether *the people support them, endorse them, like them, and are receptive to them*, we will know whether we have a firm grip on the fundamental objective of implementing the important thinking of the 'Three Represents'" (emphasis added).[54] Hu thus gave the Three Represents a more populist twist than anything Jiang had implied in the past.

The apparent tension between Jiang Zemin and Hu Jintao was further highlighted as Army Day (August 1, the anniversary of the Red Army's establishment in 1927) approached. The military normally stays out of politics, at least overtly, but, as noted above, the PLA had intervened the previous year to lobby on behalf of Jiang staying on as head of the CMC. In the summer of 2003, the PLA again showed its support for Jiang by hosting a major forum to tout the publication of the *Study Outline for Jiang Zemin's Thinking on National Defense and Army Building*. Jiang Zemin stayed away from the meeting, but vice-chairmen Guo Boxiong and Cao Gangchuan were there, as were members Xu Caihou, Liang Guangjie, Liao Xilong, and Li Jinai. In other words, the only member of the CMC, other than Jiang Zemin, *not* to attend the forum was Hu Jintao – whose name was not mentioned in the various reports.[55]

Jiang Zemin, who had no military experience prior to being named head of the CMC in 1989, was lauded for creating a body of military ideas on a par with those of Mao Zedong and Deng Xiaoping. His military thought was now an "important part" of the Three Represents, which previously had no military component. "Jiang Zemin's thinking on national defense and army building," according to CMC Vice Chairman Guo Boxiong, "is

54 "Hu Jintao zai 'sange daibiao' yantaohui shang de zhongyao jianghua (quanwen)" (Important talk by Hu Jintao at the symposium on the "Three Represents" [complete text]), *Renmin ribao*, July 1, 2003, pp. 1–2.
55 "Zhongyang junwei zhaokai 'Jiang Zemin guofang he jundui jianshe sixiang xuexi gangyao' chuban zuotanhui."

a scientific guide to our army building and military development at a new stage in the new century."[56] It seemed that the military establishment was playing an independent role in elite politics.

THE THIRD PLENUM

The Third Plenary Session of the Sixteenth Central Committee, which convened October 11–14, 2003, was in fact the first plenary session since Hu had been named general secretary for which he had been able to set the agenda (the Second Plenary Session, which met in February, approved the personnel arrangements for the March NPC meeting). The Third Plenum was also the first Party enclave during which Hu could impose his own personal style, something he did by presenting a report from the Politburo to the Central Committee. The Politburo is theoretically subordinate to the Central Committee, but it never reported as a body to its superior organization. However, Hu, who would make "Party building" and regularization of Party procedures a major feature of his administration, gave a work report on behalf of the Politburo. Unfortunately, it was not published.

More importantly, or at least more observable, was the plenum's decision on economic reform, which set a markedly different tone than had the Sixteenth Party Congress only a year earlier. Whereas the Sixteenth Party Congress stressed creating a high-tech, urbanized, globalized, economically competitive, professional, middle-class society, the Third Plenum set out a vision of a more balanced strategy, a theme that would be more fully developed two years later when the Fifth Plenary Session of the Sixteenth Central Committee articulated a plan for the Eleventh Five-Year Program. Whereas the Sixteenth Party Congress had talked in terms of *economic* development, the Third Plenum stressed "economic and *social* development" (emphasis added), a phrase it used seven times.[57]

In particular, the plenum demanded "comprehensive planning" (*tongchou*) in five areas: urban and rural development, regional development, economic and social development, man and nature (i.e., the environment), and domestic development and international trade. The Chinese-owned Hong Kong paper *Wen wei po* asserted that the notion of "comprehensive planning" came directly from China's experience with SARS, despite Hu's

[56] Wang Wenjie, "Guo Boxiong zai 'Jiang Zemin guofang he jundui jianshe sixiang xuexi gangyao' chuban zuotanhui shang qiangdiao."

[57] "Zhonggong zhongyang guanyu wanshan shehui zhuyi shichang jingji tizhi ruogan wenti de jueding."

use of the term at the late 2002 Politburo meeting (see above). But perhaps the SARS crisis had allowed Hu to better make the case for comprehensive planning as the crisis showed that jolts to economic development could come just as easily from society as from the economy, and "such unfavorable factors cannot be eliminated by seeking growth alone" – what sociologists such as Li Peilin and Lu Xueyi had long been saying.[58]

Just as importantly, the Third Plenum decision called for more thoroughgoing marketization, particularly in the area of property rights. The plenum decision noted that the better definition of property rights, protected by law, would facilitate the development of the non-public (that is, private) economy. The decision also laid out a number of measures to aid the rural economy, including further reducing taxation of peasants, giving peasants reasonable compensation when their land was requisitioned, and supporting migration to the cities. In short, the Third Plenum began to establish a developmental vision that contrasted significantly with that pursued under Jiang Zemin.

In political terms, the Third Plenum also marked a milestone. Although Hu had continuously supported Jiang's Three Represents, he also began introducing his own vocabulary. In addition to the notion of comprehensive planning, Hu used such phrases as "building a Party that serves the interests of the public and governs for the people" that took the Three Represents in a more populist direction. The Third Plenum decision also introduced the phrase "people centered" (*yiren weiben*), that comes from Mencius, Confucius' third-century BCE disciple, who introduced the philosophy of taking the "people as the root" (*minben*) into Chinese philosophical discourse. In addition, the plenum endorsed the idea of "comprehensive, coordinated, sustainable development, and promot[ing] comprehensive economic, social, and human development," a phrase that was later identified as the origin of Hu's "scientific development concept," which would be formally endorsed by the Politburo in November.[59]

The ability to impose ideological constructs is an important part of politics in China (and arguably in other countries as well). That Hu was able to introduce such constructs as "people-centered" and the "scientific development concept" into China's political vocabulary within a year of being named general secretary suggests that he had moved quickly, despite being surrounded by Jiang's protégés, to enhance his ideological authority. He did so by never directly challenging Jiang's legacy, preferring instead to

---

[58] Jen Hui-wen, "Zhonggong qiangdiao luoshi quanmian fazhan guan." See also "Quanmian jianshe xiaokang shehui de tizhi bazhang."

[59] Joseph Fewsmith, "Promoting the Scientific Development Concept."

Table 4: *Frequency of formulations*

Political Slogan	2000	2001	2002	2003	2004	2005	2006
"Three Represents"							
In title	175	419	360	366	99	23	11
Of which on p. 1	50	111	77	82	19	2	3
In full text	780	2678	3151	2982	1804	1222	931
Of which on p. 1	218	600	649	734	485	344	269
"People-Centered"							
In title	14	11	12	23	65	28	41
Of which on p. 1	2	0	1	2	6	4	3
In full text	132	131	164	259	1006	891	924
Of which on p. 1	16	8	13	40	184	139	158
"Scientific Development Concept"							
In title	0	0	0	10	181	151	191
Of which on p. 1	–	–	–	2	45	34	35
In full text	0	0	0	45	1370	1978	2203
Of which on p. 1	–	–	–	15	320	580	492
"Harmonious Society"							
In title	0	0	0	0	21	237	218
Of which on p. 1	–	–	–	–	5	49	40
In full text	0	0	0	0	144	1982	2277
Of which on p. 1	–	–	–	–	45	398	400

The data in this table were compiled by Nancy Hearst.

reshape it. After all, the issues that Hu focused on – reducing the burdens on the peasants, legal construction, fighting corruption, Party building, and so forth – were all issues that had been given attention, if not sufficient weight, during the Jiang era. Nevertheless, terms like the "scientific development concept" implicitly cast aspersions on Jiang by suggesting that planning under Jiang had been less than scientific.

The Third Plenary Session of the Sixteenth Central Committee marked an important turning point. Without ever repudiating Jiang Zemin and his Three Represents – indeed, all the while arguing that the new administration was carrying out the Three Represents – references to Jiang's doctrine began to decline conspicuously in the pages of the *People's Daily*, especially on the front page, while use of Hu Jintao's favorite tropes – "scientific development concept" (*kexue fazhan guan*), "people-centered" (*yiren weiben*), and "harmonious society" (*hexie shehui*) (introduced at the Fourth Plenary Session) (see Table 4) – increased notably. Although Hu would continue to pay public homage to the "Three Represents" and to use many people associated with Jiang's so-called "Shanghai faction," Hu's political strength was becoming more evident (though it would not go unchallenged).

JIANG RETIRES FROM THE CMC

If Hu Jintao was making substantial, indeed remarkable, progress on the ideological front (not insignificant in a system in which defining the ideology is a major tool of power), he still had to complete the takeover of power by persuading Jiang Zemin to step down as head of the CMC and to better define what his own administration would stand for. Neither of these tasks was easy or self-evident.

It is unlikely that there was any understanding within the Party about how long Jiang Zemin would continue to head the CMC. Although the military had become more professionalized over the years, the possibility of it influencing power arrangements, or being brought into politics to support one leader or another, could not be discounted – as the PLA's touting of Jiang Zemin's military expertise the year before suggested. Perhaps more importantly, if Hu Jintao did not assume leadership of the CMC, eventually the rumor mill would begin working overtime in Beijing, sowing doubts about Hu's power and longevity as leader. Such doubts, left unaddressed, could become self-fulfilling prophecies. In short, the transfer of power would not be complete until Hu had taken over as head of the military.

The military, as noted above, had given Jiang Zemin very vocal, very public, and very inappropriate support in 2003. What changed? Why did Jiang decide to retire in 2004? Until revealing memoirs are written or the archives opened, the answer will not be known with certainty. But the overall situation seems clear enough. Jiang had set out to copy the Deng model of "overseeing politics from behind the screen," but Deng himself had given up control of the CMC after two years, in part to enable his successor – Jiang Zemin – to consolidate power. This was a powerful precedent. And there were those, including Deng Xiaoping's daughter, Deng Lin, who would remind Jiang of Deng's legacy. As she put it, Deng had believed that "since he [had] handed over his work to the younger generation he should have faith in them, trust them, and let them get tempered and grow in the course of doing the work."[60]

Moreover, there were indications that the military itself was uncomfortable with the divided lines of authority. Two military delegates to the NPC meeting in March 2003 had complained: "Having one center is called

---

[60] China Central Television, July 28, 2004.

'loyalty,' while having two centers will result in 'problems.' Having multi-ple centers is the same as having no center, and having no center results in having no success in any area." Long-time PLA analyst James Mulvenon concludes from this and other indications that "dissension within the ranks over Jiang's retention of the chairmanship of the Central Military Com-mission is deep and real."[61]

Jiang may well have wanted to promote his confidant Zeng Qinghong to vice-chairman of the CMC, much as he had hoped to promote him to the PBSC in 2000 and 2001, but, if so, he was thwarted in this effort as well. Had Zeng been promoted, he would have held the fifth-ranked position on the PBSC, the vice-presidency, and a CMC vice-chairmanship – precisely the positions Hu Jintao had held before becoming general secretary, and the signal would have been unmistakable. With Jiang's retirement, and Zeng's non-promotion, it was possible to speak of Hu as finally coming into his own – though the degree to which he can consolidate power will not be known until after the Seventeenth Party Congress in 2007.

ENHANCING GOVERNING CAPACITY

The other issue that the Fourth Plenum tackled was Party building, and again Hu Jintao was able to begin to put his stamp on the Party organization. Party building, of course, was a very old topic in the CCP, as it is in all Leninist parties, but it had been given special urgency by the demonstrations of 1989 and the subsequent collapse of socialism in Eastern Europe and the Soviet Union. China had spent much of the following decade studying – and debating – the lessons of that collapse.[62] Following the Sixteenth Party Congress, Hu Jintao asked the Central Party School and other research organizations to examine the longevity of ruling parties, and by 2004 he and other leaders were ready to draw some conclusions.

In an unusually telling reflection of Party thinking, the *People's Daily* published a long article that discussed the difficulties facing the Party in the "crucial period" between 2004 and 2020, when, it predicted, per capita income would rise to $3,000. This analysis comported remarkably well with the work being generated by sociologists during the same period, some of which is cited at the beginning of this chapter. The crux of the analysis was that this critical period would determine China's long-term future. Some

---

[61] James Mulvenon, "Reduced Budgets, the 'Two Centers,' and Other Mysteries of the 2003 National People's Congress."

[62] David Shambaugh, "The Lessons of Collapse: CCP Assessments of the Soviet and East European Implosions."

countries entering this period of uncertainty when per capita incomes rise from \$1,000 to \$3,000 succeed and go on to be highly developed countries, and others fall into the "Latin American trap," that is, countries with a small group of high-income people surrounded by impoverished masses, plagued by social instability, and unable to sustain development. "On the chessboard of modernization," the article said, "reform, development, and stability are three closely linked strategic pieces, and we must pay particular attention to moving well the stability piece during the crucial period."[63]

Development, the article went on, would be largely determined by how well the Party could meet the complex challenges of the coming years. For this, strengthening the Party's "ability to govern" would be critical. And that was the issue that the Fourth Plenary Session of the Sixteenth Central Committee addressed.

THE FOURTH PLENUM

The Fourth Plenum met from September 16–19, 2004, and endorsed a resolution on strengthening the Party's ability to govern. Laying out the complexity of the situation facing the CCP, much as the *People's Daily* article had done, the resolution talked in terms of "reforming and perfecting the Party's leadership structure and work mechanism as the focal point." It was, it said, necessary to build a "harmonious society," a new term in the Hu Jintao vocabulary, which had already emphasized "serving the interests of the public and governing for the people," the "scientific development concept," and "people-centered" government. It was necessary to "institutionalize, standardize, and regularize" the practice of "socialist democracy."[64]

The core of the resolution lay in the final section, which discussed Party building. It was important to "deepen reform of the cadre and personnel systems" by promoting such mechanisms as "democratic recommendation, democratic assessment, multi-candidate examination, public announcement before appointment, open selection and competition for posts, [and] voting by the entire Party committee." Developing "inner-Party democracy" was an "important part of political structural reform."[65]

---

[63] Ren Zhongping, "Zai gan yige ershi nian: Lun woguo gaige fazhan de guanjian shiqi." "Ren Zhongping" is an abbreviation of "*Renmin ribao* zhongyao pinglun," or "important *People's Daily* commentary." Such articles are usually written by a writing team and express the views of the central leadership rather than the paper itself. They are quite authoritative, even if they do not bear the imprimatur of the Party as do such vehicles as "editorials" and certainly the resolutions of Party plenary sessions or congresses.

[64] "Zhonggong zhongyang guanyu jiaqiang dang de zhizheng nengli jianshe de jueding."

[65] Ibid.

Whereas the reformers in the 1980s had stressed the separation of Party and government, the Fourth Plenum, building on the experience of the 1990s, vigorously asserted that the Party itself would rule – by writing Party policy into state law and by invoking Party discipline to control the government bureaucracy, the people's congresses, and the CPPCC bodies at various levels – but that the Party would adhere more closely to formal procedure and "socialist democracy," including – to an unspecified degree – the participation of the non-Party "masses."

It was thus no coincidence that as the Party was preparing for the Fourth Plenum new regulations governing the Party were released. The most important regulations were those governing inner-Party supervision. These regulations, the first such regulations adopted in the Party's 82-year history, were intended to address the single most important problem in the Party – the concentration of power in the hands of individual leaders who were unconstrained in its use and abuse. Such individualized power was a major source of corruption, of bad decision-making (as leaders adopted projects that brought personal benefits), of local-level networks, and of the central authorities' inability to supervise or control sub-provincial officials. In keeping with the thinking of the Fourth Plenum, the regulations were intended to curtail corruption and improve decision-making through inner-Party democracy. The regulations tried to establish rules for collective decision-making and supervision, outlining the duties of individual Party members and the discipline inspection committees at various levels. They also included provisions for supervision by "public opinion," including the media.[66]

Unfortunately, the regulations did not establish a real division of power within the Party (much less between the Party and the government). For instance, there had been numerous calls for the regulations to establish a permanent office for Party congresses at various levels, which would have given Party delegates an institutional base from which to supervise the behavior of Party committees and others, but the proposal was found to contravene the Party constitution and thus was not accepted. The result was that the regulations ended up summarizing practices that had long been endorsed, if not necessarily adhered to, by the Party organization.[67]

But the Party's intention to enhance governing power through greater institutionalization of the Party itself was clear. Other regulations, including on disciplinary punishment, forbidding Party and government officials

[66] "Zhongguo gongchandang dangnei jiandu tiaoli (shixing)."
[67] Sun Yafei, "Zhizhengdang diyibu ziwo jiandu tiaoli jijiang chutai."

from concurrently holding posts in enterprises, and bringing the discipline inspection commissions at various levels under higher-level control, were instituted.[68]

Although new and vigorous efforts seemed to be directed at fighting corruption, there was little evidence by 2006 that there was any significant change in the situation. Writing for the 2004 annual survey on the social situation published by CASS, Wen Shengtang of the Supreme People's Procuratorate argued that corruption was getting worse. According to Wen, the number of "number one officials" (*yibashou*) arrested for corruption had been increasing, the length of time corruption was going on before being detected was lengthening, the illegal sale of offices was increasing, and the age of corrupt officials was declining.[69] Two years later, Wen was no more optimistic. Profits in coal mines were so great that it was almost impossible to make officials give up their shares in coal mines, even under direct orders; indeed, some officials quit their official postings rather than give up their holdings. Moreover, gambling had become an extremely common method of extending bribes without appearing to violate regulations (it was only necessary to lose to the person one wanted to bribe).[70]

LIBERALISM, NEOLIBERALISM, AND ILLIBERALISM

In economic terms, the Third Plenum was very liberal, as its support for property rights and further development of shareholding showed, but ideologically Hu Jintao was proving to be extremely cautious, some would say draconian. Hu Jintao has no interest in presiding over the demise of the CCP. Party concerns about foreign efforts to undermine the CCP were compounded by the various "color" revolutions – Rose, Orange, and Tulip – that overturned autocratic governments in Georgia and Ukraine in 2004 and Kyrgyzstan in 2005.[71]

China had long been conscious of the threat posed by "soft power"; that is, after all, the basis of "peaceful evolution." As the economic reforms deepened, the "threat" posed by Western economic theory became increasingly

---

[68] Xia Changyong, "Zhonggong zhongyang ban bu 'Zhongguo gongchandang dangnei jiandu tiaoli (shixing)' he 'Zhongguo gongchandang jilu chufen tiaoli'"; "Party Bans Officials from Conflicting Posts"; and Ye Jundong, "Yanfang quanli shikong."

[69] Wen Shengtang, "2003 nian de fanfubai douzheng."

[70] Wen Shengtang, "Fanfubai: Jianli jianquan zhengzhi he yufang tixi."

[71] See Jiang Zemin's harsh warnings about foreign efforts to "Westernize" and "divide" China in his January 2000 report to the Politburo, "Tongbao zhongyang zhengzhiju changwei 'sanjiang' qingkuang de jianghua."

apparent, at least to those on the left, as the discussion in the previous chapter on China's accession to the WTO shows. These concerns apparently found a growing audience in Zhongnanhai. In the summer of 2003, just as the country was emerging from the SARS crisis and studying Jiang's Three Represents, the "center" approved the establishment of a Study Group on Neoliberalism at CASS. The purpose of this study group was to show either that neoliberalism – left largely undefined – did not work in general or that it would be inappropriate for China in particular. A year later the first product of this group's efforts, *Neoliberalism: Commentaries and Analyses*, was published by CASS.

According to this book, neoliberalism is an ideological trend of thought that meets the demands of "state monopoly capitalism" as it transforms itself into "international monopoly capital." More specifically, the "Washington Consensus" marked the transformation of an academic theory into an economic model and political program for international monopoly capitalism. Neoliberalism, the book went on, is not just the promotion of globalization but specifically of "globalization under the leadership of a superpower."[72] The book also argued that the September 11, 2001, terrorist attacks had provided an opening for the United States to whip up a "political globalization" or a "global unification" (*quanqiu yitihua*).[73] As John Williamson, who drew up the list of "best practices" for the Latin American reforms as they were understood by international financial organizations in Washington in 1989, said, the "Washington Consensus" has long been used by critics who have distorted the original meaning beyond recognition, asserting that it refers to a set of policies (often not contained in the original) that Washington hopes to impose on the world.[74] Such was the case here, and it was an increasingly popular position in Beijing.

More discussion of the Washington Consensus was prompted by the publication of a paper called "The Beijing Consensus" in 2004 by Joshua Ramo, formerly an editor at *Time* magazine.[75] Written with verve, Ramo's analysis was certainly correct that whether or not its policy-makers wanted a "peaceful rise" China's rise was having an impact on the outside world. But it was certainly wrong when it argued that there was a consensus in Beijing – as the sharp debates about to burst across Beijing would demonstrate. In any event, Ramo's piece was generally interpreted to support the argument

---

[72] He Bingmeng (ed.), *Xinziyou zhuyi pingxi*, p. 5. [73] Ibid., p. 12.
[74] John Williamson, "The Washington Consensus as Policy Prescription for Development."
[75] Joshua Cooper Ramo, "The Beijing Consensus."

that China should find its own route to development and, to a certain extent, to discredit "neoliberals" in China.[76]

By the fall of 2004, as concern in Beijing about the so-called color revolutions increased in the wake of the Orange Revolution in Ukraine, China's control over ideology, never loose, was tightened further. On September 2, 2004, Xiao Weibi, editor of the liberal, Guangdong-based journal *Tongzhou gongjin* (Moving Forward on a Single Ship), was dismissed for publishing a no-holds-barred interview with Ren Zhongyi, a former Guangdong Party secretary who had voiced strong criticisms in recent years.[77] Shortly thereafter, Jiao Guobiao, a journalism professor at Beijing University who had created a sensation with his hard-hitting Internet piece harshly criticizing the Propaganda Department, was suspended from teaching (later he was dismissed from Beijing University, allegedly for staying too long in the United States). At roughly the same time, the popular bulletin board service (BBS) at Beijing University, *Yitahutu*, was closed down, as was the journal *Strategy and Management*, apparently because it published an article critical of North Korea. Wang Guangze, a journalist at the *21st-Century Economic Report*, was dismissed after he gave a speech in the United States entitled "The Development and Possible Evolution of Political Ecology in China in the Age of the Internet."[78]

On September 8, 2004 *Southern Personalities Weekly* (*Nanfang renwu zhoukan*), inspired by a listing of the 100 most influential public intellectuals published by the British periodical *Prospect*, ran its own list of the 50 most influential Chinese public intellectuals. Those enumerated constituted a diverse list, from the liberal economists Mao Yushi and Wu Jinglian to liberal historians Zhu Xueqin and Qin Hui to environmentalist Liang Congjie and poet Bei Dao. On September 30, the Propaganda Department reportedly submitted a report to the Central Committee and then, with the Central Committee's approval, issued "Document No. 29" on November 11. This document reportedly criticized economist Mao Yushi, writer Yu Jie, deceased economist Yang Xiaokai, and others, and it cited the journals *Strategy and Management*, *Yanhuang chunqiu*, *Tongzhou gongjin*, and *Tushu zhoubao* and the web site *Yitahutu* for going beyond official guidelines.[79]

---

[76] Huang Ping and Cui Zhiyuan (eds.), *Zhongguo yu quanqiuhua: Huashengdun gongshi haishi Beijing gongshi*. See also, Yu Keping, Huang Ping, Xie Shuguang, and Gao Jian (eds.), *Zhongguo moshi yu "Beijing gongshi": Chaoyue "Huashengdun gongshi."*

[77] Reporters without Borders, "Five Resign from Editorial Board in Solidarity with Dismissed Magazine Editor."

[78] Paul Mooney, "Gaging China's Intellectuals," *Asia Times Online*.

[79] "Weixian xinhao: Zhongxuanbu 29 hao wenjian yinxiang fubi daotui de kuihao."

On September 22 Liu Yunshan, head of the Propaganda Department, said, "If [the ideological and cultural fronts] are not taken over by Marxist ideas, then all kinds of non-Marxist and even anti-Marxist ideas will take over."[80] Liu kept up this old, hardline Marxist rhetoric during his November tour of Henan province. According to Liu, ideology was "an area of strategic importance, contended for by rival forces."[81] Soon Shanghai's *Liberation Forum (Jiefang luntan)* published an article by the pseudonymously named Ji Fangping (homophone for "*Jiefang ribao* commentary") titled, "A Delusive Slogan – Response to the 'Theory of Media as a Public Institution'."[82] Three days later, on November 15, Shanghai's Party paper, *Liberation Daily*, ran an article under Ji Fangping's byline titled, "See through the Appearance to Perceive the Essence – An Analysis of the Theory of 'Public Intellectuals'." Employing the harsh language of class struggle, the article declared that the concept of public intellectuals had been touted to "drive a wedge between the intellectuals and the Party and between the intellectuals and the general public." Far from being "independent" and above faction or class, as was often claimed, such public intellectuals, the article asserted, have "certain interest groups" supporting them.[83] Ten days later, the *People's Daily* threw its weight behind the emerging campaign to criticize public intellectuals by reprinting the article.

On December 14, *Enlightenment Daily* published an article called "Beware of the Intellectual Tide of 'Public Intellectuals'" that repeated the charge that public intellectuals seek to be "independent and critical," but that in fact, the article asserted, intellectuals, like everyone else, reflect their social backgrounds and interests.[84] The harsher ideological atmosphere established by these commentaries was reflected in the continuing repression of intellectuals. In December, the well-known writers Yu Jie and Liu Xiaobo were taken into custody, interrogated, and released the next day, apparently because the Chinese chapter of PEN, headed by Liu, had given its award to Zhang Yihe for her memoir *The Past Is Not Like (Dissipating) Smoke*, which details the 1957 anti-rightist campaign. The political theorist Zhang Zuhua was also detained. Also in December, some 1,287

[80] "Liu Yunshan zai quanguo xuanchuan buzhang zuotanhui shang qiangdiao renzhen xuexi xuanchuan guanche shiliujie sizhong quanhui jingshen"; Jiang Xun, "Zhongguo zhishijie you miandui hanleng de dongtian."
[81] "Liu Yunshan zai Henan kaocha shi qiangdiao tigao jianshe shehuizhuyi xianjin wenhua nengli wei quanmian jianshe xiaokang shehui tigong sixiang baozheng he yulun zhichi"; Jiang Xun, "Zhongguo zhishijie you miandui hanleng de dongtian."
[82] Jiang Xun, "Zhongguo zhishijie you miandui hanleng de dongtian."
[83] Ji Fangping, "Tuoguo biaoxiang kan shizhi."
[84] Zhan Tianyang, "Jingti 'gonggong zhishi fenzi' sichao."

web sites were shut down, most for pornography and gambling but others for promoting "superstition" (religion).[85]

In January 2006, *Freezing Point* (*Bingdian*), the weekly supplement of the widely read *China Youth Daily*, was closed by authorities for printing an article that disputed official interpretations of modern Chinese history, particularly the Boxer Rebellion. The action aroused much controversy among intellectuas in Beijing, and the editor of *Freezing Point*, Li Datong, took the unusual step of issuing an open letter, criticizing the Propaganda Department's high-handed behavior as not in accord with the constitution. Li's dissent was joined by well-known Taiwan writer Lung Ying-tai, who declared that the closing of the weekly "crushed the last hopes of many Taiwanese that Mr. Hu would allow a more open society."[86] Shortly thereafter, thirteen senior intellectuals, including Li Rui, former secretary to Mao Zedong, and Zhu Houze, former head of the Propaganda Department, issued a declaration criticizing the closing of *Freezing Point*.[87] The Party finally staunched the criticism by allowing the supplement to resume publication – but without Li Datong as editor. Li and a deputy were transferred to a news research institute, so the once outspoken supplement was reduced to a shell of its former self.[88]

THE LARRY LANG "WHIRLWIND"

It was in this ideologically charged atmosphere that Larry Lang (Lang Xianping), professor in the Department of Business Administration of the Chinese University of Hong Kong, gave a talk on August 9, 2004, at Fudan University in Shanghai. In that talk, Lang charged specifically that Gu Chujun, chairman of Kelon (Greencool), had pocketed large sums of money by manipulating a management buyout (MBO) of a state-owned enterprise. Lang had made similar charges before against other high-profile SOEs, such as TCL and Haier, but this time, after the media reported on his remarks, Gu initiated legal proceedings against Lang – thus turning what might have been an academic debate into a feeding frenzy as academics of different persuasions jumped in on different sides of the debate.

Charges that state-owned assets were being stripped were nothing new. "Non-mainstream" economists such as Yang Fan, Zuo Dapei, and Han Deqiang had been making similar arguments for years. This time, however,

---

[85] "China Shuts Down 1,287 Pornographic and Cult Websites."
[86] "Editor Challenges Party to Justify Weekly's Axing."
[87] "Veteran Cadres in Support of Closed Weekly."
[88] Vivian Wu, "Weekly Relaunches, but Without Its Editors."

the charges set off an enormous public debate because of the growing sensitivity to growing income inequalities and corruption that had been building in recent years and because Larry Lang seemed extraordinarily well qualified to speak to the issue. The son of a nationalist general, he had been raised in Taiwan before pursuing a Ph.D. at the Wharton School of the University of Pennsylvania, teaching at several universities in the United States, and finally taking up a position at the Chinese University of Hong Kong while concurrently serving as a professor at Beijing's Cheung Kong Graduate School of Business (*Changjiang shangxueyuan*). Western scholars generally support privatization (part of the Washington Consensus), so news that a Western-trained economist was opposed to privatization gave non-mainstream economists a credibility they had previously lacked.

Lang's point was that China's SOEs needed better management, not a change of property rights. In an oft-used metaphor, Professor Lang questioned whether the "nanny" should take over as the "boss" – whether managers of SOEs had the right to replace the state through MBOs and enrich themselves. Ice cream was another popular metaphor, invoked on the other side of the argument: in the hands of incompetent owners who didn't know what to do with them, SOEs would waste away like melting ice cream, but if they were sold to a competent "nanny," they could be turned into money-making ventures.[89]

Lang's views were quickly echoed by a number of non-mainstream economists. On September 15, ten academics signed a statement supporting Lang and criticizing the "neoliberal views" that supposedly lay behind China's efforts to restructure SOEs.[90] A few days later, Zuo Dapei, Yang Fan, and Han Deqiang wrote a letter to the Chinese leadership demanding that an investigation be conducted into the companies criticized by Lang, that hearings be held on the loss of state assets, and that China rethink the direction of state enterprise reform.[91] An article in the English-language *China Daily* argued that protecting state-owned assets affected the interests of the "common people" and observed that laid-off and retired workers had a "particularly huge stake in how the current property rights reform is carried out."[92] A number of mainstream economists, including Wu Jinglian, Zhang Weiying, and Zhang Wenkui, eventually weighed in

---

[89] Chi Sho-ming, "Guaqi gaige fansi."
[90] "Guanyu Lang Xianping jiaoshou zhiyi liuxing chanquan lilun he qindun guoyou zichan wenti de xueshu shengming."
[91] "Zuo Dapei, Yang Fan, Han Deqiang jiu zuzhi guoyou zichan liushi, gaohao guoyou qiye zhidang he guojia lingdaoren de gongkaixin."
[92] "Seeking Cure for Property Reform."

to oppose Lang's views, but as another article in *China Daily* noted, the "overwhelming majority of Internet opinions support the neoleftists headed by Lang."[93] Larry Lang's criticisms were not unrelated to the criticism of neoliberalism discussed above. Lang placed the blame for many of China's economic ills on the neoliberal ideology, criticized the state withdrawal from the economy, and argued that SOEs were at least as efficient as privately owned enterprises. Thus his criticisms echoed those that had been in the official press for at least the previous year.

Lang's views were partially vindicated – and the debate re-energized – following the China Securities Regulatory Commission's (CSRC) investigations into Kelon. After three months of investigation, the CSRC in early August issued a report that found the earnings figures in Kelon's annual reports for 2002, 2003, and 2004 to be false. Gu Chujun and six other senior figures at Kelon were arrested in September 2005.[94]

In December 2004, the State Council ruled that MBOs would be forbidden among China's large SOEs and those among small and medium-sized SOEs must clarify who is funding a buyout and who will manage the business before any MBO can be approved. Those rules came in April 2005, when the State-owned Assets Supervision and Administration Commission (SASAC) and the Ministry of Finance announced new regulations that continued the ban on MBOs in large SOEs and closed a number of loopholes in MBOs for small and medium-sized enterprises.[95] Putting MBOs on a sounder basis was necessary, and Larry Lang and others were correct that insiders had been abusing their positions to enrich themselves at the expense of the state and public. But it was troubling that a combination of non-mainstream economists and popular pressures was slowing reforms of SOEs. Not since the period following Tiananmen had the political atmosphere been so negative toward economic reform.

This atmosphere only got worse when Liu Guoguang, former vice-president at CASS, published an article in *Economic Research* stressing the need for Marxism in teaching economics. Expressing consternation at the increasing dominance of Western economic theory in China's economic circles, Liu warned that if these trends were to continue, "this will ultimately alter the direction of development of socialism and eliminate the leadership

[93] "Revamp Rules to Promote Equality."
[94] Hu Yuanyuan, "CSRC: Kelon Chief Did Wrong"; Hu Yuanyuan, "Kelon Gets Fined for Accounting Fraud."
[95] Sun Min, "Standards Released for State Firm Buyouts"; Tan Wei, "Fresh Start for Management Buyout: New Regulation Puts an End to the Prolonged Debate on MBO Feasibility and Ushers in New Era for the Practice."

of the Communist Party, or else change its color." Liu was particularly critical of "neoliberalism," saying that the "core theory of neoliberal economics is something we cannot accept."[96]

Liu had been an important proponent of reform in the late 1970s before trimming his sails as the more orthodox thinking associated with Chen Yun became dominant in the early 1980s. By the mid-1980s, Liu had settled down safely in the middle of the political spectrum, but he had never come out with such a conservative manifesto. There may have been personal reasons for his willingness to do so now – since retiring, his prestige had declined as younger, better-trained economists took over the field – but this was clearly an effort to align himself with conservative ideological trends. And Liu's position within the economics community gave a political weight to the debate that Lang Xianping's populist critiques had lacked.

There was no doubt that the tone of public discourse had been drifting to the left at least since the critiques of neoliberalism began in 2003. These trends were particularly worrisome to liberal thinkers in China, who worried that the new populism would make it difficult to carry out the sort of reforms that would bring about a more competitive economy and more democratic institutions.

On July 10, 2005, the Xinhua News Agency released the text of a draft property rights law that was to be considered by the National People's Congress in its annual session the following March.[97] The law, which had already been revised three times over the previous three years, was an effort to fulfill the commitment of the Third Plenum of 2003 and to reduce societal conflict by better defining property rights. But it proved to be a fuse for the most contentious debate yet. On August 12, Beijing University law professor Gong Xiantian posted a virulent letter on the Internet accusing the draft of being in violation of the constitution. The draft law, Gong wrote, did not affirm that "socialist public property is sacred and inviolable" and thus acted to protect private property, not socialism. Gong accused those who wanted to reform the state-owned economy by selling off SOEs of "pursuing the capitalist road" and being "under the influence of Western liberalist economic studies and the 'Washington Consensus'." Asking rhetorically "Is not privatization the greatest cause of the current social instability in China?" Gong declared that the "masses" were saying that the "Communist Party" had become the "private property Party."[98]

---

[96] Liu Guoguang, "Jingjixue jiaoxue he yanjiu de yixie wenti."
[97] "Zhonghua renmin gongheguo wuquanfa (cao'an)."
[98] Gong Xiantian, "Yibu weibei xianfa he beili shehui zhuyi jiben yuanze de 'wuquanfa (cao'an)'."

Gong's letter set off a heated debate on the Internet and in seminars around the country. "Non-mainstream" economists quickly came out in support of Gong Xiantian, while "mainstream" economists fired back. In November, the influential financial journal *Caijing* carried an article by senior economists Wu Jinglian, Gao Shangquan, and others pointing out that the populist effort to level the social system would have dire consequences for the economy and the society.[99] As the reform-minded *Southern Weekend* pointed out:

the key difference in understanding in the argument is that one side holds that the problems are caused by the marketizing reforms, and so it is necessary to turn back in an all-round fashion; while the other side holds that the problems are caused by the fact that the reforms are not thought through and incomplete, hence it is essential to speed up promotion of the reforms, and there can be no wavering over the direction.[100]

Arguments do not get more fundamental than that.

Gong Xiantian's letter crystallized opposition to the property law. Hence, the NPC Standing Committee did not further consider the law in its December meeting, and it was not put on the agenda of the full meeting of the NPC in the spring, as originally planned. This was the first time in China's legislative history that a proposed law had been derailed by a rising tide of public opinion in conjunction with more conservative law-makers. Intellectuals talked about a "leftward" turn in Chinese politics, and Gao Shangquan, almost pleadingly, said that the "top central leaders should speak out at the critical moment."[101]

Almost simultaneously with Gao's appeal, "Huangfu Ping" published a hard-hitting piece in the influential financial magazine *Caijing* called "Reform Must Not Be Shaken." Huangfu Ping is the pen name of Zhou Ruijin, a former editor-in-chief of the *People's Daily*, who had co-written the dramatic articles in 1991 that had conveyed Deng Xiaoping's impatience with the conservative turn in Chinese politics (see Chapter 2). The reappearance of the name "Huangfu Ping" underscored the parallel between the crisis reform faced in the post-Tiananmen period and that in the current period when reforms were being criticized for exacerbating social inequalities.

Zhou Ruijin acknowledged problems with reform, problems that he attributed largely to vested interests that had distorted reform and contributed to the prevalence of "trading power for money" and "local

---

[99] Wu Jinglian, "Xiang furen kaiqiang hui daozhi hen yanzhong de shehui houguo."
[100] Li Liang and Xu Tonghui, "2004–2006 'disanci gaige lunzheng' shimo."   [101] Ibid.

interests," but he was adamant that reform itself was not the problem and that attacking reform was not the solution. As Zhou put it, "Negating the practice of reform by criticizing neoliberalism is to fundamentally negate the history of China's reform, and it also negates Deng Xiaoping Theory and the important thinking of the 'Three Represents'."[102]

In other articles, Zhou put the contemporary debate in the context of previous debates over the course of the reforms. The first great debate was in the early 1980s, revolving around the issue of the socialist commodity economy (which was adopted as ideological orthodoxy in the decision of the Third Plenary Session of the Twelfth Central Committee in 1984). The second debate took place between 1989 and 1992, which was settled, at least on the surface, by Deng's southern journey and the Fourteenth Party Congress, which affirmed the "socialist market economy." The third debate was the present one, which still involved the issue of whether reform was "socialist" or "capitalist." Ideological issues had not died out as they continued to represent different interests in the political system and society. Zhou's position was clear. He argued that this third round of debate had emerged because there had not been any reform of the political and legal systems to support the ongoing economic reforms.[103]

REFORM AND SOCIAL JUSTICE

By this time, public debate was both broad and vituperative. It had already had an impact on public policy, both in the new rules governing MBOs and in the temporary shelving of the property rights law, which was eventually passed in amended version by the NPC meeting in March 2007.[104] Public opinion was beginning to have an impact on public policy and in a way that might threaten continued reform and foreign investment. It is no wonder that the leadership felt a need to speak out to curtail the public debate. When the annual meeting of the NPC met in March 2006, Hu Jintao strongly endorsed reform. He told the delegates, "We should unswervingly adhere to the reform orientation, further strengthen our determination and confidence in the reforms, repeatedly perfect the socialist market economy structure, and fully exercise the basic role of the market in the allocation of resources."[105] Similarly, Wen Jiabao told reporters, "we should unswervingly

---

[102] Huangfu Ping, "Gaige bu ke dongyao."
[103] Zhou Ruijin, "Ruhe kandai gaige disanci dazhenglun."
[104] Joseph Kahn, "China Approves Property Law, Strengthening its Middle Class."
[105] "Hu Jintao, Wu Bangguo, Wen Jiabao, Jia Qinglin, Wu Guanzheng, Li Changchun, Luo Gan fenbie canjia shenyi he taolun."

push forward the reform and opening up . . . Although in our way ahead there will be difficulties, we cannot stop, retrogression offers no way out."[106]

These strong affirmations of reform, made to regain control of a debate that seemed to be spinning out of control, did not mean that Hu and Wen were retreating from their vision of "people-centered" development, as the March 2006 NPC's discussions on the Eleventh Five-Year Program showed.

The Eleventh Five-Year Program adopted the term "program" to distinguish itself from its predecessors, known as "plans," and to de-emphasize the pursuit of GDP figures. The Eleventh Five-Year Program had been approved in principle at the Party's Fifth Plenary Session in October 2005 and then elaborated on at the winter's planning meetings before being approved at the NPC in March 2006. Explaining the proposal to the Fifth Plenum, Wen Jiabao had emphasized that the scientific development concept should be "put in command of economic and social development as a whole" and "extensive" economic growth, with its high inputs, must be changed to "intensive" growth, with more attention to economic efficiency and environmental impact. Wen called for creating a "new socialist countryside," with increased incomes for the peasants, better coordinated regional development, and changed functions of government. The five "comprehensive plannings" (urban and rural development, regional development, economic and social development, man and nature, and domestic development and international trade) that the Party had adopted at the Third Plenum were central to the Eleventh Five-Year Program.[107]

For both economic and political reasons, addressing the problems in the countryside was central to the Hu–Wen vision of social justice, and their policies over the previous two years brought some improvements. Grain production was up and, more importantly, so were rural incomes. In 2004, farmers' incomes had increased 6.8 percent over the previous year, the highest increase since 1997. Despite falling grain prices, rural incomes had still increased about 6 percent in 2005. These income increases were partially due to the elimination of the agricultural tax and other fees in the countryside. As of 2005, the aggregate tax burden of peasants had declined by 120 billion yuan, most of which was made up for by increased central transfers to the rural areas.[108] The agricultural policies for 2006, set out in "Document No. 1," called for eliminating the remaining taxes on peasants and for industry and the cities to support agriculture and the countryside. It

---

[106] "Wen Jiabao zongli da zhongwai jizhe wen."

[107] Wen Jiabao, "Guanyu zhiding guomin jingji he shehui fazhan dishiyi wunian guihua jianyi de shuoming."

[108] Chen Xiwen, "Dangqian de nongye jingji fazhan xingshi yu renwu."

also called for eliminating the "discriminatory and irrational restrictions" on migrant workers and expanding compulsory education in the rural areas.[109] In his report to the March 2006 NPC, Wen Jiabao promised to increase support to the rural areas by spending 340 billion yuan – up 42 billion yuan over 2005 – and another 103 billion yuan to support township governments and rural education.[110]

Although the Eleventh Five-Year Program reflected changed social and economic priorities, it also demanded changes in the way government functioned. The need to reduce government interference in the economy and to better provide public goods had long been recognized, suggesting that meeting such goals would be difficult indeed. As Wang Mengkui, head of the State Council's Development Research Center, put it, there are "deeper systemic and policy reasons" why the model of extensive growth has not changed:

When market prices do not reflect real costs, it leads to a serious waste of water and energy resources, and taxation based on actual output and not on recoverable reserves is the direct reason for the low rate of return on mineral resources. The flawed land requisition system and method of "recruiting businesses and attracting investments" by setting low or even zero price for land have abetted the reckless expansion of the scope of investment and the one-sided pursuit of speed at the expense of quality and efficient growth.[111]

In other words, the problems underlying distorted economic growth and the lack of social fairness in the society were, at bottom, governmental and political.

TOWARD A HARMONIOUS SOCIETY?

By the summer and fall of 2006, the Seventeenth Party Congress, scheduled for the fall of 2007, was beginning to loom large. That Congress, for better or worse, would largely define Hu Jintao's legacy as he set out the themes of his policies and promoted the leaders who will carry them out. It is evident that Hu Jintao had made much progress in advancing his more populist agenda in the first years of his stewardship, but consolidating his authority would mean that he would have to confront the "Shanghai gang" more directly. Jiang Zemin's close associates remained influential in the highest

---

[109] "Zhonggong zhongyang, Guowuyuan guanyu tuijin shehui zhuyi xinnongcun jianshe de ruogan yijian."
[110] Wen Jiabao, "Zhengfu gongzuo baogao."
[111] Wang Mengkui, "Quanmian jianshe xiaokang shehui de guanjian shike."

reaches of the Party and continued to run important places, including the east coast metropolis of Shanghai.

Hu stepped up his campaign against corruption in June 2006 by suddenly dismissing Liu Zhihua, the vice-mayor of Beijing in charge of construction for the Olympic Games.[112] Not long thereafter, Wang Yeshou was removed as deputy commander of the Navy, and He Minxu, a vice-governor in Anhui province, and Li Baojin, the president of Tianjin's Procuratorate, were detained for corruption.[113] In at least three of these four cases, "bad morals" were included in the reports by the Xinhua News Agency. At the same time, Hu consolidated his hold on the military by promoting ten senior officers to the rank of full-general.[114]

Just as this news was coming out in the Chinese press, Hu Jintao raised the stakes in his speech on the eighty-fifth anniversary of the CCP's founding. The speech was ostensibly intended to sum up the eighteen-month campaign to "maintain the advanced nature of Communist Party members," which had been launched in January 2005.[115] Originally promoted as an effort to implement the Three Represents, it had increasingly been infused with Hu Jintao's formulations about building a "people-centered" society and employing the "scientific development concept." By the time Hu summed up the campaign, the Three Represents were defined wholly in terms of Hu's rhetoric. Most important from an immediate standpoint, however, were Hu's warnings against various corrupt practices, such as the buying and selling of offices and promoting cadres who had problems.[116]

Ironically, just as Hu was moving to consolidate his authority in the Party and the military, he spoke at a major meeting to launch the publication of the three volumes of Jiang Zemin's *Selected Works*. Hu praised Jiang's concept of the Three Represents as reflecting the "common aspiration of the broadest masses of the Chinese people." A major publicity campaign ensued, with meetings called at all levels to propagate – and buy – Jiang's works.[117] For a moment it seemed as if the elder statesman was staging a comeback, but it turned out that this was Hu's way of giving Jiang "face" while continuing to erode his authority.

Although it was not clear at the time, a major corruption scandal in Shanghai's Social Security Bureau was about to quickly balloon into a political imbroglio that would bring down Shanghai's Party leader. In July it was

[112] Benjamin Kang Lim, "China's Hu Orders Sacking of Vice Mayor – Source."
[113] Vivian Wu, "Ex-Naval Chief Expelled by NPC."
[114] Minnie Chan, "Hu Tightens Grip with Promotion of Generals."
[115] Joseph Fewsmith, "CCP Launches Campaign to Maintain the Advanced Nature of Party Members."
[116] Hu Jintao, "Zai qingzhu Zhongguo gongchandang chengli 85 zhounian ji zongjie baochi gongchan-dangyuan xianjin jiaoyu huodong dahui shang de jianghua."
[117] Hu Jintao, "Zai xuexi 'Jiang Zemin wenxuan' baogaohui shang de jianghua."

reported that Zhu Junyi, the director of the bureau, had been accused of receiving bribes and misusing some three billion yuan (about $400 million) in funds.[118] The Shanghai case took on a more political color when Qin Yu, a former secretary to Party Secretary Chen Liangyu, was arrested in August.[119] Finally, on September 24, Chen himself was removed from office for his involvement in a pension fund scandal.[120] Chen, who had been elevated to Party secretary and then Politburo member when Huang Ju was promoted at the Sixteenth Party Congress, had long been a thorn in the side of the Hu–Wen administration, repeatedly refusing to slow investment in accordance with Beijing's directives. Chen Liangyu was also the highest ranking Party official to be cashiered since Jiang Zemin had removed Chen Xitong in 1996, and his arrest marked a significant diminution in the influence of the so-called Shanghai gang. According to many reports, Jiang Zemin himself approved of Chen's removal, but Jiang was under tremendous pressure, including apparently investigations into the financial activities of his own son, Jiang Mianhong. Jiang would continued to be publicly honored, as the publication of his *Selected Works* illustrated, but his influence was fading.

With this campaign against corruption in full swing, the Sixteenth Central Committee convened its Sixth Plenary Session in Beijing on October 8–11. The plenum approved a resolution calling for the creation of a "harmonious society," bringing together the various themes that Hu had been emphasizing since his elevation to general secretary four years earlier: creating a "people-centered" society, using the scientific development concept to guide the economy, developing socialist democracy, the rule of law, and social justice, and improving the governing capabilities of the Party. Far more than the Sixteenth Party Congress report of 2002, the Sixth Plenum resolution emphasized the need to "gradually reverse" the increasing regional income gaps, promising to use transfer payments from the central treasury to improve the infrastructure, educational facilities, health care, and other needs in the central and western regions of the country.[121] The Jiang Zemin era was clearly waning as Hu Jintao moved to consolidate political and ideological authority.

[118] Guo Liqing, "Zhongnanhai tiewan zhengzhi jingjinhu tanfu an," and "'Dakuan fuhao' Zhang Rongkun."
[119] Poon Siu Tao, "Shanghai Gang Losing Power Struggle."
[120] "Zhonggong zhongyang jueding: Dui Chen Liangyu tongzhi yanzhong weiji wenti li'an jiancha."
[121] "Zhonggong zhongyang guanyu goujian shehui zhuyi hexie shehui ruogan zhongda wenti de jueding."

Conclusion

Eighteen years have passed since the events associated with Tiananmen. Deng Xiaoping passed away in 1997, Zhao Ziyang in 2005, and Li Peng retired from his last official post in 2003. Zhao's successor as general secretary, Jiang Zemin, officially retired in 2002, though he retained some important influence in the years after. Other leaders associated with Tiananmen – such as Beijing city leaders Chen Xitong and Li Ximing, conservative elders Li Xiannian and Chen Yun, and military leaders such as Yang Shangkun – have all either left office or passed away.

At the same time, the economy has developed more rapidly than anyone expected. On average, the Chinese economy had expanded by over 9 percent per year for 16 years. In 1989, China had a GDP of 1.7 trillion yuan; by year-end 2006 its GDP stood at 20.9 trillion yuan. Foreign trade had expanded even faster than the domestic economy. In 1989 China had a foreign trade of $415 billion; at year-end 2006, foreign trade stood at $1.76 trillion, making China the third largest trading nation in the world. Foreign reserves stood at over a trillion US dollars, causing trade frictions with the US, but insuring against the risks of any sort of economic upheaval such as the Asian financial crisis. Visitors to China were dazzled not only by the modernity of Shanghai (recall that the Pudong financial district was only begun in 1992) and the imposing architecture of Beijing, but also of secondary cities, places like Suzhou and Wuxi in Jiangsu and Wenzhou in Zhejiang. Jiang Zemin may not have presided over political reform, but he took considerable pride in leading China through the crises of the early 1990s, through the Asian financial crisis, and into the front ranks of economic powers in the world.

China did remarkably well in the 1990s and into the new century. Jiang Zemin may not have been "the man who changed China"[1] (that honor clearly goes to Deng Xiaoping), but his performance was generally good, at least in keeping the country on track economically and politically stable.

[1] Robert Lawrence Kuhn, *The Man Who Changed China*.

Despite his early diatribes against "peaceful evolution" (and his continuing warnings of "hostile" efforts to "divide" China and "Westernize" it), Jiang presided over a remarkable improvement in China's diplomatic position, led China into the WTO, and deflected the pressures that stemmed from the Asian financial crisis. Perhaps his greatest contribution was to reverse the Party's 1989 ban on private entrepreneurs joining the Party. This move pushed the Party definitively away from atavistic ideological ideas and toward – but not to – the idea of a "party of the whole people" (as much as Chinese ideologues tried to deny it) and closer to global norms. If Jiang never captured people's imagination, and, indeed, tended to alienate many with his over-the-top personality and windy speeches, he nevertheless performed considerably better in office than any dared hope when he moved to Beijing in those dark days after Tiananmen.

Jiang and his colleagues adopted a neoconservative approach to governing, but neoconservatism promised stability rather than inspiring hope. As time passed, neoconservatism seemed to cover up more problems than it resolved. Politically the early hope offered by village-level elections faded as expectations that they would move up the political hierarchy at least to the township level never materialized (despite a few pioneering efforts in places like Buyun in Sichuan and Dapeng in Shenzhen). Ideologically, neoconservatism moved away from Marxism but offered no idealism in its place. The Three Represents jettisoned notions of class conflict, but it inspired much cynicism as it looked to many as transparent cover for solidifying the place of an emerging bureaucratic capitalist class. Socially, growing income inequality, corruption, and worsening relations between cadres and peasants were generating growing numbers of social conflicts and petitions to higher levels.

If there was a premise underlying neoconservativism, it was that China would be able to outgrow the social and political tensions that had underlain Tiananmen. But by the early years of the new century, people were complaining that health care reform had meant that doctors were too expensive to see, that housing reform meant that homes were too expensive to purchase, and that educational reform meant that parents could not afford to send their children to school. China's GDP continued to grow, but each percentage point of newly generated growth generated fewer jobs than it had previously. China was moving up the production scale in technological terms, but that movement was not producing the labor-intensive jobs the interior needed. People began talking darkly about the "Latin American disease" – great gaps between rich and poor and stagnating growth after early promise.

Although Jiang called for "ruling the country through law," he seemed to tolerate an enormous amount of corruption, even among his closest colleagues and family members. If Jiang was able to forge an informal coalition among political, economic, and intellectual elites, unanticipated in the wake of Tiananmen, he also presided over a vast growth in vested interests – those who had done well, sometimes very well, by cooperating with, and being coopted by, the political system. The "never left out class," as Sun Liping called it (Chapter 6), benefited from these arrangements. The growth of vested interests distinguished China in the early twenty-first century from the situation in 1989 when societal interests were much weaker. The growth of interests, one could argue, provided a sort of political stability under a neoconservative framework, but it also stood in the way of efforts to deepen reform, particularly thorough-going legal and political reforms.[2] At the same time, such interests generated intense societal opposition.

The growth of the New Left was a response to these trends. In contrast to political liberals, who believed that closer ties with the West would undermine such vested interests by reinforcing legal norms and institutions and eventually bring about democracy, the New Left saw elite interests in China combining, even colluding, with international interests to strengthen the hold of socioeconomic elites and reinforce the gap between rich and poor. That was why they viewed the WTO with such suspicion, and, as we saw, reacted with such virulence when Zhu Rongji's commitments to the US were made public in 1999 – especially when the bombing of the Belgrade Embassy followed so quickly. The New Left saw itself as representing China's dispossessed and aligned itself with emerging populist movements. The New Left and nationalist critiques explored in Chapters 4 and 5 anticipated the populist support for Larry Lang and the opposition to the Property Rights Law.

Some of the criticisms of reform that have emerged over the past few years are certainly justified. Many of the corruption cases that have been exposed in recent years reflect the incestuous relationship that often exists between the economic elite and the political leadership. And Larry Lang, whatever his intent, was certainly right that many, if not most, MBOs were insider deals that benefited a few entrepreneurs (mostly former officials) at the expense of both workers and the state. Better rules, including better accountancy, could certainly improve China's political economy.

Hu Jintao clearly appealed to this constituency, as the themes that he has touted suggest – opposing corruption, upholding rule of law, social

---

[2] Minxin Pein, *China's Trapped Transition*.

justice, balanced growth, environmental protection, Party building, and now harmonious society. Certainly much of this emphasis was long overdue. Urban areas, and especially urban elites, had benefited tremendously from the development of the east coast economy and their close relations with the political elite. Rural areas had suffered from neglect, not only in economic terms but also from the lack of public services. Education was expensive and of poor quality, as was the health care system. Welfare benefits enjoyed by many urbanites were not extended to the rural areas.

But it is not clear, four years after Hu was named general secretary, whether this populist agenda will be combined with harsher criticism of liberal ideas. Although the Third Plenary Session of the Sixteenth Central Committee suggests a willingness to adopt more thorough-going marke-tization measures, Hu's apparent support for criticism of neoliberalism, the creation of a new Marxism-Leninism Academy at CASS, tolerance of the sharp criticism of reform as it has developed over the previous two decades, and his retreat on the Property Rights Law, even if the law was eventually adopted, indicate a desire to bolster ideological legitimacy, even at the expense of economic reform. Hu certainly tolerated criticism of "public intellectuals" and consistently took measures to exert control over the media, including the Internet. Although China's integration into the global economy continues apace, these developments suggest an effort to build legitimacy by undercutting the credibility of many Western ideas. After a quarter of a century of looking to the West for inspiration, one senses that there is a turn inward to find a more "Chinese" model of development.

The populist critique of reform that has grown up in recent years bears the potential to slow the sort of reforms China needs – improving the efficiency of the market at the expense of cronyism – as it attempts to redress some of the imbalances that have grown up. Hu Jintao and Wen Jiabao appear aware of this potential, hence their reaffirmation of reform at the March 2006 meeting of the NPC. But a combination of forces appears to be making deepening reform more difficult.

The problem is that under the auspices of neoconservatism, when neither press nor a popular electorate could check the implementation of reform, powerful interests grew up. In an uncertain legal environment, such as in China, economic actors inevitably cultivate relations with powerful offi-cials, and officials, in turn, direct economic opportunities to such insiders. Enforcing the provisions of the law through an impartial judiciary, estab-lishing better accountancy, passing "sunshine" regulations so that officials are required to account for their income, allowing the press more freedom to investigate and report on the relations between economic actors and the political elite, and allowing the general public to have a greater say in the political system – all measures that would improve the fairness and competitiveness of China's economy – are not things that this economic-political elite desires. And they have the power and influence to stall such reforms.

Ironically, the populist critique of reform, which could be directed at pushing through precisely such measures, appears to working in precisely the opposite direction, as the dilution of the Property Rights Law suggests. It seems unlikely that critiques of "neoliberal" economics and the Washington Consensus, pushed by nationalists on the one hand and ideologues interested in bolstering the legitimacy of the political system on the other, will promote the sort of reforms that China needs in order to prevent precisely the sort of outcomes that critics say they want to avoid – a highly unequal society with the sort of crony capitalism that has the potential to diminish or further distort economic growth in the future. Thus, reforms have encountered difficulties arising from societal pressures, disaffected intellectuals, and the structural needs of the still Leninist state that are unlike those confronted in earlier stages of reform.

This does not mean that reforms will grind to a halt or be reversed – those same interests that oppose further marketization will also oppose retrenchment, just as political elites who need to continue economic growth to enhance performance legitimacy (including job creation) and a technocracy that is largely, but not wholly, immune to societal pressures, are likely to continue to press for marketizing reforms. In addition, the continual growth of the non-state economy and other societal pressures will continue to press against the constraints of the Leninist party-state. But the social and political pressures supporting and opposing various sorts of reform measures are clearly more complicated than they were just a few years ago. What is at question is not so much reform per se, but what is understood by reform. That argument is likely to last a considerable length of time.

At the same time that post-1989 China has witnessed a shift in public policy from the highly ideological and politically contentious debates of the immediate post-Tiananmen period to the neoconservatism and east coast developmentalism of Jiang Zemin to the more populist and inland-directed policies of Hu Jintao, the political process has remained fraught with difficulties. Because ideological issues are not as contentious as they were and because the political elite seem more conscious of their collective vulnerability to political breakdown, elite politics appears to be more institutionalized than in years past. Indeed, the Party has passed many regulations governing the selection and promotion of cadres and many informal norms have emerged over the years. Nevertheless, in the absence of electoral mechanisms, elite politics appears to be a matter of coalition building and back-room deals. Hu Jintao succeeded to power because Deng Xiaoping had picked him as successor, because he made no visible errors, and because a number of actors in China's elite circles preferred him to Zeng Qinghong, Jiang's apparent preferred heir.

As the last chapter in the book shows, Hu has worked carefully to lay out his agenda as an "extension" of Jiang's Three Represents rather than as a direct challenge, then maneuvered successfully to persuade Jiang to retire from the CMC, and finally struck hard at the "Shanghai gang" by detaining Chen Liangyu on corruption charges. No doubt the use of corruption charges to undermine one's opposition is preferable to Mao's use of ideological campaigns, but it nevertheless suggests that there are real limits to the degree of institutionalization that has taken place in China's political system. Indeed, it opens a major question about the future: if Hu has used corruption charges to undermine Jiang's power, Hu has to be aware that someday somebody else may use similar charges to curtail whatever residual power Hu retains after his retirement. This conundrum suggests that succession is likely to become a more difficult, not less difficult, issue to resolve in the future.

Epilogue: the Seventeenth Party Congress

The CCP convened its Seventeenth Party Congress, October 15–20, 2007, followed on October 21 by the First Plenary Session of the newly elected Central Committee. The Seventeenth Party Congress was the fourth Party Congress held since the tragic events of June 1989, and it marked a new stage in the political evolution of the CCP. Following the Tiananmen upheaval, it will be recalled, Deng Xiaoping, in consultation with Chen Yun and Li Xiannian, selected Jiang Zemin as the "core" of the third generation of leadership. Despite the seeming long odds of holding onto power, Jiang managed to maneuver, build coalitions, and gradually consolidate his power. Nevertheless, in 1992, Deng Xiaoping selected Hu Jintao, then only 50 years of age, to the Politburo Standing Committee (PBSC) at the Fourteenth Party Congress, apparently naming him internally as Jiang's successor. Deng was striving to build a balance in the Party that would outlast himself and one that would contrast with the bitterly divisive leadership situation Mao Zedong had left behind when he died in 1976. Given the different interests in the Party, Deng's arrangements stuck, despite Jiang's palpable desire to pass power on to Zeng Qinghong. As we saw in Chapter 8, Hu Jintao's succession to power was smooth by historical standards but not without friction. Contestation was inevitable given that Jiang surrounded Hu with many of his (Jiang's) own protégés. Hu nevertheless maneuvered with considerable skill to articulate his own ideology and begin to promote people from his own power base, the Communist Youth League (CYL).

Thus, there were three interesting questions to be tackled at the Seventeenth Party Congress. First, could the post-revolutionary generation manage leadership succession issues in the absence of the revolutionary giants of the past? For the first time, the Party's leadership would have to manage succession to a younger generation without the shadow of Deng Xiaoping and others handing over them. What mechanisms would they use to select Hu Jintao's successor? This is a question that necessarily will continue to hang over the Party through at least the next Party Congress in 2012.

Second, in part because Jiang Zemin was so successful in promoting his protégés to the Politburo at the Sixteenth Party Congress, the Seventeenth Party Congress could not rely simply on promotion by seniority to choose a new leadership. If Hu Jintao was to be able to put his own stamp on the new leadership, there would have to be some mix of institutional procedures and non-institutional bargaining. The ouster of Shanghai Party Secretary Chen Liangyu in September 2006 (see Chapter 8) was the inevitable opening shot in the informal political bargaining that would take place. Third, to what extent would the Seventeenth Party Congress ratify Hu Jintao's ideas, such as the scientific development concept? Would Hu be able to get this and other ideas into an amended Party constitution? The evidence coming out of the Congress suggests that Hu Jintao was quite successful, if not as successful as he perhaps would have wanted to be. Compromises were made. But the Seventeenth Party Congress left open questions about the institutionalization of the Chinese political system; there was the sort of bargaining necessary to achieve compromise but which thereby suggested the uninstitutionalized aspects of elite politics. These uninstitutionalized aspects may yet come back to haunt the Party in the future.

When the results of the Congress and Plenary Session were announced, it was apparent that Hu had made important gains even while making important compromises (see Tables 5 and 6). Perhaps the single most important gain was to enforce the retirement age of 68. It will be recalled that at the Fifteenth Party Congress in 1997, Jiang Zemin had been able to force Qiao Shi's retirement by imposing a retirement age of 70 (only to have Bo Yibo say that the 71-year-old Jiang should be exempted from this rule) (see Chapter 7). Five years later, Jiang lowered the retirement age to 68, which necessitated Li Ruihuan's stepping down. Until the CCP is willing to commit itself on paper to a rule governing retirement at the highest level, it has to be assumed that the retirement age adopted at any given Party Congress is subject to negotiation. In the case of the Seventeenth Party Congress, enforcing a retirement age of 68 was important because Zeng Qinghong was 68. Despite reports that Zeng and Hu were working effectively together, Zeng remained a formidable political actor, one who could effectively constrain Hu's power and plans. But enforcing the retirement age of 68 also had its costs. It meant that Jia Qinglin, 67, and Li Changchun, 63, would remain on the Politburo Standing Committee (PBSC), taking up positions that might otherwise have been used for allies of Hu. In addition, Jia's continuance on the PBSC is awkward at best because Hu has been campaigning vigorously against corruption whereas many Chinese remember Jia's apparent involvement in the Yuan Hua scandal of 1999.

Table 5: *Politburo membership before and after the Seventeenth Party Congress*

	Selected in 2002		Selected in 2007	
	DOB	Position	DOB	Position
Standing Committee (in rank order)				
Hu Jintao	1942	General Secretary	Hu Jintao	1942	General Secretary
Wu Bangguo	1941	NPC	Wu Bangguo	1941	NPC
Wen Jiabao	1942	Premier	Wen Jiabao	1942	Premier
Jia Qinglin	1940	Chr., CPPCC	Jia Qinglin	1940	CPPCC
Zeng Qinghong	1939	Secretariat	Li Changchun	1944	Propaganda
Huang Ju	1938	Vice-premier	Xi Jinping	1953	Secretariat
Wu Guanzheng	1938	CDIC	Li Keqiang	1955	Vice premier
Li Changchun	1944	Propaganda	He Guoqiang	1943	CDIC
Luo Gan	1935	Pol.-Legal Affairs	Zhou Yongkang	1942	Pol.-Legal Affairs
Other Full Members (Listed Alphabetically)				
Cao Gangchuan	1935	Vice-chair, CMC	Bo Xilai	1949	Chongqing CCP sec.
Chen Liangyu	1946	Shanghai CPP sec.	Guo Boxiong	1942	V. Chr., CMC
Guo Boxiong	1942	V. Chr., CMC	Hui Liangyu	1944	Vice premier
He Guoqiang	1943	Organization	Li Yuanchao	1950	Organization
Hui Liangyu	1944	Vice-Premier	Liu Qi	1942	Beijing CCP sec.
Liu Qi	1942	Beijing CCP sec.	Liu Yandong	1945	
Liu Yunshan	1947	Propaganda	Liu Yunshan	1947	Propaganda
Wang Lequan	1944	Xinjiang CCP sec.	Wang Gang	1942	
Wang Zhaoguo	1941	United Front	Wang Lequan	1944	Xinjiang CCP sec.
Wu Yi	1938	Vice-Premier	Wang Qishan	1948	Vice premier
Yu Zhengsheng	1945	Hubei CCP sec.	Wang Yang	1955	Guangdong CCP sec.
Zeng Peiyang	1938	Vice-Premier	Wang Zhaoguo	1941	United Front
Zhang Dejiang	1941	Guangdong CCP sec.	Xu Caihou	1943	V. Chr., CMC
Zhang Lichang	1939	Tianjin mayor	Yu Zhengsheng	1945	Shanghai CCP sec.
Zhou Yongkang	1942	Public Security	Zhang Dejiang	1941	Vice premier
			Zhang Gaoli	1946	Tianjin CCP sec.
Alternate				
Wang Gang	1942			

Table 6: *The Secretariat*

Sixteenth Party Congress	Seventeenth Party Congress
Zeng Qinghong	Xi Jinping
Liu Yunshan	Liu Yunshan
Zhou Yongkang	Li Yuanchao
He Guoqiang	He Yong
Wang Gang	Ling Jihua
Xu Caihou	Wang Huning
He young	

Zeng Qinghong's retirement also came at the cost of the promotion of two other people close to the Jiang Zemin group – He Guoqiang and Zhou Yongkang. Since four people had left the nine-person PBSC (Huang Ju through death, in 2006), these personnel arrangements left only two slots open. It has long been rumored creditably that Hu would like to pass power on to Li Keqiang, the former head of the CYL who has subsequently served as Party secretary in Henan and Liaoning provinces, two of the most difficult assignments in Chinese politics. But the rest of the leadership was not prepared to acquiesce in this arrangement. The result of the bargaining that ensued was the selection of two people – Xi Jinping, the 54-year-old son of reform leader Xi Zhongxun, and Li Keqiang – as possible successors, with neither appointed to the Central Military Commission, an appointment that would have suggested that a decision had been made. As of the moment, Xi Jinping appears to have the edge; not only was he ranked one position higher than Li in the PBSC, he was also named to head the Secretariat, the powerful body that implements Politburo decisions and oversees much of the day-to-day handling of party affairs. Nevertheless, the contest to be Hu's successor appears to be open. In addition, Hu was able to secure the appointments of Ling Jihua, Hu's former secretary, and Li Yuanchao, another protégé from the CYL, to the Secretariat (see Table 6), enhancing Hu's control over the day-to-day operation of the Party.

Personnel changes in the rest of the Politburo followed the same pattern of age-based retirements and bargaining over new appointments. The four people born before 1940 retired. With the decision to promote He Guoqiang and Zhou Yongkang to the PBSC, there were seven slots (including that opened by Chen Liangyu's arrest). These were filled by Li Yuanchao, who will take over the Organization Department and help shape a Party leadership more in Hu's image; Wang Qishan, an experienced banker who is likely to be named a vice-premier at the NPC meeting in March 2008;

Liu Yandong, a CYL cadre who has good ties with Zeng Qinghong for historical reasons; Bo Xilai, the son of the late Party elder Bo Yibo; Zhang Gaoli, who replaced Zhang Lichang as Party secretary of Tianjin, one of the three municipalities that are granted seats on the Politburo; and Xu Caihou, a vice-chairman of the CMC who replaces the retiring Cao Gangchuan and maintains the PLA tradition of having two seats on the Politburo. A decision not to name any alternates to the Politburo allowed Wang Gang to be elevated to full membership.

In addition to selecting a new leadership, Party congresses typically revise the Party constitution to reflect changed political thinking and listen to the general secretary give a report that lays out the Party's vision for the next five years. Hu's achievements at this Party Congress were reflected in both these events. The revisions to the Party constitution were the most extensive in the reform era and incorporated Hu's scientific development concept, calling it "a major strategic thought that must be upheld and applied in developing socialism with Chinese characteristics." Given how long it took to incorporate Deng Xiaoping's "theory" into the constitution and Jiang Zemin's "Three Represents," this rapid enshrinement of Hu Jintao's scientific development concept and demand to build a harmonious society marks a major achievement and suggests that Hu will be able to put an even greater stamp on the Chinese political system over the next five years.

The political report that Hu delivered to the Congress did at least three things. First, it reaffirmed "reform and opening up." This reaffirmation may not seem strange until one recalls the very heated debates about reform policy discussed in Chapter 8. The discussion grew so heated that both Hu Jintao and Wen Jiabao were forced to make strong statements reaffirming reform and opening up at the NPC meeting in March 2006. These statements, however, did not quell discussion. Over the summer of 2007, tens of retired cadres wrote a strongly worded letter to the Central Committee, "Have we lost our correct orientation?" The letter goes on and says that "The reforms now being carried out in China are reforms for turning the public ownership system into the private ownership system and for turning socialism into capitalism."[1]

This letter evidently stirred great debate in leadership circles. As an article in the PRC-owned Hong Kong paper, *Ta Kung Pao*, put it, "as reform goes deeper, it becomes harder for reform to continue, the contradictions become

---

[1] "Proposal from 17 Veteran Ministers and their Comrades for the 17th Party Congress," translated by Open Source Center (OSC), CPP20070717442001, July 17, 2007.

more conspicuous, the number of difficult issues become more numerous, and problems at a deeper level and of structural and essential nature are beginning to impact on the in-depth reform." In response to the current difficulties, the article continued, the government will launch another "great debate on emancipating the mind" and introduce new theories, new ideas, and new policies to push reform deeper.[2] So Hu's work report needs to be read in the context of the debates discussed in Chapter 8, debates that were, at least to some extent, stirred up by the populist rhetoric Hu himself had used since becoming general secretary.

Second, Hu discussed his scientific development concept at length (if not in depth), stressing that it "shares the same lineage as Marxism, Mao Zedong Thought, Deng Xiaoping Theory, and the important thinking of the 'Three Represents'." Hu defined his scientific development concept as being "people centered" and as requiring the development of a "socialist harmonious society." Hu stressed the need to strengthen sustainable development by moving more quickly from extensive development, which relies on a high rate of investment, to intensive development, which relies on the more efficient use of resources. He declared the need to build a "resource-saving and environment-friendly society." Such calls are consistent with the policies Hu and Wen have been articulating in recent years, but implementing policies based on these goals with be difficult.

Finally, and potentially most interesting, in a section on building "socialist democracy," Hu called for an "organic integration of CCP leadership, the position of the people as masters of the country, and the rule of law," though he did not note the seeming incompatibility of these goals. Nevertheless, his call for improving "restraint and supervision" over power, especially his invocation of "sunlight" provisions give hope that more efforts will be made to finds ways to make the exercise of power less arbitrary. Particularly intriguing in this regard was his support for the "practice in which candidates for leading positions in grassroots party organizations are recommended by both Party members and the public in an open manner and by the Party organization at the next highest level" and to "gradually extend direct election [*zhijie xuanju*] of leading members in grass-roots party organizations to more places."[3] Although the text makes clear that Hu's reference to "direct election" was limited to inner-Party elections of grassroots leaders, his use of the term "public" (*qunzhong*, literally, the masses) in reference to

[2] *Ta Kung Pao*, October 10, 2007.
[3] "Hu Jintao zai Zhongguo gongchandang di shiqi ci quanguo daibiao dahui shang de baogao (quanwen)" (Hu Jintao's report to the Seventeenth National Delegates Congress of the Chinese Communist Party), retrieved from http://cpc.people.com.cn/GB/64162/64168/106155/106156/6430009.html.

recommending local leaders appears to give the green light to local experiments in which non-Party members of the public have played some role in selecting local Party leaders. Such experiments have been highly controversial, and while this statement falls far short of what many outside observers would like, it nevertheless represents an important affirmation of inner-Party reform thinking.

The bottom line is that as Hu Jintao moves into his second term as general secretary, the Seventeenth Party Congress has given him a substantial, but not unlimited, mandate to pursue his agenda of addressing inequity in society, pursuing growth in ways that are more compatible with sustainable development, and the implementation of Party building efforts that will incorporate a greater degree of inner-Party democracy. Perhaps the subtext of the Party conclave, however, is that Hu must pursue these goals within the context of recognizing the different interests that exist within the Party. This context implies a long period of navigating among competing interests. China has come a long way from the deep divisions that were so apparent in the period before and after Tiananmen; power is now exercised in a way that both allows for both a *primus inter pares* and also a balancing of competing interests within the Party. But before celebrating the apparent stability of the political system, it is important to keep in mind the very deep debates of recent years – debates that seem likely to continue into the future – and the risks that could develop if stability develops into stasis.

Bibliography

"Adhere Better to Taking Economic Construction as the Center." *Renmin ribao* editorial, February 22, 1992, trans. FBIS-CHI, February 24, 1992, pp. 40–1.

Amnesty International. "China: The Olympics Countdown – Failing to Keep Human Rights Promises." http://www.amnestyusa.org/countries/china/document.?id=ENGASA170462006

Anderson, Perry. *The Origins of Postmodernism*. London: Verso, 1998.

Bai Mu. "'Foreign Winds' Invade China." In *Minzhu yu fazhi* 6 (March 21, 1996): 8–10, trans. Stanley Rosen (ed.), *The Contention in China over "Cultural Colonialism"* (*Chinese Sociology and Anthropology* 31(4): 58–67, Summer 1999).

Barmé, Geremie R. *In the Red: On Contemporary Chinese Culture*. New York: Columbia University Press, 1999.

Shades of Mao: The Posthumous Cult of the Great Leader. Armonk, NY: M. E. Sharpe, 1996.

Barnett, A. Doak. *The Making of Foreign Policy in China: Structure and Process*. Boulder, CO: Westview, 1985.

Baum, Richard. *Burying Mao: Chinese Politics in the Age of Deng Xiaoping*. Princeton, NJ: Princeton University Press, 1994.

"The Fifteenth National Party Congress: Jiang Takes Command?" *The China Quarterly* 153 (March 1998): 141–56.

"Be More Daring in Carrying Out Reform." *Renmin ribao* editorial, February 24, 1992, trans. FBIS-CHI, February 24, 1992, pp. 41–2.

"Beijing Shanghai Chongqing shiwei zhuyao fuze tongzhi zhiwu tiaozheng" [Adjustment in positions of important responsible comrades in the Beijing, Shanghai, and Chongqing Party committees]. *Renmin ribao*, October 23, 2002.

Berger, Peter L., and Hsin-Huang Michael Hsiao (eds.). *In Search of an East Asian Development Model*. New Brunswick, NJ: Transaction Books, 1988.

Bernstein, Richard, and Ross H. Munro. *The Coming Conflict with China*. New York: Knopf, 1997.

Boutros-Ghali, Boutros. *Unvanquished: A US–UN Saga*. New York: Random House, 1999.

"Build Up a Great Wall of Steel against Peaceful Evolution." *Renmin ribao* commentator, August 16, 1991, trans. FBIS-CHI, August 19, 1991, pp. 27–8.

Cao Jinqing. *Huanghe bian de Zhongguo: Yige xuezhe dui xiangcun shehui de guancha yu sikao* [China along the Yellow River: A scholar's observations and thoughts about rural society]. Shanghai: Shanghai wenyi chubanshe, 2000.

    China along the Yellow River, trans. Nicky Harman and Huang Ruhua. London and New York: RoutledgeCurzon, 2005.

"Central Authorities Urge Banks to Draw Bank Loans and Stop Promoting the Bubble Economy." *Ta kung pao*, July 1, 1993, trans. FBIS-CHI, July 1, 1993, pp. 31–2.

Chan, Afred L. "The *Tiananmen Papers* Revisited," with a rejoinder by Andrew J. Nathan. *The China Quarterly* 177 (May 2004): 190–214.

Chan, Minnie. "Hu Tightens Grip with Promotion of Generals." *South China Morning Post*, June 25, 2006.

Chang, Carson. *The Third Force in China*. New York: Bookman, 1952.

Chang, Jung. *Wild Swans: Three Daughters of China*. New York: Simon & Schuster, 1991.

Chen Chien-ping. "China Stresses Modernization of Science and Technology." *Wen wei po*, March 12, 1991, p. 1, trans. FBIS-CHI, March 12, 1991, p. 21.

    "Zhu Rongji Urges Paying Attention to Negative Effects of Reform." *Wen hui po*, January 13, 1993, trans. FBIS-CHI, January 15, 1993, pp. 27–8.

Chen Fong-ching, and Jin Guantao. *From Youthful Manuscripts to River Elegy: The Chinese Popular Cultural Movement and Political Transformation 1979–1989*. Hong Kong: Chinese University Press, 1997.

Chen Guidi, and Chun Tao. *Zhongguo nongmin diaocha* [Investigation into China's Peasants]. Beijing: Renmin wenxue chubanshe, 2004.

Chen Guidi, and Wu Chuntao. *Will the Boat Sink the Water? The Life of China's Peasants*, trans. Zhu Hong. New York: Public Affairs, 2006.

Chen Kang, Gary Jefferson, and Inderjit Singh. "Lessons from China's Economic Reform." *Journal of Comparative Economics* 16 (June 1992): 201–25.

Chen Xianyi, and Chen Ruiyao. *Zhongguo youge Nanjiecun* [In China, there is a Nanjie Village]. Beijing: Jiefangjun wenyi chubanshe, 1999.

Chen Xitong. "Report on Checking the Turmoil and Quelling the Counter-Revolutionary Rebellion." Xinhua, July 6, 1989, in FBIS-CHI, July 6, 1989, pp. 20–36.

Chen Xiwen. "Dangqian de nongye jingji fazhan xingshi yu renwu" [Current situation and tasks in the development of the rural economy]. *Nongye jingji wenti* (January 23, 2006): 7–11.

Chen Yizi, Wang Xiaoqiang, and Li Jun. "The Deep-Seated Questions and the Strategic Choice China's Reform Faces." In Rosen and Zou (eds.), "The Chinese Debate on the New Authoritarianism (II)," pp. 39–60.

Chen Yuan. "Several Questions on Methods and Theory Regarding Studies in Economic Operations in China." *Jingji yanjiu* 2 (February 1992): 29–37, trans. FBIS-CHI, May 27, 1992, pp. 32–41.

    "Wo guo jingji de shenceng wenti he xuanze (gangyao)" [China's deep-seated economic problems and choices (outline)]. *Jingji yanjiu* 4 (April 1991): 18–26.

Cheng Jo-lin. "Short But Strange Coup (Part I)." *Wen wei po*, August 23, 1991, trans. FBIS-CHI, August 27, 1991, pp. 8–9.

Cheng Nien. *Life and Death in Shanghai*. New York: Grove Press, 1986.

Cheng Te-lin. "Yao Yilin Launches Attack against Zhu Rongji, Tian Jiyun." *Ching pao* 1, January 5, 1993, pp. 44–5, trans. FBIS-CHI, January 22, 1993, pp. 46–7.

Cheng Weigao. "Further Emancipate the Mind and Renew the Concept, and Accelerate the Pace of Reform and Development." *Hebei ribao*, April 18, 1991, trans. FBIS-CHI, June 7, 1991, pp. 60–8.

Cheng Zhi'ang. "Beware of So-Called Popular Culture." *Zhongliu* 6 (June 1996): 54–8, trans. Stanley Rosen (ed.), *The Contention in China over "Cultural Colonialism" (Chinese Sociology and Anthropology* 31(4): 42–57, Summer 1999).

Cheong, Ching. "Big Trouble in Xiamen." *The Straits Times*, January 30, 2000.

"Scandal Rocks Jiang's Leadership Plans." *The Straits Times*, February 5, 2000, p. 30.

Chi Sho-ming. "Guaqi gaige fansi" [Larry Lang's whirlwind prompts rethinking on reform]. *Yazhou zhoukan* 39 (September 2, 2004): 48–50.

CCP Central Propaganda Department. *"Sange daibiao" zhongyao sixiang xuexi gangyao* [Study outline for important thinking of the "Three Represents"]. Beijing: Xuexi chubanshe, 2003.

"The CCP Issues Document No. 4, Fully Expounding Expansion of Opening Up." *Ta kung pao*, June 18, 1992, trans. FBIS-CHI, June 18, 1992, pp. 19–20.

"China Shuts Down 1,287 Pornographic and Cult Websites." Agence France-Presse, December 23, 2004.

"China Warns Off Foreign Investment in Internet." *Financial Times*, September 14, 1999.

China Youth Daily Ideology and Theory Department. "Realistic Responses and Strategic Options for China after the Soviet Upheaval," trans. David Kelly, *Chinese Law and Government* 29 (March/April 1996): 13–31.

Ching Wen. "Abnormal Atmosphere in *Renmin ribao*," *Ching pao* 178, May 5, 1992, pp. 46–7, trans. FBIS-CHI, May 18, 1992, p. 22.

Chong, Woei Lien (ed.). *Li Zehou (Contemporary Chinese Thought* 31, [Winter 1999/2000]).

Clinton, William Jefferson. "Address to the National Assembly of the Republic of Korea." Retrieved from www.pub.whitehouse.gov

"Remarks to Students and Faculty of Waseda University." Retrieved from www.mofa.go.jp/region/n-america/us/archive/1993/remarks.html

"Clinton's China Syndrome." *Weekly Standard*, April 27, 1998, pp. 7–8.

Commentator. "Dajia lai taolun zhege zhongda keti – Cong pijiu hezi yinqi de sikao" [Everybody come discuss this important topic – Thoughts derived from joint ventures in the beer industry]. *Jingji ribao*, June 20, 1996, p. 1.

"Communiqué of the Fifth Plenary Session of the Fifteenth Central Committee of the Communist Party of China." Xinhua, October 11, 2000, in FBIS-CHI-2000-1011, October 11, 2000.

"Communiqué of the Fifth Plenary Session of the Fourteenth Central Committee of the CCP." Xinhua, September 28, 1995, in FBIS-CHI, September 28, 1995, pp. 15–17.

Cooper, Helene, and Bob Davis. "Barshefsky Drove Hard Bargain, but Lost to Politics." *Wall Street Journal*, April 12, 1999, p. 24.

"Overruling Some Staff, Clinton Denies Zhu What He Came For." *Wall Street Journal*, April 9, 1999, pp. A1, A6.

"Crimes Behind the Power: Analyzing the Serious Crimes Committed by Yan Jianhong." *Renmin ribao*, January 14, 1995, trans. FBIS-CHI, January 24, 1995, pp. 29–31.

Cui Zhiyuan. "Angang xianfa yu houfute zhuyi" [The Angang constitution and post-Fordism]. In Cui Zhiyuan, *Di'erci sixiang jiefang*, pp. 143–56.

Di'erci sixiang jiefang [The second liberation of thought]. Hong Kong: Oxford University Press, 1997.

"Jiaru shijie maoyi zuzhi bushi Zhongguo dangwu zhiji" [Entering the WTO is not an urgent task for China]. In *Zhongguo yu shijie* [China and the World], Internet journal, www.chinabulletin.com/99/zs9908c.htm#2

"Lusuo xin lun" [A new discussion on Rousseau]. In Han Shuifa (ed.), *Shehui zhengyi shi ruhe keneng de – Zhengzhi zhexue zai Zhongguo* [How is social justice possible? Political philosophy in China]. Guangzhou chubanshe, 2000.

"Meiguo ershijiu zhou gongsifa biange de lilun beijing" [The theoretical background to the change in the company law in twenty-nine American states]. *Jingji yanjiu* 4 (April 1996): 35–40, 60.

"Zailun zhidu chuangxin yu di'erci sixiang jiefang" [Again discussing institutional innovation and the second emancipation of thought]. In Cui Zhiyuan, *Di'erci sixiang jiefang*, pp. 21–40.

"Zhidu chuangxin yu di'erci sixiang jiefang" [Institutional renovation and the second emancipation of thought]. In Cui Zhiyuan, *Di'erci sixiang jiefang*, pp. 1–19.

Cui Zhiyuan, Deng Yingtao, and Miao Zhuang. *Nanjiecun* [Nanjie village]. Beijing: Dangdai Zhongguo chubanshe, 1996.

"Current World Economic Situation – Chinese Scholar He Xin's Talk with Japanese Professor Yabuki Susumu." *Beijing Review* 33 (1990). Part I (November 19–25): 8–11; Part II (November 26–December 2): 14–19; Part III (December 3–9): 7–14.

Dai Qing. "From Lin Zexu to Jiang Jingguo." In Rosen and Zou (eds.), "The Chinese Debate on the New Authoritarianism (II)," pp. 61–6.

"'Dakuan fuhao' Zhang Rongkun" ["Loan tycoon" Zhang Rongkun]. *Nanfang zhoumo*, August 21, 2006, pp. 42–5.

Dangdai sichao Editorial Department. "Guanyu jianchi gongyouzhi zhuti diwei de ruogan lilun he zhengce wenti" [Several theoretical and policy questions concerning upholding the primary position of public ownership]. *Kaifang* 123 (March 1, 1997): 54–63.

Davis, Deborah S., Richard Kraus, Barry Naughton, and Elizabeth J. Perry (eds.). *Urban Spaces in Contemporary China*. Cambridge: Cambridge University Press, 1995.

"Decision of the Central Committee of the Communist Party of China Concerning Some Major Issues on Strengthening Party Building." Xinhua, October 6, 1994, in FBIS-CHI, October 6, 1994, pp. 13–22.

"Decision of the Central Committee of the Communist Party of China on Reform of the Economic Structure." Xinhua, October 20, 1984, in FBIS-CHI, October 22, 1984, pp. K1–K9.

"Deepen the Struggle against Bourgeois Liberalization." *Renmin ribao* editorial, May 17, 1987, trans. FBIS-CHI, May 18, 1987, pp. K2–K4.

"The Defense Capabilities Initiative and NATO's Strategic Concept." Sub-Committee on Future Security and Defense Capabilities, www.nato.int

Deng Liqun. "Have Correct Understanding of Contradictions in Socialist Society, Grasp Initiative in Handling Contradictions." *Renmin ribao*, October 23, 1991, p. 5, trans. FBIS-CHI, October 29, 1991, pp. 22–9.

Deng Xiaoping. *Deng Xiaoping wenxuan, di san juan* [Selected works of Deng Xiaoping, vol. 3]. Beijing: Renmin chubanshe, 1993.

"Disandai lingdao jiti de dangwu zhiji" [Urgent tasks of the third generation leadership collective]. In *Deng Xiaoping wenxuan*, vol. 3, pp. 309–14.

"Jiesu yanjun de ZhongMei guanxi yao you Meiguo caiqu zhudong" [Resolving the serious situation in Sino–US relations requires that the US take the initiative]. In *Deng Xiaoping wenxuan*, vol. 3, pp. 330–3.

"On the Reform of the System of Party and State Leadership." In *Selected Works of Deng Xiaoping (1975–1982)*, pp. 302–25. Beijing: Foreign Languages Press, 1983.

"Shicha Shanghai shi de tanhua" [Talks when inspecting Shanghai]. In *Deng Xiaoping wenxuan*, vol. 3, pp. 366–7.

"Speech at the Opening Ceremony of the National Conference on Science." In *Selected Works of Deng Xiaoping (1975–1982)*, pp. 101–16. Beijing: Foreign Languages Press, 1983.

"Women you xinxin ba Zhongguo de shiqing zuode genghao" [We are confident that we can do even better in China's affairs]. In *Deng Xiaoping wenxuan*, vol. 3, pp. 324–7.

"Zai jiejian shoudu jieyan budui junyishang ganbu shi de jianghua" [Talk on receiving martial law cadres at the army level and above in the capital]. In *Deng Xiaoping wenxuan*, vol. 3, pp. 302–8.

"Zai Wuchang, Shenzhen, Zhuhai, Shanghai dengdi de tanhua yaodian" [Essential points from talks in Wuchang, Shenzhen, Zhuhai, and Shanghai]. In *Deng Xiaoping wenxuan*, vol. 3, pp. 370–83.

"Zucheng yige shixing gaige de you xiwang de lingdao jiti" [Organizing a reformist, hopeful leadership collective]. In *Deng Xiaoping wenxuan*, vol. 3, pp. 296–301.

"*Deng Xiaoping lun wenyi* yantaohui zaijing juxing" [Discussion meeting on *Deng Xiaoping on literature and art* convened in capital]. *Renmin ribao*, December 23, 1989, pp. 1, 3.

"Deng Xiaoping on Neoauthoritarianism." *Zhongguo tongxun she*, April 7, 1989, trans. FBIS-CHI-89-066, April 7, 1989, p. 15.

"Deng Xiaoping's Visit to Special Zones Shows China Is More Open." *Wen wei po*, January 28, 1992, trans. FBIS-CHI, January 28, 1992, pp. 23–4.

Deng Yingtao. *Deng Yingtao ji* [Collected essays of Deng Yingtao]. Harbin: Heilongjiang chubanshe, 1989.

   Xin fazhan fangshi yu Zhongguo de weilai [A new model of development and China's future]. Beijing: Zhongxin chubanshe, 1991.

Deyo, Frederic C. (ed.). *The Political Economy of the New Asian Industrialization.* Ithaca, NY: Cornell University Press, 1987.

Di Yinqing, and Guan Gang. "Guanjian shi yao zhangwo jingji fazhan de zhudongquan" [What is critical is grasping the initiative in economic development]. *Gaige neican* 11 (May 20, 1999): 35–9.

   "Meiguo wei shenma jiyu yu Zhongguo chongkai ruguan tanpan" [Why is the US anxious to reopen negotiations on entering the WTO?]. *Gaige neican* 8 (April 20, 1999): 39–42.

   "Ruguan dui Zhongguo changyuan liyi jiujing yiweizhe shenma" [What after all are the implications of entering WTO for China's long-term interests?]. *Gaige neican* 9 (May 5, 1999): 34–8.

Ding, X. L. *The Decline of Communism in China: Legitimacy Crisis, 1977–1989.* Cambridge: Cambridge University Press, 1994.

Ding Xueliang. "Dangdai Zhongguo de daode kongbai" [The moral vacuum in contemporary China]. *Kaifang zazhi* (April 1994): 9–11.

   Gongchanzhuyihou yu Zhongguo [Post-communism and China]. Hong Kong: Oxford University Press, 1994.

Dong Jinguan. "The Main Characteristics of Class Struggle at the Present Stage." *Guangming ribao*, September 11, 1989, p. 3, trans. FBIS-CHI, September 11, 1989, pp. 41–5.

"East Wind Brings Spring All Around: On-the-Spot Report on Comrade Deng Xiaoping in Shenzhen." *Renmin ribao*, March 31, 1992, trans. FBIS-CHI, April 1, 1992 (suppl.), pp. 7–15.

Eckholm, Erik. "After an Attack, Chinese Won't Print Expatriate's Novel." *New York Times*, June 24, 2000, pp. A17, A22.

   "China's Inner Circle Reveals Big Unrest, and Lists Causes." *New York Times*, June 3, 2001.

   "China's New Leader Promises Not to Sever Tether to Jiang." *New York Times*, November 21, 2002, p. A16.

   "The SARS Epidemic: China; Quarantine Ends for Some in Beijing, but the Infection is Still Spreading." *New York Times*, May 9, 2003, p. 13.

Economy, Elizabeth, and Michel Oksenberg (eds.). *China Joins the World.* New York: Council on Foreign Relations, 1999.

Evans, Peter. *Embedded Autonomy: States and Industrial Transformation*. Princeton, NJ: Princeton University Press, 1995.

Fan Gang. "Liangzhong gaige chengben yu liangzhong gaige fangshi" [Two reform costs and two reform forms]. *Jingji yanjiu* 1 (1993): 3–15.

Fang Jue. "Zhongguo xuyao xinde zhuanbian" [China needs a new change]. Unpublished letter.

Fang Li. "Meiguo quanqiu zhanlüe zhong de wenhua kuozhang yu cantuo" [Cultural expansion and penetration in America's global strategy]. *Lilun dongtai* [Theoretical Trends] 1446 (June 15, 1999).

Fang Ning. "Ershiyi shiji de liangzhong qushi" [Two trends in the twenty-first century]. In Fang Ning et al. (eds.), *Quanqiuhua yinyingxia de Zhongguo zhilu*, pp. 230–41.

Fang Ning, Wang Xiaodong, and Song Qiang (eds.). *Quanqiuhua yinyingxia de Zhongguo zhilu* [China under the shadow of globalization]. Beijing: Shehui kexue chubanshe, 1999.

Fang Sheng. "Opening Up to the Outside World and Making Use of Capitalism." *Renmin ribao*, February 23, 1992, trans. FBIS-CHI, February 24, 1992, pp. 37–9.

Fei Hsiao-t'ung. *Peasant Life in China: A Field Study of Country Life in the Yangtze Valley*. New York: Oxford University Press, 1946.

Feng Baoxing. "Zhe shi yiben shenmayang de zhuzuo?" [What type of work is this?]. In Shi Liaozi (ed.), *Beijing dixia "wanyanshu,"* pp. 231–40.

Fewsmith, Joseph. "CCP Launches Campaign to Maintain the Advanced Nature of Party Members." *China Leadership Monitor* 13 (Winter 2005). Retrieved from http://media.hoover.org/documents/clm13ˑjf.pdf

  Dilemmas of Reform: Political Conflict and Economic Debate. Armonk, NY: M. E. Sharpe, 1994.

  "Historical Echoes and Chinese Politics: Can China Leave the Twentieth Century Behind?" In Tyrene White (ed.), *China Briefing, 2000*, pp. 11–48. Armonk, NY: M. E. Sharpe, 2000.

  "The Impact of the Kosovo Conflict on China's Political Leaders and Prospects for WTO Accession." *National Bureau of Asian Research*, Seattle, WA, 1999.

  "The Impact of Reform on Elite Politics." In Joseph Fewsmith, *Elite Politics in Contemporary China*, pp. 86–117. Armonk, NY: M. E. Sharpe, 2001.

  "Jiang Zemin Takes Command." *Current History* 97 (1998): 250–6.

  "Neoconservatism and the End of the Dengist Era." *Asian Survey* 35 (July 1995): 635–51.

  "Promoting the Scientific Development Concept." *China Leadership Monitor* 11 (Summer 2004). Retrieved from www.hoover.org/publications/clm/issues/2904171.html

  "Reform, Resistance, and the Politics of Succession." In William A. Joseph (ed.), *China Briefing, 1994*, pp. 7–34. New York: The Asia Society, 1994.

Fewsmith, Joseph, and Stanley Rosen. "The Domestic Context of Chinese Foreign Policy: Does 'Public Opinion' Matter?" In David M. Lampton (ed.), *The*

Making of Chinese Foreign and Security Policy, 1978–2000, pp. 151–87. Stanford, CA: Stanford University Press, 2001.

"Firmly Implement the Independent Foreign Policy of Peace." Xinhua, June 2, 1999, in FBIS-CHI-1999-0602, June 2, 1999.

Foucault, Michel. *The Order of Things: An Archaeology of the Human Sciences*. New York: Vintage, 1994.

Fukayama, Francis. "The End of History?" *The National Interest* 16 (Summer 1989): 3–18.

The End of History and the Last Man. New York: Free Press, 1992.

"A Reply to My Critics." *The National Interest* 18 (Winter 1989): 21–8.

"'Full Text' of Speech delivered by Zhao Ziyang." *Hsin pao*, June 4, 1994, trans. FBIS-CHI, June 7, 1994, pp. 13–20.

Furth, Charlotte (ed.). *The Limits of Change: Essays on Conservative Alternatives in Republican China*. Cambridge, MA: Harvard University Press, 1976.

"Gaige buneng likai gongyouzhi zhege jichu" [Reform cannot depart from the pillar of public ownership]. *Zhenli de zhuiqiu* (September 1995).

Gan Yang."Ping Zhu Rongji fangMei de shiwu yu wenti" [Critiquing the mistakes and problems of Zhu Rongji's trip to the US]. *Zhongguo yu shijie* [China and the World] 5 (May 1999). Retrieved from www.chinabulletin.com/99/zs9905a.htm

Gao Xin. *Jiang Zemin de muliao* [Jiang Zemin's counselors]. Hong Kong: Mingjing chubanshe, 1996.

Jiang Zemin quanli zhi lu [Jiang Zemin's road to power]. Hong Kong: Mingjing chubanshe, 1997.

Gao Xin, and He Pin. "Tightrope Act of Wei Jianxing." *Tangtai* 23 (February 15, 1993): 42–5, trans. FBIS-CHI, February 24, 1993, pp. 24–6.

Zhonggong "taizidang" ["Princelings" of the CCP]. Taipei: Shibao wenhua, 1992.

Zhu Rongji zhuan [Biography of Zhu Rongji]. Taipei: Xinxinwen, 1993.

Gereffi, Gary, and Donald L. Wyman (eds.). *Manufacturing Miracles: Paths of Industrialization in Latin America and East Asia*. Princeton, NJ: Princeton University Press, 1990.

Gilley, Bruce. *China's Democratic Future: How It Will Happen and Where It Will Lead*. Columbia: Columbia University Press, 2004.

Tiger on the Brink: Jiang Zemin and China's New Elite. Berkeley, CA: University of California Press, 1998.

Goldman, Merle. *Sowing the Seeds of Democracy in China*. Cambridge, MA: Harvard University Press, 1994.

Gong Xiantian. "Yibu weibei xianfa he beili shehui zhuyi jiben yuanze de 'wuquanfa (cao'an)'" [A "[draft] property law" that violates the constitution and deviates from the fundamental principles of socialism]. Retrieved from www.wyzxsx.com/xuezhe/gongxiantian/ShaArticle.asp?ArticleID=62

Gong Yantao. "The Essence of 'Transformation' Is to Abolish Ideological and Political Work." *Renmin ribao*, August 9, 1989, trans. FBIS-CHI, August 10, 1989, pp. 9–11.

Gong Yuzhi. "Emancipate Our Minds, Liberate Productive Forces – Studying Comrade Deng Xiaoping's Important Talks." *Wenhui bao*, April 15, 1992, trans. FBIS-CHI, April 20, 1992, pp. 25–8.

Gries, Peter Hays. *China's New Nationalism: Politics, Pride, and Diplomacy.* Berkeley, CA: University of California Press, 2004.

Gu Xin. "Xin quanwei zhuyi de lilun kunjing" [The theoretical dilemmas of new authoritarianism]. *Ming pao* 6 (June 1989): 46–50.

Gu Xin, and David Kelly. "New Conservatism: Intermediate Ideology of a 'New Elite'." In David S. G. Goodman and Beverly Hooper (eds.), *China's Quiet Revolution: New Interactions Between State and Society*, pp. 219–33. Melbourne: Longman Cheshire, 1994.

"Guangfan dongyuan henzhua luoshi chunfang chunkong da yichang fangzhi yibing de renmin zhanzheng" [Widely mobilize and firmly grasp mass prevention and mass control; Fight a people's war against contagious diseases]. *Renmin ribao*, May 2, 2003, p. 1.

"Guanyu Lang Xianping jiaoshou zhiyi liuxing chanquan lilun he qindun guoyou zichan wenti de xueshu shengming" [Academic statement regarding the issue of Professor Larry Lang questioning popular property rights theories and the grabbing of state assets]. Retrieved from http://finance.sina.com.cn/jingjixueren/20040915/13451025392.shtml

Guo Liqing. "Zhongnanhai tiewan zhengzhi jingjinhu tanfu an" [Zhongnanhai cracks down on corruption in Beijing, Tianjin, and Shanghai]. *Yazhou zhoukan* 31 (August 6, 2006).

Guo Shuqing. "Zhongguo shichang jingji zhong de zhengfu zuoyong" [The government's role in China's market economy]. *Gaige* 3 (1999): 48–57, trans. Joseph Fewsmith (ed.), *The Role of Government in a Period of Economic Reform* (*The Chinese Economy* 32(5): 26–8, September/October 1999).

Hamrin, Carol Lee, and Timothy Cheek (eds.). *China's Establishment Intellectuals.* Armonk, NY: M. E. Sharpe, 1986.

Harding, Harry. *The Fragile Relationship: The United States and China Since 1972.* Washington, DC: Brookings, 1992.

Harris, John F., and Michael Laris. "'Roller Coaster Ride' to an Off-Again, On-Again Trade Pact." *Washington Post*, November 16, 1999, p. A26.

He Bingmeng (ed.). *Xinziyou zhuyi pingxi* [Neoliberalism: commentaries and analyses]. Beijing: Shehui kexue wenxian chubanshe, 2004.

He Degong, Pu Weizhong, and Jin Yong. *Qingxiang Zhongguo* [Biased toward China]. Guangzhou: Guangdong renmin chubanshe, 1997.

He Jie, Wang Baoling, and Wang Jianji (eds.). *Wo xiangxin Zhongguo* [I believe in China]. Beijing: Chengshi chubanshe, 1997.

He Po-shih. "The Army Reshuffle Was Carried Out to Pacify the Leftist Faction: Commentary on the Post-14th Party Congress Political Situation in China." *Tangtai* 21 (December 15, 1992): 32–6, trans. FBIS-CHI, January 7, 1993, pp. 15–18.

He Qinglian. *Xiandaihua de xianjing: Dangdai Zhongguo de jingji shehui wenti* [The pitfalls of modernization: The economic and social problems of contemporary China]. Beijing: Jinri Zhongguo chubanshe, 1998.

He Xin. "Aiguo de Qu Yuan yu ruguo de 'He Shang'" [The patriotic Qu Yuan and the national shame of "River Elegy"]. *Beijing ribao*, August 26, 1989.

"Dangdai shijie jingji xingshi fenxi" [Analysis of the contemporary world's economic situation]. In He Xin, *Zhonghua fuxing yu shijie weilai*, vol. 1, pp. 56–65.

"Dangqian jingji xingshi pinglun (zhi yi)" [An evaluation of the current economic situation (part I)]. In He Xin, *Zhonghua fuxing yu shijie weilai*, vol. 2, pp. 542–5.

"Dangqian Zhongguo neiwai xingshi fenxi ji ruogan zhengce jianyi (zhaiyao)" [Analysis of the domestic and international situation facing contemporary China and some policy suggestions (outline)]. In He Xin, *Zhonghua fuxing yu shijie weilai*, vol. 1, pp. 1–6.

"Dui woguo shinian gaige de fansi" [Reflecting on the ten years of China's reform]. In He Xin, *Zhonghua fuxing yu shijie weilai*, vol. 2, pp. 401–13.

"'He Shang' de piping" [Criticism of "River Elegy"]. In He Xin, *Weiji yu fansi* [Crisis and reflection], vol. 1, pp. 282–99. Beijing: Guoji wenhua chuban gongsi, 1997.

"Lun woguo jingji gaige zhidao lilun de shiwu" [The mistakes of guiding theory of China's economic reform]. In He Xin, *Zhonghua fuxing yu shijie weilai*, vol. 2, pp. 503–12.

"Lun Zhongguo xiandaihua de guoji huanjing yuwaijiao zhanlüe" [The international environment of China's modernization and its diplomatic strategy]. In He Xin, *Zhonghua fuxing yu shijie weilai*, vol. 1, pp. 7–27.

"Lun ZhongMeiRi guanxi de zhanlüe beijing yu duice" [On the strategic background of Sino–US–Japanese relations and countermeasures]. In He Xin, *Zhonghua fuxing yu shijie weilai*, vol. 1, pp. 28–47.

"Tan dangdai ziben zhuyi" [Contemporary capitalism]. In He Xin, *Zhonghua fuxing yu shijie weilai*, vol. 1, pp. 66–79.

"Wo xiang nimen de liangzhi huhuan" [My call to your conscience]. In He Xin, *Zhonghua fuxing yu shijie weilai*, vol. 2, pp. 466–97.

"Wode kunhuo yu youlu" [My doubts and fears]. In He Xin, *Zhonghua fuxing yu shijie weilai*, vol. 2, pp. 421–42.

"Woguo duiwai kaifang zhanlüe de yizhong shexiang" [A concept for our strategy for opening to the outside world]. In He Xin, *Zhonghua fuxing yu shijie weilai*, vol. 1, pp. 80–5.

Zhonghua fuxing yu shijie weilai [China's renaissance and the future of the world], 2 vols. Chengdu: Sichuan renmin chubanshe, 1996.

He Yijun, Jiang Bin, and Wang Jianwei. "Speed Up Pace of Reform, Opening Up." *Jiefangjun bao*, March 25, 1992, trans. FBIS-CHI, April 22, 1992, pp. 30–3.

Ho Te-hsu. "China Has Crossed the Nadir of the Valley but Is Still Climbing Up from the Trough – Liu Guoguang Talks about the Current Economic Situation in China." *Jingji daobao* 38/39, October 1, 1990, pp. 12–13, trans. FBIS-CHI, October 12, 1990, pp. 27–30.

Ho Yuen. "CCP's 'Five Adherences' and 'Five Oppositions' to Prevent Peaceful Evolution." *Ming pao*, August 29, 1991, trans. FBIS-CHI, August 29, 1991, pp. 23–5.

Hsia Yu. "Beijing's Intense Popular Interest in CPC Document No. 4." *Ta kung pao*, June 12, 1992, trans. FBIS-CHI, June 12, 1992, pp. 17–18.

Hsu Szu-min. "On the Political Situation in Post-Deng China." *Ching pao* 210, January 5, 1994, pp. 26–9, trans. FBIS-CHI, January 30, 1994, pp. 13–17.

Hu Angang. "Background to Writing the Report on State Capacity." In Joseph Fewsmith (ed.), *Hu Angang on China's 1994 Tax Reform* (*The Chinese Economy* 31(4): 5–29, July/August 1998).

"Zhizai cujin jingji fazhan de Zhongguo zhengzhi gaige" [The aim of political reform in China is to promote economic development]. *Gaige* 3 (1999): 58–64, trans. Joseph Fewsmith (ed.), *The Role of Government in a Period of Economic Reform* (*The Chinese Economy* 32(5): 5–25, September/October 1999).

Hu Angang, and Wang Shaoguang. *Jiaqiang zhongyang zhengfu zai shichang jingji zhuanxing zhong de zhudao zuoyong: Guanyu Zhongguo guojia nengli de yanjiu baogao* [Strengthen the leading role of the central government in the transition to a market economy: A research report on China's state capacity]. Shenyang: Liaoning renmin chubanshe, 1993. Trans. in Joseph Fewsmith (ed.), *The Chinese Economy* 28, nos. 3 and 4 (May/June and July/August 1995); cited as *Wang Shaoguang Proposal (I) and (II)*.

Hu Angang, Wang Shaoguang, and Ding Yuanchu. "Jingji fangrong beihou de shehui bu wending" [The social instability behind economic prosperity]. *Zhanlüue yu guanli* 3 (May/June 2002): 26–33.

Hu Angang, Wang Shaoguang, and Kang Xiaoguang. *Zhongguo diqu chaju baogao* [Report on regional inequalities in China]. Shenyang: Liaoning renmin chubanshe, 1995.

Hu Angang, Zhao Tao, and Yao Zengqi. *Guoqing yu juece* [National conditions and policy]. Beijing chubanshe, 1990.

Hu Jintao. "Zai qingzhu Zhongguo gongchandang chengli 85 zhounian ji zongjie baochi gongchandangyuan xianjin jiaoyu huodong dahui shang de jianghua" [Talk at the meeting to celebrate the eighty-fifth anniversary of the founding of the CCP and to sum up the educational activities on preserving the advanced nature of Communist Party members]. *Renmin ribao*, July 1, 2006, pp. 1–2.

"Zai xuexi 'Jiang Zemin wenxuan' baogaohui shang de jianghua" [Speech at the report meeting to study the *Selected Works of Jiang Zemin*]. *Renmin ribao*, August 16, 2006.

"Hu Jintao he zhongyang shujichu tongzhi dao Xibaipo xue kaocha" [Hu Jintao and the Central Secretariat inspect and study at Xibaipo]. *Renmin ribao*, December 8, 2002, p. 1.

"Hu Jintao, Wu Bangguo, Wen Jiabao, Jia Qinglin, Wu Guanzheng, Li Changchun, Luo Gan fenbie canjia shenyi he taolun" [Hu Jintao, Wu Bangguo, Wen Jiabao, Jia Qinglin, Wu Guanzheng, Li Changchun, and Luo Gan take part separately in deliberation and discussion]. *Renmin ribao*, March 8, 2006, p. 1.

"Hu Jintao zai Neimenngu kaocha shi qiangdiao shenke renshi zhizheng weimin de zhongda yiyi qieshi jiejue hao qunzhong shengchan shenghuo wenti" [During an investigation of Inner Mongolia, Hu Jintao stresses deeply recognizing the major significance of governing for the people and earnestly solving well the production and living problems of the masses] *Renmin ribao*, January 6, 2003, p. 1.

"Hu Jintao zai 'sange daibiao' yantaohui shang de zhongyao jianghua (quanwen)" [Important talk by Hu Jintao at the symposium on the "Three Represents" (complete text)]. *Renmin ribao*, July 1, 2003, pp. 1–2.

"Hu Jintao zai xianfa shixing ershi zhounian dahui shang de jianghua" [Hu Jintao's talk at the commemoration for the twentieth anniversary of the promulgation of the constitution]. *Renmin ribao*, December 5, 2002, p. 1.

Hu Jiwei. *Cong Hua Guofeng xiatai dao Hu Yaobang xiatai* [From Hua Guofeng's stepping down to Hu Yaobang's stepping down]. Hong Kong: Mingjing chubanshe, 1997.

"Despotic Dictatorship Lingers On – Notes on Studying the Political Report of the 15th Party Congress." *Hsin pao*, December 30, 1997, trans. FBIS-CHI, December 30, 1997.

"Given a Good Central Committee, We Will Have a Good Party; Given a Good Party, We Will Have a Good State – Notes on Studying the Political Report of the 15th Party Congress." *Hsin pao*, December 31, 1997, trans. FBIS-CHI, December 31, 1997.

"If the Party Is Correct, Bad Things Can Be Turned into Good Things; If the Party Is Wrong, Good Things Can Be Turned into Bad Things." *Hsin pao*, December 29, 1997, trans. FBIS-CHI, December 29, 1997.

Hu Ping. "Special Zone Construction and Opening to the Outside." In *Zhonggong zhongyang dangxiao baogao xuan* [Selected reports from the Central Party School], trans. Stanley Rosen (ed.), *Debates over Special Economic Zones, Income Polarization, and Other Related Issues* (*Chinese Economic Studies* 29(3), May/June 1996).

Hu Qiaomu. "Act in Accordance with Economic Laws, Step Up the Four Modernizations." *Xinhua*, October 5, 1978, in FBIS-CHI, October 11, 1978, pp. E1–E22.

Hu Weixi. "Zhongguo jinxiandai de shehui zhuanxing yu mincui zhuyi" [Populism and social transformation in modern China]. *Zhanlüe yu guanli* 5 (October 1994): 24–7.

Hu Yuanyuan. "CSRC: Kelon Chief Did Wrong." *China Daily*, August 4, 2005.

"Kelon Gets Fined for Accounting Fraud." *China Daily*, July 6, 2006.

Hua Jinzhong. "Guoxue, zai Yanyuan you qiaoran xingqi" [National studies have appeared quietly again in the Yan garden]. *Renmin ribao*, August 16, 1993, p. 3.

Huang Ping, and Cui Zhiyuan (eds.). *Zhongguo yu quanqiuhua: Huashengdun gongshi haishi Beijing gongshi* [China and globalization: Washington Consensus or Beijing Consensus?]. Beijing: Shehui kexue wenxian chubanshe, 2005.

Huang, Yasheng. *Inflation and Investment Controls in China: The Political Economy of Central-Local Relations During the Reform Era.* Cambridge: Cambridge University Press, 1996.

Huangfu Ping. "The Consciousness of Expanding Opening Needs to Be Strengthened." *Jiefang ribao*, March 22, 1991, trans. FBIS-CHI, April 1, 1991, pp. 39–41.

"Gaige bu ke dongyao" [We must not waver in reform]. *Caijing* 151 (January 23, 2006).

"Reform and Opening Require a Large Number of Cadres with Both Morals and Talents." *Jiefang ribao*, April 12, 1991, trans. FBIS-CHI, April 17, 1991, pp. 61–3.

Huntington, Samuel. "The Clash of Civilizations?" *Foreign Affairs* 72 (Summer 1993): 22–49.

The Clash of Civilizations and the Remaking of World Order. New York: Simon & Schuster, 1996.

Political Order in Changing Societies. New Haven, CT: Yale University Press, 1968.

"Increase Weight of Reform, Promote Economic Development: Speech Delivered by Wu Guanzheng at the Provincial Structural Reform Work Conference." *Jiangxi ribao*, May 4, 1991, trans. FBIS-CHI, June 12, 1991, pp. 45–9.

International Monetary Fund. *World Economic Outlook.* Washington, DC: IMF, 1993.

Ishihara, Shintaro. *The Japan That Can Say No: Why Japan Will Be First among Equals.* New York: Simon & Schuster, 1989.

Jacobson, Harold K., and Michel Oksenberg. *China's Participation in the IMF, World Bank and GATT: Toward a Global Economic Order.* Ann Arbor, MI: University of Michigan Press, 1991.

Jameson, Fredric. *The Cultural Turn: Selected Writings on the Postmodern, 1983–1998.* London: Verso, 1998.

Postmodernism, or, The Cultural Logic of Late Capital. Durham, NC: Duke University Press, 1991.

Jen Hui-wen. "Deng Xiaoping Urges Conservatives Not to Make a Fuss." *Hsin pao*, January 1, 1993, trans. FBIS-CHI, January 4, 1993, pp. 43–4.

"Political Bureau Argues over 'Preventing Leftism'." *Hsin pao*, April 14, 1992, p. 6, trans. FBIS-CHI, April 17, 1992, pp. 28–9.

"There Is Something Behind Chen Yun's Declaration of His Position." *Hsin pao*, May 12, 1992, p. 22, trans. FBIS-CHI, May 13, 1992, pp. 21–2.

"What Is the 'Bottom Line' of CCP Political Reform?" *Hsin pao*, November 4, 1990, p. 30, trans. FBIS-CHI, November 10, 1990, pp. 24–6.

"Zhonggong qiangdiao luoshi quanmian fazhan guan" [CCP emphasizes implementing an outlook on comprehensive development]. *Hsin pao*. November 7, 2003.

Ji Fangping. "Tuoguo biaoxiang kan shizhi: Xi 'gonggomg zhishi fenzi' lun" [Seeing through the appearance to perceive the essence: An analysis of the theory of "public intellectuals"]. *Jiefang ribao*, November 15, 2004.

Ji Xianlin. "Dongxifang wenhua de zhuanzhedian" [The turning point between Eastern and Western civilizations]. *Ershiyi shiji* 3 (February 1991): 4–5.

"'Tianren heyi' fang neng chengjiu renlei" [Humanity can be saved through "unity of nature and man"]. *Dongfang* 1 (1993): 6.

"'Tianren heyi' xinjie" [A new interpretation of "unity of man and nature"]. *Chuantong wenhua yu xiandaihua* 1 (1993): 9–16.

Jia Pingwa. *Fei du* [Abandoned capital]. Beijing chubanshe, 1993.

"Jianchi gongyouzhi de zhuti diwei buneng dongyao" [The primary position of upholding public ownership must not be shaken]. *Jiefangjun bao*, April 29, 1996, pp. 1, 6.

"Jianchi he fazhan you Zhongguo tese de shehui zhuyi minzhu" [Uphold and develop socialist democracy with Chinese characteristics]. *Jiefangjun bao*, April 1, 1996, pp. 1, 4.

"Jiang Must Act Fast." *The Straits Times*, February 5, 2000, p. 30.

Jiang Po. "Guochan pijiu you biyao gao zhema duo hezi ma?" [Must Chinese beer form this many joint ventures?]. *Jingji ribao*, June 20, 1996, p. 1.

Jiang Qing. *Gongyangxue yinlun* [An introduction to the study of the Gongyang commentary]. Shenyang: Liaoning jiaoyu chubanshe, 1997.

Jiang Xun. "Zhongguo zhishijie you miandui hanleng de dongtian" [China's intelligentsia is facing yet another frigid winter]. *Yazhou zhoukan* 51 (December 19, 2004): 32–6.

Jiang Yihua. "Lun dongya xiandaihua jinchengzhong de xinlixing zhuyi wenhua" [On the new rationalist culture Asia [developed] in the course of modernization]. *Shanghai wenhua* 4 (1994); reprinted in Wang Jisi (ed.), *Wenming yu guoji zhengzhi*, pp. 259–80.

Jiang Zemin. "Gongtong zujin shijie de heping yu fazhan" [Promote world peace and development together]. *Renmin ribao*, January 1, 2002, p. 1.

Jiang Zemin wenxuan [The selected works of Jiang Zemin]. 3 vols. Beijing: Renmin chubanshe, 2006.

"Leading Cadres Must Pay Attention to Politics." Excerpted from Jiang Zemin's speech to the Fifth Plenum of the Fourteenth Central Committee by Xinhua, January 17, 1996, in FBIS-CHI, January 17, 1996.

"Memorial Speech at Deng Xiaoping's Memorial Meeting." *Beijing Review* 40 (March 10–16, 1997): 14–22.

"Quanmian jianshe xiaokang shehui, kaichuang Zhongguo tese shehui zhuyi shiye xin jumian" [Build a well-off society in an all-round way and create a new situation in building socialism with Chinese characteristics]. *Renmin ribao*, November 18, 2002.

"Text of Political Report by General Secretary Jiang Zemin at the 15th CPC National Congress." Beijing television service, September 12, 1997, trans. FBIS-CHI-97-255, September 12, 1997.

"Tongbao zhongyang zhengzhiju changwei 'sanjiang' qingkuang de jianghua" [Talk to the Politburo Standing Committee on the situation in the "three stresses" campaign]. *Jiang Zemin wenxuan*, vol. 2, pp. 519–86.

"Zai dang de shisanjie qizhong quanhui bimushi de jianghua" [Address to the closing session of the Seventh Plenary Session of the Thirteenth CCP Central Committee]. In *Shisanda yilai*, vol. 2, pp. 1427–36.

"Zai dang de shisanjie wuzhong quanhui shangde jianghua" [Address to the Fifth Plenary Session of the Thirteenth CCP Central Committee]. In *Shisanda yilai*, vol. 2, pp. 709–20.

"Zai qingzhu Zhongguo gongchandang chengli qishi zhounian dahui shang de jianghua" [Talk celebrating the 70th anniversary of the founding of the CCP]. In *Shisanda yilai*, vol. 3, pp. 1627–60.

"Zai qingzhu Zhonghua renmin gongheguo chengli sishi zhounian dahui shang de jianghua" [Talk celebrating the 40th anniversary of the establishment of the PRC]. In *Shisanda yilai*, vol. 2, pp. 609–35.

"Jiang Zemin Delivers an Important Speech at the Fourth Plenary Session of the Central Discipline Inspection Commission." Xinhua, January 14, 2000, in FBIS-CHI-2000-0115, January 15, 2000.

"Jiang Zemin huijian Yindu guofang buzhang" [Jiang Zemin receives India's defense minister]. *Renmin ribao,* April 27, 2003, p. 1.

"Jiang Zemin: Shizhong jianchi yushi jujin shizhong jianchi jianku fendou" [Jiang Zemin: Persist in upholding keeping up with the times, persist in upholding hard struggle]. *Renmin ribao*, March 7, 2003, p. 1.

"Jiang Zemin zai Guangdong kaocha gongzuo qiangdiao jinmi jiehe xinde lishi tiaojian jiaqiang dangde jianshe shizhong dailing quanmin renmin cujin shengchanli de fazhan" [Inspecting work in Guangdong, Jiang Zemin emphasized firmly integrating the new historical conditions, strengthening Party building, and continuously leading the whole people to speed development of productive forces]. In *Shenru xuexi "sange daibiao" quanmian luoshi "sange daibiao"* [Study deeply the "three represents"; comprehensively implement the "three represents"], pp. 1–8. Beijing: Xuexi chubanshe, 2000.

Jiefang wenxuan (1978–1998) [Essays of liberated [thought] – 1978–1998)]. 2 vols. Beijing: Jingji ribao chubanshe, 1998.

Jin Longde. "Zhongyuan dadi de yimian hongqi – Henan Linyingxian Nanjie fangwen jishi" [A bright red flag in the land of middle China – A true report of Nanjie, Linying county, Henan]. *Dangdai sichao* 3 (March 1994): 2–10.

Johnson, Chalmers. *MITI and the Japanese Miracle: The Growth of Industrial Policy, 1925–1975*. Stanford, CA: Stanford University Press, 1982.

Kahn, Joseph. "China Approves Property Law, Strengthening its Middle Class." *New York Times*, March 16, 2007, pp. A1, 11.

Kang Xiaoguang, Wu Yulun, Liu Dehuan, and Sun Hui. *Zhongguoren dushu toushi: 1978–1998 dazhong dushu shenghuo bianqian diaocha* [A perspective on the reading habits of the Chinese: An investigation of the changes in the reading habits of the masses from 1978–1998]. Nanning: Guangxi jiaoyu chubanshe, 1998.

Katzenstein, Peter (ed.). *Between Power and Plenty*. Madison, WI: University of Wisconsin Press, 1978.

Kennedy, Paul M. *The Rise and Fall of the Great Powers: Economic Change and Military Conflict from 1500 to 2000*. New York: Random House, 1987.

Kuhn, Robert Lawrence. *The Man Who Changed China: The Life and Legacy of Jiang Zemin*. New York: Crown Publishers, 2004.

Kynge, James. "Smuggling Row Rocks Chinese Politburo." *Financial Times*, January 22, 2000, p. 7.

"Top Investigator to Probe Smuggling." *Financial Times*, January 24, 2000, p. 4.

Lake, Anthony. "From Containment to Engagement." Address at the School of Advanced International Studies, Washington, DC, September 23, 1993.

Lam, Willy Wo-lap. *China after Deng Xiaoping: The Power Struggle in Beijing Since Tiananmen*. Hong Kong: PA Professional Consultants, 1995.

The Era of Jiang Zemin. New York: Prentice-Hall, 1999.

Lan Zhongping. "Why Do We Say That Special Economic Zones Are Socialist Rather than Capitalist in Nature?" *Jiefangjun bao*, May 22, 1992, trans. FBIS-CHI, June 11, 1992, pp. 25–6.

Lardy, Nicholas R. *China's Unfinished Economic Revolution*. Washington, DC: Brookings, 1998.

Foreign Trade and Economic Reform in China, 1978–1990. Cambridge: Cambridge University Press, 1992.

Lee, Hong Yung. "China's New Bureaucracy?" In Arthur Lewis Rosenbaum (ed.), *State and Society in China: The Consequences of Reform*. Boulder, CO: Westview, 1992.

From Revolutionary Cadres to Party Technocrats in Socialist China. Berkeley, CA: University of California Press, 1991.

Lei Yi. "Beijing yu cuowei" [Background and reversed positions]. *Dushu* (April 1995): 16–20.

"Jingti faxisi" [Beware of fascism]. Unpublished manuscript.

"Zhongguo xiandaihua de 'huaxia zhongxinguan' yu 'minzu zhuyi'" ["Sinocentrism" and "nationalism" in China's modernization]. *Zuojia shuzhai* 3 (March 1999): 163–7.

Leng Rong. "To Realize Lofty Aspirations and Great Ideals of the Chinese Nation – Studying Comrade Deng Xiaoping's Ideas Concerning Strategic Goals for China's Modernization and Development." *Renmin ribao*, April 27, 1992, trans. FBIS-CHI, April 28, 1992, pp. 17–23.

Li Changchun. "Zai quanguo xuanchuan buzhang huiyi shang de jianghua" [Talk at the national conference of propaganda department heads]. *Dangjian* (Party building) 2 (2003): 6.

"Li Changchun zai zhongyang xinwen xuanchuan bumen fuzeren huiyi shang qiangdiao zhongzhi chengcheng tuanjie fengxian kexue qiushi zhansheng kunnan duoqu shengli" [At a meeting of responsible people for news and propaganda, Li Changchun stresses uniting wills, contributing together, seeking facts through science, conquering difficulties, and winning a victory]. *Renmin ribao*, April 26, 2003, p. 1.

Li Changping. *Wo xiang zongli shuo shihua* [Telling the truth to the premier]. Beijing: Guangming ribao chubanshe, 2002.

Li, Cheng. *China's Leaders: The New Generation.* Lanham, MD: Rowman & Littlefield, 2001.

"Promises and Pitfalls of Reform: New Thinking in Post-Deng China." In Tyrene White (ed.), *China Briefing 2000: The Continuing Transformation.* Armonk, NY: M. E. Sharpe, 2000, pp. 123–58.

Li, Cheng, and Lynn White. "The 15th Central Committee of the Chinese Communist Party: Full-Fledged Technocratic Leadership with Partial Control by Jiang Zemin." *Asian Survey* 38 (April 1988): 231–64.

Li Chengrui. "Some Thoughts on Sustained, Steady, and Coordinated Development." *Renmin ribao,* November 20, 1989, trans. FBIS-CHI, December 12, 1989, pp. 32–4.

Li Liang, and Xu Tonghui. "2004–2006 'disanci gaige lunzheng' shimo" [The whole story of the 2004–2006 "third argument over reforms"]. *Nanfang zhuomo,* March 16, 2006.

Li Peilin. "Zhongguo jingji shehui fazhan de wenti he qushi" [Problems and trends in China's economic and social development]. In Ru Xin, Lu Xueyi, and Li Peilin (eds.), *2004 nian: Zhongguo shehui xingshi fenxi yu yuce,* pp. 71–80.

Li Peilin, Zhan Yi, Zhao Tingdong, and Liang Dong (eds.). *Shehui chongtu yu jieji yishi: Dangdai Zhongguo shehui maodun wenti yanjiu* [Social conflict and class consciousness: Social contradictions in contemporary China]. Beijing: Shehui kexue wenxian chubanshe, 2005.

Li Peng. "Explanations of the Proposal for the Formulation of the Ninth Five-Year Plan and the Long-Term Target for the Year 2010." Xinhua, October 5, 1995, in FBIS-CHI, October 6, 1995, pp. 17–28.

"Wei woguo zhengzhi jingji he shehui de jinyibu wending fazhan er fendou" [Struggle to take another step for the stable development of China's politics, economics, and society]. In *Shisanda yilai,* vol. 2, pp. 948–94.

"Li Peng's Life-Taking Report Lays Blame on Zhao Ziyang." *Tungfang jihpao,* July 16, 1989, p. 3, trans. FBIS-CHI, July 18, 1989, pp. 16–23.

Li Ping. *Zhongguo xiayibu zenyang zou* [How will China take its next step?]. Hong Kong: Mingjing chubanshe, 1998.

Li Rui. *Li Rui fan "zuo" wenxuan* [Li Rui's essays opposing the "left"]. Beijing: Zhongyang bianyi chubanshe, 1998.

"Li Ruihuan Meets with Hong Kong Journalists." *Ta kung pao,* September 20, 1989, trans. FBIS-CHI, September 20, 1989, pp. 10–12.

Li Shenzhi. "Bian tongyi, hedongxi" [Differentiating what is the same and what is different; synthesizing East and West]. *Ershiyi shiji* (1993); reprinted in *Jiefang wenxuan,* vol. 2, pp. 818–29.

"Chongxin dianran qimeng de huoju – Jinian 'wusi' bashi zhounian" [Relight the torch of enlightenment – Commemorating the eightieth anniversary of "May Fourth"]. *Dangdai Zhongguo yanjiu* 3 (September 1999): 2–15.

"Ershiyi shiji de yousi" [Worries about the twenty-first century]. *Dushu* (April 1996); reprinted in *Jiefang wenxuan,* vol. 2, pp. 934–43.

"Faxian lingyige Zhongguo" [Discovering another China]. Reprinted in *Jiefang wenxuan,* vol. 2, pp. 1242–54.

"Fengyu canghuang wushi nian – Guoqingye duyu" [Fifty years of storms and clouds – Solitary words on the evening of national day]. Unpublished manuscript.

"Guanyu wenhua wenti de yixie sikao" [Some thoughts about the question of culture]. *Tianjin shehui kexue* (1998); reprinted in *Jiefang wenxuan*, vol. 2, pp. 1125–35.

"Hongyang Beida de ziyou zhuyi chuantong" [Extol Beijing University's tradition of liberalism]. Preface to Liu Junning (ed.), *Beida chuantong yu jindai Zhongguo*, pp. 1–5.

"Quanqiuhua yu Zhongguo wenhua" [Globalization and China's culture]. *Taipingyang xuebao* 2 (December 1994): 3.

"Shuliang youshixia de kongju – Ping Hengtingdun disanpian guanyu wenming chongtu de wenzhang" [Under the fear of numerical superiority – Critiquing Huntington's third essay on the clash of civilizations]. *Taipingyang xuebao* 2 (1997): 3–7.

"Yeyao tuidong zhengzhi gaige." *Gaige* 1 (1998); reprinted in *Jiefang wenxuan*, vol. 2, pp. 1002–5.

"Zhongguo chuantong wenhuazhong jiwu minzhu yewu kexue" [There is no democracy or science in China's traditional culture]. *Zhongguo jingji shibaô* (1998); reprinted in *Jiefang wenxuan*, vol. 2, pp. 1118–24.

"Zhongguo yingqu shenmayang de fengfan?" [What sort of attitude should China adopt?]. *Xiandai chuanbo* (1997); reprinted in *Jiefang wenxuan*, vol. 2, pp. 952–7.

"Zhongguo zhexue de jingshen" [The spirit of Chinese philosophy]. *Chuantong wenhua yu xiandaihua* 2 (1993); reprinted in *Jiefang wenxuan*, vol. 2, pp. 805–17.

Li Shuyi, and Yong Jianxiong (eds.). *Ershiyi shiji Zhongguo jueqi* [The rise of China in the twenty-first century]. Beijing: Zhonggong zhongyang dangxiao chubanshe, 1997.

Li Zehou. *Zhongguo xiandai sixiangshi lun* [History of contemporary Chinese thought]. Beijing: Dongfang chubanshe, 1987.

Li Zehou, and Liu Zaifu. *Gaobie geming* [Farewell to revolution]. Hong Kong: Cosmos Books, 1996.

Lim, Benjamin Kang. "China's Hu Orders Sacking of Vice Mayor – Source." *Reuters*, June 22, 2006.

Lin, Min. *The Search for Modernity: Chinese Intellectuals and Cultural Discourse in the Post-Mao Era*, with Maria Galikowski. New York: St. Martin's, 1999.

Lin Ruo. "Dui fazhan shehui zhuyi shangpin jingji de jidian renshi" [Some points of understanding regarding the development of the socialist commodity economy]. *Renmin ribao*, March 1, 1999, p. 5.

Lin Wu. "Deng's Faction Unmasks Face of 'Ultraleftists'." *Zhengming* 175, May 1, 1992, pp. 17–18, trans. FBIS-CHI, May 12, 1992, pp. 27–8.

Lin Yifu, Cai Fang, and Li Zhou. "On the Gradual-Advance Style of Economic Reform in China." *Jingji yanjiu* 9 (1993), trans. *Chinese Economic Studies* 26 (November/December 1995): 5–39.

Ling Hsueh-chun. "Wang Zhen and Li Xiannian Set Themselves Up against Deng." *Zhengming* 175, May 1, 1992, pp. 14–15, trans. FBIS-CHI, May 12, 1992, p. 26.

Ling Zhen. "Zugepai de xingdong xinhao" [Signs that the faction to form a cabinet is acting]. *Kaifang* (October 1994): 20–3.

Ling Zhijun. *Chenfu: Zhongguo jingji gaige beiwanglu (1989–1997)* [Turmoil: A record of China's economic reform (1989–1997)]. Shanghai: Dongfang chuban zhongxin, 1998.

Link, Perry. "China's 'Core' Problem." *Daedalus* 122 (Spring 1993): 189–206.

"The Old Man's New China." *New York Review of Books* 41 (June 9, 1994): 31–6.

Lishi de chaoliu bianweihui (ed.). *Lishi de chaoliu: Xuexi Deng Xiaoping nanxun zhongyao jianghua fudao cailiao* [Historical trends: Supplementary materials for the study of Deng Xiaoping's important talks during his southern tour]. Beijing: Zhongguo renmin daxue chubanshe, 1992.

Liu Guoguang. "Jingjixue jiaoxue he yanjiu de yixie wenti" [On certain issues in teaching and researching economics]. *Jingji yanjiu* 10 (October 2005): 4–11.

Liu Ji. "Lun juece kexuehua" [On making decision-making scientific]. *Zhongguo shehui kexue zazhi* 3 (1982): 3–25.

Liu Ji (ed.). *Shehui zhuyi gaige lun* [On the reform of socialism]. Shanghai: Renmin chubanshe, 1997.

Liu Jun, and Li Lin (eds.). *Xinquanwei zhuyi: Dui gaige lilun gangling de zhenglun* [New authoritarianism: Debates on the principles of reform theory]. Beijing: Jingjixueyuan chubanshe, 1989.

Liu Junning (ed.). *Beida chuantong yu jindai Zhongguo* [Beijing University and modern China]. Beijing: Zhongguo renshi chubanshe, 1998.

Liu Junning. "Caichanquan de baozhang yu youxian zhengfu – Cong zhengfu de zongzhi kan zhengti gaige" [Guaranteeing property rights and limited government – Looking at political reform from the commitments of government]. *Fangfa* 3 (1998): 11–13.

"Feng neng jin, yu neng jin, guowang buneng jin!" [The wind and rain can enter, but the king may not!]. In Liu Junning, *Gonghe, minzhu, xianzheng*, pp. 38–62.

Gonghe, minzhu, xianzheng: Ziyou zhuyi sixiang yanjiu [Republicanism, democracy, and constitutionalism: Studies in liberal thought]. Shanghai: Sanlian shudian, 1998.

"Minzu zhuyi simianguan" [Viewing nationalism from four perspectives]. In Liu Junning, *Gonghe, minzhu, xianzheng*, pp. 250–9.

"Quanqiuhua yu minzhuhua" [Globalization and democratization]. In Liu Junning, *Gonghe, minzhu, xianzheng*, pp. 243–9.

"Zhijie minzhu yu jianjie minzhu" [Direct democracy and indirect democracy]. In Liu Junning, *Gonghe, minzhu, xianzheng*, pp. 199–215.

"Zhongguo jiaru WTO de zhengzhi yiyi" [The political meaning of China's entry into the WTO]. *Duowei xinwen wang* (November 16, 1999), www.chinesenewsnet.com

Liu Kang. "Quanqiuhua 'peilun' yu xiandaixing 'qitu'" [The "paradox" of global-ization and modernity's "wrong roads"]. *Dushu* (July 1995): 98–105.

"Quanqiuhua yu Zhongguo xiandaihua de butong xuanze" [Globalization and the different choices of China's modernization]. *Ershiyi shiji* 37 (October 1996); reprinted in Wang Hui and Yu Guoliang (eds.), *90 niandai de "houxue" lunzheng*, pp. 31–42.

Liu Kang, and Li Xiguang. *Yaomo Zhongguo de beihou* [Behind the demonization of China]. Beijing: Zhongguo shehui kexue chubanshe, 1996.

Liu Pi. "Deng Xiaoping Launches 'Northern Expedition' to Emancipate Mind; Beijing, Shanghai, and Other Provinces and Municipalities 'Respond' by Opening Wider to the Outside World." *Ching pao* 166, May 10, 1991, trans. FBIS-CHI, May 6, 1991, pp. 26–9.

Liu Runwei. "Zhimin wenhua lun" [On colonial culture]. *Qiushi* 5 (March 1, 1996): 26–33.

Liu Shi. "The Purpose of 'Transformation' Is to Pave the Way for Capitalism – On Comrade Zhao Ziyang's Erroneous Guiding Ideology for Ideological and Political Work among Staff Members and Workers." *Gongren ribao*, September 5, 1989, p. 1, trans. FBIS-CHI, September 5, 1989, pp. 30–2.

Liu Xiaofeng. *Geti xinyang yu wenhua lilun* [Individual belief and cultural theory]. Chengdu: Sichuan chubanshe, 1997.

"Liu Yunshan zai Henan kaocha shi qiangdiao tigao jianshe shehui zhuyi xian-jin wenhua nengli wei quanmian jianshe xiaokang shehui tigong sixiang baozheng he yulun zhichi" [On an investigation of Henan, Liu Yun-shan stresses the need to raise the ability to construct a socialist advanced culture and provide ideological guidance and public opinion support for fully building a well-off society]. *Renmin ribao*, November 15, 2004, p. 4.

"Liu Yunshan zai quanguo xuanchuan buzhang zuotanhui shang qiangdiao renzhen xuexi xuanchuan guanche shiliujie sizhong quanhui jingshen" [At a seminar of propaganda heads, Liu Yunshan emphasizes earnestly studying propaganda and implementing the spirit of the Fourth Plenary Session of the Sixteenth Party Congress]. *Renmin ribao*, September 24, 2006, p. 4.

Liu Zhifeng. "Disizhi yanjing kan Zhongguo – Wang Shan fangtanlu" [Looking at China through a fourth eye – Interview with Wang Shan]. In Liu Zhifeng (ed.), *Jieshi Zhongguo*, pp. 293–343.

Liu Zhifeng (ed.). *Jieshi Zhongguo: "Disanzhi yanjing kan Zhongguo" pipan* [Explaining China: Criticism of "Looking at China through a Third Eye"]. Beijing: Jingji ribao chubanshe, 1998.

Lo Ping. "The Anti-Deng Meeting Incident in Hebei." *Zhengming* 205, November 1, 1994, pp. 9–14, trans. FBIS-CHI, November 17, 1994, pp. 16–18.

"Blowing of the 'Left' Wind, and the Four-Horse Carriage." *Zhengming* 183, January 1, 1993, pp. 6–8, trans. FBIS-CHI, January 7, 1993, pp. 12–14.

"Report on Deng Xiaoping's Behind-the-Scenes Activities." *Zhengming* 159, January 1, 1991, trans. FBIS-CHI, December 31, 1990, pp. 20–1.

Lo Ping, and Li Tzu-ching. "Chen Yun Raises Six Points of View to Criticize Deng Xiaoping." *Zhengming* 171, January 1, 1992, pp. 18–19, trans. FBIS-CHI, January 3, 1992, pp. 22–3.

Long Yongtu. "Guanyu jiaru shijie maoyi zuzhi de wenti" [On the question of our joining the World Trade Organization]. *Zhonggong zhongyang dangxiao baogaoxuan* 11, July 22, 1998, pp. 1–6, trans. Joseph Fewsmith (ed.), *China and the WTO, Part I* (*The Chinese Economy* 33(1): 5–52, January/February 2000).

Lu Jiandong. *Chen Yinke de zuihou ershi nian* [The last twenty years of Chen Yinke]. Beijing: Sanlian, 1995.

Lu Jianhua. "Zhuanjia yanli de shehui xingshi jiqi qianjing" [The social situation and its prospects in the eyes of specialists]. In Ru Xin, Lu Xueyi, and Li Peilin (eds.), *2004 nian: Zhongguo shehui xingshi fenxi yu yuce*, pp. 13–21.

Lu Ming-sheng. "Inside Story of How *Historical Trends* Was Banned." *Zhengming* 177, July 1, 1992, pp. 33–4, trans. FBIS-CHI, July 7, 1992, pp. 19–21.

Lu Yu-shan. "Chen Yun Responds to Document No. 2." *Tangtai* 14, May 15, 1992, pp. 21–2, trans. FBIS-CHI, May 21, 1992, pp. 18–20.

Lu Xueyi (ed.). *Dangdai Zhongguo shehui liudong* [Social mobility in contemporary China]. Beijing: Shehui kexue wenxian chubanshe, 2004.

Dangdai Zhongguo shehui yanjiu baogao [Research report on contemporary Chinese society]. Beijing: Shehui kexue wenxian chubanshe, 2002.

Lubman, Stanley. *Bird in a Cage: Legal Reform in China after Mao*. Stanford, CA: Stanford University Press, 1999.

Luo Xiaolu. "Chen Xitong tan jiefang sixiang" [Chen Xitong talks about liberating thought]. *Banyuetan* 6 (March 25, 1991): 16–18.

Luo yi ning ge er. *See* Wang Shan.

Ma Hong. "Have a Correct Understanding of the Economic Situation, Continue to Do a Good Job in Economic Improvement and Rectification." *Renmin ribao*, November 17, 1989, trans. FBIS-CHI, December 5, 1989, pp. 37–9.

Ma Licheng. "Xinwen jiandu buxing 'zi'" [Press supervision is not "capitalist"]. *Fangfa* 3 (1998): 6–7.

Ma Licheng, and Ling Zhijun. *Jiao feng: Dangdai Zhongguo sance sixiang jiefang shilu* [Crossed swords: A true account of the three emancipations of thought in contemporary China]. Beijing: Jinri Zhongguo chubanshe, 1998.

Ma Ling. "Who Starts Rumors about Jia Qinglin's Divorce?" *Ta kung pao*, January 27, 2000, trans. FBIS-CHI-2000–0127, January 27, 2000.

Mahathir, Mohamad, and Shintaro Ishihara. *The Voice of Asia: Two Leaders Discuss the Coming Century*. Tokyo: Kodansha, 1995.

"Major Revisions to the Government Work Report." *Wen wei po*, March 16, 1993, p. 3, trans. FBIS-CHI, March 16, 1993, pp. 23–4.

"Make Fresh Contributions on 'Protecting and Escorting' Reform, Opening up, and Economic Development – Warmly Congratulating Conclusion of the Fifth Sessions of the Seventh National People's Congress and Seventh Chinese People's Political Consultative Conference." *Jiefangjun bao*, April 4, 1992, trans. FBIS-CHI, April 21, 1992, pp. 36–7.

"Makesi zhuyi yongyuan shi women shengli de qizhi" [Marxism is our victorious banner forever]. *Jiefangjun bao*, May 6, 1996, pp. 1, 6.

Mao Zedong. "The Yenan Forum on Literature and Art." In *The Selected Works of Mao Tse-tung*, vol. 3, pp. 69–98. Peking: Foreign Languages Press, 1967.

"March toward the New Scientific and Technological Revolution." Xinhua, May 2, 1991, in FBIS-CHI, May 3, 1991, pp. 23–6.

McMillan, John, and Barry Naughton. "How to Reform a Planned Economy: Lessons from China." *Oxford Review of Economic Policy* 8 (1992): 130–43.

Mei Qiren (ed.). *Three Interviews with Zhao Ziyang. Chinese Law and Government* 38 (3) (May–June 2005).

Meng Fanhua. *Zhongshen kuanghuan – Dangdai Zhongguo de wenhua chongtu wenti* [Bacchanalia of culture – The clash of cultures in contemporary China]. Beijing: Jinri Zhongguo chubanshe, 1997.

Meng Lin. "Deng Liqun Reaffirms Disapproval of Phrase 'Deng Xiaoping Thought'." *Ching pao* 180, July 5, 1992, p. 42, trans. FBIS-CHI, July 6, 1992, pp. 28–9.

Mercuro, Nicholas, and Steven G. Medema. *Economics and the Law*. Princeton, NJ: Princeton University Press, 1997.

Metzger, Thomas A. *A Cloud Across the Pacific: Essays on the Clash between Chinese and Western Political Theories Today*. Hong Kong: The Chinese University Press, 2005.

"Miandui 'shengtu de yingdi' – Yu women de qingnian jiaoliu" [Facing "the camp of the saints" – An exchange with our youth]. *Beijing qingnian bao*, August 11, 1995, p. 8.

Migdal, Joel. *Strong Societies and Weak States*. Princeton, NJ: Princeton University Press, 1988.

Mooney, Paul. "Gaging China's Intellectuals." *Asia Times Online*, December 15, 2004.

"More than 120 Government Officials Punished over SARS in China." Xinhua, May 8, 2003. Reported by Agence France-Presse, May 8, 2003.

"More than Seventy Writers and Artists Attend a Forum to Study the Spirit of the Fourth Plenary Session." *Renmin ribao*, July 13, 1989, p. 2, trans. FBIS-CHI, July 24, 1989, pp. 26–7.

Mufson, Steven. "Former Chinese Official Advocates Democracy." *Washington Post*, January 12, 1998, p. A3.

Mufson, Steven, and Robert G. Kaiser. "'Blue Team' Draws a Hard Line on Beijing: Action on Hill Reflects Informal Group's Clout." *Washington Post*, February 22, 2000, p. A1.

"Missed US–China Deal Looms Large." *Washington Post*, November 10, 1999, p. A1.

Mulvenon, James. "Reduced Budgets, the 'Two Centers,' and Other Mysteries of the 2003 National People's Congress." *China Leadership Monitor* 7 (Summer 2003). Retrieved from www.hoover.org/publications/clm/issues/2906056.html

Myers, Steven Lee. "Chinese Embassy Bombing: A Wide Net of Blame." *New York Times*, April 17, 2000, pp. A1, A10.

Nathan, Andrew, Perry Link (eds.), and Zhang Liang (Comp.). *The Tiananmen Papers: The Chinese Leaderships' Decision to Use Force Against Their Own People – In Their Own Words*. New York: Public Affairs, 2001.

Naughton, Barry. "Causes et conséquences des disparités dans la croissance économique des provinces chinoises" [Causes and consequences of differential economic growth of Chinese provinces]. *Revue d'économie du Développement* (Juin 1999): 33–70.

  Growing Out of the Plan: Chinese Economic Reform, 1978–1993. Cambridge: Cambridge University Press, 1995.

  "The Third Front: Defence Industrialization in the Chinese Interior." *The China Quarterly* 115 (1988): 351–61.

"New Stage of China's Reform and Opening to the Outside World." *Renmin ribao* editorial, June 9, 1992, trans. FBIS-CHI, June 9, 1992, pp. 17–18.

Observer. "Humanitarianism or Hegemonism?" Xinhua, May 16, 1999, in FBIS-CHI, May 16, 1999.

Observer. "On the New Development of US Hegemonism." *Renmin ribao*, May 27, 1999, trans. in FBIS-CHI, May 27, 1999.

Observer. "We Urge Hegemon Today to Take a Look at the Mirror of History." *Renmin ribao*, June 22, 1999, trans. in FBIS-CHI-1999-0622, June 22, 1999.

Oi, Jean. "Fiscal Reform and the Foundations of Local State Corporatism in China." *World Politics* 45 (October 1992): 99–126.

  Rural China Takes Off: Institutional Foundations of Economic Reform. Berkeley, CA: University of California Press, 1999.

O'Neill, Mark. "Fairwell to the Smuggler King." *South China Morning Post*, January 25, 2000.

"Politburo Closes Ranks." *South China Morning Post*, January 29, 2000, p. 17.

Pearson, Margaret M. "The Case of China's Accession to GATT/WTO." In David M. Lampton, *The Making of Chinese Foreign and Security Policy in the Era of Reform, 1978–2000*, pp. 337–70. Stanford, CA: Stanford University Press, 2001.

  "China's Integration into the International Trade and Investment Regime." In Elizabeth Economy and Michel Oksenberg (eds.), *China Joins the World*, pp. 161–205.

Pei, Minxin. *China's Trapped Transition: The Limits of Developmental Autocracy*. Cambridge, MA: Harvard University Press, 2006.

  From Reform to Revolution: The Demise of Communism in China and the Soviet Union. Cambridge, MA: Harvard University Press, 1994.

Peng Qian, Yang Mingjie, and Xu Deren. *Zhongguo weishenma shuobu?* [Why does China say no?]. Beijing: Xinshijie chubanshe, 1996.

Perlez, Jane. "A Visitor from China Eclipses Bush's Stop in Australia." *The New York Times*, October 25, 2003, p. A3.

Petracca, Mark P., and Mong Xiong. "The Concept of Chinese NeoAuthoritarianism." *Asian Survey* (November 1990): 1099–117.

Pi Mingyong. "Zhongguo jindai minzu zhuyi de duozhong jiagou" [The multiple frameworks of modern Chinese nationalism]. *Zhanlüe yu guanli* 3 (June 1994): 22–5.

"Political Report" to the Fourteenth Party Congress. Beijing Television Service, October 12, 1992, trans. FBIS-CHI, October 13, 1992, pp. 23–43.

Pomfret, John. "China's Crisis Has a Political Edge." *Washington Post*, April 27, 2003, p. A33.

"Chinese Tie Leaders to Smuggling; Party, Military Chiefs Among Suspects." *Washington Post*, January 22, 2000, p. A1.

"Doctor Says Health Ministry Lied about Disease." *Washington Post*, April 10, 2003, p. A26.

Qi Mo (ed.). *Xinquanwei zhuyi: Dui Zhongguo dalu weilai mingyun de lunzheng* [New authoritarianism: Debates on the fate of the Chinese mainland]. Taipei: Tangshan chubanshe, 1991.

Qian Jun. "Saiyide tan wenhua" [Said on culture]. *Dushu* (September 1993): 10–17.

Qin Hui. "Bainian zhuanhuan – 'Shangren' yu 'jiaoshi' de Zhongguoguan" [Hundred years' transformation – "Merchants" and "missionaries" views of China]. In Qin Hui, *Wenti yu zhuyi: Qin Hui wenxuan* [Problems and isms: Essays by Qin Hui], pp. 3–7. Changchun: Changchun chubanshe, 1999.

Qin Si. "Wenyiwen 'xingshe haishi xingzi'" [Asking whether this is "capitalist or socialist"]. *Guangming ribao*, August 7, 1991, p. 3.

Ramo, Joshua Cooper. "The Beijing Consensus." The Foreign Policy Centre (London), 2004.

Ren Zhongping. "Wei jingji jianshe he shehui fazhan tigong qiangyouli de zhengzhi baozhang" [A powerful political guarantee for economic construction and social development]. *Renmin ribao*, April 1, 1996, pp. 1, 3.

"Zai gan yige ershi nian: Lun woguo gaige fazhan de guanjian shiqi" [Do another twenty years: On the crucial period in China's reforms and development]. *Renmin ribao*, July 12, 2004, p. 1.

Reporters without Borders. "Five Resign from Editorial Board in Solidarity with Dismissed Magazine Editor." December 6, 2004. Retrieved from www.rsf.org/article.php3?id˙article=11726

"Resolution of the Central Committee of the Communist Party of China on the Guiding Principles for Building a Socialist Society with Advanced Culture and Ideology." Xinhua, September 28, 1986, in FBIS-CHI, September 29, 1986, pp. K2–K13.

"Resolution of the CPC Central Committee Regarding Important Questions on Promoting Socialist Ethical and Cultural Progress." *Beijing Review* 39 (November 4–10, 1996): 20–31.

"Revamp Rules to Promote Equality." *China Daily*, January 7, 2005.

Reyes, Alejandro. "A Caning in Singapore Stirs Up a Fierce Debate about Crime and Punishment." *Asiaweek*, May 25, 1994.

Roemer, John (ed.). *Property Relations, Incentives, and Welfare*. New York: St. Martin's, 1996.

Rosen, Stanley. "Youth and Social Change in the PRC." In Ramon H. Myers (ed.), *Two Societies in Opposition: The Republic of China and the People's Republic of China after Forty Years*, pp. 288–315. Stanford, CA: Hoover Institution Press, 1990.

Rosen, Stanley, and Gary Zou (eds.). "The Chinese Debate on the New Authoritarianism (I), (II), (III), (IV)." *Chinese Sociology and Anthropology* (Winter 1990, Spring 1991, Summer 1991, and Fall 1991).

Rosen, Stanley, and Gary Zou. "The Road to Modernization in China Debated: The Origins, Development and Decline of Neoauthoritarianism and Direct Democracy Schools." Unpublished manuscript.

Ru Xin, Lu Xueyi, and Li Peilin (eds.). *2004 nian: Zhongguo shehui xingshi fenxi yu yuce* [Chinese social situation: Analysis and forecast, 2004]. Beijing: Shehui kexue wenxian chubanshe, 2004.

2006 nian: Zhongguo shehui xingshi fenxi yu yuce [China's social situation: Analysis and forecast, 2006]. Beijing: Shehui kexue wenxian chubanshe, 2006.

Said, Edward. *Culture and Imperialism*. New York: Knopf, 1993.

Orientalism. New York: Pantheon, 1978.

Sanger, David E. "The Trade Deal: The Drama." *New York Times*, November 16, 1999, p. A14.

Schneider, Axel. "Bridging the Gap: Attempts at Constructing a 'New' Historical-Cultural Identity in the PRC." Unpublished manuscript.

Schram, Stuart R. "General Introduction." In *Mao's Road to Power: Revolutionary Writings 1912–1949* (vol. 1: *The Pre-Marxist Period, 1912–1920*), pp. xv–xx. Armonk, NY: M. E. Sharpe, 1992.

Schwarcz, Vera. *The Chinese Enlightenment: Intellectuals and the Legacy of the May Fourth Movement of 1919*. Berkeley, CA: University of California Press, 1986.

Schwartz, Benjamin. *In Search of Wealth and Power: Yen Fu and the West*. Cambridge, MA: Harvard University Press, 1964.

"Seeking Cure for Property Reform." *China Daily*, September 22, 2004.

Sha Feng. "Ultraleftists within CCP Launch Comeback by Criticizing Five New Rightists." *Ming pao*, August 20, 1994, p. A2, trans. FBIS-CHI, August 22, 1994, pp. 17–18.

Shambaugh, David. "The Lessons of Collapse: CCP Assessments of the Soviet and East European Implosions." Paper presented at the Association for Asian Studies Annual Meeting, San Francisco, April 6–9, 2006.

Shang Dewen. "Cong eryuan jiegou kan Zhongguo" [Viewing China from the perspective of a dual structure]. Unpublished letter.

"Guanyu Zhongguo zhengzhi tizhi gaige de ruogan wenti yu jiben duice" [Several questions about and fundamental measures for China's political structural reform]. Unpublished letter.

Shao Ren. "Zhongguo: Ruguan buru tao" [China: Joining the WTO without falling into the trap]. *Tianya* 3 (May 1999): 4–15, 90.

Shen Hongpei. "Ershi shijimo gongchan zhuyi dalunzhan" [A great Communist debate at the end of the twentieth century]. Introduction to Shi Liaozi (ed.), *Beijng dixia "wanyanshu,"* pp. 1–24.

Shen Jiru. *Zhongguo bu dang "bu xiansheng"* [China should not be "Mr. No"]. Beijing: Jinri Zhongguo chubanshe, 1998.

Shen Liren, and Dai Yuanchen. "Woguo 'zhuhou jingji' de xingcheng ji qi biduan he genyuan" [The emergence of China's "feudal lord" economy: Its harm and resolution]. *Jingji yanjiu* 3 (March 1990): 12–19, 67.

Shi Bonian, and Liu Fang. "Unswervingly Implement the Party's Basic Line." *Jiefangjun bao*, March 18, 1992, trans. FBIS-CHI, April 15, 1992, pp. 44–7.

Shi Liaozi (ed.). *Beijing dixia "wanyanshu"* [Beijing's underground "ten thousand character manifestos"]. Hong Kong: Mingjing chubanshe, 1997.

Shi Xiuyin. "Zhongguo xinshiqi siyou qiyezhu jieceng baogao" [Report on the private entrepreneurial stratum in China in the new period]. In Li Peilin (ed.), *Zhongguo xinshiqi jieji jieceng baogao* [Reports on classes and strata of China in the new period], pp. 221–91. Shenyang: Liaoning renmin chubanshe, 1995.

Shi Zhong. *See* Wang Xiaodong.

Shinn, James (ed.). *Weaving the Net: Conditional Engagement with China.* New York: Council on Foreign Relations, 1996.

Shirk, Susan. *How China Opened Its Door: The Political Success of the PRC's Foreign Trade and Investment Reforms.* Washington, DC: Brookings, 1994.

Shisanda yilai zhongyao wenxuan bian [Selected important documents since the Thirteenth Party Congress], 3 volumes. Beijing: Renmin chubanshe, 1991, 1991, and 1993.

Smith, Craig R. "Shanghai Journal; Sex, Lust, Drugs: Her Novel's Too Much for China." *New York Times*, May 11, 2000, p. A4.

Solinger, Dorothy. *Contesting Citizenship in Urban China: Peasant Migrants, the State, and the Logic of the Market.* Berkeley, CA: University of California Press, 1999.

Song Ping. "Zai quanguo zuzhi buzhang huiyi shang de jianghua" [Talk to a national meeting of organization department heads]. In *Shisanda yilai*, vol. 2, pp. 566–77.

Song Qiang, Zhang Zangzang, and Qiao Bian. *Zhongguo haishi neng shuobu* [China can still say no]. Hong Kong: Ming bao, 1996.

Zhongguo keyi shuobu [China can say no]. Beijing: Zhonghua gongshang lianhe chubanshe, 1996.

"Speech by Jiang Zemin at the Fourth Plenary Session of the Commission for Discipline Inspection." *Dangjian yanjiu* 4, as transmitted by Xinhua, April 1, 2000, in FBIS-CHI-2000-0401, April 1, 2000.

Steinfeld, Edward. *Forging Reform in China.* Cambridge: Cambridge University Press, 1998.

Stiglitz, Joseph E. *Whither Socialism?* Cambridge, MA: MIT Press, 1997.

Su Shaozhi (ed.). *Marxism in China.* Nottingham, UK: Russell Press, 1983.

Su Shaozhi. *Shinian fengyu: Wengehou de dalu lilunjie* [Ten years of storms: The mainland's theoretical circles after the Cultural Revolution]. Taipei: Shibao chuban gongsi, 1996.

Su Xiaokang, and Wang Luxiang. *He Shang* [River Elegy]. Beijing: Xiandai chuban-she, 1988.

"Summary of Tian Jiyun's Speech before Party School." *Pai hsing* 266, June 16, 1992, pp. 4–5, trans. FBIS-CHI, June 18, 1992, pp. 16–18.

Sun Hong. "Anecdotes about Deng Xiaoping's Political Career and Family Life." *Ching pao* 11, November 5, 1993, pp. 26–31, trans. FBIS-CHI, November 18, 1993, pp. 34–9.

Sun Liping. "Pingmin zhuyi yu Zhongguo gaige" [Populism and China's reform]. *Zhanlüe yu guanli* 5 (October 1994): 1–10.

"Zhongguo shehui jiegou zhuanxing de zhongjinqi qushi yu yinhuan" [Trends and hidden difficulties in the transformation of China's social structure in the near and mid-term]. *Zhanlüe yu guanli* 5 (October 1998): 1–17.

Sun Min. "Standards Released for State Firm Buyouts." *China Daily*, April 15, 2005.

Sun Yafei. "Zhizhengdang diyibu ziwo jiandu tiaoli jijiang chutai" [Ruling Party finalizes its first "inner-Party supervision regulations"]. *Nanfang zhoumo*, December 4, 2003.

Sun Yushan. "Chen Xitong Points Out at a Municipal Supervision Work Conference That Supervision Departments Should Emancipate Their Minds in Carrying Out Work." *Beijing ribao*, March 8, 1991, pp. 1–2, trans. FBIS-CHI, March 29, 1991, p. 38.

Tan Shaowen. "Emancipate the Mind, Seek Truth from Facts, Be United as One, and Do Solid Work." *Tianjin ribao*, April 17, 1991, trans. FBIS-CHI, June 18, 1991, pp. 62–8.

Tan Wei. "Fresh Start for Management Buyout: New Regulation Puts an End to the Prolonged Debate on MBO Feasibility and Ushers in New Era for the Practice." *Beijing Review*, May 13, 2005.

Tanner, Murray Scott. *The Politics of Lawmaking in China: Institutions, Processes, and Democratic Prospects*. Oxford: Oxford University Press, 1999.

Tao, Poon Siu. "Shanghai Gang Losing Power Struggle." *Asia Times Online*, August 31, 2006.

Tseng Hui-yen. "*Looking at China With a Third Eye* Reportedly Written by Pan Yue." *Lien ho pao*, September 16, 1994, p. 10, trans. FBIS-CHI, September 16, 1994, p. 31.

Tseng Pin. "Party Struggle Exposed by Senior Statesmen Themselves; Meanwhile, the New Leading Group is Trying Hard to Build New Image." *Ching pao* 145, August 10, 1989, trans. FBIS-CHI, August 10, 1989.

Tsou, Tang. "Chinese Politics at the Top: Factionalism of Informal Politics? Balance-of-Power Politics or a Game to Win All?" *China Journal* 34 (July 1995): 95–156.

The Cultural Revolution and Post-Mao Reforms: A Historical Perspective. Chicago: University of Chicago Press, 1986.

"Political Change and Reform: The Middle Course." In Tang Tsou, *The Cultural Revolution and Post-Mao Reforms*, pp. 219–58.

"Prolegomenon to the Study of Informal Groups in CCP Politics." In Tang Tsou, *The Cultural Revolution and Post-Mao Reforms*, pp. 95–111.

"The Tiananmen Tragedy: The State–Society Relationship, Choices, and Mechanisms in Historical Perspective." In Brantly Womack (ed.), *Contemporary Chinese Politics in Historical Perspective*. Cambridge: Cambridge University Press, 1991, pp. 265–327.

Unger, Roberto Mangabeira. *Democratic Experimentalism*. London: Verso, 1998.

Wakeman, Frederic. "All the Rage in China." *New York Review of Books*, March 2, 1989, pp. 19–21.

Wallerstein, Immanuel. *The Modern World System: Capitalist Agriculture and the Origins of the European World-Economy in the Sixteenth Century*. New York: Academic Press, 1974.

Wan Li. "Juece minzhuhua he kexuehua shi zhengzhi tizhi gaige de yige zhongyao keti" [Making decision-making democratic and scientific is an important subject in political structural reform]. Xinhua, August 14, 1986, in FBIS-CHI, August 19, 1986, pp. K22–K34.

Wang Chi, Zhao Zhiwen, and Zheng Hongfan. "Trading Power for Money Is Not Tolerated by Law." Xinhua, June 7, 1999, in FBIS-CHI, June 14, 1999.

Wang Hui. *China's New Order: Society, Politics, and Economy in Transition*. Ed. Theodore Huters. Cambridge, MA: Harvard University Press, 2003.

"Contemporary Chinese Thought and the Question of the Modern. In Wang Hui, *China's New Order*, pp. 139–87.

"Dangdai Zhongguo de sixiang zhuangkuang yu xiandaixing wenti" [The circumstances of contemporary Chinese thought and the problem of modernity]. *Wenyi zhengming* 6 (November 1998): 7–26.

"Guanyu xiandaixing wenti dawen" [An interview on the question of modernity]. *Tianya* 1 (January 1999):18–34.

"Wenhua pipan lilun yu dangdai Zhongguo minzu zhuyi wenti" [Cultural critical theories and the problems of contemporary Chinese nationalism]. *Zhanlüe yu guanli* 4 (1994): 17–20.

Wang Hui, and Yu Guoliang (eds.). *90 niandai de "houxue" lunzheng* ["Post-ism" in the nineties]. Hong Kong: Chinese University Press, 1998.

Wang Huning. "Chuji jieduan yu zhengzhi tizhi gaige" [The initial stage and political structural reform]. In *Wang Huning ji*, pp. 28–9.

"Jifen pingheng: Zhongyang yu difang de xietong guanxi" [Equilibrium between concentration and dispersal: Harmonizing relations between the center and localities]. *Fudan xuebao* 2 (1991): 27–36.

"Juece gongneng de shehuihua ji qi tiaojian" [The socialization of the policy-making function and its conditions]. In *Wang Huning ji*, pp. 74–80.

"Lun minzhu zhengzhi jianshe" [On building democratic politics]. In *Wang Huning ji*, pp. 30–8.

"Shehui ziyuan zongliang yu shehui tiaokong: Zhongguo yiyi" [Aggregate social resources and social control]. *Fudan xuebao* 4 (1990): 2–11, 35.

Wang Huning ji [Collected essays of Wang Huning]. Harbin: Heilongjiang jiaoyu chubanshe, 1989.

"Wenhua guozhang yu wenhua zhuquan: Dui zhuquan guannian de tiaozhan" [Cultural expansionism and cultural sovereignty: A challenge to the concept of sovereignty]. *Fudan xuebao* 3 (1994); reprinted in Wang Jisi (ed.), *Wenming yu guoji zhengzhi*, pp. 340–56.

"Zhengzhi shenmei yu zhengzhi fazhan" [Political aesthetics and political development]. *Shehui kexue zhanxian* 1 (January 1991): 134–41.

"Zhiwei fenlei yu ganbu guanli tizhi" [Types of posts and the cadre management system]. In *Wang Huning ji*, pp. 88–95.

"Zhongguo bianhua zhong de zhongyang he difang zhengfu de guanxi: Zhengzhi de hanyi" [Governmental relations between the center and localities in the course of China's changes: The political implications]. *Fudan xuebao* 5 (1988): 1–8, 30.

"Zhongguo zhengzhi tizhi gaige de beijing yu qianjing" [The background and prospects for the reform of China's political system]. In *Wang Huning ji*, pp. 3–14.

"Zhongguo zhengzhi – Xingzheng tizhi gaige de jingji fenxi" [Chinese politics – An economic analysis of the reform of the administrative structure]. *Shehui kexue zhanxian* 2 (1988): 107–15.

Wang, Jing. *High Culture Fever: Politics, Aesthetics, and Ideology in Deng's China.* Berkeley, CA: University of California Press, 1996.

Wang Jisi (ed.). *Wenming yu guoji zhengzhi: Zhongguo xuezhe ping Hengtingdun de wenming chongtu lun* [Culture and international relations: Chinese scholars critique Huntington's cultural clash thesis]. Shanghai: Renmin chubanshe, 1995.

Wang Jiye. "Several Questions on Achieving Overall Balance and Restructuring." *Renmin ribao*, December 8, 1989, trans. FBIS-CHI, January 19, 1990, pp. 30–3.

Wang Mengkui. "Quanmian jianshe xiaokang shehui de guanjian shike" [Critical stage of building an all-round well-off society]. *Zhongguo jingji shibao*, October 24, 2005.

Wang Renzhi. "Guanyu fandui zichan jieji ziyouhua" [On opposing bourgeois liberalization]. *Renmin ribao*, February 22, 1990.

"Lilun gongzuo mianlin de xin qingkuang he dangqian de zhuyao renwu" [The new situation confronting theoretical work and the primary task at the moment]. *Xuexi, yanjiu, cankao* 11 (1990): 8–17.

Wang Ruoshui. *Hu Yaobang xiatai de beijing* [Behind Hu Yaobang's stepping down]. Hong Kong: Mingjing chubanshe, 1997.

Wei rendao zhuyi bianhu [In defense of humanism]. Beijing: Sanlian, 1986.

Wang Shan [Luo yi ning ge er]. *Disanzhi yanjing kan Zhongguo* [Looking at China through a third eye]. Taiyuan: Shanxi renmin chubanshe, 1994.

Wang Shaoguang. "'Jiegui' haishi 'nalai': Zhengzhixue bentuhua de kaolu" ["Joining tracks" or "borrowing": Thoughts about the nativization of political science]. Part 1, *Zhongguo yu shijie*, October 2000, www.chinabulletin.com/2000/zs0010b.txt; Part 2, *Zhongguo yu shijie*, November 2000, www.chinabulletin.com/2000/zs0011b.htm

"The Social and Political Implications of China's WTO Membership." *Journal of Contemporary China* 9 (2000): 373–405.

Wang, Shaoguang, and Hu Angang. *The Political Economy of Uneven Development: The Case of China.* Armonk, NY: M. E. Sharpe, 1999.

Wang Shuo. *Playing for Thrills*, trans. Howard Goldblatt. New York: Penguin, 1998.

Please Don't Call Me Human, trans. Howard Goldblatt. New York: Hyperion East, 2000.

"Wang Shuo zibai" [Wang Shuo's self-defense]. *Wenyi zhengming* 1 (1993): 65–6.

Wang Wenjie. "Guo Boxiong zai 'Jiang Zemin guofang he jundui jianshe sixiang xuexi gangyao' chuban zuotanhui shang qiangdiao: Yi gaodu zhengzhi zerengan xuexi guanche Jiang Zemin guofang he jundui jianshe sixiang" [At a forum on the publication of the "Study Outline for Jiang Zemin's Thinking on National Defense and Army Building" Guo Boxiong stresses studying and implementing Jiang Zemin's thinking on national defense and army building with a great sense of political responsibility]. *Jiefangjun bao*, August 3, 2003, p. 1.

Wang Xiaodong [Shi Zhong], no title. Posting under "Guanyu Zhongguo minzu zhuyi de taolun (er)" [Discussion of China's nationalism (two)] on www.jczs.com.cn, June 9, 1999.

"Ping liangzhong butong de gaige guan" [Evaluating two different views of reform]. *Dangdai sichao* 1 (January 1992): 10–26.

"Weilai de chongtu" [The coming clash]. *Zhanlüe yu guanli* 1 (November 1993): 46–50.

"The West in the Eyes of a Chinese Nationalist." *Heartland: Eurasian Review of Geopolitics* 1 (2000): 17–30.

"Zai pingmin yu jingying zhijian xunqiu pingheng" [Seeking a balance between populism and elitism]. *Zhanlüe yu guanli* 5 (October 1994): 11–14.

"Zhongguo de minzu zhuyi he Zhongguo de weilai" [Chinese nationalism and the future of China]. *Mingbao yuekan* 9 (1996); trans. Stanley Rosen (ed.), *Chinese Law and Government* 30 (November/December 1997): 8–27.

Wang Xiaodong, and Qiu Tiancao. "Jiqing de yinying: Ping dianshi xiliepian 'He shang'" [The shadow of passion: Critique of the television series "River Elegy"]. *Zhongguo qingnianbao*, July 10, 1988, p. 4.

Wang Xiaoming. "Kuangyeshang de feixu" [Ruins on the wilderness]. In Wang Xiaoming (ed.), *Renwen jingshen xunsilu* [Pondering the humanistic spirit]. Shanghai: Wenhui chubanshe, 1996.

Wang Yizhou. "Minzu zhuyi gainian de xiandai sikao" [Contemporary reflections on the concept of nationalism]. *Zhanlüe yu guanli* 3 (June 1994): 7–12.

Wang, Yong. "China's Accession to WTO: An Institutional Perspective." Unpublished manuscript.

Wang Youfu. "Wang Zhen Inspects Xinjiang." *Renmin ribao*, August 26, 1991, p. 1, trans. FBIS-CHI, August 29, 1991, p. 21.

Wang Yungui. "Kan RiMeiFa zhengfu ruhe baohu benguo gongye" [Looking at how Japan, the United States, and France protected their domestic industries]. *Jingji ribao*, July 17, 1996, pp. 1, 3.

"We Must Not Only Persevere in Reform and Opening Up but Also Speed Them Up." *Renmin ribao* editorial, May 22, 1987, trans. FBIS-CHI, May 22, 1987, pp. K1–K3.

Wei Ming. "Yijiu jiu'er nian yilai zichan jieji ziyouhua de dongtai he tedian" [The movements and characteristics of bourgeois liberals since 1992]. *Zhongguo yu shijie*, March 1998, www.chinabulletin.com/98/zs9803d.htm

Wei Yung-cheng. "Reveal the Mystery of Huangfu Ping." *Ta kung pao*, October 7, 1992, trans. FBIS-CHI, October 16, 1992, p. 19.

"Weilai yi, ershinian woguo guojia anquan de neiwai xingshi ji zhuyao weixie de chubu tantao" [A preliminary investigation of China's domestic and international situation and primary threats in the next ten to twenty years]. In Shi Liaozi (ed.), *Beijing dixia "wanyanshu,"* pp. 134–5.

Weiskopf, Michael. "Chief Rose by Following Prevailing Political Winds." *The Washington Post*, June 25, 1989, p. A25.

"Weixian xinhao: Zhongxuanbu 29 hao wenjian yinxiang fubi daotui de kuihao" [A dangerous signal: The Propaganda Department's document 29 signals a backward turn]. Retrieved from www.peacehall.com/news/gb/china/2004/12/200412150317.shtml

Wen Jiabao. "Guanyu zhiding guomin jingji he shehui fazhan dishiyi wunian guihua jianyi de shuoming" [Explanation on the formulation of the Eleventh Five-Year National Economic and Social Development Program]. *Renmin ribao*, October 20, 2005, p. 1.

"Renzhen guanche shiliuda jingshen, wei tuijin nongcun xiaokang jianshe er fendou" [Seriously implement the spirit of the Sixteenth Party Congress, strive to build relative affluence in the rural areas]. *Renmin ribao*, February 8, 2003.

"Zhengfu gongzuo baogao" [Report on the work of the government]. *Renmin ribao*, March 16, 2006, pp. 1–3.

"Wen Jiabao zhuchi zhaokai Guowuyuan changwei huiyi" [Wen Jiabao presides over meeting of State Council Standing Committee]. *Renmin ribao*, April 3, 2003, p. 1.

"Wen Jiabao zongli da zhongwai jizhe wen" [Premier Wen Jiabao answers questions from Chinese and foreign reporters], *Renmin ribao*, March 15, 2006, p. 1.

Wen Jin (ed.). *Zhongguo "Zuo" huo* [China's 'leftist' peril]. Beijing: Chaohua chubanshe, 1993.

Wen Shengtang. "2003 nian de fanfubai douzheng" [The struggle against corruption in 2003]. In Ru Xin, Lu Xueyi, and Li Peilin (eds.), *2004 nian: Zhongguo shehui xingshi fenxi yu yuce*, pp. 158–71.

"Fanfubai: Jianli jianquan zhengzhi he yufang tixi" [Anti-corruption: Establishing a healthy system to punish and prevent it]. In Ru Xin, Lu Xueyi, and Li Peilin (eds.), *2006 nian: Zhongguo shehui xingshi fenxi yu yuce*, pp. 123–43.

Weng Jieming, Zhang Ximing, Zhang Qiang, and Qu Kemin (eds.). *Yu zongshuji tanxin* [Heart-to-heart talks with the general secretary]. Beijing: Zhongguo shehui kexue chubanshe, 1996.

"Why Must We Unremittingly Oppose Bourgeois Liberalization?" *Renmin ribao*, April 24, 1991, p. 5, trans. FBIS-CHI, April 26, 1991, pp. 18–21.

Williamson, John. "The Washington Consensus as Policy Prescription for Development." Lecture delivered at the World Bank, January 13, 2004. Retrieved from www.petersoninstitute.org/publications/papers/williamson0204.pdf

World Bank. *The State in a Changing World*. New York: Oxford University Press, 1997.

Wu Bangguo. "Guanyu guoyou qiye gaige yu fazhan de jige wenti" [Several problems regarding the reform and development of SOEs]. *Zhongyang dangxiao baogaoxuan* 18 (1996): 3.

Wu, Guoguang. "Documentary Politics: Hypotheses, Process, and Case Studies." In Carol Lee Hamrin and Suisheng Zhao (eds.), *Decision-Making in Deng's China: Perspectives from Insiders*. Armonk, NY: M. E. Sharpe, 1995, pp. 24–38.

Zhulu shiwuda: Zhongguo quanli qiju [Toward the Fifteenth Party Congress: China's power game]. Hong Kong: Taipingyang shiji yanjiusuo, 1997.

Wu Jiaxiang. "Xin quanwei zhuyi shuping" [Discussing the new authoritarianism]. *Shijie jingji daobao*, January 16, 1989; reprinted in Qi Mo (ed.), *Xin quanwei zhuyi*, pp. 4–8.

Wu Jinglian. "Guanyu gaige zhanlüe xuanze de ruogan sikao" [Some thoughts about choices in reform strategy]. *Jingji yanjiu* 2 (February 1987): 3–14.

Jihua jingji haishi shichang jingji [Planned economy or market economy]. Beijing: Zhongguo jingji chubanshe, 1993.

"Xiang furen kaiqiang hui daozhi hen yanzhong de shehui houguo" [Opening fire on the rich will lead to very serious social consequences]. Retrieved from http://news.cnfol.com/051125/101,1604,1559725,00.shtml

Wu, Vivian. "Ex-Naval Chief Expelled by NPC." *South China Morning Post*, June 30, 2006.

Wu Yan, and Gu Zhaonong. "Jiji yinzi mo panghuang" [We should not hestitate to import capital]. *Renmin ribao*, July 16, 1996, pp. 1–2.

Xia Changyong. "Zhonggong zhongyang ban bu 'Zhongguo gongchandang dangnei jiandu tiaoli (shixing)' he 'Zhongguo gongchandang jilu chufen tiaoli'" [CCP regulations on inner-Party supervision and rules for disciplinary punishment]. *Renmin ribao*, February 18, 2004.

Xiang Jingquan. "Review and Prospects of China's Economic Development." *Guangming ribao*, trans. FBIS-CHI, March 19, 1993, pp. 48–50.

"Xiangqile 'zai mai yetian xin butong'" [Thinking of "the lout who sells his grandfather's land without remorse"]. *Baokan wenzhai*, April 27, 2000, p. 2.

Xiao Gongqin. "Jingti jiduan minzu zhuyi" [Be careful of extreme nationalism]. Posted under "Guanyu Zhongguo minzu zhuyi de taolun (yi)" [Discussion of China's nationalism (one)] on www.jczs.com.cn, June 9, 1999.

"Qingmo xinzheng yu Zhongguo xiandaihua yanjiu" [The new policies of the late Qing and the study of Chinese modernization]. *Zhanlüe yu guanli* 1 (November 1993): 61–6.

Weijizhong de biange: Qingmo xiandaihua jinchengzhong de jijin yu baoshou [Change in the midst of crisis: Radicalism and conservatism in the course of modernization in the late Qing]. Shanghai: Sanlian, 1999.

"Wuxu bianfa de zai fanxing" [A new reflection on the reform of 1898]. *Zhanlüe yu guanli* 4 (1995): 11–20.

Xiao Gongqin ji [Collected essays of Xiao Gongqin]. Harbin: Heilongjiang jiaoyu chubanshe, 1995.

"'Yan Fu beilun' yu jindai xinbaoshou zhuyi biange guan" [The "Yanfu paradox" and the neoconservative view of change]. In *Xiao Gongqin ji*, pp. 18–41.

Xiao He. "Yuanhua an he dangjun gaoceng de guanxi" [The relationship between the Yuanhua case and the upper echelons of the Party and army]. *Kaifang*, October 2000, pp. 15–18.

Xibu dakaifa zhanlüe juece ruogan wenti [Several issues concerning the strategic decision to open widely the west]. Beijing: Zhongyang wenxian chubanshe, 2000.

Xin Mao. "Gaige yu jingjiren" [Reform and economic man]. In Shi Liaozi (ed.), *Beijing dixia "wanyanshu,"* pp. 201–30.

Xing Bensi. "Emphasis on Study, Politics, and Uprightness as Fine Party Traditions." *Qiushi* 7 (April 1997): 2–10, trans. FBIS-CHI-97-106, June 5, 1997.

"Jianchi Makesi zhuyi bu dongyao" [Uphold Marxism without wavering]. *Renmin ribao*, June 6, 1996, p. 9.

Xu, Ben. *Disenchanted Democracy*. Ann Arbor, MI: University of Michigan Press, 2000.

"Shenma shi Zhongguo de 'houxin shiqi'?" [What is China's "post-new period"?]. *Ershiyi shiji* 8 (1996): 74–83.

"Wang Shan qi ren" [This person, Wang Shan]. In Liu Zhifeng, *Jieshi Zhongguo*, pp. 25–63.

Xu Jilin. *Ling yizhong qimeng* [Another type of enlightenment]. Guangzhou: Huacheng chubanshe, 1999.

"Xunqiu 'disantiao daolu' – guanyu 'ziyouzhuyi' yu 'xinzuopai' de duihua" [Searching for a "third way" – a conversation on "liberalism" and the "new left"]. In Xu Jilin, *Ling yizhong qimeng* [Another type of enlightenment], pp. 276–302.

Xu Ming (ed.). *Guanjian shike: Dangdai Zhongguo jindai jiejue de ershiqi ge wenti* [The critical moment: Twenty-seven problems in contemporary China that need solving urgently]. Beijing: Jinri Zhongguo chubanshe, 1997.

Yan Jiaqi. *Toward a Democratic China: The Intellectual Biography of Yan Jiaqi*, trans. David S. K. Hong and Denis C. Mair. Honolulu, HI: University of Hawaii Press, 1992.

Yan Yunxiang. "The Politics of Consumerism in Chinese Society." In Tyrene White (ed.), *China Briefing 2000: The Continuing Transformation*, pp. 159–93. Armonk, NY: M. E. Sharpe, 2000.

Yang Jian, and Liu Siyang. "Hu Jintao tong Guangdong yiwu gongzuozhe zuotan, qiangdiao yao shizhong ba renmin qunzhong anwei leng nuan fang zai xin shang, quanli yifu zuohao feidianxing feiyan fangzhi gongzuo" [In a talk to medical workers in Guangdong Hu Jintao stresses keeping in mind the safety and well-being of the people and attending to the prevention of SARs]. *Renmin ribao*, April 15, 2003, p. 1.

Yang Ping. "The Third Eye – Commenting on *Seeing China through a Third Eye*," *Beijing qingnian bao*, June 25, 1994, p. 3, trans. FBIS-CHI, August 11, 1994, pp. 20–1.

Yang Shangkun. "Zai jinian Xinhai geming bashi zhounian dahuishang de jianghua" [Talk at the meeting to commemorate the eightieth anniversary of the Revolution of 1911]. In *Shisanda yilai*, vol. 3, pp. 1713–19.

Yang Zhongmei. *Jiang Zemin zhuan* [Biography of Jiang Zemin]. Taipei: Shibao wenhua, 1996.

Yao Fan. "How Comrade Zhao Ziyang Weakened the Party's Ideological and Political Work." *Guangming ribao*, August 25, 1989, p. 1, trans. FBIS-CHI, August 29, 1989, pp. 8–10.

Ye Jundong. "Yanfang quanli shikong" [Rigorously guard against a loss of control of power]. *Liaowang*, April 12, 2004, p. 11.

Yen Shen-tsun. "Deng Xiaoping's Talk during His Inspection of Shoudu Iron and Steel Complex." *Kuang chiao ching* 238, July 16, 1992, pp. 6–7, trans. FBIS-CHI, July 17, 1992, pp. 7–8.

"Yi gaige cu wending zhong fazhan," *Jingji yanjiu* 7 (July 1990): 3–19.

Yi jia yan [pseud.]. "'He Shang' xuanyangle shenma?" [What is "River Elegy" propagating?]. *Renmin ribao*, July 19, 1989.

Yi Ren. "Zhuozhuo huiyi de qianqian houhou" [Before and after the Zhuozhuo meeting]. *Renmin ribao*, February 14, 1990.

Yin Baoyun. "Minzu zhuyi yu xiandai jingji fazhan" [Nationalism and contemporary economic development]. *Zhanlüe yu guanli* 3 (June 1994): 13–15.

Yin Yen. "Hu Jiwei Served with Warning after Releasing Articles Criticizing CCP Autocracy and Exposing Its Errors in June 4 Incident." *Sing tao jih pao*, January 23, 1998, trans. FBIS-CHI, January 27, 1998.

"Yingxiang woguo guojia anquan de ruogan yinsu" [Several factors influencing our country's national security]. In Shi Liaozi (ed.), *Beijing dixia "wanyanshu,"* pp. 25–48.

"Yiwei yanjiusheng guanyu gaoxiao sixiang zhandi wenti de laixin" [A letter from a graduate student on the question of the ideological front at schools of higher learning]. *Guangming ribao*, March 29, 2000, p. 1.

"Yongyuan baochi he fayang jianku fendou jingshen" [Hold on to and develop the spirit of bitter struggle forever]. *Jiefangjun bao*, April 22, 1996, pp. 1, 6.

Yu Guanghua. "Xinquanwei zhuyi de shehui jichu ji huanxiang" [The social foundation and illusions of the new authoritarianism]. *Zhengming* 4 (1989): 42.

Yu Haocheng. "Zhongguo xuyao xin quanwei zhuyi ma?" [Does China need the new authoritarianism?]. In Rosen and Zou (eds.), "The Chinese Debate on the New Authoritarianism (III)," pp. 44–55.

Yu Jianrong. "Nongcun hei'e shili he jiceng zhengquan tuihua: Hunan diaocha" [The evil forces in rural areas and the deterioration of grassroots administration: An investigation of Hunan]. *Zhanlüe yu guanli* 5 (September/October 2003): 1–14.

  "Nongmin you zuzhi kangzheng jiqi zhengzhi fengxian: Hunan sheng H xian diaocha" [Organized struggles of the peasants and the political risks involved:

An investigation of county H of Hunan province]. *Zhanlüe yu guanli* 3 (May/June 2003): 1–16.

Yuecun zhengzhi: Zhuangxingqi Zhongguo xiangcun zhengzhi jiegou de bianqian [The politics of Yue village: The changes in the political structure of the Chinese countryside in a period of transition]. Beijing: Shangwu yinshuguan, 2001.

Yu Keping, Huang Ping, Xie Shuguang, and Gao Jian (eds.). *Zhongguo moshi yu "Beijing gongshi": Chaoyue "Huashengdun gongshi"* [The Chinese model and the "Beijing Consensus": Transcending the "Washington Consensus"]. Beijing: Shehui kexue wenxian chubanshe, 2006.

Yu Quanyu. "Qianyan: Women de guojia dayou xiwang" [Preface: There is great hope for China]. In Fang Ning et al. (eds.), *Quanqiuhua yinyingxia de Zhongguo zhilu*, pp. 1–4.

"Zan dangdai qingnian de 'sixiang jiefang'" [Praising the "open-mindedness" of contemporary youth]. *Zhenli de zhuiqiu* 1 (January 2000): 1–3.

Yu Xinyan [pseud. Xu Weicheng]. *"Preface to Practice and Future of Contemporary Socialism."* *Renmin ribao*, August 19, 1991, trans. FBIS-CHI, August 27, 1991, pp. 29–30.

Yu Yingshi. "Zailun Zhongguo xiandai sixiang zhongde jijin yu baoshou" [Again discussing radicalism and conservatism in the history of modern Chinese thought]. *Ershiyi shiji* 10 (1992): 143–9.

"Zhongguo jindai sixiangshi zhongde jijin yu baoshou" [Radicalism and conservatism in the history of modern Chinese thought]. *Lishi yuekan* 6 (June 1990): 135–46.

Yuan Mu. "Firmly, Accurately, and Comprehensively Implement the Party's Basic Line – Preface to 'Guidance for Studying the Government Work Report to the Fifth Session of the Seventh NPC'." *Renmin ribao*, April 14, 1992, trans. FBIS-CHI, April 16, 1992, pp. 20–3.

"Zhongguo gongren jieji shi Zhongguo gongchandang bu ke dongyao de jieji jichu" [China's working class is the unshakable class basis of the Communist Party of China]. *Dangdai sichao* 1 (February 20, 1997): 2–19.

Yuan Yongsong, and Wang Junwei (eds.). *Zuoqing ershinian, 1957–1976* [Twenty years of leftism, 1957–1976]. Beijing: Nongcun duwu chubanshe, 1993.

Yueh Shan. "Central Advisory Commission Submits Letter to CCP Central Committee Opposing 'Rightist' Tendency." *Zhengming* 175, May 1, 1992, pp. 13–14, trans. FBIS-CHI, April 30, 1992, pp. 15–16.

"Zai duiwai kaifang zhong hongyang aiguo zhuyi jingshen" [Continue to hold high the patriotic spirit in the course of opening to the outside world]. *Jiefangjun bao*, April 8, 1996, pp. 1, 6.

Zha, Jianying. *China Pop: How Soap Operas, Tabloids, and Bestsellers are Transforming a Culture.* New York: New Press, 1995.

Zhan Tianyang. "Jingti 'gonggong zhishi fenzi' sichao" [Beware of the intellectual tide of "public intellectuals"]. *Guangming ribao*, December 14, 2004.

Zhang Bingjiu. "Jingji tizhi gaige he zhengzhi tizhi gaige de jincheng yu xietiao" [The progress and coordination between economic and political system reform]. In Liu Jun and Li Lin (eds.), *Xinquanwei zhuyi*, pp. 1–26, trans. Rosen and Zou (eds.), "The Chinese Debate on the New Authoritarianism (I)," pp. 8–35.

Zhang Fa, Zhang Yiwu, and Wang Yichuan. "Cong 'xiandaixing' dao 'Zhonghuaxing'" [From "modernity" to "Chineseness"]. *Wenyi zhengming* 2 (March 1994): 10–20.

Zhang Kuan. "OuMeiren yanzhong de 'feiwo zulei'" ["Other races" in the eyes of Europeans and Americans]. *Dushu* (September 1993): 3–9

"Sayide de 'dongfang zhuyi' yu xifang de hanxue yanjiu" [Said's "Orientalism" and Western sinology]. *Liaowang* 27 (July 3, 1995): 36–7.

"Wenhua xinzhimin de keneng" [The possibility of cultural neocolonialism]. *Tianya* 2 (1996): 16–23.

"Zaitan Sayide" [Another discussion of Said]. *Dushu* (October 1994): 8–14.

Zhang Longxi. "Duoyuan shehui zhongde wenhua piping" [Cultural criticism in a pluralistic society]. *Ershiyi shiji* 2 (1996): 18–25.

Zhang Ming, and Li Shitao (eds.). *Zhishi fenzi lichang* [The standpoint of intellectuals], 3 vols. Changchun: Shidai wenyi chubanshe, 1999.

Zhang Weiguo. "Chen Xitong an yu quanli douzheng" [The Chen Xitong case and the struggle for power]. *Beijing zhi chun* 30 (November 1995): 30–2.

Zhang Weiying. *Qiye de qiyejia – Qiyue lilun* [Entrepreneurs of enterprises – Contract theory]. Shanghai: Sanlian, 1995.

"Suoyouzhi, zhili jiegou ji weituo – daili guanxi – jian ping Cui Zhiyuan he Zhou Qiren de yixie guandian" [Ownership, management structure, and principal–agent relations – Also critiquing some views of Cui Zhiyuan and Zhou Qiren]. *Jingji yanjiu* 9 (September 1996): 3–15, 53.

Zhang Wenmin et al. (eds.). *Zhongguo jingji dalunzhan* [Great debates on the Chinese economy]. Beijing: Jingji guanli chubanshe, 1996 (vol. 1) and 1997 (vol. 2).

Zhang Xiangping. "Qimeng, mincui, daminzhu de lishi fansi" [Reflections on the history of enlightenment, populism, and great democracy]. *Zhanlüe yu guanli* 5 (October 1994): 15–19.

Zhang Ximang. "Xinwen fazhi yu shehui fazhan" [Journalism, rule by law, and social development]. *Fangfa* 3 (1998): 4–6.

Zhang Xueli. *Zhongguo heyi shuobu* [How China says no]. Beijing: Hualing chubanshe, 1996.

Zhang Xuwu, Li Ding, and Xie Minggan (eds.). *Zhongguo siying jingji nianjian, 1996* [Yearbook of China's private economy, 1996]. Beijing: Zhonghua gongshang lianhe chubanshe, 1996.

Zhang Zhuoyuan. "Promoting Economic Rectification by Deepening Reform." *Renmin ribao*, November 27, 1989, trans. FBIS-CHI, December 7, 1989, pp. 28–31.

Zhao Guoliang, and Cui Jianlin (eds.). *Lixiang zhi guang – Nanjieren kaizhan gongyouzhi dataolun* [A ray of idealism – People of Nanjie open a discussion on public ownership]. 3 vols. Beijing: Zhonggong zhongyang dangxiao chubanshe, 1998.

Zhao Shilin (ed.). *Fang "zuo" beiwanglu* [Memorandum on opposing "leftism"]. Taiyuan: Shuhai chubanshe, 1992.

Zhao Shukai. "Lishixing tiaozhan: Zhongguo nongcun de chongtu yu zhili" [A historic challenge: Conflict and governance in China's villages]. In Ru Xin, Lu Xueyi, and Li Peilin (eds.), *2004 nian: Zhongguo shehui xingshi fenxi yu yuce*, pp. 212–23.

"Nongcun zhili: Zuzhi he chongtu" [Governance in villages: Organization and conflict]. *Zhanlüe yu guanli* 6 (November/December 2003): 1–8.

Zhao, Suisheng. *A Nation-State by Construction: Dynamics of Modern Chinese Nationalism*. Stanford, CA: Stanford University Press, 2004.

"Chinese Intellectuals' Quest for National Greatness and Nationalistic Writing in the 1990s." *The China Quarterly* 152 (Dec. 1997): 725–45.

"Deng Xiaoping's Southern Tour: Elite Politics in Post-Tiananmen China." *Asian Survey* 33 (August 1993): 739–56.

In Search of a Right Place? Chinese Nationalism in the Post-Cold War World. Hong Kong Institute for Asia–Pacific Studies, Chinese University of Hong Kong, 1997.

Zhao Yiheng. "'Houxue' yu Zhongguo xinbaoshou zhuyi" ["Post-ism" and China's neoconservatism]. *Ersihyi shiji* 2 (1995): 4–15.

Zhao Ziyang. "Further Emancipate the Mind and Further Liberate the Productive Forces." *Renmin ribao*, February 8, 1988, trans. FBIS-CHI, February 8, 1988, pp. 12–14.

Zheng Bijian. "'Sange daibiao' zhongyao lunshu yu mianxiang ershiyi shiji de Zhongguo gongchandang" [The important exposition of the "three represents" and the CCP facing the twenty-first century]. In *Shenru xuexi "sange daibiao" quanmian luoshi "sange daibiao"* [Study deeply the "Three Represents"; comprehensively implement the "Three Represents"], pp. 119–33. Beijing: Xuexi chubanshe, 2000.

Zheng Hongfan. "Zeng Qinghong zai zhongyang dangxiao shengbuji ganbu jinxiuban biye dianli shang qiangdiao wei shixian shiliuda queding de mubiao renwu nuli fendou" [At the graduation ceremony of the Central Party School's provincial-ministerial-level cadre training class, Zeng Qinghong stresses the need to work hard to realize the goal and tasks set at the Sixteenth Party Congress], *Renmin ribao*, November 30, 2002.

Zheng, Yongnian. *Discovering Chinese Nationalism in China*. Cambridge: Cambridge University Press, 1999.

"Zhonggong zhongyang guanyu goujian shehui zhuyi hexie shehui ruogan zhongda wenti de jueding" [CCP Central Committee decision on several problems in constructing a socialist harmonious society]. *Renmin ribao*, October 19, 2006.

"Zhonggong zhongyang guanyu jiaqiang dang de zhizheng nengli jianshe de jueding" [CCP decision on enhancing the Party's ability to govern]. *Renmin ribao*, September 26, 2004, pp. 1–2.

"Zhonggong zhongyang guanyu jinyibu zhili zhengdun he shenhua gaige de jueding (zhaiyao)" [CCP Central Committee decision on furthering improvement and rectification and deepening reform (outline)]. In *Shisanda yilai*, vol. 2, pp. 680–708.

"Zhonggong zhongyang guanyu wanshan shehui zhuyi shichang jingji tizhi ruogan wenti de jueding" [The CCO Central Committee decision on several issues related to perfecting a socialist market economy system]. *Renmin ribao*, October 22, 2003, pp. 1–2.

"Zhonggong zhongyang guanyu zai quandang xingqi xuexi guanche 'sange daibiao' zhongyao sixiang xin gaochao de tongzhi" [CCP Central Committee circular on whipping up a new high tide in the study and implementation of the "Three Represents"]. *Renmin ribao*, June 23, 2003, p. 1.

"Zhonggong zhongyang, Guowuyuan guanyu jinqi zuo jijian qunzhong guanxin de shi de jueding" [Decision of the CCP Central Committee and State Council regarding doing a few things of concern to the masses in the present period]. In *Shisanda yilai*, vol. 2, pp. 555–7.

"Zhonggong zhongyang, Guowuyuan guanyu tuijin shehui zhuyi xinnongcun jianshe de ruogan yijian" [Some opinions of the CCP Central Committee and the State Council on advancing the building of a socialist countryside]. *Renmin ribao*, February 22, 2006, pp. 1–2.

"Zhonggong zhongyang jueding: Dui Chen Liangyu tongzhi yanzhong weiji wenti li'an jiancha" [CCP Central Committee decision: Open an investigation into Comrade Chen Liangyu's serious violation of discipline]. *Renmin ribao*, September 26, 2006, p. 1.

Zhonggong zhongyang wenxian yanjiushi (ed.). *Shehui zhuyi jingshen wenming jianshe wenxian xuanbian* [Selected documents on building a socialist spiritual civilization]. Beijing: Zhonggong zhongyang wenxian yanjiushi, 1996.

"Zhonggong zhongyang zhengzhiju changwei weiyuanhui zhaokai huiyi yanjiu jinyibu jiaqiang feidianxing feiyan fangzhi gongzuo" [Politburo Standing Committee convenes meeting to study ways to strengthen SARS prevention work]. *Renmin ribao*, April 18, 2003, p. 1.

Zhonggong zhongyang zuzhibu ketizu (ed.). *Zhongguo diaocha baogao: 2000–2001 xin xingshi xia renmin neibu maodun yanjiu* [China research report: Contradictions among the people under the new circumstances of 2000–2001]. Beijing: Zhongyang bianyiju chubanshe, 2001.

"Zhongguo gongchandang dangnei jiandu tiaoli (shixing)" [Regulations of the Communist Party of China on inner-Party supervision (provisional)]. *Renmin ribao*, February 18, 2004, pp. 1–2.

"Zhongguo gongchandang dishiliuci quanguo daibiao dahui zai Jing bimu." *Renmin ribao*, November 15, 2002, p. 1.

"Zhongguo gongchandang dishisanjie zhongyang weiyuanhui diqice quanti huiyi gongbao" [Communiqué of the Seventh Plenary Session of the thirteenth CCP Central Committee]. In *Shisanda yilai*, vol. 2, pp. 1420–6.

"Zhongguo gongchandang dishisanjie zhongyang weiyuanhui disice quanti huiyi gongbao" [Communiqué of the Fourth Plenary Session of the Thirteenth CCP Central Committee]. In *Shisanda yilai*, vol. 2, pp. 543–6.

Zhongguo jingji nianjian, 1995 [Chinese economic yearbook 1995]. Beijing: Zhongguo jingji nianjianshe, 1995.

Zhongguo jushi fenxi zhongxin (ed.). *Beijing zaochun de jiaofeng* [Crossing swords in the early spring in Beijing]. Hong Kong: Mingjing chubanshe, 1998.

Zhongguo kexueyuan guoqing fenxi yanjiu xiaozu. *Shengcun yu fazhan* [Survival and development]. Beijing kexue chubanshe, 1996.

"Zhonghua renmin gongheguo wuquanfa (cao'an)" [Draft Property Law of the People's Republic of China]. *Renmin ribao*, July 11, 2005.

"Zhongliu Loses Lawsuit against 'Jiaofeng'." *Ming pao*, April 23, 1999, p. B15, trans. FBIS-CHI-1999-0423, April 23, 1999.

"Zhongxuan bu fachu tongzhi yaoqiu dali hongyang he peiyu minzu jingshen, qieshi jiaqiang fangzhi feidian xuanchuan sixiang gongzuo" [Central Propaganda Department issues a notice asking to make a great effort to develop and train the people's spirit, and earnestly strengthen propaganda work to prevent SARS]. *Renmin ribao*, April 27, 2003, p. 4.

"Zhongyang junwei zhaokai 'Jiang Zemin guofang he jundui jianshe sixiang xuexi gangyao' chuban zuotanhui" [Central Military Commission holds forum on publication of "Study Outline for Jiang Zemin's Thinking on National Defense and Army Building"]. *Renmin ribao*, August 1, 2003, p. 1.

Zhou Ruijin. *Ning zuo tongku de qingxingzhe* (I'd rather be clear-headed, if in pain). Shanghai: Wenhui chubanshe, 2003.

"Ruhe kandai gaige disanci dazhenglun" (How to think about the third great debate on reform).Dongfang wang (June 2, 2006). Retrieved from www.wyzxwyzx.com/Article/Class4/200606/7167.html

Zhu Jianhong, and Jiang Yaping. "Development and Standardization Are Necessary – Perspective of Real Estate Business." *Renmin ribao*, May 11, 1993, trans. FBIS-CHI, May 24, 1993, pp. 56–7.

Zhu Rongji. "Summarize Experiences in Clearing Debt Defaults and Preventing New Defaults to Ensure Sound Development of the National Economy." Xinhua, December 25, 1992, in FBIS-CHI, December 28, 1992, pp. 36–9.

Zhu Tao. "A Brief Introduction to the Special Zones Debate." *Neibu wengao*, trans. Stanley Rosen (ed.), *Debates over Special Economic Zones, Income Polarization, and Other Related Issues* (*Chinese Economic Studies* 29(3):36–46, May/June 1996).

Zi Yu. "Shei zai zhanling daxuesheng de sixiang zhandi" [Who is occupying the ideological front of university students?]. *Zhongliu* 4 (April 2000): 42–4.

Zou Dang [Tsou Tang]. *Ershi shiji Zhongguo zhengzhi: Cong hongguan lishi yu weiguan xingdong jiaodu kan* [Twentieth-century Chinese politics: Viewed from the perspective of macro history and micro action]. Hong Kong: Oxford University Press, 1994.

"Zuo Dapei, Yang Fan, Han Deqiang jiu zuzhi guoyou zichan liushi, gaohao guoyou qiye zhidang he guojia lingdaoren de gongkaixin" [Zuo Dapei, Yang Fan, and Han Deqiang letter to Party and state leaders urging an end to the loss of state property and an improvement of state-owned enterprises]. Retrieved from www.wyzxwyzx.com/2005/ShowArticle.asp?ArticleID=6179

Zysman, John. *Government, Markets, and Growth*. Ithaca, NY: Cornell University Press, 1983.

OTHER SOURCES

AFP. Agence France-Presse
Beijing qingnian bao
Beijing radio
Beijing television service
Beijing zhi chun
China Central Television
China Daily
Ching chi tao pao
Ching pao
FBIS-CHI. Foreign Broadcast Information Service, *Daily Report: China*
Financial Times
Guangdong radio
Guangming ribao
Hong Kong Standard
Hsin pao
Jiefangjun bao
Jingji daobao
Jingji ribao
Jinrong shibao
Kaifang
Kuang chiao ching
Lien ho pao
Ming pao
Minzhu yu fazhi
Nanfang ribao
New York Times
Renmin ribao
Shijie ribao
Sing tao jih pao
South China Morning Post
Ta kung pao
Tangtai
Wall Street Journal
Washington Post
Wen wei po
Xinhua News Service
Xinjiang television
Xinwanbao
Zhengming
Zhongguo qingnian bao
Zhongguo tongxun she

Index

1898 Reform Movement, 91, 101, 102
1911 Revolution, 60, 92, 101

Academy of Chinese Culture, 8
agriculture
   2006 policy, 268–9
   farming population, 17, 236
   peasants, 154–5, 232–3, 236, 273
   seizure of land, 244
Allbright, Madeline, 217
Asian values, 148–52
Australia, 2

Bao Zunxin, 8
Barshefsky, Charlene, 217
Bei Dao, 260
'Beijing Consensus', 259–60
Beijing Spring, 201, 204–8
Beijing University, 15, 207–8, 260
Beijing Young Economists Association, 93
Berger, Samuel, 217
Bo Xicheng, 93
Bo Xilai, 282
Bo Yibo, 61, 69, 76, 93, 201, 279, 282
Boutros-Ghali, Boutros, 222
Boxer Rebellion, 262
Brazil, 143
Brezhnev, Leonid, 191
Buchanan, James, 89
Bush, George H., 213
Bush, George W., 2, 119, 149

Cai Yuanpei, 134
Cao Gangchuan, 250, 282
Cao Jinqing, 233
Cao Siyuan, 193
Central Advisory Commission, 61, 65, 74, 76
Central Military Commission, 63–4, 241, 250,
   254–5, 277, 281
Central Work Conference (1980), 38
Chang Jung (Zhang Rong), 126

Chen Daixi (Yi Ren), 40
Chen Duxiu, 134, 187
Chen Guidi, 233
Chen Haosu, 93
Chen Liangyu, 240, 271, 277, 279, 281
Chen Xitong
   career, 25, 74
   corruption, 172–3, 271
   downfall, 208, 272
   hardliner, 24, 51
   ideological debate, 77
   Jiang and, 203
   Mayor of Beijing, 93, 172
   relations with Deng, 51, 77
   successors, 195
   on Tiananmen, 31
Chen Yi, Marshal, 93
Chen Yinke, 135
Chen Yuan, 54, 93–5, 110, 112, 113, 140, 166
Chen Yun
   career, 26, 54–5, 74
   conservative critique, 11, 22n1, 35–6, 38, 48–9,
      59, 61, 63, 94
   death, 168, 198, 272
   ideological debate, 65, 69, 265
   power, 24, 165, 278
   relations with Jiang Zemin, 76
   state planning, 88
   Tiananmen and, 34
Chen Zhili, 27
Chen Ziming, 26
Cheng Nien (Zheng Nian), 126
Cheng Weigao, 50–1
Chiang Kai-shek, 193
China Can Say No, 159–62, 166, 225
China Democracy Party, 214
Chinese Academy of Social Sciences, 43, 77
Chinese Communist Party
   3rd Plenum (2003), 243–4, 251–4, 258, 265,
      275
   4th Plenum (1994), 168–71

Chinese Communist Party (*cont.*)
    4th Plenum (2004), 255, 255–8
    5th Plenum (1996), 183–4
    5th Plenum (2005), 251, 268
    6th Plenum (1996), 188–9
    6th Plenum (2006), 271
    12th Congress (1982), 38
    13th Congress (1987), 23, 28n, 29, 31, 40, 64,
        179, 200
    14th Congress (1992), 14, 64, 70, 71–7, 79, 135,
        175, 177, 199, 267, 278
    15th Congress (1997), 137, 185, 198–203, 205,
        210, 242, 279
    16th Congress (2002), 231, 238–45, 243, 251,
        255, 271
    17th Congress (2007), 238, 269, 278–84
    39 Points, 38
    Beijing University and, 208
    constitution, 4, 282
    core, 22–3, 169, 196, 278
    governance, 256–7
    Guiding Rules on Inner Party Life, 4
    inner-party democracy, 171, 256, 257, 284
    legitimacy, 5, 111, 139
    May Fourth and, 134, 192
    PBSC 1992 members, 73
    PBSC 1997 members, 202
    PBSC 2002 members, 241
    PBSC 2007 members, 280
    PBSC retirement age, 279
    private entrepreneurs as members, 193, 273
    role, 1–2, 87
    Secretariat 1992, 73
    Secretariat 1997, 202
    Secretariat 2002, 241
    Secretariat 2007, 281
    Seeking Truth, 226–7
    third generation, 168–71, 278
Christianity, 120
Christopher, Warren, 149, 191
Chun Tao, 233
Ci Xi, Empress, 102
Clinton, Bill, 15, 148, 149, 191, 213, 214–15, 217–18
Coase, Ronald, 89
collective leadership, 4, 54
colonialism, 103, 104, 125, 127, 128, 151–2, 226
colour revolutions, 260
Columbus, Christopher, 135
commercialism, 114–15, 116
Communist Manifesto, 83
Communist Youth League, 238, 278
Confucian capitalism, 121, 149–50
Confucianism, 13, 91, 101, 121, 127, 192, 193,
    250
consumerism, 114–15, 116

corruption
    Chen Xitong, 172–3, 271
    Cheng Weigao, 50
    fight against, 171–4, 257, 258, 270
    growth, 121
    Jiang and, 271, 277
    political use, 277
    reform and, 167, 274
    scale, 16–17
    scandals, 271, 277, 279
    SOEs, 262–4
cosmopolitanism, 7, 16, 91, 103, 107, 108, 109,
    123, 136
Cox, Christopher, 215
critical legal studies, 130
Cuba, 3
Cui Zhiyuan, 129–31, 132, 133, 138, 140, 152, 166,
    222
cultural fever, 8, 11, 106–7, 108
Cultural Revolution, 4, 7, 25, 45, 91, 122, 129–30,
    153, 155–6, 159
culture
    1980s debates, 91
    Chinese tradition, 136
    colonial culture, 128
    commercialization, 13, 116–17, 120
    consumerism, 114–15, 116
    cultural imperialism, 106, 151, 226–7
    cultural liberalism, rejection, 106–9
    cultural nationalism, 90, 150
    elite, 115, 120, 155
    harmony, 90
    Westernization, 105, 108–9, 138–9

Dai Yuanchen, 92
decentralization, 43–5, 86, 94, 96
deconstructionism, 125
democracy
    activists, 118–19, 166, 219
    Beijing Spring, 204
    democracy wall movement, 110
    democratic centralism, 196
    direct democracy, 138
    economic and cultural, 129, 130, 131, 138
    elite democracy, 11, 85
    globalization and, 129
    inner-party democracy, 171, 256, 257, 284
    Jiang and, 201
    liberal democracy, 124, 141
    neoauthoritarianism and, 85–7, 97, 98
    political debate, 185
    post-Tiananmen expectations, 7
    Russia, 114
    social democracy, 130
    socialist democracy, 256, 271, 283–4

United States and, 149
Wang Xiaodong, 226
Deng Lin, 254
Deng Liqun
  allies, 188
  career, 77
  foreign investment, 185
  leftism, 23, 55, 61, 63, 65, 71, 88, 124, 175, 176
  reform and, 72
Deng Nan, 49, 142
Deng Xiaoping
  1980s reforms, 103, 171
  allies, 172, 196
  choice of new leadership, 24–5
  collective leadership and, 4
  critics, 35–6, 109, 154, 156
  death, 193, 198, 272
  devolution of power, 183
  end of career, 63–4
  Hu Jintao and, 239, 277, 278
  ideology, 111, 175, 177, 186, 193, 267, 283
  illness, 168, 169
  intellectuals and, 7, 114
  June 4 incident, 205
  legacy, 200, 267, 272
  monetary policies, 114
  neostatism and, 142
  new authoritarianism, 71, 85
  Party status, 23, 36, 171
  post-Tiananmen period, 23–47
  power, 165, 203
  principles, 28–9
  regional policy, 147
  relations with Jiang Zemin, 76, 168, 174–5,
    199–200, 206
  revival of reform, 48–79, 88, 109, 114,
    172
  rule of law, 243
  southern tour, 14, 17, 62–3, 65, 71, 72, 74,
    109, 145, 153, 165, 168, 176, 178, 200, 206,
    267
  strategy, 35–7, 45, 165
  succession, 3, 239, 254, 278, 282
  Tiananmen and, 35, 241
Deng Zhifang, 172
developing countries, 151
development
  centrality, 239
  East Asian model, 87, 95, 96
  four small dragons, 63, 86, 121
  social stability and, 237–8
Ding Guan'gen, 30, 77, 174, 207, 220
Ding, X. L., 8
Ding Xueliang, 88
diplomacy, 2, 209–10

documentary politics, 60, 70
Duan Ruofei, 55

Eagleburger, Lawrence, 46
East Asian development model, 87, 95, 96
economic reform. *See* reform
Economic Work Conference (1990), 44–5
education, 237
elitism, 100, 108, 109
embassy bombing, 16, 167, 197, 217, 218–21,
    224–7, 274
enclosure movement, 178
Engels, Friedrich, 182
English Revolution, 92
Enlightenment
  1980s project, 123
  challenge, 113–39
  Chinese Enlightenment, 8–11
  contemporary Chinese liberalism, 131–9
  critique of May Fourth project, 124–31
  May Fourth tradition, 8, 11, 121–3, 134
  rejection, 88, 107–9
  Western thought, 123, 124
Enterprise Law, 51

Fang Jue, 204
Fang Li, 227
Fang Lizhi, 35, 47, 214
Fang Ning, 161, 225, 226
Fang Sheng, 65
Fang Weizhong, 77
Fay, Michael, 150
Feng Baoxing, 193–4
Fernandes, George, 249
feudal lord economy, 92
feudalism, 97, 107, 111, 122, 123
five-year plans
  seventh, 143, 145
  eighth, 43–5, 53
  ninth, 183
  eleventh, 268–9
foreign investment, 179–81
Foucault, Michel, 125
four small dragons, 63, 86, 121
France, 96, 143
French Revolution, 92
Friedman, Milton, 95
Fukuyama, Francis, 148, 149

gambling, 262
Gan Yang, 107, 222
Gang of Four, 33, 76
Gang Yang, 8
Gao Di, 60, 66, 71, 76, 175
Gao Shangquan, 266

Ge Yang, 26
Georgia, 258
Germany, 104–5, 154
globalization
   democracy and, 129
   effect on China, 124
   intellectual support, 135–6
   opposition, 9, 15–16
   political globalization, 259
   WTO and, 222–4
Goldman, Merle, 11
Gong Xiantian, 265–6
Gorbachev, Mikhail, 31, 52, 56, 61, 177, 191
Great Leap Forward, 78, 122, 154, 155, 159
Greenspan, Alan, 215
Gromyko, Andrei, 206
Gu Chujun, 262
Gu Mu, 157
Guerra, Alfonso, 35
Gulf War (1991), 56–7, 161
Guo Boxiong, 250–1

Han Deqiang, 262, 263
harmonious society, 253, 256, 269–71, 275, 282, 283
harmony, 90
Hayek, Friedrich von, 110
He Dongchang, 77
He Guoqiang, 281
He Jingzhi, 175
He Minxu, 270
He Qinglian, 178, 182
He Xin, 102, 103–6, 108, 113, 140, 152, 166
health care reform, 273
Holocaust, 127
Hong Kong, 63, 86, 222–3
Hong Xuezhi, 75, 76
housing reform, 273
Hu Angang, 140, 141–8, 152, 166, 197, 234
Hu Jintao
   3rd Plenum (2003), 251–4
   4th Plenum (2004), 255–8
   17th Party Congress, 278–84
   advisers, 113
   agenda, 274–5, 278
   allies, 74, 242, 246
   Australian speech 2003, 2
   background, 238
   career, 74, 240
   education, 12
   harmonious society, 253, 256, 269–71, 275, 282, 283
   Jiang Zemin and, 252–5, 269–70
   military control, 270

"people-centred" society, 252, 253, 255, 268, 270, 283
populism, 276
repression, 258–62, 275
SARS, 245–8
scientific development, 252, 253, 268, 279, 282, 283
social justice, 267–9, 271, 275
social stability concerns, 238
socialist democracy, 256, 271, 283–4
state capacity, 6, 255–6
succession, 278, 281
Three Represents, 243, 247, 248–51, 253, 270, 277, 283
transfer of power to, 6, 16, 239–45, 277, 278
Hu Jiwei, 71, 133, 205
Hu Qiaomu, 88, 124, 168, 198
Hu Qili, 24, 29, 30, 74, 84
Hu Shi, 134, 135
Hu Weixi, 159
Hu Yaobang
   1980s reformist, 11, 26
   Deng succession and, 3, 239
   downfall, 24, 28, 35, 40, 76, 85, 171, 187
   Hu Jintao and, 74
   intellectual allies, 192
   new authoritarianism and, 84
   spiritual civilization, 189
Hua Guofeng, 1, 3, 23, 200, 206, 239
Huang Ju, 169–70, 240, 271, 281
Huangfu Ping commentaries, 49, 55, 56, 58, 61
human rights, 105, 149, 150, 160, 217
Human Rights Commission, 160, 225
humanism, 120, 127
Hundred Flowers Movement, 155
Hungary, 96
Huntington, Samuel, 97, 99, 148–52

identity issue, 13
ideology
   control, 260–2
   decline, 105, 276–7
   definitions, 33
   importance, 5, 15, 261
IMF, 149–50, 223
imperial China, 3
incrementalism, 89–92, 102, 111, 112
India, 143, 226
individualism, 124, 134
Indonesia, 209
inequality, 144–8, 179, 182, 243–4, 268–9
institutional economics, 89
institutional fetishism, 131

intellectual property rights, 18, 222
intellectuals
 1990s shift, 15–16, 119–23, 165–8
 control, 260–2
 elite politics and, 165–8, 189
 ideological debate, 71
 impact, 113
 internationalization of discourse, 117
 loss of values, 120
 marginalization, 115–17
 national studies, 120–1
 neoconservatism, 83–112
 post-Tiananmen concerns, 2, 6–11
 pre-Tiananmen, 22
 professionalism, 12, 13
 public intellectuals, 261, 275
 state and, 2, 11–16
 Tiananmen shock, 9, 14, 21, 118–19
 traditional role, 13
 United States and, 119
international relations, 2, 209–10
internationalism, 117
Internet
 control, 261–2
 embassy bombing and, 224
 emergence, 10
 foreign firms, 218
 internationalization of discourse, 117
 Larry Lang affair, 264
 political criticism, 260
 property rights debate, 266
 SARS crisis, 247–8
Iraq, 226
Ishihara, Shintaro, 148, 150

Jameson, Fredric, 125
Japan
 alliance with, 104
 Asian values, 148
 East Asian crisis and, 222–3
 economic growth, 121
 global ambitions, 104
 Sino-Japanese War, 23, 88, 219
Ji Fangping, 261
Ji Xianlin, 121–2
Jia Pingwa, 116
Jia Quinglin, 195, 240, 279
Jiang Chunyun, 170, 196
Jiang Hong, 110
Jiang Mianhong, 271
Jiang Qing, 156
Jiang Shangqing, 25, 75
Jiang Yanyong, 245, 246
Jiang Yihua, 151–2

Jiang Zemin
 9th NPC, 208–13
 16th Party Congress, 238–45
 advisers, 113, 207
 allies, 27, 76, 168, 174, 190, 207, 213, 238, 240, 246, 255, 269–70, 279, 281
 Beijing Spring, 204–8
 career, 24–6, 74–6
 Chen Zitong and, 203, 271
 CMC, retirement from, 254–5, 277
 consolidation of power, 198–203, 239
 corruption and, 271, 277
 critics, 68–9, 193–6
 education, 12, 25
 embassy bombing, impact, 224
 era, 1–2, 5–6
 general secretary, 23–7, 30, 39, 64
 ideological debate, 70, 77, 78, 185
 international relations, 46
 legacy, 252–3, 272–3
 military support, 75–6
 neoconservatism, 276
 origins, 238
 reform and, 33, 48, 57, 60, 63, 66, 70, 188, 189–95
 regional policy, 146–7
 retirement, 272, 279
 rise to power, 165–96, 278
 SARS crisis, 247–8, 249
 Selected Works, 270, 271
 succession, 6, 239–45, 277, 278
 Three Represents, 5, 243, 248–51, 253, 270, 277, 282
 WTO membership, 211–21
Jiao Guobiao, 260
Jin Guantao, 8
Jing Wang, 107

Kang Youwei, 91, 101, 102, 135
Keynes, John Maynard, 95
Klein, Joe, 154
Kosovo, 216–17
Kyrgyzstan, 258

Lake, Anthony, 148–9, 191
land sales, 178
Lang Xiangping (Larry Lang), 262–7, 274
law
 growth, 5
 rule of law, 137, 205, 242–3, 271, 274
 Western concept, 124
Lee Hsien Loong, 146
Lee Kuan Yew, 108, 146, 150
Lee, T. D., 37
Lee Teng-hui, 160, 184, 211

Lei Yi, 138–9, 205
Leng Rong, 68
Leninism, 3, 6
Li Baojin, 270
Li Changchun, 247, 248, 279
Li Changping, 233
Li Chengrui, 42
Li Datong, 262
Li Jinai, 250
Li Keqiang, 242, 281
Li Lanquing, 213, 214
Li Peilin, 234, 237–8, 252
Li Peng
　5th Plenum, 183–4
　16th Party Congress, 240–1
　conservative reaction, 23–4, 30, 44, 45, 52, 53,
　　61
　eclipse, 168, 170, 202–3, 208, 212, 221
　ideological debate, 67, 78, 200
　Korean trip (1994), 169
　opposition to WTO, 213–14, 218
　retirement, 272
　State Council, 180
　state planning, 40–1, 42, 53
　succession, 75
　Tianjin Party Secretary, 25
　Zhao downfall and, 29–32, 33
Li Qeqiang, 281
Li Qiyan, 172
Li Rui, 133, 262
Li Ruihuan, 24, 27, 30, 37, 50, 52, 54, 60, 61, 279
Li Shenzhi, 133–7, 139
Li Xiannian, 24, 33, 49, 69, 75, 76, 168, 198, 213,
　　272, 278
Li Xiaoming, 116
Li Ximing, 74, 76, 173, 175, 272
Li Yuanchao, 242, 281
Li Zehou, 92, 107, 122–3, 187
Li Zemin, 54
Li Zhonghua, 8
Liang Congje, 260
Liang Guangjie, 250
Liang Qichao, 91, 101
Liao Xilong, 250
liberalism
　14th Party Congress, 72–7
　contemporary Chinese liberalism,
　　131–9
　cultural liberalism, rejection, 106–9
　Hu Jintao repression, 258–62
　intellectuals and, 8–11
　liberal democracy, 124, 141
　liberal economics, 114, 131, 259, 263–7
　May Fourth tradition, 123
　new authoritarianism and, 85–7

New Left and, 125
Study Group on Neoliberarlism, 259
World Economic Herald, 26–7, 31, 190
WTO and, 221–2, 223–4
Lin Biao, 3, 52, 156, 239
Lin Ruo, 50
Ling Jihua, 281
Ling Zhijun, 206
literature crisis, 120
Liu Binyan, 35
Liu Guoguang, 43, 264–5
Liu Huaqing, 74, 76, 110
Liu Huaqiu, 191
Liu Ji, 27, 174, 190, 192, 200, 206, 207
Liu Junning, 205, 223–4
Liu Qi, 240
Liu Shaoqi, 3, 31, 239
Liu Xiabao, 261
Liu Xiaofeng, 8, 120
Liu Yandong, 282
Liu Yunshan, 261
Liu Zaifu, 92, 187
Liu Zhengwei, 172
Liu Zhifeng, 156
Liu Zhihua, 270
Lou Jiwei, 147
Lu Jianhua, 235
Lu Xueyi, 234–5, 236–7, 252
Lu Xun, 134
Lung Ying-tai, 262
Luo Gan, 210, 240–1

Ma Hong, 42, 93
Ma Licheng, 205, 206
Ma Xiaowei, 245
Mahathir, Mohamad, 150
Malaysia, 223
management buy-outs, 262–4, 274
Mao Yushi, 260
Mao Zedong
　Deng and, 68
　historiography, 133, 153, 154–6
　Hunan province, 232
　ideology, 122, 187, 277
　intellectuals and, 7–8, 129–30
　legacy, 76, 129–30, 139, 189, 199
　Marxism, 111, 128
　metaphors, 52, 62, 220, 243
　populism, 159
　power, 4, 23, 54, 183, 200, 240
　succession, 3, 239, 278
　"Ten Great Relationships," 189
marketization of politics, 182
martial law, 29–30, 47
Marx, Karl, 182

Marxism, 8, 14, 34, 39, 77, 111, 115, 128, 130, 182, 185, 186, 189, 199, 226, 261, 264, 273
Marxism-Leninism, 5, 109, 132, 139, 148, 156, 175, 182, 192, 200, 275
Marxism-Leninism Academy, 68
Marxism-Leninism-Mao Zedong Thought, 28, 31, 58, 68, 77, 189, 283
mass disturbances, 231–2
May Fourth Movement
  critique, 106–7, 124–31, 139
  intellectual mission, 115
  nationalism, 158
  radicalism, 91
  rejection of Confucianism, 192
  tradition, 8, 11, 121–3, 134
Mencius, 132, 252
Meng Xuenong, 245–6
middle class, 235–6, 251
Migdal, Joel, 141
military
  CMC, 63–4, 241, 250, 254–5, 277, 281
  Hu Jintao control, 270
  ideological debate, 67
  New Fourth Army, 75–6
  PLA, 67, 250, 282
  support for Deng, 69, 71, 75
Milosevic, Slobodan, 216
modernity, 122, 123, 124, 128, 139, 140, 272
monetary policies, 114
Mulvenon, James, 255

National People's Congress
  9th Congress, 208–13
  1993 meeting, 75
  2003 meeting, 240
  2006 meeting, 275, 282
  Li Peng report (1989), 32
  political debate, 67, 68, 195–6
  role, 5, 201
nationalism
  anti-Americanism, 104–6, 141
  Asian values, 148–52
  China Can Say No, 159–62
  cultural nationalism, 90, 121
  embassy bombing, 224–7
  Enlightenment and, 123
  globalization and, 15
  intellectuals, 113–14
  national studies, 120–1
  new nationalism, 135–6
  popular nationalism, 108, 109, 152–7, 159, 167
  response to Huntington, 148–52
  rise, 10, 15
  River Elegy, 107–8

state-centred, 103–6
  Strategy and Management, 157–9, 225, 234, 260, 272
  WTO entry and, 18, 212–21
NATO, 105, 119, 216–17, 226
Naughton, Barry, 42
neoclassical economics, 89–90, 106, 124, 130, 141
neoconservatism
  emergence, 83–112
  incrementalism, 89–92, 111, 112
  Jiang Zemin, 273
  local–central relations, 92–5, 148
  meaning, 88–9
  nature of movement, 113
  new authoritarianism and, 95–103
  political results, 273–7
  "Realistic Responses," 109–14, 158
  rejection of cultural liberalism, 106–9
  state-centred nationalism, 103–6
neoliberalism, 9, 259, 263–7
neostatism, 140–8
new authoritarianism, 71, 83–7, 95–103
"new cat thesis," 49
New Confucianism, 127
New Culture Movement, 8, 107
New Enlightenment, 8, 9
New Left, 13, 16, 124–32, 134–5, 137–9, 140, 141, 147, 151, 158, 166, 167, 177, 195, 213, 221–4, 274
New Life Movement, 193
Nixon, Richard, 46
North, Douglass, 89
North Korea, 3, 27, 217, 260
nouveaux riches, 17, 22, 181–2
Nye, Joseph, 151

observer articles, 220
Occidentalism, 127
Old Left, 14, 88, 103, 108, 110, 132, 174–7, 197, 208, 225
Olson, Mancur, 89
Olympics, 119, 270
Orange Revolution, 258, 260
Orientalism, 126, 127, 128, 151

Pan Yue, 110
Pang Xianzhi, 77
Park Chung Hee, 159
peasants, 154–5, 232–3, 236, 273
PEN, 261
Peng Zhen, 33, 69, 172, 196
"people-centred" society, 252, 253, 255, 268, 270, 283
People's Liberation Army, 67, 250, 282
personality cult, 4

Pi Mingyong, 158
Ping, Huangfu (Zhou Ruijin), 56, 266–7
Podesta, John, 217
politics
    elite politics, 2, 2–6, 165–8, 277
    elite politics and public opinion, 221
    marketization, 182
Pomfret, John, 246
Popper, Karl, 110
populism, 138
pornography, 37, 262
postcolonialism, 103, 104, 125, 151–2,
    226–7
postmodernism, 124, 125, 139
poverty, rural poverty, 233, 237
power
    balance, 165, 278
    collective leadership, 4, 54
    monistic power, 3, 6
    pluralization, 5
    retirement age, 279
    retreat of state control, 4–5
    soft power, 2, 151, 258–9
    transfers, 238, 239–45, 277–82
pragmatism, 61
press
    freedom, 276
    reform papers, 26–7
    repression, 262
private enterprise
    conservative critique, 282–3
    growth, 5, 114, 179–80, 210–11
    membership of CCP, 193, 273
    ratio, 236
privatization, 88, 178, 263, 265
property rights, 130–1, 138, 252, 258, 265–7, 274,
    275, 276
protectionism, 191
provinces
    8th five-year plan and, 43–5
    decentralization, 43–5, 86, 94, 96
    economic reform and, 50–1
    localism, 99
    mass disturbances, 231–2
    regional inequalities, 144–8, 179, 244
    relations with centre, 92–5, 98, 104
    rural education, 237
    rural governance, 232–3
    rural inequalities, 243–4, 268–9
public intellectuals, 261, 275
public opinion, 13, 14, 16, 17, 31, 83, 161, 197,
    206, 219, 221, 234–5

Qian Jun, 128
Qian Qichen, 47, 220

Qiao Shi
    on democracy, 170, 184
    liberalism, 195–6
    martial law and, 29, 30
    political positions, 61, 66, 68–9
    power, 24, 195
    retirement, 201, 203, 279
Qin Benli, 27
Qin Chaoying, 157–8
Qin Chuan, 157, 158
Qin Hui, 260
Qin Jiwei, 74
Qin Yu, 271
Qu Yuan, 13

Rambouillet Agreement, 216
Ramo, Joshua, 259–60
rationalism, 110–11, 113
"Realistic Responses," 109–14, 158
Red Guard, 153
reform
    1980s failure, 83, 117–19
    central–local relations, 92–5
    Chinese model, 89, 90
    conservative critique, 21–47, 193–5, 282–3
    Deng revival, 48–79
    disillusionment, 166–7
    economic and social results, 273–7
    growth, 78, 272–3
    health care, 273
    housing, 273
    incrementalism, 89–92, 102
    inequalities, 144–8, 179, 182, 243–4, 268–9
    institutional economics, 89
    Jiang revival, 189–95
    liberal economics, 9, 114, 131, 259, 263–7
    middle path, 185–8
    neoconservatism, 83–112
    Old Left critique, 174–7
    pace, 1–2
    populist critique, 275–6
    post-Tiananmen debate, 14, 41–3, 49
    privatization, 4–5
    property rights, 130–1, 138, 252, 258, 265–7,
        274, 275, 276
    SARS effect, 247
    social justice, 16, 141, 147, 267–9, 271, 273, 275
    socioeconomic changes, 177–83
    stages of debate, 267
    state-centred nationalism, 103–6
    winners and losers, 115
regions. *See* provinces
religion, 262
Ren Jianxin, 195
Ren Zhongyi, 260

River Elegy, 88, 105, 107–9, 115, 128, 152
Roemer, John, 130
Rousseau, Jean-Jacques, 138
Rubin, Robert, 217
Rui Xingwen, 30
rule of law, 137, 205, 242–3, 271, 274
rural governance, 232–3
rural inequalities, 237, 243–4, 268–9
Rural Work Conference, 243–4
Russell, Bertrand, 110
Russia, 10, 111, 114, 119, 137, 166, 222, 223

Said, Edward, 125, 126, 127, 128
SARS, 10, 245–8, 249, 251–2
scientific development, 252, 253, 268, 279, 282, 283
Scowcroft, Brent, 46, 149
semi-authoritarianism, 84–5, 103
Serbia, 216–17, 218–19, 226
Shang Dewen, 204
Shao Huaze, 175
Shao Ren, 222–3
Shen Jiru, 206
Shen Liten, 92
Sheng Hong, 89–90, 90, 112, 113
Singapore, 63, 72, 86, 209
Sino-Japanese War, 23
small dragons, 63, 86, 121
Smith, Adam, 100
soap operas, 115–16
social change, 2, 16–18, 177–83
social justice, 16, 141, 147, 267–9, 271, 273, 275
social stability, 86, 87, 88, 92, 97, 112, 115, 120, 156–7, 198, 234–8
social structures, 235–8
soft power, 2, 151, 258–9
Song Jiaoren, 85
Song Ping, 30, 34, 55, 66, 73–4, 76, 207
Song Qiang, 225
Song Renqiong, 66
South Korea, 63, 86, 96, 210
Soviet Union
    1991 coup, 58–61, 109
    alliance with, 104
    collapse, 3, 22, 88, 89, 104, 114, 135, 148, 165, 175, 191, 193, 206, 255
    Communist Party, 57
    Gorbechev era, 56
    ideological debate and, 68
    price reform, 106
    Stalinism, 4, 122, 144
Special Enterprise Zones, 48, 62, 69, 70, 144–6
Sperling, Gene, 217
spiritual civilization, 188–9, 194

stability, 115
Stalinism, 4, 122, 144
state control
    See also five-year plans
    centralization, 144, 146
    decentralization and, 43–5
    intellectual debate, 124
    intellectuals and state, 11–16
    Jiang Zemin era, 5–6, 194
    Larry Lang affair, 262–7
    neostatism, 140–8
    planned economy, 38, 40–1, 72, 93, 132, 251–2
    relations with provinces, 92–5, 98
    retreat, 4–5
    state capacity, 140–8, 255–6
    state-centred nationalism, 103–6
State Council Production Commission, 40–1, 52–3
State Economic and Trade Commission, 53, 210, 214
State Economic Commission, 41, 52
State Economic Restructuring Commission, 41
state-owned enterprises
    5th Plenum (1996), 183–4
    decrease, 4–5
    Jiang policy, 57, 200
    Leftist officials, 29
    losses, 43, 114, 168–9, 198–9
    management buy-outs, 262–4, 274
    political debate, 193
    privatization, 88, 178, 263, 265
    reform, 170, 200, 208–9, 214, 216
    Shanghai, 179
State Planning Commission, 41, 44, 52
Strategy and Management, 157–9, 225, 234, 260, 272
Su Shaozhi, 26, 27
Sun Changjiang, 71
Sun Liping, 138, 159, 274
Sun Yat-sen, 100, 135
sustainable development, 283

Taiwan, 63, 86, 209, 217
Taiwan Straits crisis, 159, 160, 176, 180, 211, 213
Tan Shaowen, 50
Tan Sitong, 91, 92
Tang Yijie, 8
television, 115–16
Teng Tong, 190
Teng Wensbeng, 174, 188, 207
think-tanks, 117, 192
Three Represents, 5, 239, 243, 247, 248–51, 253, 267, 270, 273, 277, 282, 283
Tian Jiyun, 51–2, 69, 74, 75, 196

Tiananmen
  Beijing University and, 207–8
  conservative critique, 21–47, 62, 88
  intellectuals and, 9, 14, 21
  nationalist analysis, 106
  neoconservative response, 89–92, 102
  origins, 26
  post-Tiananmen expectations, 1–2, 7
  role of Chen Xitong, 173
  role of Li Peng, 203
  US involvement, 46
Tibet, 160, 217
township and village enterprises, 17, 40
transition economics, 90

Ukraine, 258, 260
Unger, Roberto, 130
United Nations, 223
United States
  anti-Americanism, 104–6, 141, 159–62,
    220–1
  central government revenues, 143
  Chinese Embassy bombing, 16, 167, 197, 217,
    218–21, 224–7, 274
  Chinese foreign reserves and, 272
  democracy and, 149
  Gulf War victory, 56–7
  hegemony, 213
  human rights policy, 105, 149, 150, 160
  intellectual property rights, 222
  intellectuals and, 119, 125, 130
  property rights, 130–1
  sanctions, 119
  September 11, attacks, 259
  triumphalism, 148–9
  US-Sino relations, 22, 45–7, 61, 138, 166, 191,
    204, 205–6, 209–10
  WTO and Chinese entry, 160, 181, 211–21,
    222–3
urbanization, 17

values, 120–2, 148–52
Vietnam, 3
Voice of America, 105

Wallerstein, Immanuel, 137–8
Wan Li, 66, 67, 74, 172, 173, 201
Wang Baosen, 172
Wang Bingqian, 43–4, 78
Wang Dan, 207
Wang Daohan, 25, 26, 174
Wang Gang, 282
Wang Guangze, 260
Wang Guowei, 135

Wang Hui, 116, 124, 128–9, 132, 134, 138, 139, 140,
  150, 166
Wang Huning, 15, 84, 96–100, 113, 151, 166, 207
Wang Jingwei, 219
Wang Jiye, 42
Wang Meng, 71, 120
Wang Mengkui, 269
Wang Qishan, 246, 281
Wang Renzhi, 39–40, 55, 61, 71, 77, 175, 190,
  207
Wang Renzhong, 198
Wang Ruoshui, 71, 133
Wang Ruowang, 35
Wang Shan, 152–7, 158, 166, 167
Wang Shao, 115–16, 120
Wang Shaoguang, 140, 141–8, 152, 166, 197, 234
Wang Shucang, 8
Wang Shuo, 152
Wang Xiaodong
  cultural fever, 128
  embassy bombing, 224–6
  impact, 113
  popular nationalism, 108, 166
  "Realistic Responses," 110–14, 158
  response to Huntington, 150–1
  River Elegy, 108, 115, 128, 152
  Strategy and Management, 158, 225
  survey of youth attitudes, 161
Wang Xiaoming, 120
Wang Yeshou, 270
Wang Zhen, 55, 58, 61, 108–9
Washington Consensus, 259, 263, 265
Wei Jianxing, 195
Wen Jiabao
  background, 238
  education, 12
  reform agenda, 267–8, 275, 282
  rural policy, 269
  SARS, 246
  social stability concerns, 238
  Zhu Rongji succession, 16, 240, 243–4
Wen Shengang, 258
Wen Yuankai, 31
West
  China's relations with, 13
  cultural hegemony, 138–9, 150
  demythification, 125
  distorted views of China, 126–8
  economic model, 131
  Enlightenment and, 123, 124
  intellectual debate, 123
  modernity, 122, 123, 124, 128, 139, 140, 272
  rationalism, 110–11, 113
  rejection, 159–62

threat, 103
triumphalism, 148–9
universalism, 152
Westernization, 105, 108–9, 138–9
Williamson, John, 259
World Bank, 223
World Economic Herald, 26–7, 31, 190
WTO membership
  anti-WTO ideologies, 9
  intellectual property rights, 18, 222
  nationalist opposition, 18, 106, 197, 212–21
  negotiations, 210–21, 246
  New Left critique, 221–4
  political decision, 181
  public opinion, 221
  terms, 16
  US opposition, 160, 181, 211–21
Wu Bangguo, 170
Wu Guanzheng, 51
Wu Jiaxing, 83–4, 95
Wu Jichuan, 218
Wu Jinglian, 260, 263–4, 266
Wu Xueqian, 51–2, 74
Wu Yi, 246
Wu Zuguang, 71

Xi Jinping, 281
Xi Zhongxun, 281
Xiamen smuggling operation, 16
Xiao Gongqin, 100–3, 113, 166, 224
Xiao Ke, 157
Xiao Weibi, 260
Xiao Xialin, 116
Xing Bensi, 186–8, 189
Xinjang, 217
Xu Ben, 138
Xu Bing, 153
Xu Caihou, 250, 282
Xu Jilin, 116, 117
Xu Weicheng, 58, 76–7, 175

Yan Fu, 100–2
Yan Jianhong, 172
Yan Jiaqi, 26, 31
Yan Mingfu, 30, 74, 157
Yan'an Forum on Literature and Art, 7–8, 23, 111, 189
Yang Baibing, 67, 75, 173
Yang Fan, 262, 263
Yang Ping, 109–14, 113, 158
Yang Rudai, 74
Yang Shangkun, 29, 30, 45, 48, 60, 64, 69, 74, 75, 76, 201, 272
Yang Shaoming, 64

Yang Xiaokai, 260
Yao Yilin, 23–4, 29–30, 33, 41, 51–2, 66, 73–4, 76, 77–8, 246
Ye Fei, 75, 76
Ye Qing, 41, 53
Ye Xuanping, 45
Yeltsin, Boris, 58–9
Yi Ren (Chen Daixi), 40
Yin Baoyun, 158–9
Yin He incident, 160
You Lin, 77
Yu Guangyuan, 93
Yu Haocheng, 85–6, 87
Yu Jianrong, 232
Yu Jie, 260, 261
Yu Quanyu, 160, 225
Yu Yingshi, 91–2, 115
Yuan Baohua, 157
Yuan Hongbing, 71
Yuan Mu, 32, 68, 175, 193
Yuan Shikai, 85, 101, 102
Yugoslavia, 99, 143, 226

Zeng Qinghong, 174, 238, 239–40, 242, 255, 277, 278, 279, 281, 282
Zeng Shan, 238
Zha, Jianying, 116
Zhang Aiping, 75–6
Zhang Bingjiu, 84–5, 103
Zhang Gaoli, 282
Zhang Kuan, 126–8
Zhang Lichang, 282
Zhang Rong (Chang Jung), 126
Zhang Weiying, 263–4
Zhang Wenkang, 245–6
Zhang Wenkui, 263–4
Zhang Yanning, 53
Zhang Yihe, 261
Zhang Yimou, 126
Zhang Zhidong, 101
Zhang Zhen, 75, 76
Zhang Zhuoyuan, 42
Zhang Zuhua, 261
Zhao Shukai, 233
Zhao, Suisheng, 125
Zhao Weichen, 53
Zhao Yiheng, 138
Zhao Zhihao, 45
Zhao Ziyang
  1987 speech, 40
  allies, 74, 75
  Chen Yun and, 93
  critics, 86
  death, 272

Zhao Ziyang (*cont.*)
  decentralization, 43–4, 86
  downfall, 1, 3, 23, 24, 27, 28–35, 38, 40, 76,
    187, 239
  economic development, 28
  house arrest, 205
  reappraising Tiananmen, 203
  reformist, 11, 21, 35, 62, 85, 96, 200
  River Elegy and, 108
  think-tanks, 192
  Tiananmen and, 29–30, 241
Zheng Nian (Cheng Nien), 126
Zheng Wanlong, 115–16
Zhou Beifang, 172
Zhou Enlai, 133
Zhou Guanwu, 70, 172
Zhou Ruijin (Huangfu Ping), 56,
    266–7
Zhou Yongkang, 281
Zhou Zhengyi land development, 16
Zhu Houze, 262

Zhu Junyi, 271
Zhu Muzhi, 225
Zhu Rongii
  career, 16, 49, 74, 75, 170, 203
  conservative critics, 59, 61, 77–8, 274
  decentralization, 45
  Deng support, 70, 72
  economic policy, 175
  education, 12, 93
  neostatism, 141
  premiership, 210, 214
  reformist, 70
  regional policy, 146–7
  successor, 240
  vice-premier, 51–3, 70, 168
  WTO entry, 215–19, 221–2
Zhu Xueqin, 260
Zhuozhuo meeting (1987), 40
Zou Jiahua, 41, 44, 51–2, 53
Zuo Dapei, 262, 263
Zysman, John, 141

Cambridge Modern China Series

Edited by William Kirby, Harvard University

Other books in the series (cont.)

Susan H. Whiting, *Power and Wealth in Rural China: The Political Economy of Institutional Change*

Xiaoqun Xu, *Chinese Professionals and the Republican State: The Rise of Professional Associations in Shanghai, 1912–1937*

Yung-chen Chiang, *Social Engineering and the Social Sciences in China, 1919–1949*

Joseph Fewsmith, *China Since Tiananmen: The Politics of Transition*

Mark W. Frazier, *The Making of the Chinese Industrial Workplace: State, Revolution, and Labor Management*

Thomas G. Moore, *China in the World Market: Chinese Industry and International Sources of Reform in the Post-Mao Era*

Stephen C. Angle, *Human Rights and Chinese Thought: A Cross-Cultural Inquiry*